DIGITAL FUTURES OF GRADUATE STUDY IN THE HUMANITIES

DEBATES IN THE DIGITAL HUMANITIES

Matthew K. Gold and Lauren F. Klein, Series Editors

DIGITAL FUTURES OF GRADUATE STUDY IN THE HUMANITIES

Gabriel Hankins, Anouk Lang, and Simon Appleford
EDITORS

DEBATES IN THE DIGITAL HUMANITIES

University of Minnesota Press
Minneapolis
London

Published by the University of Minnesota Press
111 Third Avenue South, Suite 290
Minneapolis, MN 55401-2520
http://www.upress.umn.edu

 Available as a Manifold edition at dhdebates.gc.cuny.edu

ISBN 978-1-5179-1691-6 (hc)
ISBN 978-1-5179-1692-3 (pb)

A Cataloging-in-Publication record for this book is available from the Library of Congress.

Printed in the United States of America on acid-free paper

The University of Minnesota is an equal-opportunity educator and employer.

33 32 31 30 29 28 27 26 25 24   10 9 8 7 6 5 4 3 2 1

To the memory of Rebecca Munson

Contents

PART VI
Disciplinary Contexts and Translations

Acknowledgments

W e would like to thank all our contributors for their work, their patience, and their generosity during the process of peer review. This is a much better volume for their collective wisdom.

We thank Lauren Klein and Matthew Gold for their invaluable help and guidance throughout the process; Leah Pennywark for her editorial work; and the copy editors and proofreaders at the University of Minnesota Press. For their examples and guidance, we thank Brian Croxall and Diane Jakacki, the original participants at the MLA Panel on the Digital Futures of Graduate Study, including many of the contributors here, Elizabeth Maddock Dillon, Roopika Risam, and Patrick Jagoda. For offering invaluable suggestions at the beginning of the project, we thank Jennifer Guiliano.

At Clemson, we thank Camille Cooper, our invaluable digital humanities librarian; the exploratory DH PhD committee that began much of this work, including Vernon Burton, Lindsay Thomas, David Blakesley, Jan Holmevik, and Diane Perpich; and the leadership of Dean Richard Goodstein and Dean Nicholas Vazsonyi throughout the debates over graduate studies within the college.

Introduction

GABRIEL HANKINS, ANOUK LANG, AND SIMON APPLEFORD

What are the digital futures of graduate study in the humanities, and how are those futures related to the institutionalization of digital humanities degrees and programs? The digital humanities has passed from its moment of insurgency to a new phase of institutionalization in an array of graduate certificate programs, MA-level programs, and doctoral programs. But how is specific graduate-level work in these programs imagined, planned, and realized? What are the available models and options, and what do we know about their outcomes for both students and faculty? What has failed, and why? How might we reimagine current models of graduate education to address ongoing challenges to the humanities? In a moment of multiple crises for graduate study more generally, how should we restructure and rethink our programs to create sustainable and humane pedagogies, classes, and institutions? The essays in this volume set out to open these debates to those outside and inside the digital humanities community, provide concrete institutional answers to often-confronted questions, and critically assess potential models. Our volume aims to be a resource for those engaged in the early twenty-first-century digital transformations of graduate study in the humanities, across a range of disciplines and institutions.

This volume centers on the ongoing debates about the future of graduate study in the digital humanities, and it connects those debates to the digital futures of graduate study in the humanities more generally. The audience for this volume is the large group of humanities scholars, students, librarians, and associated academic staff in institutions engaged in reimagining graduate study in the humanities, not just those involved in creating and directing graduate programs and not just those working in digital humanities or digital education. We are now all implicated in the digital mediation of our research, teaching, and service and must now consider how those mediations should transform our graduate programs and pedagogies, as well as when and how they should be resisted. Our contributors write in the painful context of multiple crises: an economic collapse likely to exacerbate existing inequalities, a job market failure with causes far preceding the current moment, political crises and nationalist insurgencies, and the aftermath of a global pandemic that has revealed and accentuated ongoing social and racial damage. We trace those lines of determination in the following essays, and their presence will be felt whether or not these emergencies are directly addressed.

This volume, planned long before the compounding viral, social, environmental, and economic crises of the 2020s, has become of necessity a series of meditations in an emergency. Such meditations require clear evidence and serious thinking about past programs and future plans, plans that avoid the "digital groundhog day" problem diagnosed by Manfred Thaller, in which we learn little from the failure of past programs and thus endlessly rediscover key problems. Serious thinking on the future of graduate education in the humanities must learn from the past and engage the controversies of the present. We have thus included a variety of voices on key issues, provided specific evidence on the life and death of programs and degrees, and asked our contributors to generalize their arguments beyond the limits of a single program or institution. We believe that engaging the digital future of graduate education requires a clear factual basis for argument, absolute clarity about distinct disciplinary and institutional situations, and strongly articulated positions.

The editors of this volume are white academics working at majority-white institutions; they were trained in research-intensive universities in the Global North that share similar values, constraints, forms of assessments, and research cultures. Our research is anchored in two historically dominant disciplines in the digital humanities: literary studies and history. We are conscious that we therefore share forms of privilege and compensation that are not extended to many of our contributors, many of whom are precariously employed and discriminated against in a variety of ways. Our volume includes a range of positions, and it features contributors outside the Anglophone academic world, beyond research institutions, and across academic ranks and hierarchies. Below we survey important volumes on digital humanities in the Black Atlantic, continental Africa, and India, and we do this to deprovincialize and reframe implicit beliefs about graduate study, its infrastructures, and its horizons. We thus begin with an account of some national, cultural, and disciplinary contexts before we describe the contributions of our essays.

What Is Digital Humanities Graduate Training, and Where Does It Happen?

In this volume, we use the term "graduate study" to denote the training that occurs after the first university degree and before the first academic appointment: what are called "graduate students" in the United States are "postgraduate students" in the United Kingdom and elsewhere in the former British Commonwealth. Digital graduate study in the humanities occurs through a wide range of institutions and settings, both inside and outside formal digital humanities programs, institutes, and certificates. Our contributors work in contexts ranging from library-based institutes to academic training networks to doctoral programs awarding the PhD, MPhil, and MSc.

Graduate training in computational approaches to the humanities is not new, nor are digital humanities degrees novel, as Thaller and others note in this volume. Research centers around what would later be termed humanities computing began to be established from the early 1960s onward.[1] The University of Glasgow began offering an MPhil in History and Computing in 1989, more than a decade after the launch of the first quantitative training programs for historians at the University of Chicago and the "cliometrics" controversy that followed them (Spaeth, "Research and Representation," 120–21).[2] In the 1990s, the first degree program in humanities computing was established at the University of Alberta, and other programs followed at University College London, King's College London, McMaster University, Gröningen, Rome, and Cologne.[3] Although graduate and undergraduate programs such as these were gradually coalescing, many who would go on to become active in the field were also learning the tools of their trade outside formal institutional settings. Training institutes including the Digital Humanities at Oxford Summer School, the Digital Humanities Summer Institute at the University of Victoria, the European Summer University in Leipzig, and the Humanities Intensive Learning and Teaching Institute, established initially at Maryland, have been crucial in offering a wide range of opportunities to acquire new expertise.

Where does graduate training in the digital humanities happen now? Surveying even formal teaching and research programs is a challenge, and one that the community has addressed through collaborative registries like the Digital Humanities Course Registry, a joint initiative of the Common Language Resources and Technology Infrastructure (CLARIN) and Digital Research Infrastructure for the Humanities (DARIAH) projects. This registry gives an overview of formal teaching at both the graduate and undergraduate levels in Europe and is designed to help potential students find the optimal course for their needs (Digital Humanities Course Registry).[4] The graduate entries in the list are mostly focused on master's-level teaching courses, with advanced research programs being less common.[5] Elizabeth Hopwood and Kyle Roberts give a robust defense of one such master's program in Brian Croxall and Diane Jakacki's *What We Teach When We Teach DH*, a volume compiling essays concerned with DH pedagogy (Hopwood and Roberts, "What's the Value of a Graduate Digital Humanities Degree?"). In 2017, Chris Alen Sula, S. E. Hackney, and Phillip Cunningham conducted an international survey of digital humanities programs and noted steady growth at both the undergraduate and graduate levels over the preceding decade. Even so, their study identified only three doctoral programs, eight master's programs, and twelve certificate programs compared to three undergraduate programs and a further ten programs listed under "other." The majority of digital humanities programs, they concluded, were in the form of certificates, which were much more common at the graduate level and made up nearly one-third of all the programs they uncovered, with minors, specializations, and concentrations in digital humanities also present. They found only a handful of doctoral programs, all located in the United Kingdom and Ireland (Sula et al., "Survey of Digital Humanities Programs"). A more recent compilation titled "Advanced Degrees in the Digital Humanities" lists three additional European PhD programs, one PhD program in the planning stage in India, and several interdisciplinary programs that teach digital humanities approaches, including the Texts and Technology PhD program at the University of Central Florida (Gil et al., "Advanced Degrees in Digital Humanities"). "Digital humanities," then, is taught quite differently depending on the graduate education structures involved. As UK universities do not commonly offer certificates, for instance, the most common graduate degree in digital humanities offered by institutions is a master's degree, which usually takes one year of full-time study to complete. Moreover, the language of "major" and "minor" is not in wide usage in European and British institutions, so graduate students proceeding to doctoral study (whether in one of the few doctoral programs that is formally designated as a PhD in digital humanities or one that is not) from undergraduate study in the United Kingdom and Europe are less likely to possess broad skills across subjects like statistics, programming, or data science compared to some of their North American counterparts. Thaller provides a valuable overview of the historical development and recurrent problems of European digital humanities degree programs in his contribution to this volume.

Beyond Europe and the Anglosphere, opportunities for formal graduate study in the digital humanities are less common, but research and community-building activities suggest that pedagogical structures may soon follow. Although there were at the time of writing no graduate programs in digital humanities in African nations, Tunde Opeibi points to "the growing and widespread interest in digital humanities scholarship and research in sub-Saharan Africa," citing initiatives such as the launch in 2017 of the Lagos Summer School in Digital Humanities, the establishment of the first Centre for Digital Humanities at the University of Lagos in Nigeria, and the Corpus of Nigeria New Media Discourse in English project ("Digitizing the Humanities," 162, 163–64). Taking a still broader view of the African continent, Babalola Titilola Aiyegbusi identifies a lopsidedness to some of the digital humanities work, deriving from the way that many of the digital projects involving Africa are initiated or executed in Europe or North America. Even where such projects are affiliated with local institutions—for instance, the Accra Mobile project at Wayne State University, which is linked with Ashesi University Ghana—the absence of digital humanities centers in African countries "tends to create a disconnect between the project and the targeted audience and users, and may reduce accessibility and incorporation into academic research circles" (Aiyegbusi, "Decolonizing Digital Humanities," 435). Infrastructure and the difficulty of getting online mean that technologies used to teach digital methods are not readily available.

Another important factor inheres in the structure of the educational systems. In African countries, according to Aiyegbusi, these tend toward conservatism and the enforcement of standardized curricula, such that practicing digital humanities is perceived as learning to use digital tools rather than participating in a discipline. Compared to the relative flexibility of the American educational system, in which students in the humanities and social sciences can switch their major or minor multiple times, or the relative protections and latitude of German graduate study, the educational model in African nations is more rigid and compartmentalized, with students admitted to study specific courses and permitted to take a minor only in selected fields. Specializing earlier on in a student's undergraduate education has an effect on the options open to them in their graduate careers. Aiyegbusi also points out that interdisciplinary collaboration is uncommon in the African model of research, in which lone scholars are still the norm within the humanities, though efforts are underway to promote collaboration. With Aiyegbusi, we recognize that many of the norms and practices that are taken for granted within much of the North American academy, such as the ease of collaboration and interaction with other scholars, emerge from the way North American educational systems are structured and thus do not necessarily pertain in other national and regional contexts ("Decolonizing Digital Humanities").

In the 2020 volume *Exploring Digital Humanities in India,* Nirmala Menon and T. Shanmugapriya describe digital humanities work as situated "in the margins of the Indian academy," with very few programs and courses exposing students to work in the field ("Digital Humanities in India," 91). They observe that though digital research has experienced steady growth in areas such as the digitization of print materials, the development of databases, and the use of digital methods for preserving Indian cultural heritage, pedagogy lags; other than at a few institutions, there are only scattered interdisciplinary opportunities at the undergraduate level that bring together disciplines in combination, such as history, economics, and computer science, which offer students at public universities the opportunity to familiarize themselves with digital tools to provide new perspectives on prevailing modes of humanities research ("Digital Humanities in India," 94–95). In Australasia, a handful of institutions including Sogang University in Korea, the University of Canterbury in New Zealand, the Australian National University, and the University of Western Sydney in Australia run master's programs or postgraduate certificates in digital humanities. Much research and teaching in the field is occurring in these locations, but where institutional centers for digital work exist, they tend to be anchored in research. Teaching, especially at the postgraduate level, is something that follows only once research activity and the infrastructure for supporting teaching are well established. Moreover, as many of the contributors to this volume note, digital humanities training often occurs outside formal educational structures, which makes it more difficult to track.[6]

The difficulty of capturing both formal and informal opportunities for digitally inflected work at the graduate level in institutions beyond the Anglosphere illustrates the point Padmini Ray Murray and Chris Hand make: just as computing resources are unevenly distributed across the developed and developing worlds, so digital humanities needs to be transposed to fit its local exigencies ("Making Culture," 142–43). Such transpositions, Murray and Hand argue, have the potential to enrich the varieties of digital humanities graduate study on offer: "As the digital humanities grows more visible in South Asia as in other regions, it is necessary to recognize the ways in which disciplinary practices might diverge in these places, owing to the exigencies of language, rate of technological growth and obsolescence, and different institutional and cultural histories, all of which combine to create an alternative definition of what the discipline might offer" (144). In her consideration of the African context, Aiyegbusi argues for the importance of exposing the western-centric roots of what too often passes for the "all-encompassing interdisciplinary practice" of digital humanities. Where digital humanities is understood, whether implicitly or explicitly, as a phenomenon practicable only in places with advanced technological infrastructure, this raises barriers to inclusion and comprehension ("Decolonizing Digital Humanities," 434). Our contributors work almost entirely within the structures and institutions of the Global North, but even there, resources, training, and infrastructure are unevenly distributed. Aiyegbusi, Menon and Shanmugapriya, and others point to the necessity for a continuing inner critique of the colonial and postcolonial roots of a neocolonial digital economy, society, and educational infrastructure, a critique that digital humanists must engage as part of their disciplinary and infrastructural thinking.

Current Debates in Graduate Education in the United States

Many of our contributors, as well as two of us as editors, are located in American universities and thus respond to the unique challenges and privileges of the U.S. academic system. Although many outside the Global North perceive graduate institutions in the United States as uniquely privileged places to develop digital humanities work, digital humanities conversations internal to North America have been dominated by crisis and scarcity long before the most recent economic and viral catastrophes, like the broader conversation on graduate education and precarity around it. Humanities graduate programs in the United States have long been trapped within contradictory demands for legitimacy, selectivity, and prestige. Three generations of academics have entered into a system still premised on the continuation of the mid-twentieth-century boom in academic positions. Elsewhere, graduate reform has been a live issue in the last two decades, after the beginning of the Bologna graduate standardization process in Europe and the growth of new degree-granting institutions throughout Asia.[7]

In the United States, by contrast, reform has only recently been taken seriously, often in response to student activism. In the U.S. academy, selectivity and research prestige were the goals of graduate programs formed in the twentieth century on the model of older elite institutions and against demands for democratic access to teaching or career-oriented degrees.[8] Those acculturated and employed within those graduate programs naturally envisioned the highest achievement of academic employment to be teaching selectively educated and admitted graduate students oriented toward research, thus recreating while mastering the conditions of their own academic maturation. Against those demands for selective, research-oriented students and programs stand the continuing call for public justifications and the broadening of career outcomes to include alternative, public sector, and nonacademic careers. The mid-twentieth-century boom in college-aged populations temporarily squared the circular contradictions between selectivity, prestige, and democracy, enabling programs to be at the same time highly selective, democratically responsive, and highly productive of new professors and new programs. In the United States in particular, public investment in higher education was tightly linked to the expanding white middle classes that were its primary beneficiaries, a link that has slowly come undone.[9] Continued if fitful expansion in higher education over the last three decades, along with a boom in international students in Anglophone university systems, allowed many of these contradictions to go unchallenged. Yet in the wake of the most recent global financial crises, state divestments, and then a global pandemic, the circle has slowly been unsquared without the tensions of the essential contradictions within graduate education undergoing any clear resolution. The collapse has given rise to a literature, inside and outside the digital humanities conversations, on these intersecting crises that we recall briefly below, as it provides an essential context for many of our contributors.

Current discussions about reform in graduate education differently negotiate the tensions between selectivity, research prestige, and democratic justifications. Only relatively recently have other entries in the list—student experiences, outcomes, and pathways—been seriously considered in books on graduate education reform, a fact that is itself an indictment of the present system.[10] The contributors to this book continue a vibrant digital humanities conversation about pedagogy and labor, thinking deeply about graduate and postdoctoral student outcomes, identities, and the meanings attached to programs and degrees by those within them.

Katina Rogers is one of our most thoughtful writers on those identities and meanings and one of the best critics of the institutional structures that produce them. Her emphasis, both in chapter 1 in this volume and in her book *Putting the Humanities PhD to Work*, centers on the close examination of the assumptions and structures of graduate study and how changing these might lead to meaningful careers outside the academy. "One of the most important things that faculty members can do is help students feel more comfortable talking about career pathways from the moment they begin their program," Rogers argues (78). This open conversation, then, needs to be reaffirmed in a number of ways: meaningful credit for collaborative, public-oriented work; credit for interdisciplinary projects; reinvestment in teaching; and a public list of *all* work placements for their graduates, not just the familiar tenure-track placement list.[11] Rogers joins other recent commentators like Anna Kornbluh, Michael Bérubé, and Jennifer Ruth who enjoin us to "reshape and strengthen" the structures of the academy from within rather than reiterate crisis talk, analysis, and catastrophizing without systematic organizing and action (Rogers, 128; Kornbluh, "Critical Building"; Bérubé and Ruth, *Humanities, Higher Education, and Academic Freedom*).

Graduate education in the digital humanities has often been seen externally and internally as one clear path to multiplying graduate outcomes and thus "usable futures." We affirm this function of digital humanities graduate education as an essential part of the many pathways our graduates take inside and outside the university. Digital humanities graduates, including the contributors to this volume, have entered into a variety of career paths inside and outside the academy. But it is clear, on the evidence of the essays in this volume and other writings, that not all forms of digital graduate education are equally usable or viable. Outside a few centers of intensive involvement in digital humanities work, students often face the prospect of isolation or outright hostility to their interests, as Sean Weidman's essay in chapter 16 in this volume notes, and temporary supports like the Mellon program fellowships—addressed by Daniel Gorman Jr., Erin Francisco Opalich, Madeline Ullrich, and Alexander Zawacki in chapter 25 in this volume—are well known for not changing institutional conditions. Even within programs featuring strong digital teaching and research components, graduate students face enormous obstacles to serious engagement with digital methods, from increased time to degree to incomprehension of their projects and interests. Nor are all advisors able to help. Even if advisors wished to take up all of the excellent suggestions of Rogers and Leonard Cassuto, most have neither the training nor the ability to advise students on career paths that look fundamentally different from their own. The internalized disdain for "alternate" or pragmatic careers for graduate students can stand in the way of the most obvious steps, such as including university career services in mandatory graduate introductory sessions (on the model of Stanford or Michigan State), maintaining lists of all alumni with all their career outcomes, and opening an account with the most common professional networking services.[12] These moves outside the internal economy of the university do not preclude us from addressing the economics of the university and our place within it, resisting managerialism and the private capture of publicly funded research, and advocating for graduate unions and labor actions.

Few commentators on the "graduate mess" are interested in simply cutting down on graduate programs and enrollments. Rogers's final recommendation in chapter 1 in this volume, in the context of the massive losses caused by both the pandemic and racialized violence within her former institution (the City University of New York), is simple: *stop* what we are doing now, and refuse the return to "normal." Many graduate programs indeed stopped admissions during the crisis, but not all will reconsider what they are doing and why. Both Rogers and Cassuto argue that we should not cut PhD admissions too far, for various reasons: PhDs have a salutary effect on society; cutting admissions will not actually change the precarious conditions of academic labor more generally; and cutting programs will lead to an antidemocratic narrowing of the professoriate to products of only the wealthiest institutions, just like the bad old days. Marc Bousquet and others have noted that most contingent faculty (at community colleges in particular) hold the MA, not the PhD, though this is not so much an argument for new PhDs as for strengthening master's programs at institutions that take that degree seriously.[13] Sidonie Smith reminds us that many applicants who were working-class, first-generation women, or students of color would never have had a chance under the old elites-only doctoral model (*Manifesto for the Humanities*). All writers agree that doctoral students have a beneficial effect on the world. What remains unclear is how graduate training should be structured to benefit those students in return.

We agree that the value of graduate study in the humanities must be actively defended, especially in the face of blunt external attacks on the teaching of critical race theory, academic freedom, and the histories of race and colonialism. Digital humanities training contributes to a variety of public goods, from public history projects to a critical understanding of digital culture and society. Simply reducing and defunding graduate programs eliminates a central pillar of our work and our disciplines and concedes, in advance, the battle over public legitimacy; moreover, a reduction of internal programs fails to address the larger structural questions of university privatization, precarity, administrative capture, and public defunding. The question remains how to restructure and strengthen programs in a way that supports both the value of the humanities and the value of our students.

Programmatic suggestions for doctoral reform are legion, in this volume and elsewhere: move to a six-year PhD, as recommended in 2014 by the Modern Language Association's *Report of the MLA Task Force on Doctoral Study in Modern Language and Literature*; imagine what it would mean to create a three-year "professional" PhD (Menand, "How to Make a PhD Matter"); envision a "20-Year Dissertation" in which one student's work would be placed within the context of a much larger ongoing project (Presner, "Welcome to the 20-Year Dissertation"). Less common are attempts to follow through on those reforms, though significant funds have been spent by the Mellon Foundation and others in the attempt.[14] In the midst of the pandemic, many programs did take the position advocated by Rogers and others and paused graduate admissions. That opens the space to think about what should come next.

Cassuto and Robert Weisbuch have called for a "public-facing PhD" that would turn outward rather than inward: toward career diversity for graduate students, toward public humanities, toward the public and private sectors, and toward what they conceive as a "liberal-arts" graduate degree (*New PhD*, 13). They propose an ambitious agenda, from expanding the outcomes of graduate education to changing degree requirements and advising norms. Less clear is how to accomplish their ambitious agenda or why graduate students would need a second such liberal arts degree. Crucially, Cassuto and Weisbuch provide a detailed examination of why previous moments of PhD reform largely failed. Learning from mistakes is a key component of the movement toward usable futures, one that Donna Bussell, Tena Helton, Thaller, and others take up in this volume. Many of our contributors implicitly or explicitly support a main contention of Cassuto, Weisbuch, and Rogers: that career diversity and planning must be addressed explicitly by faculty at the beginning of a graduate career and then reaffirmed by faculty advising. Finally, there is value in departments and advisers showcasing and affirming the diversity of actual routes taken by their students.

Cassuto and Weisbuch approach the question of graduate futures primarily from the "administrative reformer" point of view rather than as a question of academic labor. Yet the question of academic labor presents itself urgently when considering the crisis from the bottom up rather than the reverse. Certainly, working to open new outcomes for graduate students in our programs, including those in the enormous public-sector and academic-adjacent or "alt-ac" labor markets with which humanities programs have some overlap, has the potential to bring many benefits. However, as Natalia Cecire cautions, rather than being content with alt-ac jobs as "shovel-ready projects just waiting to put our PhDs back to work," we need to think carefully about what order of jobs we are imagining. For Cecire, those in digital humanities are well positioned to understand how such jobs form part of the postindustrial precaritization of academic labor, seen for instance in "the rise of contingent and modular work, interstitiality, the hegemony of immaterial labor, the monetization of affect" and more, and have a responsibility to critique and change, rather than reproduce, such practices ("Introduction"). In their discussion of whiteness and labor in academic libraries, Anne Cong-Huyen and Kush Patel offer one such critique, flagging the "silences, absences, erasures, and quiet traumas" that have accompanied their journeys from PhDs in English and architecture and subsequent postdoctoral fellowships to "Brown digital humanities–adjacent librarians" ("Precarious Labor," 265, 264). They note how exclusionary politics and practices have hampered efforts to diversify digital humanities, with diversity initiatives too often grounded in precarious labor practices. The temporary nature of posts such as resident librarians, fellowships, and postdocs means that postholders do not have the opportunity to make sustained changes, and precarious jobs are largely limited to U.S. citizens and permanent residents (Cong-Huyen and Patel, "Precarious Labor," 264). The rise of a new precarious class of academic workers must be openly addressed and redressed, not only by faculty with permanent positions but in solidarity with members of the precarious faculty majority themselves. Here the growing field of critical university studies is important as is the practical experience of renewed academic labor activism for graduate student unions and adjunct faculty in recent years.[15]

Graduate student workers are educating themselves in a system that also employs and frequently exploits their labor. At the same time, that education has real individual and systemic benefits we must defend. The futures of graduate education arise out of these constitutive contradictions of "student labor" itself. Our volume hopes to contribute to the discussion of student labor practices along with the central problems of digital humanities education confronted by recent volumes in the Debates in the Digital Humanities series. Many of our contributors think through the problem of the emotional, affective, and self-organizational work that goes into academic self-presentation: this kind of (largely) immaterial labor both converges with and diverges from the forms of self-branding and self-presentation required by the neoliberal economies of precarity more generally. Such labor is of course also gendered, classed, localized, and raced, as Sethunya Mokoko's essay in chapter 18 in this volume on self-policing in digital rhetoric demonstrates. We invite our readers and writers to think through the forms, structures, and solidarities that mediate digital graduate education within broader social and economic transformations while not losing sight of the particular positions from which our contributors speak.

Specific positions and institutional arrangements matter here, as does clarity about the changes underway, so this volume advocates for arguments about the actual systems of graduate education that exist, not their imagined others. Despite the common wisdom that tenure and permanent contracts are withering away, for example, in the United States, the number of degree-granting institutions with a tenure system actually increased in the decade from 2007 to 2017, especially in public systems; this occurred even as the total numbers of contingent faculty increase and the conditions of tenure have come under attack.[16] Fixed-term contracts are on the rise everywhere, yet the terms of those contracts can be challenged by collective actions. Graduate systems vary dramatically across national and linguistic contexts, and they interact unevenly and occasionally: even as the European PhD system has moved closer to the Anglo-American model (as Thaller notes in chapter 6 in this volume), Cassuto and Weisbuch advocate for a move to small-group tutorials for graduate students, like those employed at undergraduate level at Oxford and Cambridge, in response to diminishing class sizes and cohorts. By putting inhabitants of widely different academic worlds and disciplines in conversation, this volume hopes to deprovincialize the discussions of digital graduate education, on the one hand, while on the other hand emphasizing the local situations and positionalities of its contributors and arguments. We echo Roopika Risam and Kelly Baker Josephs, the editors of *The Digital Black Atlantic,* in acknowledging that assumptions anchored in the white and predominantly Anglophone cultures of the Global North have had an overwhelming and undue influence in shaping the epistemologies of the field (Josephs and Risam, "Introduction," xiii), and if this is true of the research out of which an at times hegemonic vision of digital humanities has emerged, it also holds for the institutions, policies, and practices that have shaped the way digital humanities is taught at both the undergraduate and graduate levels. Both digital futures and graduate study should be understood here as always in the plural; as a set of institutionalized practices and beliefs located within particular disciplines, practices, and identities; as racialized, classed, and gendered; and as differently structured by dominance in the Global South and North. Nonetheless, and as a result of that history of domination, graduate study in the humanities shares a surprisingly solid core of habits and practices across identities, national boundaries, and political orientations.[17] One of the aspirations of this volume is to think about, and not just within, such habits and practices.

The Structure of This Book

This volume is organized into six sections. Part I, "Positions and Provocations," offers a set of concrete proposals and provocations on shaping the digital futures of graduate studies in the humanities, understood as plural and in a useful set of contradictions and tensions. Rogers notes that power hierarchies in the academy can exacerbate the way care work is rendered invisible and uncompensated, thus erasing a burden that often falls disproportionately on women, especially women of color. She advocates for shifting from a system that is oriented toward prestige to one that is instead rooted in generosity, a shift that requires not only a significant change in values but a change in the structures that underlie and have proceeded from those values. Alison Booth, the director of the Scholars' Lab at the University of Virginia, argues for an expansive vision of graduate studies in the humanities, but one in which practical difficulties and false binaries are addressed head-on rather than being ignored so as to offer a "Digital-AND-Humanities" model with the potential to reinvent and reimagine the way universities organize graduate education. Brandon Walsh, the head of student programs at the Scholars' Lab, makes the case for a digital humanities practice that flattens power hierarchies in the academy by understanding administrative interventions as pedagogical acts and finding ways to connect student projects with community action and activism. In the final essay of this section, Travis Bartley advocates for a vision of the public university as public infrastructure and a version of graduate study that would refuse the privatization of public education in the neoliberal academy, instead affirming its role as an infrastructural resource for the common good.

The authors featured in Part II, "Histories and Forms," offer a reconsideration of the past and the present of graduate education to examine institutional and curricular variations within digital humanities programs and certificates. The first two essays explore the reasons why digital humanities programs may fail and offer guidance as to how their long-term sustainability can be ensured. Bussell and Helton share their experiences at the University of Illinois Springfield, exploring how a combination of institutional, geographical, and curricular challenges were arrayed against the dedication and energy of faculty members tasked with setting up a digital humanities program. Offering a *longue durée* perspective on a similar set of issues in the European context, Thaller looks back at the recurring cycles of hype and deflation in humanities computing degrees. He argues that unless newly established digital humanities programs can maintain the long-term institutional support that makes them more than a means of learning a series of tools that happen to be popular in the moment, they risk suffering the same fate as their predecessors and disappearing. Local context emerges as a key factor in Maria José Afanador-Llach and Camilo Martínez's account of establishing the first graduate program in digital humanities in Latin America; they describe building a program from the ground up without an established departmental home while initiating student projects that reach across other domains, such as law and activism, to address concerns specific to local and regional communities. In the final essays in this section, Stuart Dunn explores how the rapid pivot to online teaching required by the pandemic has the potential to transform our conceptualization of the use of technology in the classroom, and Stephen Robertson evaluates the differences between teaching a certificate in digital public humanities in person and offering the same content in an online setting.

Graduate education has been an intermittent concern of the field's often boisterous conversations around pedagogy, as Croxall and Jakacki note, yet the goals and rationales of graduate pedagogy often remain implicit in those debates.[18] The essays in Part III, "Pedagogical Implications," consider these goals and rationales alongside the ways in which graduate students are introduced to a wide range of digital methodologies and theories and the implications of different learning and teaching approaches. In many programs, the graduate research methods seminar is a critical building block in teaching students how to think, research, and write as scholars. Laura Estill argues that as more of the resources that humanities researchers encounter are digital in form, these classes must be adapted to equip students with the skills they need to critically engage with digital materials in the same way a researcher might when faced with any other unfamiliar resource. Another argument frequently made by proponents of digital humanities programs is that their benefits include transferable technical skills and experience creating digital forms that make students more marketable for academic and nonacademic jobs, a claim taken up by authors elsewhere in this volume. One such form that boasts increasing popularity is project-based learning, in which students demonstrate their mastery of digital methods by creating their own digital projects. Cecily Raynor evaluates the effectiveness of these projects in achieving this mastery and proposes ways of assessing the quality of project work being done at the graduate level. Brady Krien proposes a series of best practices aimed at strengthening the developmental infrastructures that institutions need to effectively integrate digital methods training into graduate education, as opposed to an approach in which such training is "jerry-rigged." Mentoring is central to Krien's vision of a more equitable, more diverse, and more collaborative vision of graduate education. Laura Crossley, Amanda Regan, and Joshua Casmir Catalano similarly posit that there exists an inherent tension between such digital methodological training and the requirements of a degree program, a tension that is often resolved by prioritizing the needs of the project. Drawing on their own experiences at George Mason University, Crossley, Regan, and Catalano suggest a series of best practices that can be adopted by program and project directors to ensure that their relationship with students is mutually beneficial and nonexploitative. Finally, Kayla Shipp argues that framing project-based pedagogies as sites for skill building puts students at risk for inefficiency in their careers, given that this work prioritizes invisible and isolated labor. Instead, she suggests, digital humanities training should emphasize creative scholarship that conveys to students that what should be valued is not simply their technical prowess but the objects that they create.

Part IV, "Forum on Graduate Pathways," centers the experiences of graduate students themselves, with the contributors to this forum bringing with them a range of positions, disciplines, and concerns across geographic and institutional boundaries. They give a vivid sense of what it is like to work on doctoral projects both within and outside institutional structures for supporting digital work, providing concrete examples of the difficulties encountered as well as glimpses of how these problems might be addressed as different pathways through the field are taken. Such challenges range from the practical—seen in the difficulties encountered by Hoyeol Kim in accessing the kind of funding and technical infrastructure that are more prevalent in computer science than humanities departments and which facilitate research collaborations—to the ideological. This latter is seen, for example, in the opposition born of disciplinary entrenchment articulated in Weidman's account of working on a digital humanities PhD from within an English department and in the structural racism repeatedly encountered by Mokoko on the way to, and within, the academic institutions that helped him to equip himself to use digital media for activist work with communities in Lesotho. As with Kim, Weidman, and Mokoko, Maria Alberto's account of working at the intersection of the digital and the humanities reinforces the way that graduate-level research in the humanities is often based on a model of the lone scholar, though her essay illustrates that even a modest level of support in the form of a fellowship for several months can go a long way in fostering sustainability for digital humanities research undertaken by individuals who are not part of preexisting projects or well-established communities or collaborations. The remaining four essays in this section move from personal and individual experiences to incorporate reflections on structural and systemic relationships. Olivia Quintanilla and Jeanelle Horcasitas chart several barriers to graduate success that, though increasingly and widely acknowledged, remain unsolved, including the effects of financial pressures and precarious employment conditions on graduate students and the struggle to build a community of digitally minded fellow humanists in institutional contexts such as community colleges where data-rich research may not be a high priority. Quintanilla and Horcasitas's account is also a testament to what can be achieved through student-led initiatives, something that is also explored by Sara Mohr and E. L. Meszaros in their account of using a digital publication to both carry out and train others in public humanities work. These essays are "where the rubber hits the road" in terms of the oft-proclaimed need for digital humanists to do interdisciplinary work, learn skills in project management and collaborative working, and connect their work to the communities and publics beyond the academy in a world in which economic forces and institutional cultures do not necessarily support or reward this kind of work. Agnieszka Backman, Quinn Dombrowski, Sabrina Grimberg, and Melissa Hosek acknowledge the difficulty of balancing these many obligations when involved in digital projects, and their use of a role-playing game as a device for interrogating what is at stake in this balancing act connects back to Rogers's argument about taking seriously the need to acknowledge the importance of care and understanding one's own time and energy as a limited resource. Their account also supports the arguments advanced by Alex Wermer-Colan to demonstrate the importance of structures like libraries and digital humanities centers in providing crucial support for graduate students and post-doctoral scholars doing interdisciplinary digital work.

The contributors to Part V: Infrastructures and Institutions raise questions about where the responsibility for driving change lies, whether with institutions, funding bodies, research infrastructures, graduate students themselves, or elsewhere. As they do so, these authors articulate shared pathways and experiences that those involved in graduate studies are well advised to learn from, some of which are congruent with the pathways showcased in Part IV. Natalia Ermolaev, Rebecca Munson, and Meredith Martin point to the value of incorporating project management into graduate student programs, not only for allowing students to think critically about process, collaboration, and contingency but also for what can be learned about the intellectual, ethical, and social dimensions of running and sustaining digital research projects. Heather Richards-Rissetto and Adrian S. Wisnicki draw on their experiences of the digital humanities program at the University of Nebraska-Lincoln to highlight some of the factors necessary to ensure its success and to assess the relative value of an "agile" approach—where students are offered a menu of curricular options that changes each year—versus that of a fixed curriculum. Although the latter has significant benefits, Richards-Rissetto and Wisnicki argue that an agile curriculum can more effectively shift students' focus from the classroom to real-world applications of digitally informed skills of critical thinking. Opalich, Gorman, Ullrich, and Zawacki explore what it looks like when graduate students themselves take up the work of integrating digital humanities into graduate programs across a range of disciplines, within the different constraints of working at a single institution with the benefit of Mellon funding, institutional legitimacy, and a ready-made community of fellow graduate students also using digital approaches. The importance of incorporating research methodologies from a range of disciplines is similarly the focus of Gabriel Viehhauser, Malte Heckelen, Claus-Michael Schlesinger, and Peggy Bockwinkel's essay, which uses feedback from students in the master's program in digital humanities at the University of Stuttgart to argue that transdisciplinary collaborations greatly enrich both digital humanities research and learning. Jennifer Edmond, Vicky Garnett, and Toma Tasovac consider graduate training in the humanities from a position outside the university, framing it in terms of professional "acculturation" and presenting the work of DARIAH in the European context as their example. They consider the role that large research infrastructures like DARIAH play in fostering experiential and student-led learning in a way that goes beyond just skills-based development. In the final essay of this section, Jacob Richter and Hannah Taylor propose that humanities programs embrace what they term hybrid infrastructures to better nurture practices, sensibilities, and orientations enabled by technology rather than focusing primarily on the technologies themselves. Underlying all these essays is a sharp awareness of both the necessity for graduate students to develop the skills needed by the ever-shifting goalposts of the academic job market and the extent to which different institutional configurations are serving, or failing to serve, their students in helping them to meet these expectations.

The essays in Part VI, "Disciplinary Contexts and Translations," examine how the task of shaping the digital futures of graduate education is inflected differently in distinct disciplinary configurations. Scholars at different career stages assess the challenges and opportunities of undertaking and facilitating graduate study outside established boundaries. They identify interdisciplinary exchange as one of the core strengths and drivers of transformation of graduate study in the digital humanities but assert that the path to successful research, pedagogy, and collaboration across disciplines is far from straightforward. Investigating interdisciplinary possibilities that arise where humanities fields intersect with computer science and information science, Ted Underwood and Benjamin Lee consider the different backgrounds and motivations that graduate students and educators bring to the encounter and the differences in what they take away. Lee gives a graduate student's perspective on how benefits flow both ways in such collaborations, pointing to the instrumentality of humanities questions and research paradigms for computer scientists in, for instance, alerting them to the ethical implications of their data analysis. Underwood, observing that the value of collaboration within digital humanities has been predominantly articulated by those in the humanities, turns the question around to examine it from the point of view of information science. He puts forward the iSchool model as one example of how these perspectives may be integrated and how robust graduate training can be put in place to serve a range of constituencies. Demonstrating how the exigencies of the local context shaped the development of the United States's first PhD program in digital history at Clemson University, Catalano, Pamela E. Mack, and Douglas Seefeldt offer a rationale for a dedicated doctoral program instead of the more common model of a certificate program or institute. Finally, Serenity Sutherland argues for the value of media studies as a field that offers access to theoretical and conceptual tools for a better understanding of the relationship between the analog and the digital, an understanding that boasts the potential for wider applicability in other disciplines. The notion of remediation, Sutherland suggests, might serve as a bridge between subfields in the digital humanities, helping to show that rather than displacing some disciplines or rendering them obsolete, interdisciplinary digital work has the power to transform and reenergize them. The volume ends with a reflective Afterword by Ken Price, codirector of the Center for Digital Research at the University of Nebraska-Lincoln.

Our volume poses a number of questions not fully addressed here but which we hope others will take up in the years ahead. What does it mean to address racism, sexism, class bias, and settler coloniality not only at the level of critical discourse but also in our structures of graduate teaching and training? How should practitioners position themselves in relation to the new paradigms of data science and data and society interdisciplinary programs? What effect will large language models and generative AI have on graduate writing and training? What does sustainability look like in graduate studies, in both human and environmental terms? How do we create the new forms, supports, solidarities, and models of writing in public that are needed as new media forms and platforms evolve? Our contributors raise these questions and many others in the essays that follow. We need to attend to their thinking in order to move beyond familiar habits and into the new pathways ahead.

Notes

1. For histories of the first decades of digital humanities work, see Nyhan and Flinn, *Computation and the Humanities,* 1–19.

2. For a brief account of the cliometrics controversy, see Schmidt, "Two Volumes."

3. For a brief history of humanities computing, see the canonical account by Hockey, "History of Humanities Computing."

4. See also Wissik et al., "Teaching Digital Humanities Around the World."

5. At the time of writing, this directory listed eighty-four programs at the bachelor's level, 164 at the master's level, eight research master's courses, and seventeen doctoral programs, as well as stand-alone courses, summer schools, and continuing education programs across nineteen European countries; see Digital Humanities Course Registry, https://dhcr .clarin-dariah.eu/. A second resource is the more informal listing of advanced degrees in digital humanities maintained by Columbia University's Group for Experimental Methods in the Humanities. At the time of writing, this resource lists only nine PhD programs—eight in Europe and one in the U.S., with a further one in development in India, but the list of master's programs is much longer; see Gil et al., "Advanced Degrees in Digital Humanities."

6. Souvik Mukherjee gives the example of the extensive Bichitra project, the online variorum edition of the Bengali poet Rabindranath Tagore, whose project team, led by Sukanta Chaudhuri, was composed almost entirely of "young scholars with good Master's degrees, nearly always in the humanities but with formal or informal computer training." See Mukherjee, "Digital Humanities, or What You Will," 112.

7. See Bitusikova, "Reforming Doctoral Education in Europe" as well as chapter 6 (Thaller) and chapter 27 (Edmond, Garnett, and Tasovac) in this volume. On the enormous growth of doctoral programs in China in particular, see Shin et al., "Challenges for Doctoral Education in East Asia."

8. Cassuto tells this story in relation to graduate education at Michigan and Berkeley in relation to Harvard in particular; see Cassuto, *Graduate School Mess,* 33–34.

9. Newfield's books are the essential point of reference here: see, for example, Newfield, *Unmaking the Public University.*

10. As Cassuto shows, at no point in the twentieth-century development of U.S. graduate systems were student outcomes seriously considered, and programs that might have

a more democratic and practical orientation were usually deprecated; see Cassuto, *Graduate School Mess,* 44.

11. On the final point, Rogers notes, "It is not uncommon for department websites to unceremoniously drop the names of their graduates who step into jobs outside the familiar ranks of assistant, associate, full—especially since only faculty job placements count toward program rankings. . . . Since graduate students excel at reading between the lines, the silences speak loudly." See Rogers, *Putting the Humanities PhD to Work,* 4.

12. See a description of Michigan State's PREP (planning, resilience, engagement, professionalism) initiative in Cassuto, *Graduate School Mess,* 126–27.

13. Bérubé notes that as of 2004, the last year of the National Study of Postsecondary Faculty, 57.3 percent of nontenure-track faculty held the MA as their highest degree in four-year institutions and 76.2 percent in two-year institutions; see Bérubé, "Among the Majority." More recent surveys do not track the terminal degree of faculty at all institutions, but for degree-granting two-year and four-year institutions, the US Digest of Education Statistics 2018 notes that over the previous decade, "the number of full-time staff increased by 11 percent, while the number of part-time staff was 8 percent higher in 2017 than in 2007. Most of the increase in part-time staff was due to increases in the number of part-time faculty (8 percent) and graduate assistants (17 percent) during this time period." See Snyder et al., *Digest of Education Statistics 2018,* 209.

14. See Cassuto and Weisbuch's thorough review of the last decades in doctoral reform in *New PhD,* 32–90.

15. Here we refer to work such as that by the New Faculty Majority and the Coalition of Academic Labor along with the new graduate student unions at Columbia (GWC-UAW 2210) and elsewhere. On the academic literature, see William, "An Emerging Field Deconstructs Academe." Critical university studies now has a number of online bibliographies and a series of books under that rubric at both Johns Hopkins Press and Palgrave.

16. "The percent of institutions with tenure systems increased from 49 percent in 2007–08 to 55 percent in 2017–18. The percentage of public institutions with a tenure system increased from 71 percent in 2007–08 to 75 percent in 2017–18." Snyder et al, *Digest of Education Statistics 2018,* 210.

17. As Cassuto notes, the rigidity of graduate training extends far beyond the humanities into the social sciences and bench sciences, where particular forms of PhD training, admission, and the "graduate funding package," innovated by Johns Hopkins University in imitation of the German research university in 1876, still live on largely unquestioned; see *Graduate School Mess,* 28–29.

18. See the comprehensive discussion of the history of digital humanities pedagogy in Croxall and Jakacki, "Introduction."

Bibliography

Aiyegbusi, Babalola Titilola. "Decolonizing Digital Humanities: Africa in Perspective." In *Bodies of Information: Intersectional Feminism and Digital Humanities,* edited by

Jacqueline Wernimont and Elizabeth Losh, 434–43. Minneapolis: University of Minnesota Press, 2018.

Bérubé, Michael. "Among the Majority." *From the President* (blog), Modern Language Association, January 2012. https://web.archive.org/web/20120722144727/http://www .mla.org/fromthepres?topic=146.

Bérubé, Michael, and Jennifer Ruth. *The Humanities, Higher Education, and Academic Freedom: Three Necessary Arguments.* New York: Palgrave Macmillan, 2015.

Bitusikova, Alexandra. "Reforming Doctoral Education in Europe." *Academe* 95, no.1 (January–February 2009): 21–23. https://www.aaup.org/article/reforming-doctoral -education-europe.

Cassuto, Leonard. *The Graduate School Mess: What Caused It and How We Can Fix It.* Cambridge, Mass.: Harvard University Press, 2015.

Cassuto, Leonard, and Robert Weisbuch. *The New PhD: How to Build a Better Graduate Education.* Baltimore: John Hopkins University Press, 2021.

Cecire, Natalia. "Introduction: Theory and the Virtues of Digital Humanities." *Journal of Digital Humanities* 1, no. 1 (Winter 2011). http://journalofdigitalhumanities.org/1-1 /introduction-theory-and-the-virtues-of-digital-humanities-by-natalia-cecire/.

Cong-Huyen, Anne, and Kush Patel. "Precarious Labor and Radical Care in Libraries and Digital Humanities." In *Knowledge Justice: Disrupting Library and Information Studies through Critical Race Theory,* edited by Sofia Y. Leung and Jorge R. López-McKnight, 263–82. Cambridge, Mass.: The MIT Press, 2021.

Croxall, Brian, and Diane K. Jakacki. "Introduction: What We Teach When We Teach DH." In *What We Teach When We Teach DH: Digital Humanities in the Classroom,* edited by Brian Croxall and Diane K. Jakacki, ix–xix. Minneapolis: University of Minnesota Press, 2023.

Gil, Alex, Dennis Yi Tenen, Austin Mason, Cole Crawford, Roopika Risam, Matthew K. Gold, Will Hanley, et al. "Advanced Degrees in Digital Humanities." GitHub. Accessed April 22, 2024. https://github.com/dh-notes/dhnotes/blob/master/pages/dh-programs.md.

Hockey, Susan. "The History of Humanities Computing." In *A Companion to Digital Humanities,* edited by John Unsworth, Ray Siemens, and Susan Schreibman, 1–19. Malden, Mass.: Blackwell, 2004.

Hopwood, Elizabeth, and Kyle Roberts. "What's the Value of a Graduate Digital Humanities Degree?" In *What We Teach When We Teach DH: Digital Humanities in the Classroom,* edited by Brian Croxall and Diane K. Jakacki, 127–42. Minneapolis: University of Minnesota Press, 2023.

Josephs, Kelly Baker, and Roopika Risam. "Introduction: The Digital Black Atlantic." In *The Digital Black Atlantic,* edited by Roopika Risam and Kelly Baker Josephs, ix–xxiv. Minneapolis: University of Minnesota Press, 2021.

Kornbluh, Anna. "Critical Building: Persistence of Ideology Critique Roundtable." Modern Languages Association Annual Meeting 2019. Chicago, January 4, 2019.

Menand, Louis. "How to Make a PhD Matter." *New York Times Magazine,* September 22, 1996. https://www.nytimes.com/1996/09/22/magazine/how-to-make-a-phd-matter.html.

Menon, Nirmala, and T. Shanmugapriya. "Digital Humanities in India: Pedagogy, Publishing and Practices." In *Exploring Digital Humanities in India: Pedagogies, Practices, and Institutional Possibilities,* edited by Maya Dodd and Nidhi Kalra, 91–104. New Delhi: Routledge India, 2020.

Modern Language Association. *Report of the MLA Task Force on Doctoral Study in Modern Language and Literature.* May 2014. https://www.mla.org/Resources/Guidelines-and -Data/Reports-and-Professional-Guidelines/Report-of-the-Task-Force-on-Doctoral -Study-in-Modern-Language-and-Literature-2014.

Mukherjee, Souvik. "Digital Humanities, or What You Will: Bringing DH to Indian Classrooms." In *Exploring Digital Humanities in India: Pedagogies, Practices, and Institutional Possibilities,* edited by Maya Dodd and Nidhi Kalra, 105–23. New Delhi: Routledge India, 2020.

Murray, Padmini Ray, and Chris Hand. "Making Culture: Locating the Digital Humanities in India." *Visible Language* 49, no. 3 (December 2015): 140–55.

Newfield, Christopher. *Unmaking the Public University: The Forty-Year Assault on the Middle Class.* Cambridge, Mass.: Harvard University Press, 2008.

Nyhan, Julianne, and Andrew Flinn. *Computation and the Humanities: Towards an Oral History of Digital Humanities.* New York: Springer, 2018.

Opeibi, Tunde. "Digitizing the Humanities in an Emerging Space: An Exploratory Study of Digital Humanities Initiatives in Nigeria." In *The Digital Black Atlantic,* edited by Roopika Risam and Kelly Baker Josephs, 162–67. Minneapolis: University of Minnesota Press, 2021.

Presner, Todd. "Welcome to the 20-Year Dissertation." *Chronicle of Higher Education,* November 25, 2013. https://www.chronicle.com/article/welcome-to-the-20-year -dissertation/.

Rogers, Katina L. *Putting the Humanities PhD to Work: Thriving In and Beyond the Classroom.* Durham, N.C.: Duke University Press, 2020.

Schmidt, Benjamin. "Two Volumes: The Lessons of Time on the Cross." *Ben Schmidt* (blog), December 5, 2019. https://benschmidt.org/post/2019-12-05-ToTC/2019-AHA/.

Shin, J. C., Gerard A. Postiglione, and K. C. Ho. "Challenges for Doctoral Education in East Asia: A Global and Comparative Perspective." *Asia Pacific Education Review* 19, no. 2 (June 1, 2018): 141–55. https://doi.org/10.1007/s12564-018-9527-8.

Smith, Sidonie. *Manifesto for the Humanities: Transforming Doctoral Education in Good Enough Times.* Ann Arbor: University of Michigan Press, 2016.

Snyder, Thomas D., Cristobal de Brey, and Sally A. Dillow. *Digest of Education Statistics 2018.* Washington, D.C.: U.S. Department of Education, 2019.

Spaeth, Donald. "Research and Representation: The M.Phil in History and Computing." *Computers and the Humanities* 37, no. 1 (2003): 119–27.

Sula, Chris Alen, S. E. Hackney, and Phillip Cunningham. "A Survey of Digital Humanities Programs." *Journal of Interactive Technology and Pedagogy* 11 (2017). https://jitp .commons.gc.cuny.edu/a-survey-of-digital-humanities-programs/.

William, Jeffrey J. "An Emerging Field Deconstructs Academe." *Chronicle of Higher Education,* February 19, 2012. https://www.chronicle.com/article/deconstructing-academe/.

Wissik, Tanja, Jennifer Edmond, Frank Fischer, Franciska de Jong, Stefania Scagliola, et al. "Teaching Digital Humanities Around the World: An Infrastructural Approach to a Community-Driven DH Course Registry." Preprint, submitted in 2020. https://hal .archives-ouvertes.fr/hal-02500871.

PART I

POSITIONS AND
PROVOCATIONS

Covid, Care, and Community
Redesigning Graduate Education in a Pandemic

KATINA L. ROGERS

Beginning in March 2020, the Covid-19 pandemic plunged educational structures into disarray, with seemingly immutable policies and procedures shifting overnight in response to urgent public health concerns. As instructors scrambled to find ways to teach students remotely with no time to prepare, concerns about technology and pedagogy opened into necessary and often painful conversations about underlying inequities in the structures of higher education that have long persisted. These rapid changes have prompted crucial conversations not only about how graduate education is structured but also about its value and purpose at a moment of significant upheaval. Matters of equity are tantamount to these discussions, as the scholarly community collectively grapples with questions of what we do, how, why, and for whom.

As the pandemic unfolded, the realities of higher education's inequities were made painfully apparent. Students who relied on computer labs were suddenly left without safe, quiet, internet-equipped spaces to work. Many juggling work and caregiving responsibilities alongside their studies confronted impossible schedules and economic hardship. Thousands of faculty and staff in precarious positions were let go, often with no medical insurance to protect them amid a public health crisis. And because of underlying structural inequalities, these faculty, staff, and students were more likely to hail from minoritized and marginalized communities.[1] In this chapter, I examine some of the fundamental inequalities of higher education and ask what it might look like to imagine otherwise.

Balancing the equation of graduate education reform requires attention to a critical variable that is often overlooked: care. In our current political and social moment, spaces of care and support are more important than ever, particularly for students whose backgrounds are typically marginalized in the academy. Regardless of a student's field or methodology, no matter how traditional or innovative a program's curriculum, the matter of how students experience and demonstrate care is a crucial element in their eventual success (where success is defined by reaching their own goals). Care work tends to be feminized in academia as it is in many other domains; as such, it is often undervalued despite its importance. Knowing how to tap into some of the academy's more typical structures of care—those found in mentoring, advising, and developing a peer network—may not be equally available to all students. Because a certain amount of educational and cultural knowledge is required to navigate the spaces of the academy, these areas of support can become part of the hidden curriculum, leaving first-generation students and students of color less likely to ask for the support they need for fear of seeming like they do not belong.

Like many U.S. institutions, from healthcare to policing, higher education is structured in a way that upholds a status quo. This is not necessarily a bad thing; institutions are often intentionally conservative, which provides stability and longevity. However, it *does* become a problem when that status quo is grounded in inequality, which I argue is the case for higher education. Although the idea of the "life of the mind" might seem to be beyond the effects of systematic injustice, in reality, higher education's prestige economy perpetuates a structure of patriarchal white supremacy and a myth of meritocracy. This structure leads to continued marginalization along axes of race, gender, sexuality, disability, and more. This is especially apparent in labor structures: for example, underpaid adjuncts are far more likely to be women from minoritized communities, but tenured professors are more likely to be white men, even at an institution as diverse as the City University of New York (CUNY), the large public university system where I worked from 2014 until 2021.

Even for those in secure positions, the nature of scholarly work has shifted unequally, particularly with regard to gender, due not only to well-documented gender bias but also to the uneven distribution of care work.[2] In colleges and universities, this work takes the shape of mentoring, guiding, supporting, and sustaining so that others may continue to advance toward their goals. Given the trauma of the pandemic, many people in the higher education community have experienced profound distress. Faculty and staff members found themselves undertaking a significant increase in care and support work to try and support vulnerable students and colleagues, all while navigating their own highly stressful pandemic realities. We know from countless sources, from anecdotes to peer-reviewed research, that women, and especially women of color, tend to perform more of the work of care and support than cis men in educational contexts.[3] In this way, it is similar to other kinds of care work in that it is reproductive, easing the friction of others' progress and accomplishments while often going unnoticed and unrewarded.

This increase in academic care work adds to imbalances in the home that have also been exacerbated during the challenges of navigating work and home life during the Covid-19 pandemic. And yet, this imbalance often goes unperceived by those who benefit from it. One recent study showed that among heterosexual couples with small children, men tended to think they were doing most of the childcare and housework, and yet in reality, most of that work continued to be performed by women.[4] The result has been a striking imbalance in research productivity, the usual mode of measuring academic success and progress. Although scholarly journal submissions from men increased during the period of isolation, submissions from women—and especially women with caregiving responsibilities—plummeted.[5]

I felt this imbalance in my own life, where especially in the early days of stay-at-home orders I took on the majority of caring for my two young children while working full-time as an administrator at The Graduate Center, CUNY.[6] I directed a group of about ten people that included graduate students, a postdoctoral fellow, and staff members. My leadership was predicated on care, and I worked hard to try and ensure that our team felt supported to the degree possible while so much was in upheaval. It was a lot. In fact, all this contributed to the difficult decision to leave my position in September 2021, despite how much I care about CUNY as an institution. In this, I was like countless others who have significantly changed their relationship to work during the Covid-19 pandemic.

And yet, even to be able to make such a decision was a tremendous privilege. My spouse and I have financial security. We live in a quiet, comfortable apartment with access to outdoor space. We can both work from home and have a choice in whether and when to take exposure risks. Our family has plenty to eat. As a white woman, it is highly unlikely that I will ever be harmed by the police, especially in my own home. Much of this nation's social, economic, and educational infrastructure was designed to protect and benefit people like me.

Many of my team members could not have said the same. As graduate students, even graduate students in a strongly unionized institution, they were in precarious financial and labor situations. Many were students of color and international students for whom the disparities of education, health, and policing are painfully clear in their daily lived realities. And in the midst of this trauma—one that follows generations of racism and inequity, brought into especially sharp relief in recent years—they are also the ones supporting their own students.

Graduate students have so little support and yet for those who are teaching, as most CUNY Graduate Center students are, they are also the first and most direct point of contact for countless undergraduate students whose lives may be even more severely upended. CUNY serves five hundred thousand students from across the five boroughs of New York City, and a significant majority of them navigate the city from a marginalized position related to their racial or ethnic background, immigration status, and socioeconomic status. The college setting sometimes provides a sense of belonging, sometimes alienation. Most of them are taking courses from graduate students and adjunct faculty who lack a living wage, job security, or office space. Yet I see these graduate students and adjuncts putting themselves out there day after day, caring deeply not only for their students' learning but also their students' well-being. They love what they do and feel a strong sense of commitment. As I argued in *Putting the Humanities PhD to Work,* however, conflating love with labor is risky because it makes it easy to minimize the value of the work and to neglect material needs. The ways in which adjuncts and graduate students show care to their students is work, and it is hugely important work. But because care work tends to be feminized and undercompensated, and because cities and states have been reducing their investment in higher education for decades, these brilliant and caring educators are at a breaking point.

Working in an underfunded public university system made it clearer than ever that public reinvestment in higher education is absolutely foundational to any kind of meaningful reform. It may be impossible to extricate educational systems from the structural inequalities they uphold, but I strongly believe that we can create and protect spaces that offer freedom and hope if there is sufficient support. CUNY faculty and staff must frequently conjure something from nothing, buying their own supplies and working in buildings with inadequate infrastructure. Yet it is not that the state has insufficient money to support education but rather that other initiatives are given higher priority. Education has long been a place where budget cuts happen first when city and state budgets are tight, something with which CUNY is intimately familiar. For example, in summer 2020, after the first brutal Covid-19 wave in New York City when many students sought affordable options for online learning, CUNY's enrollment increased by 17 percent. Yet CUNY was subjected to massive system-wide budget cuts, which resulted in significant course reductions and the layoffs of nearly three thousand adjunct faculty.[7] The program I codirected had its operating budget cut by 80 percent; other programs were hit even harder. It almost goes without saying that students from marginalized racial, ethnic, and socioeconomic backgrounds were hurt most significantly by these cuts, given that many were already in precarious positions not only with respect to their education but also with respect to their health, safety, and financial well-being.

All of our social systems—including education, health, and policing—are connected. Rather than creating a robust safety net, though, the deeply rooted inequity in each of these structures compound with one another. The result is an exponentially greater risk for people whose identities are marginalized in one or more ways. At the same time, the Covid-19 pandemic has disproportionately struck the Black and Latinx communities because of a lack of access to quality health care, a predominance of low-wage work that cannot be performed remotely, resulting either in joblessness or exposure, and high-risk comorbidities resulting from generations of social and health disparities.[8] In addition to these health and economic impacts, the ongoing trauma of racialized violence at the hands of the state continues unabated.[9] As protests in support of Black Lives Matter underscored, there is a glaring discrepancy between the willingness of city and state leaders to continually increase funding to police departments as a proportion of public spending, but other public services—including health care, social services, transportation, and education— sustain budget cuts year after year.[10] Shifting funds from punitive measures like policing and incarceration would immediately open significant opportunities to better support individuals and communities.

Education is supposed to be a "way out" of poverty, a ticket to greater opportunities; CUNY has indeed been shown to propel many students into more financially stable lives than their parents had, with many of the CUNY colleges near the top of lists of institutions providing social mobility.[11] But when education continues to perpetuate the same violence, and the same inequity, as every other social system, is it worth it? My work focuses on transforming graduate education, with a particular focus on equity, sustainability, and even joy. But it is impossible to skip equity in trying to reach the other goals. Sustainability and joy can only emerge when programs reckon with the racism and inequity that are woven into the fabric of their competitive, hierarchical structures. The possibility of joy in graduate education, for me, is pressed tightly against my anger at a system that does so much harm to so many brilliant, caring students and educators.

A significant portion of my work as an administrator was likely invisible to anyone except my team. Some of this work would likely have been categorized as service in a faculty position—mentorship, advising, and guiding the graduate students and postdocs on our team, for instance. Given the intensity of graduate school, this involves a great deal of care work, helping each member of our team to manage their competing obligations and reach their goals. For many students on our team, these elements of support and the resulting joy of the community were a welcome counterbalance to the toll of graduate school, which too often causes students to experience significant emotional, psychological, and physical challenges that have nothing to do with their studies. Our team worked hard; our weekly meetings included a sometimes daunting agenda of upcoming events and responsibilities. Yet the meetings became a source of sustenance for the staff members and graduate students who made up the core program team during an especially challenging year. This was not alchemy. The program I codirected emphasized elements that could be applied to any graduate education context, whether in a department, a workplace, or an extracurricular group. These translatable elements include trust, material support, and a shared mission.

A major challenge in creating holistic and sustaining programs is that higher education operates on an economy of prestige. In this economy, the so-called life of the mind takes center stage, leaving little room for attention to physical and emotional well-being. A different orientation—one that prioritizes people over prestige—is essential to creating supportive and sustainable structures. However, programs in interstitial spaces often have greater flexibility than those with longstanding institutional mandates. The bigger challenge, then, is how to build lasting change by incorporating similar methods into academic departments, where students and faculty put down intellectual and professional roots. Although elements of our work at the Futures Initiative could absolutely be used in academic and extracurricular or cocurricular programs, other elements may simply not be possible in a core academic department. Academic departments tend to be competitive spaces with finite resources that are unevenly distributed. This is fundamentally different from a space like the Futures Initiative. Despite the program's location within the competitive space of a research institution, within the program, the values shift. In a program like the Futures Initiative, there is no weeding out or formal evaluation, as such programs are not gatekeepers to students' degrees or careers. Students are not vying for resources or faculty time, nor are they jockeying for position. Perhaps the inherently competitive and evaluative nature of academic programs means that work like this can only exist in interstitial spaces.

That said, with the pandemic's effects still fresh in mind, we have a unique opportunity to try. As institutions nationwide rapidly shifted to emergency online instruction in spring 2020, it became clear that sweeping change was possible in institutions that often seem resistant to reform. These changes were undertaken in a crisis and were far from perfect, yet they suggested the possibility that deep reform might be possible. The question that remains is how might we (scholars, administrators, and graduate students) take action to redesign graduate education in favor of more holistic and sustaining systems. Opportunities like those afforded by the Futures Initiative are rare in academe, but they do not have to be. The collaborative nature of the program has proven to be intellectually generative and has sparked new scholarly insights. Graduate fellows in the program often reported that they were waiting for this kind of opportunity; they found that it brought their work to life in a new way. This suggests there is an alternative to the more dominant, prestige-oriented model of graduate education. I look to Kathleen Fitzpatrick's exhortation in *Generous Thinking* to replace the default scholarly position of competition with one of generosity. I also look to bell hooks's earlier assertion in *Teaching Community*, "Educating is always a vocation rooted in hopefulness" (xiv). Hope and joy are not a way of sugarcoating reality; on the contrary, hope is at its most powerful when the circumstances seem bleak. I think of Toni Cade Bambara's reflection on what she perceived as her responsibility: "As a culture worker who belongs to an oppressed people my job is to make revolution irresistible."[12] To extend Bambara's framework for arts and culture, I would argue that the beauty, joy, and hope of education are predicated on the possibility of change. To go a step further, perhaps graduate education can be a source of joy if it is also a lever of social justice. Enabling doctoral students to pursue deep and rigorous education that also furthers goals they have within their multiple communities may help to reduce feelings of alienation and isolation that often accompany doctoral work and to spark a sense of meaning and contribution that brings the research to life.

As these examples suggest, generosity, abundance, hope, and joy can form a foundation on which our educational principles are grounded. Feminist scholarship by Black women, Indigenous women, and women of color offers especially rich perspectives on the praxis of hope and joy, even (and especially) in difficult times. Scholarly work is all about creating new knowledge, new ways of being, and new possibilities. Such goals could create a mindset of curiosity and abundance, but higher education has come to be dominated by a sense of scarcity and competition.

Yet a sense of scarcity is necessary for the university's value when that value is predicated on prestige. Shifting from a prestige-oriented system to one that is fundamentally rooted in abundance and generosity would require a massive change not only in values but also in the structures that have been developed on the basis of those values.[13]

I think the first step may be to simply stop for a moment. There is power in collective action, in a protest, in a strike, and in the act of saying, "No more." Before we can build new systems and structures and incentives and task forces, I think we need to pause and say no. No, some of this work does not matter, and we can let it drop. No, we will not continue to exploit adjunct labor. No, we will not ask the impossible of our underfunded institutions, constantly pressured to do more with less. For me, there is hope in this refusal because it says that a different way is possible.

Notes

1. For a look at the numbers, see Finkelstein et al., "Taking the Measure of Faculty Diversity." To understand some of the dynamics of how this has come to be, even in an era with increased diversity efforts, see Matthew, *Written/Unwritten* and Ahmed, *On Being Included.*

2. See Savonick and Davidson, "Gender Bias in Academe" for a comprehensive (and growing) annotated bibliography.

3. See Social Sciences Feminist Network Research Interest Group, "Burden of Invisible Work"; Conesa, "How Are Academic Lives Sustained?"; Mason, Wolfinger, and Goulden, *Do Babies Matter?*; Guarino and Borden, "Faculty Service Loads and Gender."

4. For a discussion about the disparity in men's and women's perspectives, see Carlson et al., "Changes in Parents' Domestic Labor During the COVID-19 Pandemic."

5. See Amano-Patiño et al., "Who Is Doing New Research?" and Malisch et al., "In the Wake of COVID-19." This is consistent with research showing that parental leave augments men's scholarly productivity, but it slows research production among women.

6. I left this role in September 2021 to launch an independent consultancy focused on graduate education reform. Although my role has changed, my work continues to focus on care, equity, sustainability, and joy.

7. See Schubert, "CUNY Sees Massive Budget Cuts." CUNY employees and students have rallied to urge city and state lawmakers to restore CUNY's full funding; for more details, see the CUNY Rising Alliance's NewDeal4CUNY movement.

8. For just a few examples of this, see Godoy, "What Do Coronavirus Racial Disparities Look Like State By State?" (based on data from the Atlantic's COVID Racial Data Tracker); American Medical Association, "Impact of COVID-19"; Centers for Disease Control and Prevention, "Health Equity Considerations"; and Oppel et al., "Fullest Look Yet."

9. See Edwards et al., "Risk of Being Killed by Police"; Obasogie, "Police Killing Black People Is a Pandemic"; Siegel, "Racial Disparities in Fatal Police Shootings."

10. For examples, see Kanik, "Reality of US City Budgets"; Ingraham, "U.S. Spends Twice as Much"; Burnette, "Schools or Police."

11. For instance, see Chetty et al., "Mobility Report Cards," where CUNY colleges make up six of the top ten institutions when ranked by intergenerational social mobility.

12. Bambara shared this comment with Kay Bonetti; see "Interview with Toni Cade Bambara."

13. I also explore these ideas in my forthcoming chapter, "Cultivating a Joyful Workplace," in Hartman and Strakovsky, eds., *Graduate Education for a Thriving Humanities Ecosystem.*

Bibliography

Ahmed, Sara. *On Being Included: Racism and Diversity in Institutional Life.* Durham, N.C.: Duke University Press, 2012.

Amano-Patiño, Noriko, Elisa Faraglia, Chryssi Giannitsarou, and Zeina Hasna. "Who Is Doing New Research in the Time of COVID-19? Not the Female Economists." *VoxEU* (blog), May 2, 2020. https://voxeu.org/article/who-doing-new-research-time -covid-19-not-female-economists.

American Medical Association. "Impact of COVID-19 on Minoritized and Marginalized Communities." Accessed September 11, 2020. https://www.ama-assn.org/delivering -care/health-equity/impact-covid-19-minoritized-and-marginalized-communities.

Bonetti, Kay. "An Interview with Toni Cade Bambara." In *Conversations with Toni Cade Bambara,* 35–47. Literary Conversations Series. Jackson: University Press of Mississippi, 2012.

Burnette, Daarel, II. "Schools or Police: In Some Cities, a Reckoning on Spending Priorities." *Education Week,* June 18, 2020. https://www.edweek.org/ew/articles/2020/06/18 /schools-or-police-in-some-cities-a.html.

Carlson, Daniel L., Richard Petts, and Joanna Pepin. "Changes in Parents' Domestic Labor During the COVID-19 Pandemic." May 6, 2020. https://doi.org/10.31235/osf.io/jy8fn.

Centers for Disease Control and Prevention. "Health Equity Considerations and Racial and Ethnic Minority Groups." July 24, 2020. https://stacks.cdc.gov/view/cdc/91049.

Chetty, Raj, John N. Friedman, Emmanuel Saez, Nicholas Turner, and Danny Yagan. "Mobility Report Cards: The Role of Colleges in Intergenerational Mobility." Working Paper Series, National Bureau of Economic Research, July 2017. https://doi.org /10.3386/w23618.

Conesa, Ester. "How Are Academic Lives Sustained? Gender and the Ethics of Care in the Neoliberal Accelerated Academy." *Impact of Social Sciences, London School of Economics* (blog), March 27, 2018. https://blogs.lse.ac.uk/impactofsocialsciences/2018/03/27 /how-are-academic-lives-sustained-gender-and-the-ethics-of-care-in-the-neoliberal -accelerated-academy/.

The COVID Tracking Project. "The COVID Racial Data Tracker." Accessed September 11, 2020. https://covidtracking.com/race.

CUNY Rising Alliance. "NewDeal4CUNY." Accessed December 13, 2021. https://cuny risingalliance.org/newdeal4cuny.

Edwards, Frank, Hedwig Lee, and Michael Esposito. "Risk of Being Killed by Police Use of Force in the United States by Age, Race–Ethnicity, and Sex." *Proceedings of the National Academy of Sciences* 116, no. 34 (August 20, 2019): 16793–98. https://doi.org /10.1073/pnas.1821204116.

Finkelstein, Martin, Valerie Martin Conley, and Jack H. Schuster. "Taking the Measure of Faculty Diversity." Accessed September 11, 2020. https://www.tiaa.org/public/insti tute/publication/2016/taking-measure-faculty-diversity.

Fitzpatrick, Kathleen. *Generous Thinking: A Radical Approach to Saving the University.* Baltimore: Johns Hopkins University Press, 2019.

Guarino, Cassandra M., and Victor M. H. Borden. "Faculty Service Loads and Gender: Are Women Taking Care of the Academic Family?" *Research in Higher Education* 58, no. 6 (2017): 672–94. https://doi.org/10.1007/s11162-017-9454-2.

hooks, bell. *Teaching Community: A Pedagogy of Hope.* New York: Routledge, 2003.

Ingraham, Christopher. "U.S. Spends Twice as Much on Law and Order as It Does on Cash Welfare, Data Show." *Washington Post,* June 4, 2020. https://www.washingtonpost .com/business/2020/06/04/us-spends-twice-much-law-order-it-does-social-welfare -data-show/.

Kanik, Alexandra. "The Reality of US City Budgets: Police Funding Eclipses Most Other Agencies." CityMetric. June 19, 2020. https://www.citymetric.com/politics/reality-us -city-budgets-police-funding-eclipses-most-other-agencies-5186.

Malisch, Jessica L., Breanna N. Harris, Shanen M. Sherrer, Kristy A. Lewis, Stephanie L. Shepherd, Pumtiwitt C. McCarthy, Jessica L. Spott, et al. "Opinion: In the Wake of COVID-19, Academia Needs New Solutions to Ensure Gender Equity." *Proceedings of the National Academy of Sciences* 117, no. 27 (July 7, 2020): 15378–81. https://doi .org/10.1073/pnas.2010636117.

Mason, Mary Ann, Nicholas H. Wolfinger, and Marc Goulden. *Do Babies Matter? Gender and Family in the Ivory Tower.* New Brunswick, N.J.: Rutgers University Press, 2013.

Matthew, Patricia A. *Written/Unwritten: Diversity and the Hidden Truths of Tenure.* Chapel Hill: University of North Carolina Press, 2016.

Obasogie, Osagie K. "Police Killing Black People Is a Pandemic, Too." *Washington Post,* June 5, 2020. https://www.washingtonpost.com/outlook/police-violence-pandemic /2020/06/05/e1a2a1b0-a669-11ea-b619-3f9133bbb482_story.html.

Oppel, Richard A., Jr., Robert Gebeloff, K. K. Rebecca Lai, Will Wright, and Mitch Smith. "The Fullest Look Yet at the Racial Inequity of Coronavirus." *New York Times,* July 5, 2020. https://www.nytimes.com/interactive/2020/07/05/us/coronavirus-latinos-african -americans-cdc-data.html.

Rogers, Katina L. "Cultivating a Joyful Workplace through Trust, Support, and a Shared Mission." In *Graduate Education for a Thriving Humanities Ecosystem,* edited by Stacy Hartman and Yevgenya Strakovsky. New York: Modern Language Association, 2023.

Rogers, Katina L. *Putting the Humanities PhD to Work: Thriving in and beyond the Classroom.* Durham, N.C.: Duke University Press, 2020.

Savonick, Danica, and Cathy Davidson. "Gender Bias in Academe: An Annotated Bibliography of Important Recent Studies." *Impact of Social Sciences* (blog), March 8, 2016. https://blogs.lse.ac.uk/impactofsocialsciences/2016/03/08/gender-bias-in-academe-an-annotated-bibliography/.

Schubert, Maya. "CUNY Sees Massive Budget Cuts in Age of COVID." *Brooklyn College Vanguard* (blog), March 12, 2021. https://vanguard.blog.brooklyn.edu/2021/03/11/cuny-sees-massive-budget-cuts-in-age-of-covid/.

Siegel, Michael. "Racial Disparities In Fatal Police Shootings: An Empirical Analysis Informed by Critical Race Theory." *Boston University Law Review* 100, no. 3 (2020): 1069–92.

Social Sciences Feminist Network Research Interest Group. "The Burden of Invisible Work in Academia: Social Inequalities and Time Use in Five University Departments." *Humboldt Journal of Social Relations* 39 (2017): 228–45.

Useless (Digital) Humanities?

ALISON BOOTH

The current crisis in the humanities and higher education, compounded by the pandemic and national politics, intensifies the longstanding pressure to justify graduate education as useful. Useful can mean that a specific degree program must help in the drive to find employment after an expensive education, or it can mean that a program must address immediate problems in society as well as in universities. In both senses of utility, graduate study in digital humanities (DH) is increasingly useful. I am convinced that DH is *a* (not the only) key to rewarding careers and flourishing interdisciplinary research relating to the humanities in decades to come. Fellowships and research assistantships in DH often lead to related positions after the master's or doctoral degree, whether or not the candidate remains in academia, as I can attest. At the University of Virginia, I was a founding co-leader of the graduate Certificate in Digital Humanities with Rennie Mapp, and since 2023 I am faculty director of the DH Center in the Shannon Library.[1] Like other programs and centers, we serve not only the vocational preparation of students but also the social uses of DH as students, faculty, and staff collaborate on initiatives promoting historical understanding and environmental and social justice.[2]

But what do we risk if we advocate digital graduate study in terms of usefulness? Perhaps the definition of usefulness needs to be reconsidered. Perhaps, even, we should listen beyond our ideological bubbles and cultivate ambivalence, uncomfortable as it may be. In an opinion piece titled "The Humanities May Seem Pointless, but That Is the Point," Santiago Ramos objects to "our quasi-utilitarian value system." Ramos states: "Under this system, the humanities are only worth studying if they are useful for something like ethical training or developing business skills. The latest version of this argument holds that Silicon Valley leaders should have studied literature and philosophy to avoid unethical applications of new technology. But thinking about literature and philosophy exclusively as *useful*—effectively, as tools—ultimately undermines the humanities."[3] Ramos voices belief in a Kantian, noninstrumental potential in humanities education that I recognize and share to an extent in this essay. Because this humanism can be heard in a conservative forum like *America: The Jesuit Review* does not mean that it has no beneficial purpose; many so-called conservative voices not only would reduce humanities to be means to ends but go further to such measures as laws policing the topic of race in public schools or surveilling wokeness in higher education. I would not make humanities merely useful but indispensable, and no more useless than a great deal of higher education, as deferred and diffusive as the humanities. Direct payoff is not required of all scientific research or work in engineering schools or quantitative social sciences, so why is it required in the humanities, which is understood to include the arts? We do not believe near-term dividends are the justification for studying history or archaeology, creating, performing, or studying music, becoming an adept interpreter of literature, or becoming a mathematician. Digital humanities is useful but also useless in terms that promote new models of engaged, accessible human inquiry in higher education and beyond.

In this essay, I resist justifications of higher education as vocational training even as I affirm the inherent value (social and political as well as economic) of the humanities. As part of a principle of principled ambivalence, I advocate digital methods and learning, certainly not because they mesh well with a corporate culture of the future but because they serve many of the aims of methods and learning in the humanities, an idea that has been contested. Further, and possibly in counterpoint to a chorus in this volume, I express some concerns about digital study in graduate education. We cannot assume it is easy to blend such education with the traditional modes of humanities scholarship in three main respects: competing for limited time, acknowledgment or credit, and the interrelated tensions between DH and more prevalent disciplinary practices. Foreseeable transformations of humanities will entail some conflicts and losses. But if we push back against emerging pressures and balance the accounts of our ambivalence, we may foster collaborative and fruitful graduate training that serves humanist learning well beyond academia.

The idea of learning that is worthwhile in its own right may seem to be a complacent myth that undergirded universities over a century ago when the elite professoriate came from the monied classes. Those universities, as Cathy N. Davidson argues, in fact made practical changes to adjust to industrialization's demand for management of literate employees; in the internet age, we need new skills and certification.[4] Davidson hopes that a nimble, un-siloed education will qualify students to find worthwhile jobs that are unlikely to be eliminated by automation. But those like Davidson who seek to remodel higher education according to standards other than the corporate bottom line also warn against sidelining subjects that seem impractical. Christopher Newfield has argued that faculty should reclaim governance of colleges and universities, especially regarding budget and planning, so that they can demystify what is affordable; they should "repudiate learning = earning" and "theorize the non-monetary and social effects" of liberal arts education.[5] Other voices outside DH similarly resist the overestimation of STEM subjects. Studies show that the skills of humanities-educated applicants are favored by businesses and that liberal arts majors earn more over their careers.[6] Even when resisting "learning = earning," it is difficult to advocate for the humanities and hence the digital approach to this spectrum of subjects, materials, and theories without falling into a utilitarian argument.

No one disputes that the future of humanities research and teaching is entwined with digital literacy, as Alexander Reid and others understood in 2012 ("Graduate Education," 353–54). But it would not be the answer to the crisis in humanities and higher education to require that all graduate students in humanities be card-carrying members of DH.[7] As Katina Rogers writes in *Putting the Humanities PhD to Work*, "Pushing all humanities students to learn to code isn't a quick fix to systemic labor issues; however, making it possible for students to pursue the kinds of projects that spark genuine interest, and making it possible for them to learn necessary skills along the way, will likely lead to more creative and interesting research projects while also building up digital literacy and skills that may be transferable to other job contexts" (xii). Rogers here, and in her advocacy of graduate work as care work in chapter 1 in this volume, articulates the spirit I aspire to in graduate education in digital humanities. Likewise, this spirit is broadly aligned with Kathleen Fitzpatrick's *Generous Thinking* and the prospects for reenvisioned, noncorporate higher education laid out by Davidson and Newfield. Digital humanities can be a means to collaborative, engaged education for careers that apply technologies for public good rather than using them to monetize consumer data or create financial instruments.[8]

Let me turn to matters that give me concern as well as hope, by way of my own observations, for the future engagement of the humanities with reflective digital methods. As a feminist critic hired into a large English department that had only recently tenured its second senior woman and that hired only its second Black colleague the next year, I felt we were unsettling entrenched tradition as we eventually launched women's studies and African American studies. But I recognize my privilege as a white, heterosexual, now-tenured faculty member at a research university with an excellent library. Until recently, this university prioritized humanities graduate programs.[9] I deplore how this place emulates neoliberal, privatizing models of higher education that create and then exploit an oversupply of humanities PhDs. My experience of course shapes the standpoint from which I see hope for careers that transform higher education as well as society. I will claim the compatibility of the digital *and* the humanities, but I also note the primary issues as follows: competition for limited time, matters of acknowledgment or credit, and interrelated tensions between DH and more prevalent disciplinary practices.

Digital and *Humanities*

Waves of critique of DH persist, not always concurring on what it is that is being opposed.[10] A Google search shows that "oxymoron digital humanities" is a frequent locution. It is easy to suppose that humanities, qualitative, cannot be served by quantitative methods. Some attacks on DH have assumed that it aspires to make C. P. Snow's two cultures of science/information and arts and letters/aesthetics into a monoculture, to the demotion of the apparently softer values. On the contrary, there is a dialectic if not an oxymoron in the term digital humanities. In positive senses, the "digital" can entail technological innovation and collaboration on publicly accessible products; "humanities" can mean state-of-the-art documentation and interpretation of the objects of humanities research, often in solitary inquiry shared with a few specialists.[11] In one of many refutations of attacks on DH within academic humanities, Sarah E. Bond, Hoyt Long, and Ted Underwood insist, as their title puts it, " 'Digital' Is Not the Opposite of 'Humanities.' " Noting that computer technology helps us explore "questions, long central to literary history . . . on a new scale," they also offer examples of "social-justice initiatives" using geographic information systems to reveal "the spatial patterns of lynching, urban segregation, and 'white flight.' Expanding the scope of our knowledge needn't make scholars less critical of power." I share this conviction that humanities research can prompt collaboration and public access with digital methods and in the process move toward the interdisciplinarity and impact that many in higher education have long advocated. My interest here is in the necessary choices, the roads taken to prepare future explorers, not to seek extraction or colonization but care, sustainability, and discoveries that respect diverse pasts.

We can agree with Alan Liu that humanists all would gain from some familiarity with developments apparently non-native to humanities: statistics; data visualization; machine learning; linked open data about peoples, objects and sites, archives, and print corpora; documenting social media in crises; born-digital literature and arts; and information architecture (Liu, "Toward a Diversity Stack"). At the same time, Liu anticipates that something in the humanities is left behind in the present dissemination of myriad bites of information. In *Friending the Past*, Liu's media archaeology and reflections on cultural studies and DH alike register the loss of a sense of collective history. Liu is far from nostalgic or technophobic; he maintains that "one needs to handle the apparatus and the code to gain a feel for the future of the sense of history" (8). The future will undoubtedly bring fewer well-written academic monographs or essays like Liu's.[12] Writing that works well in grants is different from journalism, blogs, or tweets and again from the diction of books by professors of literature, which, however readable, must introduce specialized terms and footnotes. How easily does a novice in the humanities or digital technology acquire the range of skills necessary to produce the research, whether in book or digital form? Digital humanities asks us to unite skills, knowledge, theory, and tolerance of the elusive in a challenging combination.

Like some other senior faculty today, I was introduced to DH gradually, at a period when the horizons of online research were opening but before the digitization of swaths of library holdings. A graduate student can now traverse that introduction in a matter of weeks, whereas training in a particular field such as American studies or French extends over years. Often, researchers turn to digital methods when they find their inquiry expands beyond what can be confirmed by travel to far-flung archives or communicated in printed prose with static tables and footnotes. I took the digital fork in the road to investigate variegated data in a neglected genre (books not yet digitized), but I was also motivated by collaboration, public access, interdisciplinarity, and impact. I was attracted by a more interactive and less hierarchical mode of teaching and scholarly communication. I always felt humanities research was diminished by its specialist print formats, slow and unlikely to reach general readers, so I was excited by the resurgence of public intellectuals in blogs and websites. Then, the large scope of a bibliography project and the obvious advantage of online searchability led me, with the help of many people, to hands-on humanities computing and immersion in the rich discourse of reflections upon this work. I was drawn to the joined effort to assemble something colorful and moving, tangible and coded, not unlike a quilt in also being useful. It was an aspiration to exceed my own graduate training, much like learning a new language. Continuing to learn on the job is a hallmark of both alt-ac and academic jobs, not least because the humanities are never constant.

Competing for Scarce Time in Digital and Humanities

Ars longa, vita brevis. Or, Liu's long list of what we need to learn runs up against the short years of a researcher's life. I have already noted that a humanities discipline requires years even without the technological skills. If the student's previous humanities education has not been global, critical of such categories as nation and period and race, and aware of media history, if it has not developed skills of close reading and writing and has not also offered experience in archival research or data collection, and if it has made the humanities appear to be about surface familiarity with a received repertoire instead of about living matters that have served different interests, well, graduate education in the humanities may be too little, too late. And while catching up and absorbing the changing global perspectives beyond nation, period, and departmental boundaries, we hope the graduate student will also master project management and Python. The educational transformation must begin earlier, as I suggest with respect to pedagogical collaborations, below.

University administrators have accepted pressures to shorten the time it takes to earn the doctorate or master's degree. In the United States, specialized studies are delayed until the third year of undergraduate school. Digital research methods are often encountered first in the MA or PhD program, when the student may be undertaking advanced humanities research for the first time. Digital skills can be learned in online tutorials or workshops and institutes, but reinforcement of this learning and enticement to keep practicing depends on a community, perhaps hardly overlapping with people in one's home humanities field (field-specific associates may be hostile to DH). Not everyone has access to resources such as fellowships, licensed software or databases, or research centers, and further obstacles come with travel restrictions, health vulnerabilities or disabilities, or family care and schooling obligations. Without the advantages of access, both training and implementation of projects will take far longer. A master's student needs to jump in immediately and may not have time to launch and complete an independent project. The doctoral candidate is advised to postpone large-scale independent DH projects to devote scarce time to completing the dissertation. This pressure intensifies with the rankings and metrics that count time to degree. As with a linguist's or anthropologist's fieldwork or learning a necessary language, a DH researcher should be allowed a focused additional year.

There are related pressures of time: all project managers can attest that "it will take longer than you think"; DH implementation, even as technology speeds up, is labor intensive. And projects should not linger and cannot survive long because technology changes so fast.[13] The schedule of research obsolescence appears to be even faster in new media: publish *and* perish. Printed articles and books, along with ephemera, periodicals, and archival materials, have been known to last decades longer than digital access or microfilm access to these materials. So, may graduate students be enthusiastic adopters of new digital applications, but may they also avoid intertwining their research profiles with the datasets or technical resources of this decade alone. Taking the time to learn the long histories and expanding perspectives of humanities disciplines prepares for an adaptable career and helps to remind that digital modes of graduate work are rapidly evolving along with the world's encounter with transformative technology.

Credit Where Credit Is Due

It requires a change of custom for humanists to take stock of the infrastructure of their research—the many other people who have saved their time, we might say. Scholarship with the solo byline (e.g., a monograph) includes acknowledgments, which sometimes mention librarians and archivists and usually name colleagues, research assistants, typists, and family members. Any scholar's book or article also needs a scaffolding of citation but often elides the crucial prior work (and bias) of databases and search engines, the building of the cathedrals of digitized materials. Originality is still at a premium in DH, and indeed the demand for novelty in tools and designs can stand in the way of perceiving the value of substantial innovation in materials and interpretation. But digital projects usually preempt any claim to solo authorship. The group effort resembles film production, even in work that looks like end user calculations; someone built that out-of-the-box software. Certainly, the ethic I observe in DH puts strong pressure on acknowledging all contributors. Citation is not enough; we need the equivalents of film credits, including all the extras, who deserve fair pay.

Acknowledgment is one thing, but evaluation in graduate school and future employment tends to be individual. And we know that DH is still hard to plug into the academic systems for evaluation and promotion (and tenure, for track faculty). After decades of guidelines from professional organizations such as the American Historical Association, the Modern Language Association, and the Association for Computers and the Humanities, review committees still claim to be unable to assess digital projects alongside published articles and books.[14] As in multiauthored articles produced by grant-funded labs, it can be difficult to tease apart one person's contributions to a digital project, but as in the natural sciences, there are ways to reconstruct the role of many participants. Giving due credit is not the main obstacle to fair evaluation. The problem is disbelief that coding and building entail intellectual and theoretical work. It may be a holdover from the gender, race, and class hierarchies that associate invention and intellect with powerful men and iteration and hand work with subordinates (Chun et al., "Dark Side," 499–500; Nowviskie, "On the Origin"). Those who evaluate digital research projects should have some familiarity with the scholarly value of each element of different sorts of project, from productive parsing of newly discovered data to whether the method itself is the experimental focus; this is all the more reason to include some digital training in any program in humanities, from archaeology to philosophy to urban planning. In the precious time of education beyond high school, students should have experience with ongoing research teams, quite the contrary to the premium placed on individual originality. Research projects should be structured to engage faculty, staff, graduate students, and undergraduates, acknowledging and compensating all contributors.

(Digital) Humanities Education Is Not Useful for Graduate Students Only

I have noted that a collaborative ethos does not mesh well with the incentive system in academia and that DH can strain the available time of humanities researchers facing these incentives. Pedagogical training and experience are often sidelined in graduate programs, as if they merely offset tuition and can be learned well enough on the fly. Instead, advanced research should interweave with pedagogy in humanities as is already the case in some areas of social and natural sciences. Graduate education in DH should not only be well taught as shared inquiry, but graduate students in DH should be trained as teachers and mentors *within* research practice and under thoughtful discussion. In light of the time compression of graduate education, undergraduates should be introduced to research applications of technology, find opportunities to collaborate on speculative projects (rather than proven pedagogical exercises), and engage in peer review as they also learn to write a single-author essay. As part of giving credit to all participants, students should move quickly to coauthor and present a project, under decent work conditions (Di Pressi et al., "Student Collaborators' Bill of Rights"). In a well-designed digital research and learning community, staff and faculty can promote long-term advanced projects (given that students stay at the institution for only a few years), projects that provide opportunities for course assignments and paid research positions at all levels.[15] Undergraduates gain experience in advanced research and graduate students gain experience as teachers and mentors as well as researchers. The faculty or staff who ostensibly lead projects also directly and indirectly learn from this multilayered team interaction.

Digital humanities collaboration, in best practice, reduces hierarchies and redistributes access to privileged knowledge. Interdisciplinary collaborative pedagogy and research can mesh with community engagement and communicate beyond universities and top research libraries. Public humanities and service learning are gaining traction at Georgetown, Yale, Rutgers, and other universities as well as the University of Virginia, which was founded in the early nineteenth century to educate white gentlemen and built and funded by the labor of enslaved and free Black men and women. Even when libraries, colleges and universities, museums, and government research agencies around the world are the main engines behind substantial DH projects, many of these projects are designed to be influential in earlier education and lifelong learning, with crowdsourcing, microcomputing, or community-guided work in precarious archives.[16] Digital humanities as a bridge to community engagement can enhance education in all our vicinities, with antiracism and diversity as guiding aims. In my experience, graduate students affiliated with the Scholars' Lab have helped me, Brandon Walsh, and other staff and faculty members mentor undergraduates in a summer program funded by Mellon for undergraduates enrolled at historically Black colleges and universities or from Latinx communities; they quickly absorb digital humanities skills and produce projects ready for graduate school.

Useless Humanities, Transformed Education

Oscar Wilde declared that arts and humanities are utterly useless. He did not want them harnessed to commercial or normative purpose, but the aesthete's paradoxical aphorisms were far from pointless. Ludic performance does not signal idle complacency. With Wilde, we might entertain an idea of uselessness beyond what programmatically counts, hoping to find ways to stump so-called artificial intelligence and to protect human records from surveillance capitalism (Zuboff, *Age of Surveillance Capitalism*). Yet data is not the enemy, nor is tech the solution, nor are humanities a refuge. Chun et al. warn against the cruel optimism (Lauren Berlant's term) of relying on DH to solve the market crisis of humanities ("Dark Side," 495–96). We should not tout digital literacy or technological skills as vocational training any more than we should suppose humanities can be a preserve of all the wild, endangered things that resist instrumentality. Digital humanities research and teaching are not the solution but a willingness to engage in the difficulty of lifelong understanding in the humanities, facing the challenge of adapting computational tools to such understanding, while also striving to shape machine learning to ethical priorities. Graduate training in DH could help model a reinvented university in which graduate students with their intense, inventive repertoires influence both undergraduates and faculty. Humanities teaching, research, and service can flourish in creative tension with the different working terms and affordances of new media. We should practice ambivalence, generating a collaborative and less hierarchical public humanities that is artfully useless and deliberately needful.

Notes

An earlier version of this essay was shared at the MLA Convention session under the book's title, January 3, 2019.

1. On experiences running DH centers, see Booth and Posner, "Materials at Hand." The DH Center (since 2023) includes the Scholars' Lab (since 2006), led by Amanda Visconti; its prominent graduate training program, Praxis, and dissertation fellowships are led by Brandon Walsh, contributor to this volume, with Jeremy Boggs, Shane Lin, Ronda Grizzle, and others (https://scholarslab.lib.virginia.edu). Also in the DH Center is the Institute for Advanced Technology in the Humanities (since 1992), led by Sarah Wells, which supports faculty fellowships (http://iath.virginia.edu). The pan-university graduate certificate in DH is now administered by Rennie Mapp in Arts and Sciences, with Library and School of Data Science support.

2. Examples involving Scholars' Lab and the University of Virginia Library include Take Back the Archive (PI Lisa Goff, English, 2014–19), https://takeback.scholarslab.org /about; Charlottesville Regional Equity Atlas (co-PI, Rebecca Coleman, Library, and Michele Claibourn, Equity Center, 2014–24), https://virginiaequitycenter.github.io /cville-equity-atlas/; community-focused events beginning in 2018 to crowdsource the transcription of the papers of the late Civil Rights leader and faculty member Julian Bond, https://woodson.as.virginia.edu/transcribebond-crowdsourcing-event, a collaboration led by the Carter G. Woodson Institute and the Center for Textual Editing.

3. Italics in the original.

4. During a 2018 lecture, Davidson offered remarks based on her book, *The New Education*. See Davidson, "New Education." The historian Adrian Johns shows that a science of reading took over American institutions to safeguard democracy and fend off race degeneration. See Johns, *The Science of Reading*.

5. Newfield also urged, "Delegitimize inequalities of research resources" because evidence shows that the humanities and some social sciences net revenues for universities, but STEM research and education cost millions of dollars not covered by the funding they bring in. I cite slides from his talk hosted by the AAUP chapter I participate in at my university. Newfield, "When Did Tenured Faculty Give Up on Governance? Notes Towards a Self-Governed University," December 2, 2020, University of Virginia.

6. Business executives and hiring managers were polled to list the qualities most valued in job applicants. They cited effective oral communication; critical thinking; ethical judgment; and working effectively both in teams and independently; see McKenzie, "Why a Humanities Degree." McKenzie notes that humanities as well as STEM education yields such skills. Another desired qualification, effective written communication, is much stronger in humanities education.

7. After decades of minuscule tenure-track job prospects, the graduate humanities degree remains worthwhile and leads to careers as researcher, teacher, librarian, editor, journalist or writer, higher education administrator, grant writer, project manager, caseworker or executive, in both nonprofit and private sectors. Arguably, work-life balance is better outside academia.

8. Along with increasing adjunctification, the pandemic has exposed more than ever the unequal labor conditions for women and people of color, from care work to staff positions whose work cannot be done remotely.

9. Since the beginnings of this volume, there have been allocations and policies supporting humanities and graduate studies at the University of Virginia.

10. Digital humanities itself is not a single discipline though it has job listings, degrees, and even departments. It may be a "para discipline"; see O'Donnell, "All along the Watchtower," 171; it includes social sciences in "reflexive understanding of knowledge production and information as process." See Clement, "Where Is the Methodology," 160. Notable takedowns usually focus on text analysis, which some call distant reading or cultural analytics. Only that narrowed focus could lead one to assert that "the digital humanities has displayed almost no specifically political interest in the world outside the university." See Lennon, "Digital Humanities," 140–41, where he cites a range of political critiques from within DH.

11. Lee traces information overload in the new age of mass print. Lennon points out that linguists and philologists were recruited for intelligence work. McPherson argues that the modular and "lenticular logics" of computation compartmentalized social critique from data processing; see McPherson, "Why Are the Digital Humanities So White?," 142–45. Proposing an MLA 2013 panel, "The Dark Side of the Digital Humanities," Chun et al. note the risk of justifying a field for "instrumental or utilitarian value" that can increase the distance between the haves and "'have-nots' of mainstream humanities" ("Dark Side," 493). Chun and Grusin anticipate some of my points here. Currently, DH does not look like it is diverting funds from humanities, from where I sit.

12. I caution that valuation of style is a shifting consensus based on the purpose of the communication and the era in which it is produced. Care for effective prose, like humanities and arts, may be treated like a luxury.

13. Sustainability is the byword of libraries and DH circles, but experience warrants skepticism about the viability of today's projects as they age.

14. The MLA Committee on Information Technology has submitted new guidelines and an extensive handbook to be adopted by the organization in 2024. See Alison Booth

et al., "Sustainab* Public H*? Thirty Years of Evaluation Guidelines for Digital Scholarship," a presentation about work in progress on thirty years of professional guidelines.

15. In the U.S., external sources of funding for DH are woefully limited. Yet the cost (other than staff and space) of some kinds of multiyear projects can be supported internally through competitive small grants, fellowships, or short-term institutes, and research and teaching assistantships built into graduate funding plans and curricular allocations.

16. Examples include One More Voice, a project launched in 2021 by Adrian Wisnicki, Heather F. Ball, Jared McDonald, and Mary Borgo Ton (https://onemorevoice.org) and the Colored Conventions Project, launched at University of Delaware in 2012, since 2020 at Penn State University, with a book of essays edited by Gabrielle Foreman, Jim Casey, and Sarah Patterson, and a range of online exhibits: https://coloredconventions.org/exhibits/.

Bibliography

Bond, Sarah E., Hoyt Long, and Ted Underwood. "'Digital' Is Not the Opposite of 'Humanities.'" *Chronicle of Higher Education Review,* November 1, 2017. https://www.chronicle.com/article/digital-is-not-the-opposite-of-humanities/?cid=gen_sign_in.

Booth, Alison, Spencer Grayson, Lucas Martinez, Brandon Walsh, and Jeremy Boggs, "Sustainab* Public H*? Thirty Years of Evaluation Guidelines for Digital Scholarship." Working paper presented at the DH Center, University of Virginia Library, March 12, 2024. https://docs.google.com/document/d/1okvU5giJZk1-ZWO9w2TMHv02Jk9LykNvebG5rL3QDL8/edit?usp=sharing.

Booth, Alison, and Miriam Posner. "The Materials at Hand." Special Topic: Varieties of Digital Humanities, *PMLA* 135, no.1 (January 2020): 9–22.

Chun, Wendy Hui Kyong, Richard Grusin, Patrick Jagoda, and Rita Raley. "The Dark Side of the Digital Humanities." In *Debates in the Digital Humanities 2016,* edited by Matthew K. Gold and Lauren F. Klein, 493–509. Minneapolis: University of Minnesota Press, 2016.

Clement, Tanya E. "Where Is the Methodology in Digital Humanities?" In *Debates in the Digital Humanities 2016,* edited by Matthew K. Gold and Lauren F. Klein, 153–75. Minneapolis: University of Minnesota Press, 2016.

Davidson, Cathy N. "The New Education." Lecture at UC Santa Cruz. March 1, 2018. YouTube video, posted May 11, 2020, 1:31. https://youtu.be/iLyupA1phME.

Davidson, Cathy N. *The New Education: How to Revolutionize the University to Prepare Students for a World in Flux.* New York: Basic Books, 2017.

Di Pressi, Haley, Stephanie Gorman, Miriam Posner, et al. "A Student Collaborators' Bill of Rights." HUMTECH. UCLA. June 8, 2015. Accessed April 7, 2024. https://humtech.ucla.edu/news/a-student-collaborators-bill-of-rights/.

Fitzpatrick, Kathleen. *Generous Thinking.* Baltimore: Johns Hopkins University Press, 2019.

Johns, Adrian. *The Science of Reading: Information, Media, and Mind in Modern America.* Chicago: University of Chicago Press, 2023.

Lee, Maurice S. *Overwhelmed: Literature, Aesthetics, and the Nineteenth-Century Information Revolution.* Princeton, N.J.: Princeton University Press, 2019.

Lennon, Brian. "Digital Humanities and National Security." *Differences* 25, no. 1 (2014): 132–55.

Liu, Alan. *Friending the Past.* Chicago: University of Chicago Press, 2019.

Liu, Alan. "Toward a Diversity Stack." *PMLA* 135, no. 1 (January 2020): 130–51.

McKenzie, Sam. "Why a Humanities Degree Isn't Career Suicide." Medium. October 11, 2019. https://medium.com/@sammckenzie/why-a-humanities-degree-isnt-career-suicide-d6f7bf3989a.

McPherson, Tara. "Why Are the Digital Humanities So White?" *Debates in the Digital Humanities,* edited by Matthew K. Gold, 139–60. Minneapolis: University of Minnesota Press, 2012.

Newfield, Christopher. "When Did Tenured Faculty Give Up on Governance?" Lecture, American Association of University Professors, University of Virginia, Charlottesville, Va., December 2, 2020.

Nowviskie, Bethany. "On the Origin of 'Hack' and 'Yack.'" *Debates in the Digital Humanities,* edited by Matthew K. Gold, 66–70. Minneapolis: University of Minnesota Press, 2012.

O'Donnell, Daniel Paul. "All along the Watchtower: Intersectional Diversity as a Core Intellectual Value in the Digital Humanities." In *Intersectionality in Digital Humanities,* edited by Barbara Baradlejo and Roopika Risam, 167–86. Amsterdam: ARC Humanities Press, 2019. https://doi.org/10.5281/zenodo.3580235.

Ramos, Santiago. "The Humanities May Seem Pointless, but That Is the Point." *America: The Jesuit Review,* November 4, 2019. https://www.americamagazine.org/arts-culture/2019/10/31/humanities-pointless-Jesuit-education.

Reid, Alexander. "Graduate Education and the Ethics of the Digital Humanities." *Debates in the Digital Humanities,* edited by Matthew K. Gold, 350–67. Minneapolis: University of Minnesota Pres, 2012.

Rogers, Katina. *Putting the Humanities PhD to Work.* Durham, N.C.: Duke University Press, 2020.

Zuboff, Shoshana. *The Age of Surveillance Capitalism: The Fight for a Human Future at the New Frontier of Power.* New York: Public Affairs: 2019.

The Futures of Digital Humanities Pedagogy in a Time of Crisis

BRANDON WALSH

Higher education has long been in crisis, both by design and by circumstance. In the United States in particular, the systematic dismantling of public higher education, the ever-increasing burden of student debt, and the growth of adjunctification and precarious labor conditions for faculty and staff have all created an unstable and toxic system.[1] As I write this essay in spring of 2020, more specific emergencies have taken hold. An international public health crisis has deepened, exacerbating already extant systemic inequality. In higher education, the Covid-19 pandemic has led, and will continue to lead, to widespread budget cuts, hiring freezes, and concerns over how we can teach without killing our students and each other. Against the backdrop of this emergency, the murder of George Floyd by police has brought renewed attention to the ongoing struggles of Black people against widespread police brutality and systemic racism, on campus and beyond.[2] To be clear, these two most recent moments of crisis intersect,[3] and they are not new: they represent merely the most immediate and emergent manifestations of longstanding systems of discrimination that will continue to persist once this news cycle fades.[4]

The future of graduate education in digital humanities (DH) lies in the field's ability—or lack of ability—to direct its pedagogy to respond to and take account of its complicity in these crises. Chris Sula, S. E. Hackney, and Phillip Cunningham note that the development of certificates and degree programs in DH in recent years might appear to be part of a growing and healthy field, but like the institutions of which they are a part, Boyles et al. assert that the field is streaked with inequitable labor practices, and Bailey points to prevalent white supremacy in the community (Sula et al., "Survey of Digital Humanities"; Boyles et al., "Precarious Labor"; Bailey, "All the Digital Humanists"). It can feel impossible to answer the questions that moments like the present ask of us. How do we teach right now? Why do we teach now? And, for this audience, what might DH pedagogy in particular have to do with and for this moment? It is impossible to ignore these questions now, but even so, we must recognize that this sense of urgency should have always been central to our practice. As Kevin Gannon notes in *Radical Hope*, "Pedagogy is political," and, "our students and our academic communities need more from us" than a pedagogy of neutrality (22, 21). In the United States, given persistent attacks on higher education from the political right, it is not a given that there will be a future for graduate training in the humanities, much less a digital one. For there to be any kind of DH teaching worth having in the years to come, the field needs to be founded on a critical and engaged pedagogy that acts beyond the classroom. This moment can be an opportunity to take actionable steps toward big change: to reevaluate the nature of the teaching we do, to stand in solidarity with those who have long struggled for a more just and equitable DH practice, and to shape a DH that labors in the midst of present crises for a better future.

The idea of reworking one's approach to teaching might seem daunting, because time is at a premium for many in the academy right now, particularly for women who have been disproportionately affected by caregiving responsibilities as schools close and demand that work and learning continue.[5] One can, however, start small, advancing a more just pedagogy in the classroom itself, following the examples set by those already engaged in this work. As Matthew Cheney and Catherine Denial argue, we can frame our syllabi and course practices as instruments of trust and community building rather than abuse.[6] Roopika Risam calls for a digital pedagogy informed by postcolonial studies that "empowers students to not only understand but also intervene in the gaps and silences that persist in the digital cultural record,"[7] and instructors might engage students in course projects that address local issues to do so. In a related blog post titled "Against Cop Shit," Jeffrey Moro calls for a movement against those pedagogical practices and technologies that rely on punishment and surveillance. These steps, even if they might feel small at times, can begin to redirect DH teaching practices toward the pursuits of freedom, hope, and self-transformation.[8]

Beyond course practices and course assignments, though, this is a time for pedagogical action, for critically engaged teaching that sees the work of pedagogy as moving beyond the classroom. Sean Michael Morris speaks of a pedagogical habitus, "embodied practice, often uninspected or subterranean to a person's own thinking about themselves," that forms the "genetic makeup" of one's teaching ("Habitus of Critical Imagination"). Accordingly, the ways we carry out projects reflect our outlooks toward students.[9] Model examples of a lived commitment to pedagogy are the African American Digital and Experimental Humanities Initiative at the University of Maryland and the US Latino Digital Humanities Center at the University of Houston, both of which center on mentoring and community building even as they advance research agendas.[10] In this line of thought, pedagogy transcends classroom practice in the same ways that students' lived circumstances outside of our courses affect their ability to learn. Sara Goldrick-Rab's work at the Hope Center on food insecurity, homelessness, and poverty among students is emblematic of the ways pedagogy can join with advocacy beyond the classroom.[11] Pedagogy is a generalizable outlook toward all that one does in relation to students, and it should lead to action beyond teaching. Teaching the whole student means caring for their lived experience and, as several essays in this collection propose,[12] helping them to fit their education to that reality rather than the other way around.

The ways we theorize and practice DH teaching and research can also intervene in the institutions around us, and they can both reflect and enact infrastructural changes. Digital humanities teaching and mentoring regularly happen in interstitial university spaces, and this positionality can be leveraged to make administrative interventions that recognize their intersections with equitable pedagogical practices. By viewing budgets as moral pedagogical documents, we can advocate for better conditions for students and postdoctoral fellows.[13] When called upon to offer professional development to students, we can make sure that the work we do with them is informed by organizations like the Academic Job Market Support Network, which offers materials and resources for a range of different career paths. We must join pedagogical innovation with an activist spirit that pushes for infrastructural change.[14]

I am especially aware of my privilege and positionality in writing this piece as a cisgender, heterosexual, white man. There are, of course, DH practitioners, largely Black, Indigenous, and people of color (BIPOC), who have already been engaged in this work for years. The work of activists involved in the creation of #TransformDH, Postcolonial Digital Humanities, and DHWOGEM, to name a few, has made the field a better space.[15] It is incumbent upon people with privilege like mine to assign and cite these projects, to amplify and support these scholars, and to take part in this work. Similarly, look to local communities to find those people already engaged in this labor. Amplify and support the student activists fighting to unionize, the adjunct and precarious faculty working toward better working conditions, and the BIPOC staff and students fighting for justice on campuses dominated by white supremacy. No one person can affect change at all levels. More than or in addition to individual efforts, this is a moment for collective action, pedagogical and otherwise. And, to echo the title of a recent piece by Arteaga et al., "We all have levers we can pull." It is all too common for higher education workers to support these actions in spirit and conversation but not in practice, to see unionization efforts but not join them, or worse, to actively undermine them. Now is the time to act in accordance with our professed political and pedagogical values. Now is the time to pull the levers.

It may appear that I am offering a mercenary argument: DH pedagogy must serve the ends of equity and justice so that it can survive. That is not my aim. Instead, I hope to echo Kathleen Fitzpatrick in "Your Institution Does Not Deserve to Survive," where she speaks of universities' plans to reopen while Covid-19 continues to spread: an institution does not deserve to survive unless it is "committed to the survival of the people who make up and serve that institution first, foremost, and above all." The same can be said for DH and its associated pedagogies: if they are unconcerned with acting toward a more just vision of the world and safeguarding better conditions for the communities they affect, then they do not deserve to survive. This is finally true of pedagogies beyond digital humanities as well. Disciplinary training is an important part of graduate education, but it cannot operate in a vacuum, closed off from the social and political world. Our students' lives do not end at the doors of our classrooms, and we cannot teach as though they do. The future of our work, if there is to be one, must act in the present.

Notes

1. For just one example of political attacks on public education, see *UW Struggle* for Rybak's personal reporting on the actions of former governor Scott Walker as they pertain to the University of Wisconsin system. On student debt, see Goldrick-Rab, *Paying the Price.* On labor precarity in higher education, see Bousquet, *How the University Works.*

2. As of July 3, 2020, "#BlackInTheIvory" on Twitter offered an ongoing chronicling of the systemic discrimination faced by BIPOC in academia.

3. For further discussion, see Risam, "Reopening Schools Safely."

4. This argument exists in the present tense, but the publication timeline for this article has forced me to reinhabit it several times over the course of subsequent months and years. The particular crises invoked here have a historic specificity to them, but they have, in many ways, only taken further hold since I first drafted this essay and given it more urgency. Digital humanities teaching—and indeed, teaching of all kinds—must act in and against the conditions of present struggles.

5. For valuable insights into this type of predicament, see "Open Letter to Editors/ Editorial Boards," accessed July 6, 2020, http://femedtech.net/published/open-letter-to -editors-editorial-boards/.

6. For more, see Cheney, "(Against) The Syllabus" and Denial's perspective in "Pedagogy of Kindness."

7. Risam explores these themes in *New Digital Worlds,* 89–90. There are many examples of using course projects to engage in local activism. For a recent example from the Scholars' Lab, see "Land and Legacy" at https://landandlegacy.scholarslab.org/, a project which asked students to engage with the Charlottesville Regional Equity Atlas, a collaboration between the library and local community members. See "Charlottesville Regional Equity Atlas," accessed July 6, 2020, https://equityatlas.lib.virginia.edu/.

8. See hooks, *Teaching to Transgress;* hooks, *Teaching Community;* and Freire, *Pedagogy of the Oppressed.* For more examples of courses assignments that could serve as models, see Davis et al., *Digital Pedagogy in the Humanities.*

9. See DiPressi et al., "Student Collaborators' Bill of Rights" for evidence of how a generalized pedagogy of equity can be enacted in project development.

10. For more information, see "AADHum @ UMD," accessed April 5, 2024, https:// aadhum.umd.edu/. See also "Digital Humanities—Arte Publico Press," accessed July 5, 2024, https://artepublicopress.com/digital-humanities/.

11. For more on these programs, see "The Hope Center," accessed July 7, 2024, https://hope.temple.edu/.

12. See, in this volume, chapters 12 (Krien), 13 (Crossley, Regan, and Catalano), and 15 (Quintanilla and Horcasitas).

13. For more on viewing budgets as moral pedagogical documents, see Walsh, "Your Budget Is a Question." See also Alpert-Abrams et al., "Postdoctoral Laborers Bill of Rights."

14. See, in particular, work by Cathy Davidson and Rogers at "The Futures Initiative," accessed July 7, 2020, https://www.gc.cuny.edu/Page-Elements/Academics-Research-Centers-Initiatives/Initiatives-and-Committees/The-Futures-Initiative.

15. For more information, see "#TransformDH," accessed July 5, 2020, https://transformdh.org/. For more insights on postcolonial studies as it intersects with the field, see "Postcolonial Digital Humanities," accessed July 5, 2020, https://dhpoco.org/blog/. And more information about gender-based advocacy in DH can be found at "Women and Gender Minorities in Digital Humanities (DH-WOGEM)," accessed July 5, 2020, http://www.dhwogem.org/.

Bibliography

"Academic Job Market Support Network." Humanities Commons. Accessed July 7, 2020. https://hcommons.org/groups/academic-job-market-support-network/.

Alpert-Abrams, Hannah, Heather Froehlich, Amanda Henrichs, Jim McGrath, and Kim Martin, eds. "Postdoctoral Laborers Bill of Rights." Humanities Commons. April 9, 2019. http://dx.doi.org/10.17613/7fz6-ra81.

Arteaga, Rachel, Brian DeGrazia, Jimmy Hamill, Stacy M. Hartman, Stephanie Malak, Ashley Cheyemi McNeil, Katina Rogers, and Beth Seltzer. " 'We All Have Levers We Can Pull': Reforming Graduate Education." Los Angeles Review of Books. Accessed October 30, 2020. https://lareviewofbooks.org/article/we-all-have-levers-we-can-pull-reforming-graduate-education/.

Bailey, Moya. "All the Digital Humanists Are White, All the Nerds Are Men, but Some of Us Are Brave." *Journal of Digital Humanities* 1, no. 1 (2011). http://journalofdigitalhumanities.org/1-1/all-the-digital-humanists-are-white-all-the-nerds-are-men-but-some-of-us-are-brave-by-moya-z-bailey/.

Bousquet, Marc. *How the University Works: Higher Education and the Low-Wage Nation.* New York: New York University Press, 2008.

Boyles, Christina, Anne Cong-Huyen, Carrie Johnston, Jim McGrath, and Amanda Phillips. "Precarious Labor and the Digital Humanities." *American Quarterly* 70, no. 3 (September 2018): 693–700. https://doi.org/10.1353/aq.2018.0054.

Cheney, Matthew. "(Against) The Syllabus As Instrument of Abuse." *Syllabus* 9, no. 1 (2020). http://www.syllabusjournal.org/syllabus/article/view/301.

Davis, Rebecca Frost, Matthew K. Gold, Katherine D. Harris, and Jentrey Sayers, eds. "Digital Pedagogy in the Humanities." Modern Languages Association. Accessed July 7, 2020. https://digitalpedagogy.hcommons.org/.

Denial, Catherine. "A Pedagogy of Kindness." Hybrid Pedagogy. August 15, 2019. https://hybridpedagogy.org/pedagogy-of-kindness/.

DiPressi, Haley, et al. "A Student Collaborators' Bill of Rights." June 8, 2015. https://humtech.ucla.edu/news/a-student-collaborators-bill-of-rights/.

Fitzpatrick, Kathleen. "Your Institution Does Not Deserve to Survive." *Kfitz* (blog), June 26, 2020. https://kfitz.info/your-institution-does-not-deserve-to-survive/.

Freire, Paulo. *Pedagogy of the Oppressed, 30th Anniversary Edition.* Translated by Myra Bergman Ramos. New York: Continuum, 2000.

Gannon, Kevin M. *Radical Hope: A Teaching Manifesto.* Teaching and Learning in Higher Education. Morgantown: West Virginia University Press, 2020.

Goldrick-Rab, Sara. *Paying the Price: College Costs, Financial Aid, and the Betrayal of the American Dream.* Chicago: University of Chicago Press, 2016. http://ebookcentral.proquest.com/lib/uva/detail.action?docID=4519377.

hooks, bell. *Teaching Community: A Pedagogy of Hope.* New York: Routledge, 2003.

hooks, bell. *Teaching to Transgress: Education as the Practice of Freedom.* New York: Routledge, 1994.

Moro, Jeffrey. "Against Cop Shit." Accessed July 5, 2020. https://jeffreymoro.com/blog/2020-02-13-against-cop-shit/.

Morris, Sean Michael. "The Habitus of Critical Imagination." October 5, 2018. https://www.seanmichaelmorris.com/the-habitus-of-critical-imagination/.

Risam, Roopika. *New Digital Worlds: Postcolonial Digital Humanities in Theory, Praxis, and Pedagogy.* Evanston, Ill.: Northwestern University Press, 2018.

Risam, Roopika. "Reopening Schools Safely Can't Happen without Racial Equity." *CNN,* Accessed July 3, 2020. https://www.cnn.com/2020/07/02/opinions/covid-19-colleges-racial-equality-risam/index.html.

Rybak, Chuck. *UW Struggle: When a State Attacks Its University.* Minneapolis: University of Minnesota Press, 2017. https://doi.org/10.5749/9781452958545.

Sula, Chris Alen, S. E. Hackney, and Phillip Cunningham. "A Survey of Digital Humanities Programs." *Journal of Interactive Technology and Pedagogy,* May 24, 2017. https://jitp.commons.gc.cuny.edu/a-survey-of-digital-humanities-programs/.

Walsh, Brandon. "Your Budget Is a Question of Pedagogy and Equity." Accessed July 7, 2020. http://walshbr.com/blog/your-budget-is-a-question-of-pedagogy-and-equity/.

Executing the Crisis
The University beyond Austerity

TRAVIS M. BARTLEY

Like my chapter co-contributors, I find myself unable to reflect upon the future of the humanities without first considering the crises defining them. Since the Covid-19 pandemic began, each week seems to have brought yet more news of layoffs and gutted funding, with particular severity facing departments in the American public university. For affiliated doctoral students like myself, it is difficult to experience this moment without a variety of emotions: employment anxieties, fear for self-preservation, and rage at the systemic mistreatment of the racialized and vulnerable (see chapter 1 in this volume by Katina Rogers). Yet one response notably absent is surprise. For, as Alison Booth and Brandon Walsh note in chapters 2 and 3 in this volume, respectively, our current state is not a novel consequence of the pandemic but instead an exacerbation of a much older crisis, one that has continued unabated for the last half-century (Smith, *Manifesto for the Humanities*, 8):[1] the defunding of the university through a neoliberal[2] rhetoric of austerity (Fabricant and Brier, *Austerity Blues*, 20). Booth's "roar of disinvestment" has sounded for decades, producing inequitable structures worsened by the university's accompanying reliance on neoliberal market logics (Newfield, "What Are the Humanities For?"; Lusin, "MLA Job Information List"). Those grand ideals of the American public university so crucial for the preservation of democratic society amidst crisis—equitable economic mobility, egalitarian access to education, defense of critical inquiry—have been diminished by years of assault, leaving us with mere gestures toward their noble promise (Brown, "End of Educated Democracy"; Newfield, "What are the Humanities For?").

It is tempting to view austerity as an aberration; we believe the public university is only momentarily compromised, hoping that once we identify an "out" we may resolve neoliberalism's onslaught and no longer be "in" crisis. But as I consider the duration of austerity in the academy, I come to question this narrative. In our categorization of crisis, we err in understanding the university's relationship to the market. Rather than seeing crisis as an auxiliary property of our disciplines,

I argue that crisis is what defines them. The very ideals through which we characterize the American public university are a crisis in the historic relations of academia and capital. To respond to austerity, we must abandon resolution and instead seek an *aggravation* of crisis, disrupting the university's neoliberal role so as to promote the egalitarian ideals that transcend it. Rather than create *producers* of intellectual capital (Miyoshi, "Ivory Tower in Escrow"; Readings, *The University in Ruins*, 1–2), the aim of academic training should evolve to fashion facilitators of public knowledge distribution, seizing upon the transformative technologies of the current era to change the very structural purpose of academic institutions. To respond to crisis, I argue here, the public university must prioritize serving as digital infrastructure for the public as a whole, providing an alternative to intellectual development outside the market sphere and wholly severing itself from the forces of austerity.

The Crisis

My inquiry begins with etymology. Were we to seek out the origin of "crisis," we would find the Greek *krisis*, a point when a sickness would abate (or permanently fail to).[3] Crisis signified "a decisive moment—a turning point between what came before and what might now follow. A crisis does not persist; it passes" (Reitter and Wellmon, *Permanent Crisis*, 1). Taking this definition in reference to American public universities, the rhetoric of crisis is misleading. True, austerity is decisive, but its persistence is hardly momentary. When comparing the current university with its precrisis "golden age," one is inclined to suppose crisis only categorizes austerity's absence. Public investment in U.S. university and humanities education follows only roughly from the postwar G.I. bill to the mid-seventies (Fabricant and Brier, *Austerity Blues*, 91; Smith, *Manifesto*, 8),[4] a scant four decades within the eighteen spanning the American system (Moses, "Humanities and Inclusion").[5] Preceding this period, the rhetoric justifying the public university's existence was centered less around equity and economic mobility than on producing a labor force to facilitate bourgeois interests (Miyoshi, "Ivory Tower"). In the Morrill Act that established land-grant universities, instruction focused on "agriculture and the mechanic arts . . . in order to promote the liberal and practical education of the industrial classes" (National Agricultural Library, "Morrill Land Grant College Act"). Such education was qualified with the progression of American industry and integration of recent acquisitions of state and private property from indigenous lands (Yang, *Third University Is Possible*; Lee and Ahtone, "How They Did It"). The public university's role was founded on capital, not egalitarianism (Yang, *Third University*).[6]

This foundation raises doubts regarding the usual narrative of a postwar period exempt from neoliberal pressures. During its post–World War II expansion, the university was hardly autonomous of market demands. That the humanities, arts, and sciences all shared in public investment owed less to a lost period of public values and more to postwar economics (Heller, *Capitalist University*). Public education transitioned the war economy into one suitable for the United States' new economic dominance on the world stage, while the promotion of humanistic critique arguably supported Cold War propaganda efforts in enforcing the hegemony of American capital and diminishing leftist influences both domestically and abroad (Fabricant and Brier, *Austerity Blues*, 40–41; Heller, *Capitalist University*, 42). That public divestment accompanied the transition from East-West adversarialism to market globalism furthers this point, as the dominance of capitalist ideologies made these propaganda efforts unnecessary and could be dismissed for new economic needs (Newfield, *Great Mistake*, 236; Heller, *Capitalist University*, 171; Readings, *University in Ruins*, 45).

This relationship between the academy and capital reveals why accounts of the midcentury academic boom are typically footnoted by admissions that the egalitarian ideals of the public university were never fully realized in practice. As Brown notes, the period's merit was "*only* that its values and practices were vastly superior to those preceding and succeeding it" (emphasis mine; Brown, "End of Educated Democracy"). The difference in continuity is relative, not absolute. Even at its peak, the university was still marred with discrimination against "white women and women and men of color" (among other forms of discrimination; Smith, *Manifesto*, 19). To say this is not to dismiss social progress but to recognize that if the fundamental consequences of neoliberal forces and the "cheapening" of the humanities lie in limiting ideals of diversity, accessibility, and opportunity, then the continual presence of these limitations throughout the academy's lifetime joinder with market forces suggest such ideals to be more exceptions than rules of the public university (Fabricant and Brier, *Austerity Blues*, 118–19). The outlier is not neoliberal capital; it is the ideals of the university that such capital undermines.

That we may locate this exception not in the perceived adversary of austerity but in our own humanistic ideals is not surprising, given the traditional relationship between crisis and the humanities. As Paul Reitter and Chad Wellmon note in their study on the subject: "Self-understanding of the modern humanities didn't merely take shape in response to a perceived crisis; it also made crisis a core part of the project of the humanities" (*Permanent Crisis*, 3). Due to the humanities' foundation in responses to crises in meaning, value judgment, and knowledge formation, the disciplines have been traditionally lodged in a discourse, where "crisis has not only been variously invoked to describe the plight of the humanities—crisis has also been the humanities' rationale" (*Permanent Crisis*, 253). We understand the humanities through a frame of permanent crisis, knowing the aims of our scholarship merely by resistance to a perceived opposition. We are prone to "contradictions, oppositions, and presumptions" that limit our ability to understand that humanistic inquiries "have always been wrapped up with the very things they only recently were purported to oppose" (*Permanent Crisis*, 254). Returning to the question of austerity, the reasons for the temporal contradiction of our rhetoric become clear: rather than understanding austerity as a dire misfortune, the genealogy of our disciplines suggests this state to be a new self-formulation that resists the politico-economic context of the American public university's history. If the American public university is founded in relationship to capitalist ideologies and market needs, then the humanities' egalitarian ideals of the university that we find in opposition are fundamentally a crisis in this relationship. Instead of responding to the university *in* crisis, we should speak of enabling the university *as* crisis.

This reformulation of crisis, the university, and the humanities' positioning illuminate why a proper response to austerity appears so unobtainable. Conceiving the university within crisis presupposes an academic existence that could be outside the crisis conditions of neoliberal capitalism. Austerity is to be abated, in this view, either by returning to previous capital relations or moving to new forms. To conceive the university as the crisis realizes this practice as both ineffectual and self-destructive, for resolution requires dismissal of the very ideals we hope to protect (along with our current rationale of humanistic inquiry). Rather, we must sustain the crisis so as to persevere in the struggle the public university has come to represent. If our lofty conceptions are outliers in the academy's market function, then we may only realize the idealized university within the actual university by an overt commitment against this market role. This raises two questions: what is this role? And what becomes of a university in opposition to it?

Programming and Open Access

Responding first to the question of market role, one is tempted to identify the university as primarily a producer of intellectual capital (Readings, *University in Ruins*, 1–2; Miyoshi, "Ivory Tower"). Indeed, that it is difficult to speak of the American public university without the implication of the American public research university suggests the sheer difficulty of displacing the academy from knowledge production. As Masao Miyoshi notes, the expansion of market logics into public domains has assisted in transforming the American university's role from "fill[ing] the need for knowledge production" to serving as "R&D" for the global market ("Ivory Tower"). Integrated into a system of "knowledge transfer" that cycles public scholarship into corporate development, the public university has an unavoidable responsibility for producing intellectual capital for the market. However, I believe this focus on production fails to encompass the university's full domain. Interrogating the academy's role in intellectual capital, previous work in scholarly communications has brought into focus the university's peculiar sensitivity regarding intellectual legitimization. Most notably demonstrated through the sine qua non of peer-reviewed scholarship, the academy defines itself by an ability to systematically legitimize knowledge via its own institutional structures (Fitzpatrick, *Planned Obsolescence*, 17). In fact, the control over legitimacy often proves more crucial than the ability to produce knowledge capital, as intellectual legitimation practices are defended even at the cost of "bottleneck[ing]" scholarship without guarantees of quality (Fitzpatrick,

Planned Obsolescence, 16, 48). When attempts to democratize the process via integration with public forums are proposed, this defensiveness acquires a particular "vehemence," construing such actions as threatening the cultural capital of scholarly prestige (Fitzpatrick, *Planned Obsolescence,* 19–20).

This coupling of quality, prestige, and legitimacy with the university's history of knowledge production suggests to me that the American public university's market role goes beyond simply the creation of intellectual capital. Rather, we may see this process of legitimization as a simultaneous process of delegitimization. In the university's capability to proclaim scholarship as valid through its internal mechanisms (peer review, university presses, the dissertation), there is an implication that scholarship produced outside these mechanisms lacks the same degree of validity. By consequence, this creates a hierarchization of knowledge in tandem with the university's intellectual production. Not only may the university expand market processes in the diversion of public intellectual resources toward private enterprise, but it may do so with the implication that these resources implicitly possess a higher claim to legitimacy as a result of their method of production. That is, not only may the university produce knowledge, its production delegitimizes alternatives.

For open-access enthusiasts, this line of reasoning may seem familiar, as similar discussions regarding public access outside traditional institutional structures also prompt concerns of lost "viability" (Eve, *Open Access and the Humanities,* 30–34; Suber, "Promoting Open Access in the Humanities"). And it is to this discourse that I would like to now pivot, for the case of digital democratization is particularly rich with potential insight into engaging with the university's market role. The telecommunication technologies of the "information era" decentralize traditional distribution models (Wesch, "From Knowledgeable to Knowledge-able"; Kelty, *Two Bits,* 6), upsetting those frameworks where knowledge production requires hierarchizing processes. Instead, these frameworks have encouraged a conceptualization of knowledge as a "commons," where rights and maintenance responsibilities may be shared among a user population. For the question of knowledge production, this conceptualization is notable, for, as Charlotte Hess and Elinor Ostrom note, "One of the critical factors of digital knowledge is the 'hyperchange' of technologies and social networks that affects every aspect of how knowledge is managed and governed, including how it is generated, stored, and preserved" ("Introduction," 4, 9). Given our interest in opposing the public university's market role in knowledge production, this disruption posed by digital technologies signals a promising avenue of approach. Of course, this is not an attempt to preach techno-evangelism and the inherent democratizing function of digital communications. Like their historical and agricultural equivalents, these digital commons are still subject to "enclosures," privatization, and their subsequent abuses (simply consider social data-mining and its effects on American politics; Holmwood, "Open Access, 'Publicity'"; Miyoshi, "Ivory Tower"; Newfield, "What are the Humanities For?"). However, this prospect of utilizing digital technologies to craft a public commons and engender a practice of intellectual production outside of and antithetical to the sphere of capital presents an opportunity to be seized upon (Kranich, "Countering Enclosure"; Rausing, "Toward a New Alexandria"; Kelty, *Two Bits,* x–xi; Federici, "Feminism and the Politics of the Commons"; Linebaugh, *Stop, Thief!,* 14).

This potential leads to a question. What could be achieved if academic training prioritized combining scholarship with this digital adversarialism? We have seen possibilities signaled by existing digital humanities centers and departments. See chapter 13 in this volume by Joshua Casmir Catalano, Amanda E. Regan, and Laura Crossley in which they describe how the Roy Rosenzweig Center for History and New Media facilitates public research and archiving efforts with the development of Zotero and Omeka. Mukurtu CMS demonstrates the vitality of archival software based in equity and social justice (Mukurtu). My home institution, the City University of New York, supports open scholarship with implementations of Manifold and Academic Commons. What would happen if the university integrated and prioritized these peripheral developments as its central scholarly mission, focusing its resources on opening alternatives to public engagement through digital services that had hitherto been limited to private enterprise? Imagine social media platforms designed by humanities scholars to enable public discourse rather than individual data mining, or an internet web archive enshrined in a public institution instead of being supported by precarious private investment (Rausing, "Toward a New Alexandria").

Execution

How should we act on this critique of the neoliberal university and its exploitation of public goods? In short, I would echo Ethan Zuckerman's call for "digital public infrastructure" and connect it to the American public university's mission ("Case for Digital Public Infrastructure"). Let the academy relinquish its history of hierarchized intellectual production and instead combat digital privatization. Rather than regulating knowledge for the market, let the university build upon its history with digital technology to transform into a utility, facilitating public intellectual development through primary investiture in digital platforms, like noncommodified messaging services, community hubs for internet access, and distribution nodes for required educational literature. Instead of leaving these essentials to mythically benevolent entrepreneurs, hard-working but precarious centers and departments (see the contribution of Donna Alfano Bussell and Tina L. Helton in chapter 5 in this volume), or extralegal necessity,[7] we should employ the fifty-plus iterations of the American public university system as a nexus for these public needs. In doing so, public universities may not only sever themselves from neoliberal complicity but also discover opportunities to increase public relevance, a significant weapon against austerity (Newfield, *Great Mistake,* 236).

Needless to say, such change will not be solely external. To internalize a new public mission requires new structures. Most crucial will be the training of academic professionals, for the university's relationship to knowledge distribution does not alter the necessity of critique. In fact, given the immediacy of the university's digital platforms, such critique will demand greater exactitude. Here, we may turn to the digital and public humanities, which have long worked to develop effective pedagogy that interrogates the transformation of critique into praxis, championing course design in project management, collaboration, and methodology; see the contributions by Meredith Martin, Natalia Ermolaev, and Rebecca Munson in chapter 23 in this volume and the work of Sara Mohr and E. L. Meszaros in chapter 19 in this volume (Davidson and Goldberg, *Future of Thinking*; Greenspan, "Scandal of Digital Humanities," 92). Academic professionalization will need to incorporate these critical digital practices into all disciplines, understanding that separation from either public engagement or digital facilitation is impractical in the academy. Indeed, the first alteration of professionalization may come in realizing redundancy in these qualifications of digital and public, with the former obvious in all scholarship that engages with contemporaneity and the latter inherent in those studies relevant beyond the lecture hall.

An example of this change would come in doctoral course design. Starting at the level of program introductions, this new form of the public university would instruct its academic hopefuls that their scholarship is in service to public need, not an individualistic "knowledge for knowledge's sake." Students would begin with introductions to the academy's public digital services, considering which services assist professional trajectories. Once acquainted with those services, these students will cycle through seminars that train them as contributors to these platforms. One course may instruct and deploy students in sustaining the community digital archive. Another may take a more physical role, prompting interactions with local social justice networks to maintain equity through the networking service utilized for public forums. What is key is that this coursework abandons the traditional program of developing individual products from the raw resources of the seminar, instead creating engagements with ongoing projects that negotiate individual contributions with long-standing goals. Along with understanding the public vitality of scholarship, these young professionals would learn early that scholarship and employment are ultimately the continuation of a prior conversation, a collaboration of individual knowing with the work of one's peers. By the time of the dissertation (or, rather, new forms that have evolved in utility beyond the monograph), we will have trained scholars not in solipsism but in collaborative, public-minded praxis, wholly capable of realizing the scholarly wealth of public academia (Smith, *Manifesto*, 132).

This is but one possible course of many. My fellow contributors have experienced such professionalizations already and have rich personal experiences to provide. All we should demand is the following: that the public university ceases its complicity in neoliberalization, that it realizes a primary responsibility to its intellectual publics, and that it is willing to begin anew in service to this responsibility. By doing so, we may decouple the university from its traditional market role and fashion a new understanding of what the interrelationship of the public and scholarly production may be. By failing to realize this responsibility, we risk bringing an end to the crisis that is our ideals and the necessary contradictions of the public university with it.

Notes

1. Smith speaks of four decades at the time she was writing in 2015.

2. For clarity, I adopt Harvey's definition of neoliberalism as "a theory of political economic practices that proposes that human well-being can best be advanced by liberating individual entrepreneurial freedoms and skills within an institutional framework characterized by strong private property rights, free markets, and free trade" that encourages state action in the free creation of new markets even when said markets affect the public domain (e.g., water, education, environment). See Harvey, *Brief History of Neoliberalism,* 2.

3. Oxford English Dictionary, s.v. "crisis (n.)," March 2024, https://doi.org/10.1093 /OED/3661901481.

4. Fabricant and Brier use the imposition of tuition rates at the City University of New York as an end date, and Smith chooses the first election of Ronald Reagan.

5. I follow Moses in taking the 1862 Morill Act Land-Grant Act as the origin of the American public university.

6. As Yang argues, "Land as *capital* and not as *campuses* is an innovation of the land-grant university." See Yang, *Third University,* 27.

7. Do we truly believe not a single student chose Library Genesis—the multimedia peer-to-peer service allowing online sharing of scholarly articles and books (without concern for pesky copyright)—over the campus bookstore?

Bibliography

Brown, Wendy. "The End of Educated Democracy." *Representations* 116, no. 1 (2011): 19–41. https://doi.org/10.1525/rep.2011.116.1.19.

Davidson, Cathy, and David Theo Goldberg. *The Future of Thinking: Learning Institutions in a Digital Age.* John D. and Catherine T. MacArthur Foundation Reports on Digital Media and Learning. Cambridge, Mass.: The MIT Press, 2010.

Eve, Martin Paul. *Open Access and the Humanities: Contexts, Controversies and the Future.* Cambridge: Cambridge University Press, 2014. https://doi.org/10.1017/CBO 9781316161012.

Fabricant, Michael, and Stephen Brier. *Austerity Blues: Fighting for the Soul of Public Higher Education.* Baltimore: Johns Hopkins University Press, 2016.

Federici, Silvia. "Feminism and the Politics of the Commons." In *The Wealth of the Commons: A World beyond Market and State,* edited by David Bollier and Silke Helfrich. Amherst, Mass.: Levellers, 2012.

Fitzpatrick, Kathleen. *Planned Obsolescence: Publishing, Technology, and the Future of the Academy.* New York: New York University Press, 2011.

Greenspan, Brian. "The Scandal of Digital Humanities." In *Debates in the Digital Humanities 2019,* edited by Matthew K. Gold and Lauren Klein. Minneapolis: University of Minnesota Press, 2019.

Harvey, David. *A Brief History of Neoliberalism.* Oxford: Oxford University Press, 2005.

Heller, Henry. *The Capitalist University: The Transformations of Higher Education in the United States since 1945.* London: Pluto Press, 2016. https://doi.org/10.2307/j.ctt1gk07xz.

Hess, Charlotte, and Elinor Ostrom. "Introduction: An Overview of the Knowledge Commons." In *Understanding Knowledge as a Commons,* edited by Charlotte Hess and Elinor Ostrom, 3–26. Cambridge, Mass.: The MIT Press, 2011.

Holmwood, John. "Open Access, 'Publicity,' and Democratic Knowledge." In *Reassembling Scholarly Communications: Histories, Infrastructures, and Global Politics of Open Access,* edited by Martin Paul Eve and Jonathan Gray. Cambridge, Mass.: The MIT Press, 2020.

Kelty, Christopher M. *Two Bits: The Cultural Significance of Free Software.* Durham, N.C.: Duke University Press, 2008.

Kranich, Nancy. "Countering Enclosure: Reclaiming the Knowledge Commons." In *Understanding Knowledge as a Commons,* edited by Charlotte Hess and Elinor Ostrom, 85–122. Cambridge, Mass.: The MIT Press, 2011.

Lee, Robert, and Tristan Ahtone. "How They Did It: Exposing How U.S. Universities Profited from Indigenous Land." Pulitzer Center. May 19, 2020. https://pulitzercenter.org/stories/how-they-did-it-exposing-how-us-universities-profited-indigenous-land.

Linebaugh, Peter. *Stop, Thief! The Commons, Enclosures, and Resistance.* Oakland, Calif.: PM Press, 2014.

Lusin, Natalia. "The MLA Job Information List, 2017–18: Final Report." November 2019. https://www.mla.org/content/download/113931/file/Report-MLA-JIL-2017-18.pdf.

Moses, Yolanda T. "Humanities and Inclusion: A Twenty-First-Century Land-Grant University Tradition." In *A New Deal for the Humanities: Liberal Arts and the Future of Public Higher Education,* edited by Hutner Gordon and Feisal G. Mohamed, 72–85. New Brunswick, N.J.: Rutgers University Press, 2016.

Miyoshi, Masao. "Ivory Tower in Escrow." *boundary 2* 27, no. 1 (2000): 7–50.

Mukurtu. https://mukurtu.org/.

National Agricultural Library. "Morrill Land Grant College Act." https://www.nal.usda.gov/topics/morrill-land-grant-college-act.

Newfield, Christopher. *The Great Mistake: How We Wrecked Public Universities and How We Can Fix Them.* Baltimore: Johns Hopkins University Press, 2017.

Newfield, Christopher. "What Are the Humanities For? Rebuilding the Public University." In *A New Deal for the Humanities: Liberal Arts and the Future of Public Higher Education,* edited by Hutner Gordon and Feisal G. Mohamed, 160–78. New Brunswick, N.J.: Rutgers University Press, 2016.

Rausing, Lisbet. "Toward a New Alexandria." New Republic. March 12, 2010. http://www.newrepublic.com/article/books-and-arts/toward-new-alexandria.

Readings, Bill. *The University in Ruins.* Cambridge, Mass.: Harvard University Press, 1996.

Reitter, Paul, and Chad Wellmon. *Permanent Crisis: The Humanities in a Disenchanted Age.* Chicago: University of Chicago Press, 2021.

Smith, Sidonie. *A Manifesto for the Humanities: Transforming Doctoral Education in Good Enough Times.* Ann Arbor: University of Michigan Press, 2015. https://doi.org/10.3998/dcbooks.13607059.0001.001.

Suber, Peter. "Promoting Open Access in the Humanities." In *Knowledge Unbound: Selected Writings on Open Access,* edited by Peter Suber and Robert Darnton. Cambridge, Mass.: The MIT Press, 2016.

Wesch, Michael. "From Knowledgeable to Knowledge-able." In *Hacking the Academy: New Approaches to Scholarship and Teaching from Digital Humanities,* edited by Daniel Cohen and Tom Scheinfeldt, 69–77. Ann Arbor: University of Michigan Press, 2013.

Yang, K. Wayne. *A Third University Is Possible.* Minneapolis: University of Minnesota Press, 2017.

Zuckerman, Ethan. "The Case for Digital Public Infrastructure." Academic Commons. January 17, 2020. https://academiccommons.columbia.edu/doi/10.7916/d8-chxd-jw34.

PART II

HISTORIES
AND FORMS

Why Our Digital Humanities Program Died and What You Can Learn about Saving Yours

DONNA ALFANO BUSSELL AND TENA L. HELTON

In 2010, Matthew G. Kirschenbaum described a convergence of six causes for the residence of the digital humanities (DH) in English departments. These included text as a data source discrete enough for computers to manipulate, the historical role of computers in composition, the interest in producing electronic editions and archives, creative projects in digital writing and hypertext, an "openness of English departments" to digital material culture as a subject of analysis, and large-scale digitization of texts (60). At a time when the death knell for the humanities, and especially English departments, was being sounded in professional and popular venues, DH was one way into the future of the humanities.

Our story is about participating in this future and about what went right, what went wrong, and the way forward. When we started discussing the possibilities in 2011, not long after the publication of Kirschenbaum's article, we were well positioned to see DH integrated into our English program's MA curriculum. Sometimes, however, moving too quickly can backfire if the institution has not fully embraced DH. Most DH programs begin with individual projects or collaborations from which programs are built incrementally. As Patrik Svensson noted in the early days of DH, the formation of meaningful projects and programs is very much a managerial task. We had DH practitioners at the University of Illinois Springfield (UIS), but no "manager" to establish and reaffirm institutional commitment to our department's graduate DH program. Institutional commitment is key to building capacity in a DH program, according to the Educause Center for Analysis and Research (ECAR). Our program was housed in one of the many institutions "beginning to explore [DH]" that "struggle[d] with how best to engage with this growing field" and that "provide[d] varying levels of administrative and faculty support" (Educause Center for Analysis and Research, "Building Capacity for Digital Humanities," 4). Had it been available to us, we could have benefited from ECAR's advice that the institution itself clarify its "priorities and goals for DH (if any) and the commitment to provide the requisite support to achieve them" (4). In 2013, as we revised our MA curriculum to have DH options in pedagogy and publishing, our liberal arts university had no such institutional focus or clarity about DH, and individual projects had not reached the critical mass necessary to move the institution toward centralized and significant support. Ours is a cautionary tale for others attempting to shift traditional expectations of a master's degree in English. We did not understand the need to build capacity and support for resources for digital humanities when we began our program, nor did we fully consider the structural and geographical disadvantages of our small teaching-oriented institution. We hope our experience helps those working in other institutions, whether in program planning, implementation, or assessment phases. We outline our curriculum design process, issues with faculty and student support, and pitfalls in establishing a strategic, collaborative foundation within the college and campus. We address managing expectations about enrollment, growth, and the integration of DH within and across the curriculum, and we highlight some successes and unfulfilled potential that point the way forward.

Revising the Traditional Curriculum

The University of Illinois Springfield is a regional public liberal arts institution in the Midwest. With an enrollment of about five thousand students split somewhat evenly between on campus and online liberal arts and professional programs, UIS is the smallest of the three campuses in the University of Illinois system. Our student population is nontraditional and increasingly diverse. Graduate programs typically enroll part-time students who attend to increase salary and broaden professional opportunities. In the UIS Department of English and Modern Languages (henceforth English department), graduate student enrollment had seen variability, but it was a small program with a brief period of expansion followed by quick contraction.[1] Early in its history (from 1993 to 2001), enrollments ranged from one to fourteen students per year with a mean of six and a median of five over these eight years; there were two outlier years with thirteen and fourteen students, respectively, according to the formal self-study conducted in 2003 by the English department. There was also a five-to-six-year period (from 2003 to 2009) that saw much larger enrollments with an influx of many part-time students, increasingly women and teachers who were seeking credit hours, if not the MA, to secure a better salary and career advancement in their school districts. Enrollments during this period ranged from a high of forty-three early in fall 2003 but began falling steadily in the first four years and then dropping precipitously the two following years so that enrollment totaled twenty-two by fall 2009 (formal department self-study, 2011). With this pattern of enrollment change, the mean of thirty-four and a median of thirty-six during our program self-study in 2011 were poor indicators of enrollment potential that contributed to our administration's perceptions of the department as declining and less than fully productive. The recession of 2008 and the subsequent changes in reimbursement by local school districts had a profoundly negative impact on this unusual era of growth, but these were not addressed as factors in enrollment patterns. Teachers from local districts no longer benefited from a state program that would pay for graduate courses. We hoped to see more enrollments by increasing direct marketing and outreach on our own, with minimal resources and pressure to improve metrics, but these efforts were ineffective. We maintained an enrollment of twenty-one to twenty-two students each year for two more years (from 2010 to 2012), most of whom were part-time.

During the next three years, we saw enrollment numbers revert to earlier levels of the 1990s to the early aughts, that is, we had six, eleven, and sixteen students, respectively, from 2013 to 2016 in the MA program. In retrospect, with the value of another departmental self-study in 2018 in which we compared the enrollments in our graduate program with the enrollments at other Illinois public universities, it became clear that by the numbers, we were not unique. Our enrollment numbers for MA programs in English placed us within the median of regional public institutions in midsize cities and followed trends observable in these programs between 2007 and 2016, according to the 2018 formal departmental self-study. Yet we felt we were paddling as fast as we could to respond to questions about the future of our MA in English, questions that required answers or efforts beyond our purview. We could not change larger trends in the number of humanities majors. We could not undertake additional marketing and outreach efforts alongside our regular responsibilities as faculty. We were also baffled by the undue emphasis given enrollment numbers from an unusual period of expansion in the department's history for which external support in school districts no longer existed. Enrollment urgency increased when the dean of the College of Liberal Arts and Sciences began talking about closing our graduate program altogether. Thus, in academic year 2010–11, our faculty of ten unanimously agreed to revise the graduate curriculum to leverage the institution's reputation as a leader in online education and integrate digital methods with our other fields of expertise to pivot our entire MA to focus on DH. We assembled a committee of four faculty members and a graduate student. After two years of research about other DH programs, our market, and best practices, our department submitted the revised MA curriculum to governance in academic year 2012–13.

Although the curricular change was undertaken because of enrollment pressures, there were also strong, positive reasons for a radical reframing of the English MA to focus on digital humanities. Some faculty had already begun expanding their scholarship into these areas. We argued at the time that faculty across the university had felt the impact of digital culture and technologies and that the impact was particularly significant in English studies. The myriad changes in reading, writing, and textual production of the past few years were as profound as those initiated by the printing press in the sixteenth century. We anticipated a sea change in the skills our students would need and the projects they could complete. Our curriculum would provide marketable textual analysis and data visualization skills, a deep understanding of classroom technologies, and a facility with digital publishing and editing. In addition to the traditional skills of a graduate degree in English, these digital meth-odologies could open doors for our students. The world was going digital, and we wanted to provide a conduit to the changes in resources, methods, and occupations at the forefront of this change. It was an exciting time to be working in a new field whose practitioners were learning together and doing so in an inspiring, generous, and collaborative fashion.

Given the enrollment pressures that initiated the program revision, we requested an economic feasibility study from the associate provost of Budget and Administra-tive Planning, the chief financial officer for our campus. We envisioned a five-year timeline for establishing and growing DH programming in English, with assess-ment toward the end of this period for further revision. The economic feasibil-ity study assessed potential tuition and course fee revenue based on assumptions of breaking even or perhaps beginning to see a slight return on investment by the third year of this new program. This analysis was predicated on increased credit hours generated over a four-year period, which entailed two enrollment periods (fall and spring), with cohorts taking a full-time load. It also was based on the increas-ing numbers of applicants with a yield of full-time registered students that would increase our ten-year historical average of eight to ten graduate students per year by 40 to 50 percent each year over four years. Costs taken into account included allo-cating substantial funds for a faculty hire (estimated $60,000 per annum for a tenure or tenure-track position) and for faculty training (estimated $10,000) and for mar-keting and other material support (estimated $10,000) during the first three years. With these investments, we hoped that this would be a strong option in the Midwest region, a "destination" program that would attract strong applicant pools over time. We had hopes, not unjustified, yet not borne out in enrollments, of attracting appli-cants both within and outside our region who might enroll full-time or nearly so.

Another early step was surveying DH programming at relevant cohort institu-tions, specifically Council of Public Liberal Arts Colleges (COPLAC) institutions, as well as the offerings at much larger sister University of Illinois campuses at Chi-cago and Urbana-Champaign (UIC and UIUC) and at large midwestern and coastal universities where DH curricula were emergent. We reviewed these institutions, in addition to assessing the local, regional, and national landscape in DH, a first step toward DH capacity (Educause Center for Analysis and Research, "Building Capac-ity," 6–8). However, the initial survey, according to ECAR, should inform an insti-tutional needs assessment. Ours, however, stood alone and untethered from any institutional focus on DH. We determined that although a smattering of specific DH courses was offered, no fully developed DH-focused MA programs existed at institutions similar to ours in the Midwest at the time, suggesting a gap we could fill. Because we had surveyed DH programs in other institutions, we knew DH at a teaching institution would be unique. As Brett D. Hirsch observes in his introduc-tion to *Digital Humanities Pedagogy: Practices, Principles and Politics,* despite the early grounding of digital humanities in pedagogy, the programs that thrive exist

largely at research institutions where pedagogy often plays second fiddle to scholarship. He posits a "(Re-)Turn" toward pedagogy (6), but, unfortunately, structural
reasons for the research-pedagogy divide continue to make implementing DH curricula in an institution such as ours a fraught endeavor. We knew that we could not
create a program comparable to those at larger research-oriented institutions. We
instead focused on our faculty's strengths, the teaching mission of our institution,
and its potential as a small, personalized program. We had hoped this focus would
recruit students more broadly from the state and beyond. Although we could envision our students going on to PhD programs in DH or at least using DH methods
in more traditional English PhD programs, we anticipated that the MA, the terminal degree for most of our students, would enhance their professional skills in
education, publishing, and other sectors where they would have the advantages of
using digital tools to understand the logic and aesthetics of print and virtual literacies, literary production, and the increasingly complex relationship between them.

Because employment in education and in publishing is important to our students, we constructed a curriculum with two tracks, one in digital pedagogy and
one in digital publishing (see Appendix). The digital pedagogy track was built upon
a burgeoning graduate certificate program in pedagogy marketed to community
college teachers who needed eighteen hours of graduate credit in English to secure
their employment and to high school instructors teaching dual credit or advanced
placement courses. In the revised English MA, all graduate students took a common core, including courses such as Computing in English Studies, an overview
and hands-on analytic approaches to using computers in English studies; Digital
Humanities Research, an introduction to research methodologies for using digital
resources, including online archives, practice in textual markup, and web design/
editing; and Textual Criticism, a study of editorial, archival, and analytic tools and
methods for English studies that pertain to digital texts and online modes of publication in an interdisciplinary context. Students selected either digital publishing
or digital pedagogy as a concentration and then completed additional coursework.
Digital publishing required courses including Rhetoric and Composition in Digital Media, The Business of Creative Writing, three creative writing workshops, a
literature elective, and a closure project. Digital pedagogy required courses including Teaching Writing, Teaching Literature, sociolinguistics, Teaching Technologies,
a teaching practicum, two literature electives, and a closure project. The faculty
all agreed that they would infuse DH methods and technologies into all of their
courses.

We recognized a successful DH program housed in the UIS English department
and oriented to English studies would still need to build connections across disciplinary boundaries and develop faculty skills. We quickly secured $5,000 through
a UIS internal funding source, the Strategic Academic Initiative Grant (SAIG),
intended to promote interdisciplinary initiatives. Our goal was to introduce ideas
and methods of new curricular DH initiatives in our respective programs, focusing

on revision of the MA curriculum in English and establishing courses or projects relevant to the graduate public history concentration in the history MA. This grant funded an initial workshop and faculty training led by a specialist from a research university with a new but strong DH center. The workshop was successful and well attended by faculty in English, history, communications, and computer science divisions and by specialists and support staff in the UIS Center for Online Learning and in information technology. Our beginning looked promising.

Expectations and Reality

Our graduate students created strong DH projects from the first years of the program initiation as they worked with a small but carefully curated set of methods and tools most relevant to their specific professional goals for teaching literature, creative writing, linguistics, or composition. We aimed to see students acquire a sufficient understanding of the various tools and methods to apply them broadly. In this, we saw success. Our core classes provided opportunities for students to apply their DH skills.[2] For example, in Digital Humanities Research Methods, the gateway course to the MA for both DH pedagogy and DH publishing concentrations, students planning to teach composition courses did sentiment analyses of composition and rhetoric texts often used in first-year writing courses. In one excellent project, Daymon Kiliman, then a graduate student in the fall 2016 DH methods course and now the director of a community college writing center, performed a textual analysis of the "model" summaries and paraphrases provided to students for a compare and contrast assignment. He found that the assignment contained lexical and syntactical features that implied a set of expectations both complementing and diverging from the written instructions, creating conflicts with assignment grading rubrics (Kiliman, "Composition Textbooks"). This had implications in the evaluation of textbooks and faculty and instructor training. In a course specific to the pedagogy track, Teaching Literature, students created syllabi and assignments using technologies and DH methods. Sheri Wingo, an experienced high school teacher, created a class about literature in digital culture. In a project that would become the basis for her thesis, she focused on "the potential of digital formats to examine questions of readership, authorship, embodiment, and power" through analysis of "content [. . .], form, user interface, interactivity, and platform" (Wingo, "Using a Hybrid Flipped-Blended Approach"). The course, then, was inclusive of both traditional literary forms, such as the novel *Ready Player One*, but also the rhizomatic structure of digital poetry and the interactive narratives of video games. If our curriculum had not provided the imaginative space for such a project, it is doubtful that she would have created assignments for students critically exploring connections between digital texts, modes of production, and critical analysis. These are but two of several sophisticated projects we were delighted to supervise. We had hoped to create stronger connections to undergraduate programming using transitional

400-level coursework and connections to the library and to peer tutoring, but these aspects of the program did not have a chance to develop. Nevertheless, our students have found their graduate work useful in their careers. In this respect, our revised curriculum met our objectives.

In the time we had, we were unable to capitalize immediately on these student successes for recruitment. Besides hiring an additional creative writer and filling a vacant line with a digital humanist or compositionist, the success of the new curriculum hinged upon four primary needs: faculty development in digital research methods and pedagogy; aggressive program marketing; one course release for managing and building the program; and a "story" (digital) lab for teaching and collaborative work. Although our hires were approved, the other needs were only partially addressed or ignored completely following the curriculum approval in 2014.

Finding faculty who fit our graduate program, the liberal arts mission of the university, and the needs of our undergraduates was more challenging than anticipated. The term "digital humanities" was new, and we struggled to write job descriptions that matched how potential candidates would describe their expertise. Searches failed for many reasons, but a primary cause was that we wanted candidates with DH expertise combined with another, more traditional field in creative writing or composition. Attempting to combine multiple areas of expertise proved unproductive. Many candidates either did not demonstrate substantive knowledge in at least one specialization in DH pedagogy or scholarship or, if they did, they were snapped up by a research institution before we could complete an initial interview. We needed candidates with experience in the analytic use of DH tools and methods who were committed to directing student projects. Ideally, we wanted someone who could also teach and learn from other faculty, working collaboratively with us and graduate students. It took longer to find those candidates than we anticipated.

Unfortunately, we did not have as long to build the program as we thought. Although our faculty had genuine pedagogical and research interests in DH and digital rhetoric, college-based economic interests shaped implementation and compressed the timeline in ways we did not anticipate. Indeed, our program did not exceed the "early stage" or "grassroots initiative" stage of capacity because we were forced to take a "catch-as-catch-can approach to resource acquisition and maintenance" (Educause Center for Analysis and Research, "Building Capacity," 17). We created and delivered a curriculum mostly in isolation and cobbled together the support and services necessary for the program. As ECAR describes, "In the absence of institutional support, grassroots initiatives tend to be siloed" (17). Although we reached out to other campus entities, building stronger capacity and alliances institutionally would have sustained our momentum and increased the potential for program success.

The first sign that we would not receive the promised resources was the lack of consistent funding for faculty development. We predicated the MA revision in part upon securing commitments for additional training, which unfortunately were not made available after the initial year except very occasionally. A few among us were the scrappy teachers who were taking on the considerable "invisible labor" of "self-pedagogy" that Brian Croxall and Diane K. Jakacki describe in their 2023 volume ("Introduction," *What We Teach*). We wanted to advance as teacher-scholars by training the next generation to use digital humanities methods in their professional paths and by reaching out to our colleagues to work collaboratively as much as we could. Although Bussell attended conferences and workshops to prepare to teach Digital Humanities Research Methods and was using campus resources such as our GIS lab in her own research, no one else was provided funding or time to do so. We hit a limit quickly after some success with a training presentation from UIUC that followed the SAIG workshop. However, we were unable to fund other workshops or "training the trainer" resources. Our faculty would have to go out to regional symposia and larger sister universities for limited resources and to national or international trainings. Unfortunately, only one—Bussell—was able to use faculty development funds for this on a limited basis. Funding dried up quickly due to state budget woes and was never reinstated. After the initial institutional interest lagged, we were unable to negotiate and secure specific budgetary commitments, nor did we continue to see faculty coalitions from various departments in these discussions on resource allocation.

The faculty time needed for leadership and program development in these efforts was not taken into account, as we had requested in the proposal. This proved to be a critical loss. Without this provision, no resources were allocated even at the college level after the first year of implementation. Nothing was committed at the provost level. We had no one on point to remind administrators of the commitments agreed upon when the proposal was accepted through multiple levels of governance. At UIS, the English department chair (Helton) was tasked with much of the implementation and follow-up. With only two course releases for the year, the chair could not also administer a newly developed graduate DH program, nor could the full-time faculty member providing much of the instruction (Bussell) do so, although we were both as active as possible in advocacy as well as training, marketing, and seeking resources. A program director could have applied for grants to develop the program's reach and collaborate across campus with units with interest in digital methods, especially computer science, communication, history, and the library.

Providing equipment was a necessary part of our initial proposal as well. We had requested a designated DH lab to include dedicated computers, printers, iPads, and software focused on data visualization, authoring, and creative design. The lab would have also supported the department's online journal, the digital work evolving in the composition program, and incentivized the integration of the digital into projects throughout the major and the graduate program. Despite several requests, however, the institution never committed the space, hardware, or software. Because our curriculum had been approved, we directed our students to use the media lab in the library, which could serve until the program had robust enrollments and created a larger demand for dedicated lab space. Those enrollments did not materialize. The better approach would have been for UIS to develop a DH lab in a central hub such as the library to support the scholarship of both faculty and students across multiple disciplines to incentivize the use of the lab.

Administrative support faltered generally, especially as DH became connected to broader visions of market-oriented innovation initiatives. Interest periodically arose in working collaboratively with computer science or business in various courses, but these were not developed. We saw intermittent interest from academic affairs in DH training and lab funding years after our program began and after our request for a "story lab" had been set aside. We tried again to secure both lab and training resources in the context of the University of Illinois system through a competitive grant process in academic year 2018–19 when we sought to be integrated into UIUC library advancements in training for DH with "training the trainer benefits" for UIS English, history, and communication departments. Unfortunately, this particular application was not funded. Several subsequent transitions in administration and research leadership, along with further budget constraints, continued to limit support for DH scholarship and teaching. Another key item on the list of must-haves, which did not materialize, was support through active marketing. In our initial proposal, we requested start-up funds for advertisement of the program at the national and regional levels. Although those funds were allocated, the dean's office did not communicate their availability or how to expense them. This resulted in delays in advertising, which meant our dollars were not as effective as they might have been if we had produced ads and direct mailings earlier in the graduate student recruitment cycle. Without such support, getting a DH foothold at an institution is a challenge, and moving beyond the early grassroots stage is nearly impossible.

The fatal blow to our MA program was pressure from the administration and our college dean to show higher enrollments in the second year and produce "proof" of a growing program in its third year through enrollment numbers and credit hour production. This unreasonable demand and conversation about closing the program emerged significantly before the end of the initial five-year framework on which the program's financial feasibility study was based. We needed a substantial number of cohorts to graduate, allowing us to assess curriculum and placement. The economic feasibility study, moreover, was based on problematic assumptions that needed to be revised; the study was too ambitious and did not reflect the realities of a program with a much slower growth curve. We were not resourced to recruit from the broader Midwest or nationally as we had hoped. Applications and inquiries increased by the end of the third year but nowhere near the number desired. Although our students produced fascinating projects, they were not enrolled full-time and were unable to complete the program in two years. Many took only one or two courses per semester. With the economy continuing to slide after the 2008 recession, graduate students had to focus on their paid jobs. Teaching fellowships that had been approved went unfunded. Without the commitment to building the program's marketing and to supporting its management, enrollment in our MA remained primarily local. Still, we enrolled five to eight new students per year. We had enough time to see about seventeen students graduate, most with the MA and a few with the one-year certificate. A few more have yet to finish, and we are teaching out these students. Some graduates were employed in sectors that highly valued their skills in DH, such as managers of social and digital media; some brought their expertise into more traditional jobs such as those in teaching; others went on to advanced graduate work in teaching, publishing, and library and information science. Finally, we found that a modest cohort split between two concentrations was not workable. It resulted in class sizes too small to teach as robust seminars. This exacerbated the enrollment inefficiencies and was institutionally and economically insupportable. Even so, by mid-spring 2018, applicant numbers had increased, and our reach was broadening. We offered admission to ten applicants. But our time was up. By May 2018, we suspended our MA program for new admits.

Moving Ahead

In hindsight, we would have done several things differently and would suggest that others consider the following as they build their DH programming.

> **Foundations.** Securing essential resources is a vital lesson of our experience. Promises of investment in hiring new faculty, training current faculty, marketing, and other support should have been formalized beyond the initial feasibility study and in discussions in governance and with our dean and the provost's office. At the institutional level, promoting DH specifically as an area of teaching and scholarship could have moved our individual program from the grassroots stage to the established and (later) the high-capacity stage where DH moves beyond individual "championing" to full support of the university, including "sustainable funding, support, and academic and political commitment" (ECAR, 19). In their IDHMC white paper for Texas A&M, Maura Ives and Amy Earhart outline hiring needs and space and infrastructure supports that, if scaled appropriately, could have improved our feasibility study and proposal, as would have more realistic expectations for enrollments, timelines, internal and external funding, and managing program responsibilities. Although individual DH practitioners' projects are important to generating excitement about using DH methods, a program director is crucial to the effort to get institutional buy-in and to hold the administration accountable for promised resources. These resources should have been itemized and included benchmarks, timelines, and processes for using these resources, reviewing progress, and assessing and revising curricula. These should have taken into account a candid discussion about return on investment from growth in credit in hours from

admissions, enrollment, and time-to-degree for graduate students managing work and family obligations. Support for additional, staged assessments of interests and needs in our local economy and regional workforce would also have been helpful, especially as students graduated and began using the knowledge and skills from our program in their careers and professional development. We suggest preparing an outline of the administrative tasks and project management skills important for building and sustaining digital humanities initiatives, as A. Miller has done, whether centered in a library or elsewhere. Administrative support, including advising and faculty development within the department is important at every step. Written commitment of release time and reimbursement is crucial.

Curriculum and Capacity Building. Scaling programmatic ambitions to fit resource allocation is another important piece of advice we can offer. We were unable to sustain two tracks. Having a more integrated, slender curriculum would have helped ease some of the enrollment pressures. A mixture of online and on campus delivery would have had a broader appeal and probably attracted more students. Ives and Earhart argue for strategic investment in building capacity of DH and emerging technologies based on existing campus initiatives. If other campus initiatives had existed, we may have been able to more effectively share resources and build capacity. It would have been prudent to begin more slowly and expand as we went. This might have started with a concentration with transdisciplinary connections in coursework to other departments or with a minor for advanced undergraduates more clearly linked to the one-year graduate certificate program. This may have helped build capacity within the college and create opportunities (and pressures) for cross-program investment. It is important to develop stakeholders outside as well as within the department. Surveying campus as well as college programming would have been helpful on this front. The opportunities will vary depending on the campus. For example, we have an honors program with a history of co-teaching its lower division core courses. There may have been some interest in piloting upper-division honors capstone courses or seminars within departments desirous of developing or expanding DH coursework.

Consortium-Building on and off Campus. Identifying and creating working relationships with multiple consortia partners would help at every stage. This is slow and time-consuming work but vital to creating and sustaining any curriculum over the long term. Working with our career center, library, and learning hub, we would like to have seen the creation of internships, tutoring, and teaching opportunities. The library could have been a key partner in building on and off campus collaborative efforts. Planning for costs should include the library, an important center in development of DH initiatives institutionally. John White and Heather Gilbert's overview of libraries as

DH hubs, especially at research institutions, and Lijuan Xu and Benjamin Jahre's case study of an example at Lafayette College, a small private liberal arts university, suggest different approaches to consolidating resources and providing support to students and faculty across disciplines. Developing complementary skill sets that are adaptable and creating support for collaborative multi-instructor teaching between departments and various units is essential (Jakacki). One of the authors (Bussell) worked on a section of an NEH grant application (on the possibility of creating a cross-disciplinary DH minor based on existing courses) in which the UIS library would serve as a central hub. At our institution, with its long history of effective faculty-driven programming in online learning, we could foresee integrating the UIS Center for Online Teaching and Learning into this hub. Costs to be taken into account include those for student workers or interns, software subscriptions and other materials, as well as space and hardware that may be purchased through and located in the library.

Currently, more opportunity exists to work with University of Illinois institutions, regional DH symposia, and COPLAC institutions. One of our frustrations was being unable to access the resources of the University of Illinois, although we found individual faculty and academic professionals very accommodating and helpful. We would have liked to see more specific planning and advanced agreements for "training the trainer" resources, as well as shared system-level funding and shared faculty development. Lisa Spiro, in her discussion of the problems of scalability and equity for faculty and students at institutions of more modest means, proposes an alternate model of networked and open program development that is very promising and becoming more feasible ("Opening Up"). Today, online opportunities exist for DH training that could have been used for faculty development and provided knowledge and skills that would have aided in student and faculty research projects. Our small program may have suffered from being at the leading edge of the curve because we did not have access to these resources now available as options. Resources such as Texas A&M University's continuing education through Programming4Humanists and its Center of Digital Humanities Research Advanced Research Consortium, as well as The Programming Historian, have emerged and continue to make it possible for those with limited resources to learn needed skills and find collaborative communities and support. The Humanities, Arts, Science and Technology Alliance and Collaboratory (HASTAC), cofounded in 2002 by Cathy N. Davidson and David Theo Goldberg, remains an invaluable resource and learning space focused on graduate students and advanced undergraduates as well as scholar-teachers. The ability to effectively use these resources for faculty development and retraining, much less for teaching and connecting students to others in an external community of fellow students and scholar-teachers, nonetheless requires commitments for curricular support, funding, and release time at one's home institution order to make it possible to use such resources. Greater access to resources across institutions within a given university system or consortia is also necessary. We have seen that putting primary or sole responsibility on individual faculty or departments for developing this open networked model in the absence of support is a recipe for failure. Even a basic, open certificate program must be grounded in meaningful material institutional resources for teaching, advising, mentoring, and program administration at the home university if the potential that Spiro envisions is to be realized ("Opening Up"). Teaching, research, and strategic implementation cannot be farmed out.

Alternative Pathways

In hindsight, we can see more clearly why our graduate DH program failed. From the remains, however, we can develop different initiatives, such as an undergraduate DH minor that uses the expertise we have gained, serves students, and more appropriately matches the mission and resources of our small, liberal arts college. Although most DH programs are housed in graduate programs at research universities focused on deliverable scholarship (the "production" model), there is still much room to maneuver at the undergraduate level at a small college. Bryan Alexander and Rebecca Frost Davis recognize the challenge of doing DH at small colleges but have found multiple examples of institutions that are "establishing their own centers, finding preexisting structures with analogous functions, and forming strategic partnerships with each other and larger institutions" ("Should Liberal Arts Campuses Do Digital Humanities?"). These are sustainable, however, when the work fits the mission of the institution, and for small, liberal arts colleges, as Alexander and Davis argue, the mission is undergraduate education that develops "student-professor interaction rather than more public, outward-facing types of sharing and publication" (371). Alexander and Davis further state that DH at small colleges capitalizes on the tradition of student-professor collaborations and encourages applied projects from problem-based assignments: "This process-over-product focus distinguishes the digital humanities as practiced at small liberal arts colleges from the production focus in much of the digital humanities community" ("Should Liberal Arts Campuses"). This may be a much more productive pathway for DH in the UIS English department, something broader in scope than the UIS History Department's successful participation in the History Harvest project (curating online exhibitions of local and regional artifacts using Omeka as part of their public history emphasis) and more similar to scope to the minor cohoused in History and Political Science Department at Saint Xavier University in Chicago. With careful scaffolding, resourcing, and time, undergraduates will still learn important and practical humanities skills applicable to multiple careers through a curriculum transformed by interdisciplinarity and digitalization.

Digital humanities methods, projects, and processes already exist at the undergraduate level. Caitlin Christian-Lamb and Anelise Hanson Shrout detail how DH is integrated with traditional curricula, even if not formalized as DH. They identify a distributed model in which undergraduate programs use "DH methods and tools throughout several courses and on smaller, more discrete projects" ("Starting from Scratch," para. 24). Indeed, this is how DH occurs at UIS: in the English department, digital literacy and DH have lived in many composition classrooms for over two decades, and DH continues to be incorporated in both freshman composition and in upper-division coursework at UIS in English. Creative writing courses have encouraged our students to design and produce online zines in collaboration with visual arts students. The faculty mentors for our literary magazine, *The Alchemist Review,* have helped students to recognize the importance of digital editorial processes and publicity, essential because we have a significant enrollment of online students in the major. Our core research class incorporates quantitative methods for language and literary analysis. At our institution, we also see initiatives in digital humanities integrated into DH and non-DH courses in history, communications, and visual arts.

Promoting student DH projects in writing, if properly curated, can help to create a second groundswell and interest in DH at the graduate level in the future. But for now, focusing on undergraduates is the future of DH at UIS. We can build capacity by teaching DH methods in our core research class, by creating classroom assignments that encourage the use of technology and data analysis and visualization, and by encouraging digital capstone projects, all in the context of interdisciplinarity and a central management paradigm that can promote DH institutionally and in the community. The integration of DH methods and assignments utilizes faculty expertise and institutional resources, but the visibility of DH and its core tenets and goals may be weaker with a distributed model than a more centralized model, perhaps administered through the library rather than a particular discipline. Whether or not our institution uses a centralized or distributed model, we are certain we can retool and refocus productively on pedagogy at the undergraduate level. The success of DH should be measured differently at a small liberal arts institution such as UIS. Alexander and Davis remind us how small institutions should value DH by "emphasizing a distributed, socially engaged *process* over a focus on publicly shared *products*" (369, emphasis in original). At our small university, we hope that process—not product—will again take center stage in DH.

Our institution has embraced online education and encouraged digital modalities of learning, teaching, and scholarship, but it has not committed sustained or consistent resources to DH leadership in scholarship or teaching. Because there has been some waxing and waning enthusiasm for the fresh approaches and innovations that DH might bring to our campus, we succeeded for a while on an early wave of that enthusiasm, but we now find ourselves teaching out the program that was not given the time and resources to take root and be adapted as needed. Our conclusion is that DH programming that is faculty-initiated but limited to department resources and the efforts or interests of particular faculty may have limited success without sustained capacity building within the college and campus.

Yet our students and our teacher-scholars deserve the opportunity to partici-pate in digital humanities in all areas of our discipline and across the curriculum. The process of designing and resourcing digital humanities initiatives that survive long term at modestly resourced teaching institutions is a complex undertaking requiring substantial commitment and planning. The good news is that there are many more resources and models now for doing so than we had available to us eight years ago. Moreover, we are beginning to see overdue discussions of diver-sity, access for BIPOC students and scholars, and work across disciplines taking place, all of which also must be integral to creating and managing DH initiatives (Posner, "Digital Humanities"; Risam, "Diversity Work and Digital Carework"). We hope that this account of our early effort will help bring about a better outcome for others going forward.

Appendix: Proposed English MA Curriculum Structure

COMMON CORE

462	Computing in English Studies		4
501	Digital Humanities Research		4
502	Textual Criticism		4
598	Closure Project		4
		Total:	16 hours

CONCENTRATIONS
Digital Publishing

409	Rhetoric and Composition in Digital Media		4
570	The Business of Creative Writing and Publishing		4
Three	Creative Writing Workshops		12
One	Literature elective		4
		Total:	24 hours
		Total for MA:	40 hours

Digital Pedagogies

550	Teaching Writing		4
551	Teaching Literature		4
552	Sociolinguistics in English Studies		4
553	Teaching Practicum		2
554	Teaching Technologies in English Studies		4
Two	Literature electives		8
		Total:	28 hours
		Total for MA:	42 hours

Notes

1. The graduate program was eventually suspended and then eliminated as of 2023 along with Modern Languages, and we became the Department of English once again in 2024.

2. All student projects are cited by permission. We would like to thank them for their contributions and also acknowledge the many original, thoughtful, and pragmatic projects we have seen from many students over the last three years, which we would happily discuss if space permitted.

Bibliography

Alexander, Bryan, and Rebecca Frost Davis. "Should Liberal Arts Campuses Do Digital Humanities? Process and Products in the Small College World." In *Debates in the Digital Humanities,* edited by Matthew K. Gold., 368–89. Minneapolis: University of Minnesota Press, 2012. https://www.jstor.org/stable/10.5749/j.ctttv8hq.24.

Christian-Lamb, Caitlin, and Anelise Hanson Shrout. "'Starting from Scratch'? Workshopping New Directions in Undergraduate Digital Humanities." *Digital Humanities Quarterly* 11, no. 3 (2017). www.digitalhumanities.org/dhq/vol/11/3/000311/000311 .html.

Croxall, Brian, and Diane K. Jakacki. "Introduction." In *What We Teach When We Teach DH: Digital Humanities in the Classroom,* edited by Brian Croxall and Diane K. Jakacki. Minneapolis: University of Minnesota Press, 2023. E-book.

Educause Center for Analysis and Research. "Building Capacity for Digital Humanities: A Framework for Institutional Planning." Accessed June 2, 2020. https://er.educause .edu/~/media/files/library/2017/5/ewg1702.pdf?la=en.

Hirsch, Brett D. "Introduction." In *Digital Humanities Pedagogy: Practices, Principles, Politics.* Cambridge: Open Book Publishers, 2012. E-book.

Kiliman, Daymon. "Composition Textbooks and the Construction of Student Identities: A Computer-Aided Textual Analysis of Model Summaries and Paraphrases." Student presentation, English 501: Digital Humanities Research Methods, University of Illinois Springfield, Springfield, Ill., December 2016; StARS presentation, University of Illinois Springfield, Springfield, Ill., April 2017.

Kirschenbaum, Matthew G. "What Is Digital Humanities and What's It Doing in English Departments?" *ADE Bulletin* 150 (2010): 55–61. www.ade.mla.org/content/down load/7914/225677.

Miller, A. "Innovative Management Strategies for Building and Sustaining a Digital Initiatives Department with Limited Resources." *Digital Library Perspectives* 34, no. 2 (April 2018): 117–36.

Posner, Miriam. "Digital Humanities." In *The Craft of Criticism: Critical Media Studies in Practice.* Report no. 27, 2018. https://escholarship.org/uc/item/1558k4vg.

Risam, Roopika. "Beyond the Margins: Intersectionality and Digital Humanities." *Digital Humanities Quarterly* 9, no. 2 (2015). http://www.digitalhumanities.org/dhq/vol/9/2/000208/000208.html.

Risam, Roopika. "Diversity Work and Digital Carework in Higher Education." *First Monday* 23, no. 3 (March 2018). https://firstmonday.org/ojs/index.php/fm/article/download/8241/6651.

Spiro, Lisa. "Opening up Digital Humanities Education." In *Digital Humanities Pedagogy: Practices, Principles, and Politics,* edited by Brett D. Hirsch, 331–63. Cambridge: Open Book Publishers, 2012. https://books.openedition.org/obp/1654?lang=en.

Svensson, Patrik. "The Digital Humanities as Humanities Project." *Arts and Humanities in Higher Education* 11 (2002): 42–60.

White, John W., and Heather Gilbert. "Introduction." In *Laying the Foundation: Digital Humanities in Academic Libraries.* West Lafayette, Ind.: Purdue University Press, 2016. ebook.

Wingo, Sheri. "Using a Hybrid Flipped-Blended Approach in an AP Literature and Composition Course, Digital Pedagogy." Student project presentation, Teaching Literature 551, University of Illinois Springfield, March 21, 2018.

Xu, Lijuan, and Benjamin Jahre. "From Service Providers to Collaborators and Partners: A Nondiscipline-Based Approach at a Liberal Arts College." *New Review of Academic Librarianship* 14, no. 3–4 (July 2018): 418–29.

Notes on Digital Groundhog Day

MANFRED THALLER

The journal *Computers and the Humanities,* which gave its name to the Association for Computers and the Humanities, began publication in September 1966. Of the six issues printed between January 1969 and January 1970, five contained announcements of courses in computing for the humanities: two of these announcements addressed all the arts and humanities, two literature, two history, and one each for musicology and anthropology.[1] Why is it that fifty years later, teaching the digital humanities is still surrounded by a flair of something new and pioneering? Having watched and participated in these announcements and discussions since the late seventies, this and some other frequently discussed questions in the digital humanities for me evoke the "groundhog day" feeling of a permanent rerun of extremely familiar discussions. Some of these reruns occur in fifteen-year cycles, some in much shorter intervals.

In a recent description of their teaching model for visualization, Dawn Opel and Michael Simeone describe a very impressive way to start an introduction to visualization by showing how visualization can mislead ("Invisible Work in Digital Humanities"). Well, already Darrell Huff's 1954 book *How to Lie with Statistics* gave a very convincing introduction to the fact that data visualization is a perfect way to create misleading impressions, even if that is not the first impression created by the title. Why is it still necessary to describe this fact explicitly in the presentation of one specific teaching module? Would it not be more productive if we as a community agree that at least certain types of digital humanities degrees *must* contain a module on visualization, which in turn must cover the pitfalls this creates? Would it not be more useful if we could not simply understand Opel and Simeone as another possible solution to a problem well known and defined to be prepared for comparison with other solutions on criteria like resources needed, possibilities to connect to other well-defined modules, and possibilities to adapt to advances in technology without changing the basic concept?

How hard it is currently to compare degrees and courses is demonstrated impressively by Chris Alen Sula et al. in their survey of digital humanities curricula

(Sula et al., "Survey of Digital Humanities Programs"). Preparing descriptions of teaching solutions in a way that emphasizes comparison with other solutions to well-understood problems might also improve the continuity of the discussions. If I look at relatively recent collections on teaching the humanities, including Brett Hirsch's *Digital Humanities Pedagogy* from 2012, Emily Murphy and Shannon Smith's 2017 special issue of *Digital Humanities Quarterly* focused on undergraduate education, and this volume, I notice that there are twenty-nine contributors to Hirsch's volume, thirty-four to Murphy and Smith's, and fifty-six to this volume (Hirsch, *Digital Humanities Pedagogy*; Murphy and Smith, "Imagining the DH Undergraduate"). None of the contributors to Hirsch appear in the later two collections, and there is exactly one contributor who appears in both of the later ones. Even allowing for the fact that Murphy and Smith's book is targeted at undergraduates and this collection at graduate studies, this seems not to indicate an ongoing discussion. Even more surprising is the lack of institutional overlap. Of the institutions represented in Hirsch, only one occurs among the twenty-one institutions contributing to Murphy and Smith. And of the twenty-nine institutions analyzed by Sula in 2017, only three appear among the twenty-one in Murphy and Smith's special issue (Sula et al., "Survey of Digital Humanities Programs"; Murphy and Smith, "Imagining the DH Undergraduate").

This essay formulates some theses about why, after all these years, we remain in a stage where courses in the digital humanities, and even more so graduate programs, are usually announced as being brand new and scarcely comparable. I consider this to be counterproductive. Acquiring an innovative degree may be cool: when it turns out that no employer within academia—or outside of it—has any idea what to expect from the holder of such a degree, it loses much of its attractiveness. I argue, therefore, for the definition of an abstract reference curriculum against which the specific properties of a concrete class of degrees in the digital humanities can be defined.

Let me emphasize the plural implied in a concrete class of "degrees." This plural is the reason that I abstain from defining, even by example, the reference curriculum I recommend and to which I refer. The definition of my academic field is the application of information technologies to enhance the epistemic possibilities of humanities disciplines, with the humanities very broadly conceived. This includes the concept that technologies, which are needed by the humanities, are not provided by computer science but have to be developed by "us." For that field, such a reference curriculum would be perfectly feasible. But for obvious reasons, it would not apply to any graduate course defining the digital humanities as the interpretation of the cultural or social meanings of developments in social media. For that latter definition, a reference curriculum would be just as easy to define, of course. When we avoid deciding between the two and hide behind the opaque label "digital humanities," we do a disservice to our students and ultimately to ourselves, as the followers of one of the two definitions will be able to formulate many stimulating arguments for why the components of the reference curriculum of the other of these definitions are definitely useless for one's own. So, everyone is on their own.

Being fully aware of the multiplicity of definitions of the digital humanities, I take this multiplicity for granted and will not discuss the individual ones.

Some Personal Background

The observations behind these theses and proposals come from a fairly long academic biography, which was spent completely within the interdisciplinary domain. All the professional positions I have held required a combination of qualifications from history (or cultural heritage) and computer science (or rather software engineering), occasionally sprinkled with a taste of sociology. After spending twenty years at the then Max-Planck-Institute for History in Göttingen (an institute dedicated to basic research) to work on software systems for the handling of historical sources, I became director of a university-wide digital humanities center in Bergen, Norway. In 2000, I became a professor at the University at Cologne for *historisch-kulturwissenschaftliche Informationsverarbeitung* (roughly, information processing for the historical-cultural disciplines). Do not worry: even native speakers do not understand this result of a convoluted name-finding process at the faculty. For some of my positions in this essay, it is important to know, however, that together with a second professor, I was responsible for the application of computational methods to disciplines across the humanities, with an understanding of the field heavily biased toward hard-core software technology. Graduates are, for example, expected to be able to program in a higher programming language.

Informationsverarbeitung (for the humanities) at the University at Cologne is understood to be a full-fledged academic subject, offering a bachelor's, master's, and doctoral degree. Bachelor students are always required to combine *Informationsverarbeitung* with another humanities discipline; master's students usually do, and doctoral students usually explore the application of information technology to one of the traditional humanities disciplines. The programs start with approximately one hundred undergraduate students and around twenty master's students each year. In 2015, around 60 percent of those earning a degree with *Informationsverarbeitung* as a major found employment outside of academia, with 20 percent in the cultural heritage sector and 20 percent in academia.

My involvement in curricular discussions went considerably beyond this program, however. I was heavily involved in a series of workshops discussing an international curriculum for history and computing in 1992 and 1993 (Spaeth et al., *Towards an International Curriculum*; Davis et al., *Teaching of Historical Computing*). Furthermore, I participated in the European "aco*hum" project, which between 1996 and 1999 prepared a report on the status of the use of computers in the humanities, identifying research issues as well as teaching models and tentative curricula (de Smedt et al., *Computing in Humanities Education*). More recently I initiated a working group of the Digital Humanities im deutschsprachigen Raum (or DHd), the German member organization of the Alliance of Digital Humanities Organizations (or ADHO), resulting in a comprehensive catalog of all German degree courses in digital humanities and a statement of principles for a reference curriculum (Sahle, *Digitale Geisteswissenschaften;* Sahle, *DH Studieren!*).[2]

Differences between the American and the European University Systems

These experiences obviously shaped the opinions expressed in this essay. A second introductory statement is required to understand some of the positions taken, which are rather obvious in a European context but possibly enigmatic in an American one.

Until 1998 or 1999, continental European university systems had widely different curricular and degree structures. Most had some significant exams at roughly the stage where one would expect a BA and an MA, but in many cases, these were intermediate checkpoints that did not result in a degree. As a result, most study programs at universities were conceptualized monolithically, with a change of universities at some stage acceptable but without any provisions for it. When I studied history in Austria in the early seventies, I had only three options from the first term onward: passing a final state examination to earn qualifications as a teacher in secondary education, getting a doctorate, or failing.

This situation changed somewhat after the seventies toward more clearly defined intermediate degrees, but the structures still varied widely across Europe. As this impeded the integration of the union—and more specifically academic exchange—a group of forty-eight countries around the European Union agreed upon a reform process that culminated in a model which, with some local variance, has led to a system that typically leads to a BA after three years and an MA after two more years; this is the so-called Bologna process.

Academia is exceptionally good at resisting change. Although the degree structure on the surface is now like the Anglo-American one, changes are much less significant under the hood. Anglo-American curricula are usually structured with the expectation that the student will switch institutions after the BA, but most European degree programs have been created with the tacit assumption that the standard case will be an MA at the institution that awarded the BA. As a result, in most European countries, MA programs have still much more narrowly defined requirements than their relatives on the other side of the Atlantic, which implies at the same time BA programs with a greater degree of specialization. Therefore, a BA with a major in digital humanities and a minor in English studies, history, or another more traditional discipline is perfectly feasible. On the other hand, MA programs also often assume a major/minor structure, so an MA program in digital humanities may concentrate considerably more on technical knowledge—with the content to be provided by the other subject chosen—than an MA in "digital X," where the digital components just provide some specialized flavor within a content driven profile.

Doctoral theses in the digital humanities are in this environment frequently co-supervised by a computational and a content-oriented supervisor.

The fact that in most European countries it is typical for students to start a bachelor's program at the age of 18, 20, or 21 also changes the climate of undergraduate courses: the separation between undergraduate and graduate teaching is much less pronounced in most European university systems. Courses that can be taken either as part of a bachelor's or a master's degree are not unheard of. This is the reason that in the following text, it may not always be obvious at which level the comments are directed.

Back to the Opening Question

Why have so many programs failed, and why do the discussions seem to form an endless loop? I do not know when the first-degree program that would fall under today's umbrella of the digital humanities was established. Leaning toward my area of specialization, in 1989 there existed three fully developed MA courses in history and computing in the United Kingdom: at Hull, at the University of London (a cooperation between three colleges), and at Glasgow (Davis, "Postgraduate Experience in the UK"). None has survived. In 1986 at the University of Utrecht, a department for computers and the humanities with twelve permanent full-time positions was founded, offering fifteen full-term courses plus thesis supervision to be integrated into all degree programs of the humanities; this allowed degrees with a heavy computational element in all study programs offered by the faculty (Mandemakers, "History and Computing at Dutch Universities"). The department was, after some time, moved to the faculty of information science and no longer boasts any connection to the humanities faculty. In 1999, at least eight universities in seven European countries offered degree programs based on dedicated departments (Orlandi, "European Studies on Formal Methods," 20–22). Beyond that, about one hundred additional offerings on various levels, where the boundary with computational linguistics is almost impossible to define, are listed under headings more closely related to individual disciplines. King's College is the only one of the eight universities where the BA minor program offered at the time shows a clear continuity with today, and by "continuity" I mean that at the end of the period, the courses offered are easily recognizable as similar to the ones offered at the start of the period. Glasgow started with a degree in history and computing then moved to a degree that referred to the digital humanities, which was so focused on digital preservation that it was more of a library degree and has since changed back to what looks more like mainstream DH.

Everyone at the various accidental and intentional meetings dedicated to curricular questions I mentioned, or implying these questions, agreed that a clearer definition of the program requirements would be needed for the sustainability and sharpness of the degree profiles offered, as well as for the ten to fifty times more courses offered at all imaginable subdegree levels. The main reasons given by participants included the following: making sure that graduates would fit the requirements of the academic job market; offering a clear profile to nonacademic employers outside of the traditional humanities labor market; making qualifications more easily comparable among different institutes of higher learning; increasing the trust of students as well as employers of graduates in the quality of degrees and qualifications offered; and making it easier to establish new degree programs (and departments) by having the ability to point to established standards when negotiating with university administration. This incomplete catalog goes back to three questions, which can be traced back to the first generation of conferences on matters computational in a humanities context: What do I have to know to profit from this fascinating movement? Where can I learn it? Whom can I hire to take over the computing part of my interdisciplinary project? The transformation of this earlier list into the later one simply reflects the realization that having learned to use digital methods for one's own research project enhances one's profile as a potential teacher of digital methods.

Why, if this interest goes back so far and if focused and organized discussions go back at least forty years, do we still not have a clear idea what a degree that provides computational skills and methodologies for humanists should consist of? The following three theses and a summarizing fourth one try to answer this question.[3]

(1) **Very few DH degrees are established due to an intrinsic epistemic interest in "the field." They are rather established because of the glamour of novelty that may coax support out of administrative/political structures reluctant to support the humanities as such.**

This is not to deny that some people, basically the primary proponents of a new degree, have epistemic interests. Rather, my claim is that when selling the degree in an administrative and political environment, this interest ceases to be important.

From the beginning, most approaches to the application of computational or digital methods to humanities fields emphasize very early in their argumentation that humanities questions must be more important in the mix than technology.

> Thus, as already indicated, the person who wants to use a computer in anthropological work of any sophistication must know a great deal of anthropology, but he doesn't require much more knowledge of computers than is contained in this paper. (Lamb and Romney, "Anthropologist's Introduction to the Computer," 88)

That not "much more knowledge of computers than is contained in this paper," originally published in 1962, referred to the ability to program in machine language gives the argument in my opinion an even sharper profile.

Try not to learn too much about the computer side of things, just what you "really need." Many found it always reassuring, at least from 1970 onward, that you had to understand computers just sufficiently that "you could talk to the technicians" (my summary of Société des Historiens Médiévistes, *La Démographie Médiévale*, 62–69).

Are you reading a paper by a techno-freak who complains that his toy is not taken seriously enough? Definitely not. But please remember that we are talking about *teaching* not *research*. When you are interested in the novel in the nineteenth century and listen to a fascinating paper at a conference applying quantitative stylistics, it is absolutely correct and sensible that you economize your knowledge reception, learning exactly as much about the method that paper has applied as you need to replicate its application for your own research question. When you are teaching a degree in "digital X," however, you are not supposed to train people to write the paper you are interested in, but to give them the knowledge they need to identify and answer questions you have *not* thought of yourself. Therefore, shrinking the wide methodological vista opened by some subgroup of digital methodologies to what you must know to show students how to answer the type of question you personally are interested in is inherently shallow. If you are not embracing a broader scope of digital methodologies and technologies relevant for a reasonably broad knowledge domain, but rather the absolute minimum of what is needed to engage with data or digitized materials, you are not teaching "digital X," you are teaching "X." And you happen to live in an era when digital tools are simply there, so knowing about *one* of them is not quite such an earth-shaking qualification.

In this "content reigns, don't talk too much about the technology" approach, there is an inherent danger when you want to attract students. When signing up for a degree in "digital X," students are almost certainly attracted at least as much by the glamour of "the digital" as by the "X." Otherwise they would have chosen a degree in "X" as it is much more easily accessible. If they then spend 90 percent of their time with the intricacies of X and are learning only very specialized details about "the digital," they will be disappointed and let others know, which puts the degree program at risk.

Probably less than 25 percent of all degree courses in "digital X" I have encountered have started with the question "what digital stuff do we have to teach the students to get better at solving the questions of our discipline?" as opposed to "how can we teach this specific technology for the research questions of interest to us?" And the more the second question drives the degree program, the shorter its life expectancy.

So, if you attract students by the glamour of "the digital" and then talk vaguely about the digital, but do not engage it seriously, you will lose them.

Can there be lurking a more general problem? That is, how many graduate programs are really driven by a consensus among the proponents that "the digital" in the humanities should be a driving interest in the study program? Is it not frequently the case that a small number of people actively identifying with "the digital" find support in the wider faculty, because that wider faculty believes that this is a good strategy to convince the administration to continue the funding level (or more simply, the department) when it is threatened? So, you teach "digital X" not because you are interested in "the digital," but because you want "X" to survive, which leads to a situation where many of those who support the plans of the digital activists have a hidden agenda to get away with as little "digital" as they possibly can. It does not help the situation, that "the digital" may be clear in the mind of the proponents but is usually cloudy in the minds of the remainder of the department or the faculty.

Here in my experience a situation arises, which at first looks weird, but at a second glance is easily explained. If you are introducing a new graduate program for, say, French studies, you would try to point the local authorities to the best-known examples and any documents of the relevant academic groups that define what a degree in French studies should constitute. You want to make sure that your new degree program can compete with the established standards. In the case of "digital X" in the countries of my experience, this did not happen in the 1980s, nor later, nor last year. The argument to convince the authorities in this case is "we are the very first ones to have ever had that idea!" at academic institutions with well-developed self-esteem. In less self-assured ones: "even the <enter-the-name-of-an-institution-you-assume-to-be-more-prestigious-than-yours> is doing that, but this is so new, by doing this now we can become even better than them."

I doubt that I have seen any prospectus for a "digital X" since 1984 that did not either claim that this was the very first of its kind worldwide, or at least emphasize that this degree course was unique, as different from all others ever, it was the very first one . . . which, since I have followed these discussions since the beginning of the 1980s, contributes much to my intimate acquaintance with groundhog days.

If your main political argument for your graduate degree is that it is a trailblazer, any existing recommendations of what a study program of this kind *should* look like invalidate that claim. A trail needing blazing has no road map. And "learning from others" is beyond counterproductive politically: if there is a standard for what you want to do, it cannot be all that unique, right?

But, once you have established your degree course, should you not have an interest in underpinning it by relating it to a consensus model that goes beyond your own campus?

(2) The concept behind many degrees and courses consists of the arbitrary bundle of skills available at a given point in time from the current staff at an institution.

The closing statement of the previous section does *not* describe my experience from the forty or fifty events during which, over the decades, I have tried to organize terms of reference for interdisciplinary degrees between history/the humanities and computer science/information technologies. Such terms of reference, or a "reference curriculum," should define what a degree has to contain to be part of a specific denomination, like "DH" (core) and in what ways it can typically be locally extended. I abstain from making that more concrete: if you give a short example of the components of such a reference curriculum, many, if not most, readers tend to misunderstand the example for the full scope of the concept.

I would like to emphasize that I write the following as a diagnosis and I hope it does not hurt the feelings of any colleagues from some of these meetings who may recognize themselves. That I did not *share* their opinions does not mean that I did not appreciate them.

My overall impression is that the implied guarantee of quality given by the possibility of referring to agreed-upon terms of reference would be appreciated. Suspicion and fear that such a recommendation might ask for something that is unavailable locally prevail, however.

This is interacting in two ways with the situation I diagnosed under my first thesis. As the "X" is much more important than "the digital" for the huge majority of the local supporters of a degree course in "digital X," local politics become more complicated if you have to work for the inclusion of an element into the degree course where it is not immediately obvious how the local brand of "X" will profit from it.

This is aggravated by the fact described in the second thesis: "the digital" is a very wide field. The parts of this very wide field represented by the staff available at any humanities institution is a kind of random sample. Say you want to implement a graduate degree for "digital philology" and you are hard-pressed to prove that the staff supporting the required number of teaching hours are available within the faculty, which you have to prove, at least in Germany, before you can start. An offer to teach an introductory course on GIS from archaeology would be extremely hard to decline in this situation. No offense against GIS intended: mappings of various types of relationships can be a valuable tool for philology. But that the capacity for that teaching is available somewhere is not really a convincing reason to include it as a mandatory component of an abstract curriculum. And if after you have collected these local resources you find a reference curriculum that does not include GIS but includes some other skill or methodology unavailable locally, it is absolutely contrary to your interests.[4]

(3) Established DH institutions have the tendency to restrict their offerings to the focus chosen at the time of their establishment. As soon as other parts of the big DH tent are hyped, the established unit tends to lose local support, which is then transferred to the glamour of the most recent novelty.

The core of the argument presented so far is that "digital X" graduate courses are short lived for two major reasons. (1) Many of them are not initiated based on a *consensus* at the home institution that "digital X" opens up broad new methodological vistas for X, if "the digital" is embraced consistently. Such an opinion of a very small group of proponents is supported by a wider group who thinks that placating "the digital" helps in a political situation difficult for X. (2) As the courses are usually built upon a rather narrow staff base, the skills and methodological specializations of very few people present locally heavily influence the content of the study programs. This results in offerings which on the one hand are anything but homogeneous, and on the other face great difficulties in implementing any abstract curricular requirements.

The very few examples of institutions that have kept up continuous graduate programs over longer periods than ten years are indeed usually built upon a more stable platform. King's College London is probably the institution with the longest-running teaching record that can claim conceptual continuity rather than a succession of fluctuating teaching models. Here the strong platform on which these courses were built is an exceptionally large research and service center for digital methods that offered a broad background of methodological knowledge and skills. At my own university at Cologne, a full-fledged BA/MA/doctoral curriculum has been running since 1997 until the present. There exists a backbone of two professorships that are *not* digital flavors that derive their reputation from the digitally flavored "real" discipline of the incumbents, but where interdisciplinary work between the humanities and computer science is the not negotiable core.

Size alone is not a guarantee of survival, though. At Utrecht, the Department for Computers and the Humanities founded in 1986 with twelve full-time positions has after some years drifted into the Faculty of Science. It implemented a very substantial program in mainly database and information retrieval-oriented skills and methods, the focal points of computer-supported work in the humanities in the founding decade. At that point, this was a very sensible focus: if we look beyond a rather narrow definition of "literary computing," database technology was for many humanities disciplines the most widely discussed technology of the day. But more recently the other departments of the Faculty of Humanities at Utrecht perceived a need for training possibilities for their student population in more recent technical and methodological waves, which turned out to be provided more easily outside of the existing structure than within.

Humanistisk Informatikk at the University of Bergen, founded in 1995 and a full-fledged department in every respect, had originally quite a few links to the digital humanities but drifted during the years towards media studies, acknowledging that with a name change in 2010, and the graduate program it offered sharing that drift.

A problem for the survival of graduate programs based on large structures is in a sense the reverse of the perspective of many proponents of "digital X." As many of them justify the engagement with "the digital" with the service it may perform for "X," it is not really surprising that the faculty of many "Xs" also conceptualizes the whole field as a kind of service unit, which only deserves support as long as it is directly useful for the short term goals of the traditional disciplines, or, rather, the personal interests of local faculty members. And the positions and funding assigned to it are seen as a convenient resource to draw upon when another fashionable trend comes along, from the embrace of which the traditional departments may profit even more.

Of course, a general program must take care of the immediate needs of the traditional disciplines. But these must not be constrained by whatsoever happens to be the current focus of local research programs. And it is *not* possible to transfer the responsibility for the more general view to another established institution or department, which is not connected to the humanities. GIS technologies are obviously useful for many applications in the humanities. Teaching "GIS" on the base of, say, ArcGIS served the immediate needs well, but became quite irrelevant for many "immediate" needs as soon as Google Maps arrived. However, when you look not at what the present technology allows, but what technology adapted to the specific needs of the humanities should allow, you soon get into problems like spatial timeline presentations, where the administrative/political units used for mapping change their spatial covering over the years, in some areas in quite tricky ways. Solving that problem goes well beyond the typical three-year project, but when you learn about the specificity of that in one technical environment, you are in a much better position to solve the problem when another such environment becomes more convenient. And there is no reason to assume that the local geography department will be interested in that problem just for the sake of the historians. This is a general problem of attempts to transfer the teaching of matters digital to other departments with agendas of their own, which also relates therefore to information science and library science researchers. They frequently support the notion that, as humanities researchers need digital libraries, researchers interested in the digital humanities should just take some courses offered by the Information Science Department.

(4) Nothing will change until some solid terms of reference are established.

So will we have to continue to watch local implementations of degree programs in "digital X," which after some years fade away while their original enthusiastic and sometimes exuberant proponents get either settled within the traditional structures or drop out from academia and their experience is lost in both cases to the next generation?

As long as the vicious mechanism "to get my local program started, I must not be hampered by any framework that hinders the compromises I have to make" working towards "as my local program derives its value not from itself, but from its usefulness to others, those others may find it eventually even more useful to abolish it" continues, I'm afraid the groundhog will remain the heraldic device of the digital humanities.

You may have noticed that I have written many more times about "digital X" rather than "digital humanities." This is for the simple reason that the digital humanities as they present themselves today are in my opinion a chimera. This may seem surprising from the person who wrote two of the chapters responsible for defining the digital humanities in the most widely used German textbook for them (Thaller, "Geschichte der Digital Humanities"). The contradiction is simple: the authors contributing to that volume are far from the ability or willingness to define the field clearly or give clear definitions what a curriculum of the field must contain. But having been written by the people responsible for five to ten of the better-established graduate programs in Germany, at least a shadowy de facto definition of the commonalities between these programs emerges from it. This in my opinion is not enough, but it is a start.

The big tent of the digital humanities at large, on the other hand, provides a very cozy climate to meet and greet friendly people. Any description of a field or fields that can be taught consistently it provides not.

"Digital humanities is not about defining, but about doing" sounds wonderful and it warms your heart as it implies that whatsoever you are doing, you are a or possibly *the* central part of this big friendly crowd. Somehow "digital humanities is what we have decided to teach" is less convincing—at least to outsiders.

As long as you are defining the justification of your degree course as some service to one of the established disciplines—even if the content you choose is the most revolutionary available—you depend on the whims of that discipline. Only if we manage to define an agenda that can meaningfully claim to be of such generality that it deserves to have people trained in it systematically, even if at the moment nobody else at the faculty profits directly from it, will we reach continuity and stability. An agenda concrete enough that it can be translated into practical administrative requirements, not another manifesto raising the spirit.

My first thesis started with the claim that very few DH degrees are established due to an intrinsic epistemic interest in "the field." The quotes around "the field" should indicate that it is unclear what "the field" consists of. Indeed between some of the different brands of presentations at a typical digital humanities conference there is such a great distance, that it is hard to find any epistemic or methodological commonalities between them, the warm embrace offered to both by a friendly community notwithstanding.

Between "digital X" and the "digital humanities" there should be room enough under the big tent for more than one definition of what a curriculum for *a* field consistent in itself should contain as a minimum. And one can only hope that we start realizing that the long-term advantages of embedding your graduate program into the more widely accepted framework of a recognized curriculum outweigh the short-term inconveniences of having to fit into such a framework. The warmth and coziness of an exuberant wide tent you can share, nevertheless. Just when it comes to serious work, move into a smaller plain seminar room.

"A degree in digital humanities": "When I use a word," Humpty Dumpty said in rather a scornful tone, "it means just what I choose it to mean—neither more nor less." Alice was unconvinced. So am I.

Notes

1. These courses were announced under the heading "New Courses Established" in *Computers and the Humanities* 3, nos. 3, 4, and 5 (1969) and 4, no. 1 (1969) and no. 3 (1970).

2. On their activities after my time—I retired in 2015—see the homepage of the working group on the activities of the "Digital Humanities im deutschsprachigen Raum" or DHd, the German equivalent of the Association for Computing and the Humanities, which is available at http://dig-hum.de/ag-referenzcurriculum-digital-humanities, accessed April 9, 2024.

3. The theses reflect my personal experiences. For records of similar ones, Cordell, "How Not to Teach Digital Humanities" and Kirschenbaum, "What Is 'Digital Humanities'" are good starting points.

4. This kind of dance can be performed on rather high levels. I once had the honor of participating in a small group that was exploring the feasibility of a framework for a European MA on digital preservation, answering an initiative from one of the directorate-generals (= ministries) of the European Union, an initiative vaguely smelling of money. The group included people from quite different disciplines, one of them a computer scientist, another a proponent of library science, both very sensitive to that smell and both

focused on the feasibility of collecting funding for an implementation at their respective home universities. Unfortunately, both were rarely present at the same time. As a result, after each meeting that included the representative of computer science, we had a draft of a curriculum that included a major part of the first two years of a computer science BA. After every meeting with the representative of library science, we had watered that down very much to the "you just have to understand enough about it to talk to the technical people" approach from 1970 quoted above. It was a beautiful dance in its way; after three or four rounds, for some reason, the representative of the commission (roughly, the European administration) lost interest.

One can perform this dance on much lower levels as well. That entering a temporary job in academia is much easier with some "digital knowledge" than without I consider to be as true today as it was when I started myself. If one has, so I observe, any technical knowledge at all within a humanities subject, it was and is always relatively easy to get a *first* job. There was and is almost always somebody who is looking for a "technician" who could do what is not easy for humanists to learn themselves. And for a distinguished member of the department, the young graduates who have read the manual of precisely one program can do magical things, which definitely qualify them as technicians, even if for reasons of politeness they are referred to as esteemed colleagues.

A *first* job. That by being hired to perform what is somewhere below the dignity of a true humanist one is implicitly disqualified from any real job should be obvious. But it is not so obvious for young researchers who enthusiastically find themselves embedded in seemingly central roles in their first research team. Five to ten years later, they are the ones raising their voices at digital humanities conferences with the sharp critique that it is extremely difficult to get into more permanent positions and the higher strata of the academic staff scheme. While five to ten years earlier they have usually been the most insistent that "just doing it" was much more important than discussing what "it" consisted of.

As staff who have begun their positions based upon a relatively narrow qualification are usually those who are most strongly motivated to work for the implementation of a degree course that depends on their qualification, they are obviously interested in ensuring that that qualification is central to the curriculum and not overshadowed.

What I describe is visible in the great reluctance to define the levels of knowledge a specialist in "digital X" should have within the fields of competence chosen. Consequently, the qualification to be awarded by a course training such specialists is usually vague, which frequently leads to some types of magical thinking and name calling, highly destructive on the project and research level but also damaging for what one can expect from somebody having a "digital X" degree and what the long-term chances of survival are for such a degree program.

I had the honor a few years ago to act as a reviewer of a funding line in the "digital humanities." Some time ago, the final reports started to trickle in, and a few had been accepted among other reasons "because all appropriate standards are recognized and applied." I was less than happy to read in one of the final reports that the promised results could not be delivered, as "applying the TEI was much more complicated than they had learned to believe." Another report containing a similar phrase with the TEI replaced by CIDOC/CRM did not increase my happiness. If the specialists consulted by the people who drew up these applications had emphasized that to apply these standards needed some serious training and work, the magical thinking that following the standard would solve all problems could have been avoided.

Bibliography

Cordell, Ryan. "How Not to Teach Digital Humanities." February 1, 2015. https://ryancor dell.org/teaching/how-not-to-teach-digital-humanities/.

Davis, Virginia. "Postgraduate Experience in the UK." In *Towards an International Curriculum for History and Computing,* edited by Donald Spaeth, Peter Denley, Virginia Davis, and Richard Trainor, 13–14. St. Katharinen: Max-Planck-Institut für Geschichte in Kommission bei Scripta Mercaturae Verlag, 1992.

Davis, Virginia, Peter Denley, Donald Spaeth, and Richard Trainor, eds. *The Teaching of Historical Computing: An International Framework.* St. Katharinen: Max-Planck-Institut für Geschichte in Kommission bei Scripta Mercaturae Verlag, 1993.

De Smedt, Koenraad, Hazel Gardiner, and Espen Ore, eds. *Computing in Humanities Education: A European Perspective.* Bergen: University of Bergen, 1999.

Hirsch, Brett D., ed. *Digital Humanities Pedagogy: Practices, Principles and Politics.* Cambridge: Open Book Publishers, 2012. https://doi.org/10.11647/OBP.0024.

Kirschenbaum, Matthew. "What Is 'Digital Humanities' and Why Are They Saying Such Terrible Things about It?" *differences* 25 (2014): 46–63.

Lamb, Sydney M., and A. Kimball Romney. "An Anthropologist's Introduction to the Computer." In *The Use of Computers in Anthropology,* edited by Dell Hymes, 37–90. The Hague: Mouton, 1965.

Mandemakers, Kees. "History and Computing at Dutch Universities." In *Towards an International Curriculum for History and Computing,* edited by Donald Spaeth, Peter Denley, Virginia Davis, and Richard Trainor, 91–105. St. Katharinen: Max-Planck-Institut für Geschichte in Kommission bei Scripta Mercaturae Verlag, 1992.

Murphy, Emily Christina, and Shannon R. Smith, eds. "Imagining the DH Undergraduate: Special Issue in Undergraduate Education in DH." *Digital Humanities Quarterly* 11, no. 3 (2017).

"New Courses Established." *Computers and the Humanities* 3, no. 3 (1969): 162.

"New Courses Established." *Computers and the Humanities* 3, no. 4 (1969): 242.

"New Courses Established." *Computers and the Humanities* 3, no. 5 (1969): 270–71.

"New Courses." *Computers and the Humanities* 4, no. 1 (1969): 24.

"New Courses Established." *Computers and the Humanities* 4, no. 3 (1970): 172.

Opel, Dawn, and Michael Simeone, eds. "Invisible Work in Digital Humanities." *Digital Humanities Quarterly* 13, no. 2 (2019).

Orlandi, Tito. "European Studies on Formal Methods in the Humanities." In *Computing in Humanities Education: A European Perspective,* edited by Koenraad de Smedt, Hazel Gardiner, and Espen Ore, 13–62. Bergen: University of Bergen, 1999.

Sahle, Patrick, ed. "DH Studieren! Auf dem Weg zu einem Kern—und Referenzcurriculum der Digital Humanities." DARIAH-DE Working Papers 1, 2013. http://webdoc .sub.gwdg.de/pub/mon/dariah-de/dwp-2013-1.pdf.

Sahle, Patrick, ed. "Digitale Geisteswissenschaften." Digital Research Infrastructure for the Arts and Humanities. 2011. Accessed April 8, 2024. https://dig-hum.de/sites/dig-hum .de/files/cceh_broschureweb.pdf.

Société des Historiens Médiévistes de l'Enseignement Supérieur Public. *La Démographie Médiévale: Sources et Méthodes: Actes du Congrès de l'Association des Historiens Médiévistes de l'Enseignement Supérieur Public, Nice, 15–16 mai 1970. Annales de la Faculté de Lettres et Sciences Humaines de Nice, 17, 1972.* Paris: Les Belles Lettres, 1972.

Spaeth, Donald, Peter Denley, Virginia Davis, Richard Trainor, and Steffen Wernicke, eds. *Towards an International Curriculum for History and Computing.* St. Katharinen: Max-Planck-Institut für Geschichte in Kommission bei Scripta Mercaturae Verlag, 1992.

Sula, Chris Alen, S. E. Hackney, and Phillip Cunningham. "A Survey of Digital Humanities Programs." *Journal of Interactive Technology and Pedagogy* 11 (2017). https://jitp .commons.gc.cuny.edu/a-survey-of-digital-humanities-programs.

Thaller, Manfred. "Geschichte der Digital Humanities" and "Digital Humanities als Wissenschaft." In *Digital Humanities: Eine Einführung,* edited by Fotis Jannidis, Hubertus Kohle, and Malte Rehbein, 3–18. Stuttgart: Metzler, 2017.

Digital Futures for the Humanities in Latin America

MARIA JOSÉ AFANADOR-LLACH AND GERMÁN CAMILO
MARTÍNEZ PEÑALOZA

In a Twitter conversation from June 2020 among the digital humanities Spanish-language community, a question was posed as to whether digital humanities (DH) teaching was necessary to become a good humanist. One participant replied: "Yes! What is difficult to answer is what must be taught, how, and what for" (Rojas Castro, "Sí!"). We ask this question frequently in an ongoing experiment to build a digital humanities curriculum and a community of practice in Colombia. Created in 2017, the MA in digital humanities at the Universidad de los Andes, a private university, is the first graduate program in the field in Latin America and is an interdisciplinary program of the School of Arts and Humanities that is not anchored in any single discipline. As DH professors and digital development staff, we are striving to sustain an MA program that was created before we arrived at the university where we work. As is the case across Latin America, we work in an academic realm in which DH is on the fringes of humanities research and pedagogy.[1] By mobilizing conversations on interdisciplinarity, research-creation, linguistic diversity, and digital infrastructures, our curriculum and epistemological foundations have attempted to engage with topics and problems that are relevant to the broader DH Latin American community. These issues inform contemporary discussions on digital scholarship among the Global South DH community and present possible pathways for emerging programs in the field.

Infrastructures and Linguistic Diversity

As Roopika Risam argues in her discussion on postcolonial digital humanities, the political dimensions of digital knowledge production include facilitating methods and epistemologies for expanding the digital cultural record of the Global South (9). In Colombia, as in most of the countries of Latin America, the allocation of computing resources is prioritized in areas of research such as those in STEM departments that guarantee a clearly applicable outcome. In most cases, the infrastructure is outsourced to established players in the technology sector at the global level, shaping a landscape of technological infrastructure that tends to ignore the needs of research-creation projects in the arts and humanities. Infrastructure for DH comprises not only computer hardware and network access but also "the more intangible layer of expertise and the best practices, standards, tools, collections and collaborative environments that can be broadly shared across communities of inquiry" (Morton and Price, *Our Cultural Commonwealth*). However, projects dedicated to creating and maintaining public cultural resources for research and education are mostly poorly funded by already limited budgets for culture. Because the promise of data mining and machine learning is unequal across the world, in the context of our MA program, we are leveraging the diversity of questions and disciplinary backgrounds of our students and professors (Crymble et al., "The Globally Unequal Promise"). Most of our students are not pursuing projects that employ text mining or perform algorithmic analysis of large amounts of cultural data, or when they do, they face substantial problems related to information access and the lack of digital skills and resources.

Cultural criticism in DH has become a backdrop to Latin American discussions about DH infrastructures, research, and programs. Hegemonic views about the field have tended to "constrain it and make invisible the work that is done in languages other than English and in latitudes other than the United States, Canada and Northern Europe" (Galina Russell, "Introducción," 10). Within this discussion, the issues of multilingualism, geographical diversity, code hegemony, infrastructures, and North-South cooperation, among others, have opened a working and thinking space both in Latin America and in our MA program (Fiormonte, "Testo Tempo Verità"; Fiormonte et al., *The Digital Humanist;* Liu, "What is Cultural Criticism"; Galina Russell, "Geographical and Linguistic Diversity"; Ortega, "Multilinguism in DH"; Del Río Riande, "Humanidades Digitales"; Rojas Castro, "Sí!"). Besides the geopolitics of DH knowledge production, we grapple in our institutional context with the fact that few researchers have the interest, skills, or incentives to participate and work in the field.

Despite these challenges, our context affords the creative opportunities and freedoms needed to engage with interdisciplinary and interinstitutional conversations (Fiormonte, "¿Por qué las Humanidades Digitales necesitan del sur?"). We are building upon ongoing conversations on other computations concerned with how to "articulate other accounts of digital design and construction that do not place regions outside of the global North on the receiving end of technology and innovation" (Cardoso Llach and Burbano, "Other Computations"). Although the regional economy is tied to the transfer of already existing technologies, we see potential in the open source and open access models as pathways to bridge some of DH's digital divides.[2]

One of the key conversations in the Global South is connected to the issue of Anglocentrism in DH. Resources, readings, and documentation for digital tools and scholarship are scarce in Spanish. To address this problem, our MA program hosted a DH writing workshop in Bogotá in 2018 in connection with the open-access online resource *The Programming Historian* and aligned with its diversity policy (Sichani et al., "Diversity and Inclusion in Digital Scholarship").[3] This initiative, which emerged from a North-South collaboration funded by the British Academy, led to the production of the first Spanish-language DH lessons written by native Spanish speakers for *The Programming Historian*, which sought to address the needs of researchers in the region (Crymble et al., "Digital Humanities Skills"). Twenty-two scholars from ten countries in North and South America attended the workshop, which led to the activation of a DH community across the region that continues to collaborate.[4] Another outcome was the publication, so far, of thirteen original Spanish-language lessons, with more underway. These lessons have become a key documentation site that we use widely in our MA curriculum and regard as a valuable outcome given the scarcity of online Spanish-language DH resources.

The workshop also mobilized a conversation around the state of the art in Latin America regarding digital infrastructures for accessing and analyzing primary sources.[5] As a result of the networks that were initiated at the Bogotá workshop, we organized another event in September 2019. This event, Abrir Colecciones en Latinoamérica (Opening Collections in Latin America), opened a space to reflect on digital infrastructures for libraries, archives, museums, and DH in Latin America. In our own institution, we also host an initiative to create a digital archive that preserves the work of Colombian artists and researchers. Banco de Archivos Digitales de Artes en Colombia (BADAC) is a faculty-level project that aims to digitize, preserve, and provide access to digitized works in the fields of visual arts, literature, film, music, and journalism. Because several projects in the archive are led by teachers with little experience in digital scholarship, the role of the team at BADAC is to help researchers realize the potential of the digital in their projects, thus helping to advance the adoption of DH among the faculty in general. We regard BADAC as a laboratory where this digital infrastructure is constantly under construction but also as a place where students, teachers, and researchers can experiment, learn, and create using digitized and born-digital materials described in Spanish and about local cultural production.

Interdisciplinarity, Experimentation, and Research-Creation

Our students come from multiple disciplinary backgrounds, including design, linguistics, computer science, arts, communications, and history, and they have disparate research and technical skills. This multiplicity of backgrounds and a flexible institutional setting and curriculum—the MA program operates across the school rather than being housed in a specific department—has allowed our students to constantly cross disciplinary boundaries. For instance, students can choose three courses outside of their school in any MA program across the university to support their projects. As a result, students have found in the program a space to develop a diverse array of forms, expressions, methods, and paths to explore research questions that are not necessarily inscribed in traditional humanities scholarship. Besides questions from art history, literature, and history, students' projects address questions related to activism, law, maker culture, environmental studies, gender inequality, civic engagement, speculative design, and the digital divide, with some seeking solutions to social problems.[6] At first, we were concerned that the diversity of these topics would cause us to drift from mainstream Global North DH curricula, but then we started listening to our context and enabling spaces for interdisciplinarity.

One of our student projects posed a research question relevant to both the fields of law and DH. In this interdisciplinary experiment, Maria Fernanda Guerrero (a lawyer) and Carlos Varón (a linguist) applied methods from computational linguistics to a corpus of legal texts to determine how its content related to fundamental rights defined in the Colombian National Constitution. They decided to tackle the problem of the selection of cases of guardianship action (in Spanish, *acción de tutela*) by the country's supreme court.[7] The court regularly selects guardianship action cases based on a review process assisted by undergraduate law students. Undergrads read through statements, sentences, evidence, and other documents and then select a case based on how it relates to or represents the defense of a fundamental right. Guerrero and Varón applied topic modeling techniques to the corpus and identified the relationship between individual sentences and an individual right. Along the way, the project encountered a series of challenges arising from poor archival practices in local courts and difficulties in information access and management, challenges faced broadly across public and memory institutions in Latin America. For example, local courts often store and add metadata to the sentences without following a standardized structure, file format, or markup schema for the documents. This experience revealed the obstacles that poor open access practices and the lack of digital infrastructures pose for digital research. However, it also made us, the teachers, realize that in extending critical methodologies to corpus creation and analysis, an interdisciplinary and critical humanistic approach helps lawyers, students, and researchers understand the problem in its ethical, political, and historical dimensions.

Our MA program is based on research-creation in which the production of knowledge is not only based on forms of academic writing and argumentation but also on the creation of artifacts that communicate and convey ideas. This model of research-creation is pursued in several arts and humanities schools across the country and responds to the need to validate the production of artists, designers, architects, curators, writers, and other cultural producers inside and outside academia. We have been able to propose and test a curriculum where digital research methodologies meet creative and experimental forms of creation and communication. Although this model poses methodological and epistemological challenges to argument-driven forms of scholarship, it is also an avenue for crossing disciplinary borders (Chapman and Sawchuk, "Research-Creation").

One of the key affordances that led us to the adoption of the research-creation model is the recurrence of projects that are based on research problems and whose goal is to intervene in a specific context by creating digital artifacts that seek to act as a form of argumentation. Another student project proposed to develop digital tools and infrastructures to allow a community to store, share, and recover their traditional knowledge while simultaneously recognizing the relationships between plants, humans, and digital devices. In the early stages of the project, Maria Juana Espinosa Menéndez used tools like MediaWiki and the FOAF vocabulary to describe these relationships and the traditional medicinal and spiritual uses of plants held by the community.[8] During this process, she realized that, in general, those tools and standards did not allow for an adequate representation of the traditional knowledge of the community and their relationships with plants ("El Lenguaje del Botsque"). Instead of uncritically applying dominant models, Espinosa turned to methodologies from the fields of critical and speculative design to develop a series of prototypes that explored questions related to the project. In her interactions with the community, she found that cell phones were more relevant devices for communication and information exchange than personal computers and tablets. Forms of communication based on narrative and orality were also more familiar to the community than technologies for data capture like web forms or spreadsheets. In the final prototype, Espinosa used a Telegram group to host the exchange of information and collective building of knowledge, and she developed a bot to assist in the recording and recovery of information based on conversational interactions with plants and the community. This project is an example of how students in our MA program can experiment with problem-based and prototype-based research and at the same time question the limits of Anglophone protocols and standards and the challenges of operating in a context characterized by digital divides.

As Isabel Galina Russell asserts, "The breadth of meaning embraced by the digital humanities inherently entails the existence of research and teaching experiences from various perspectives, no longer multidisciplinary, but more broadly cultural" ("Introducción," 12). Our students' questions and interests have compelled us to rethink the role of DH in local contexts, reflecting as it does the limitations and potentialities of the many places in the Global South. In a context characterized by rampant social inequality and the challenges of overcoming a long-lasting armed conflict, attaching academic efforts to civic engagement has allowed us to reimagine the role of the humanities for the twenty-first century and drawn us away from definitions of DH toward an acceptance of, and a desire to play with, its elusive nature. A core aim of our emerging interdisciplinary research-creation praxis is for DH scholarship in the form of textual or digital artifacts to contribute to the ongoing conversations on humanities research, infrastructures, cultural production, inter-disciplinarity, and digital transformation more broadly in Latin America. We believe that having students connect their DH work with entities such as the publishing industry, design studios, hackerspaces, memory institutions, art collectives, software companies, and the public sector in general is a possible path to revamping the relevance of the humanities in the contemporary world.

Our advice to other emerging DH programs is to listen to their context and promote conversations about digital culture beyond academia. Building curricula that reflect a set of discipline-specific tools, methodologies, and workflows developed elsewhere is fine, but we also need to keep a "childlike sense of wonder" attitude while paying attention to and engaging in technology appropriation processes arising in Latin America (Baladrón, "Apropiación de Tecnologías"). We are aware that this process requires us to reimagine the ways we teach, guide, and assess digital projects, as well as to acknowledge the role of the academy and DH networks in fostering communities of practice in the region. We imagine a DH future for Latin America in which practitioners critically assess the institutional, cultural, techno-logical, economic, and political dimensions of digital scholarship and work around an open definition of what digital scholarship can look like in the region. In this process, we must keep a self-critical stance to keep asking what must be taught, how, and what for.

Notes

1. The first DH organization in the region was created in 2011 in Mexico as the *Red de Humanidades Digitales:* http://www.humanidadesdigitales.net/. In Argentina, the *Asociación Argentina de Humanidades Digitales* was created in 2013: http://aahd.net.ar/. Colombia followed with the creation of the *Red Colombiana de Humanidades Digitales* in 2016: http://www.rchd.com.co/. A couple of MA programs recently created in the region include Maestría en Humanidades Digitales, Tec de Monterrey in 2019, and Maestría en Comunicación y Humanidades Digitales, Universidad del Claustro de Sor Juana in 2017.

2. A project involving our students and former participants of a DH writing work-shop that we held in 2018 was the construction of a DIY scanner with open source designs, software, and hardware. The tutorial and guidance for this activity was provided by Matías Butelman, a participant in the workshop and a member of the Bibliohack project, an Argentinian initiative that develops designs, documentation, and community around the task of building and putting to work DIY open-source scanners for digitization projects. Neogranadina is another organization that works with DIY scanners for digitizing colo-nial records in Colombia.

3. *The Programming Historian* is an online, peer-reviewed publication that publishes tutorials that help humanists learn a wide range of digital tools, techniques, and workflows to facilitate research and teaching. To date, it has published ninety-seven English-language tuto-rials, forty-seven translations into Spanish, and fifteen original Spanish-language lessons.

4. The constitution of a Spanish-speaking community around *The Programming Historian* has also sparked key conversations about diversity within a global DH community. See Sichani et al., "Diversity and Inclusion."

5. Priani defines digital infrastructures as basic ecosystems where materials and the systems and processes necessary for research, teaching and the dissemination of culture can be accessed; see Priani, "¿Infraestructura de Cómputo para las Humanidades?"

6. Examples of student projects include data modeling and textual analysis of topics such as femicide and the archival activism of LGBT communities; participatory digital archives of local neighborhood stories; storytelling around Colombian musical heritage; and textual analysis of newspaper accounts of Latin America's armed conflict, among others. A sample list of MA projects can be found at https://humanidadesdigitales.uniandes.edu.co/.

7. Guardianship action is the most widely used instrument of law to defend fundamental rights in Colombia such as healthcare access and fair labor conditions, among others. See Guerrero Mateus and Varón Castañeda, "¿Un Sistema Automatizado?"

8. FOAF, or Friend of a Friend, is a machine-readable ontology used to describe people and their relationships with other people, objects, or organizations. It implements the RDF/XML syntax to share FOAF descriptions.

Bibliography

Abrir Colecciones en Latinoamérica. "Diálogos Regionales sobre Bibliotecas, Archivos, Museos y Tecnología Digital." Universidad de los Andes. September 24, 2019.

Baladrón, Mariela Inés. "Apropiación de Tecnologías en las Redes Comunitarias de Internet Latinoamericanas." *Trípodos* 46 (2020): 56–76.

Banco de Archivos Digitales de Artes en Colombia. https://badac.uniandes.edu.co.

Bibliohack. http://bibliohack.org/.

Camburn, Bradley, Vismal Viswanathan, Julie Linsey, David Anderson, Daniel Jensen, Richard Crawford, Kevin Otto, and Kristin Wood. "Design Prototyping Methods: State of the Art in Strategies, Techniques, and Guidelines." *Design Science* 3 (2017): e13. https://doi.org/10.1017/dsj.2017.10.

Cardoso Llach, Daniel, and Andrés Burbano. "Other Computations: Digital Technologies for Architecture from the Global South." *Dearq* 27 (2020): 6–19.

Chapman, Owen, and Kim Sawchuk. "Research-Creation: Intervention, Analysis and 'Family Resemblances.'" *Canadian Journal of Communication* 37, no. 1 (2012): 5–26.

Crymble, Adam, and Maria José Afanador Llach. "The Globally Unequal Promise of Digital Tools for History: UK and Colombia Case Study." In *Teaching History for the Contemporary World,* edited by Adele Nye, 85–98. Singapore: Springer, 2021.

Crymble, Adam, Maria José Afanador Llach, and José Antonio Motilla. "Digital Humanities Skills for Latin American Scholarship." Bogotá: Universidad de los Andes, 2018. https://doi.org/10.5281/zenodo.1473414.

Del Río Riande, Gimena. "Humanidades Digitales: Infraestructuras Visibles e Invisibles." Laboratorio de Humanidades Digitales del Centro Argentino de Información Científica y Tecnológica, CONICET, December 9, 2020. *Computers and Culture* 1 (April 2023): 18–29. https://hdl.handle.net/10468/14426.

Endres, Bill. "A Literacy of Building: Making in the Digital Humanities." In *Making Things and Drawing the Boundaries: Experiments in the Digital Humanities,* edited by Jentery Sayers. Minneapolis: University of Minnesota Press, 2017.

Espinosa Menéndez, Maria Juana. "El Lenguaje del Botsque: Relaciones Plantas-Seres Humanos en Entornos Digitales de Aprendizaje Colaborativo Interespecies." Master's thesis, Universidad de los Andes, 2020. http://hdl.handle.net/1992/64473.

Fiormonte, Domenico. "¿Por qué las Humanidades Digitales Necesitan del Sur?" In *Humanidades Digitales: Construcciones Locales en Contextos Globales: Actas del I Congreso Internacional de la Asociación Argentina de Humanidades Digitales (AAHD),* edited by Gimena del Rio Riande, Gabriel Calarco, Gabriela Striker, and Romina De León, 17–38. Ciudad Autónoma de Buenos Aires, Editorial de la Facultad de Filosofía y Letras, Universidad de Buenos Aires, 2018. https://doi.org/10.5281/zenodo.1239201.

Fiormonte, Domenico. "Testo Tempo Verità." *Humanist Studies and the Digital Age* 2, no. 1 (2012): 57–70. https://doi.org/10.5399/uo/hsda.2.1.2996.

Fiormonte, Domenico. "Towards a Cultural Critique of Digital Humanities." In *Debates in the Digital Humanities 2016,* edited by Matthew K. Gold and Lauren F. Klein. Minneapolis: University of Minnesota Press, 2016.

Fiormonte, Domenico, Teresa Numerico, and Francesca Tomasi. *The Digital Humanist: A Critical Inquiry.* Brooklyn: Punctum Books, 2015.

FOAF Vocabulary Specification. http://xmlns.com/foaf/spec/.

Galina Russell, Isabel. "Geographical and Linguistic Diversity in the Digital Humanities." *Literary and Linguistic Computing* 29, no. 3 (September 2014): 307–16. https://doi .org/10.1093/llc/fqu005.

Galina Russell, Isabel. "Introducción." In *Humanidades Digitales: Recepción, Institucionalización y Crítica,* edited by Isabel Galina Russell, Miriam Peña Pimentel, Ernesto Priani Saisó, José Francisco Barrón Tovar, David Domínguez Herbón, and Adriana Álvarez Sánchez, 8–11. Tlalpan, Ciudad de México: Bonilla Artigas Editores, 2018.

Guerrero Mateus, María, and Carlos Varón Castañeda. "¿Un Sistema Automatizado Podría Asistir la Selección de Tutelas Realizada por Estudiantes de Derecho en la Corte Constitucional?" Master's thesis, Universidad de los Andes, 2019. https://repositorio.uni andes.edu.co/handle/1992/44057.

Liu, Alan. "What is Cultural Criticism in the Digital Humanities?" In *Debates in the Digital Humanities 2016,* edited by Matthew K. Gold and Lauren F. Klein. Minneapolis: University of Minnesota Press, 2016.

Mediawiki. https://www.mediawiki.org/.

Morton, Herbert C., and Anne J. Price. *Our Cultural Commonwealth: The Report of the American Council of Learned Societies Commission on Cyberinfrastructure for the*

Humanities and Social Sciences. New York: American Council of Learned Societies, 2006. https://www.acls.org/past-programs/commission-on-cyberinfrastructure/.

Neogranadina. http://www.neogranadina.org/.

Norton, David. "Making Time: Workflow and Learning Outcomes in DH Assignments." *Debates in the Digital Humanities 2019,* edited by Matthew K. Gold and Lauren F. Klein. Minneapolis: University of Minnesota Press, 2019.

Ortega, Élika, "Multilingualism in DH." *2015 MLA Position Papers,* December 31, 2014. https://www.disruptingdh.com/multilingualism-in-dh/.

Priani, Ernesto. "¿Infraestructura de Cómputo para las Humanidades?" *Red de Humanidades Digitales* (blog), March 10, 2012. http://humanidadesdigitales.net/infraestructura-de -computo-para-las-humanidades/.

Ramsay, Stephen, and Geoffrey Rockwell. "Developing Things: Notes toward an Epistemology of Building in the Digital Humanities." In *Debates in the Digital Humanities,* edited by Matthew K. Gold. Minneapolis: University of Minnesota Press, 2011.

Risam, Roopika. *New Digital Worlds: Postcolonial Digital Humanities in Theory, Praxis, and Pedagogy.* Evanston, Ill.: Northwestern University Press, 2018.

Rojas Castro, Antonio. "FAIR Enough? Building DH Resources in an Unequal World." Presentation, Digital Humanities Kolloquium, Berlin, Germany, August 4, 2020. https:// hcommons.org/deposits/item/hc:32187/.

Rojas Castro, Antonio (@RojasCastroA). "Sí! Lo difícil de contestar es qué hay que enseñar, cómo o para qué." Twitter, June 23, 2020. https://twitter.com/RojasCastroA /status/1275383783253061637.

Sichani, Anna-Maria, James Baker, Maria José Afanador Llach, and Brandon Walsh. "Diversity and Inclusion in Digital Scholarship and Pedagogy: The Case of *The Programming Historian.*" *Insights: The UKSG Journal* 32, no. 16 (2019): 1–16. https://doi .org/10.1629/uksg.465.

What versus How
Teaching Digital Humanities before and after Covid-19

STUART DUNN

Any student, in any part of the world, will be able to sit with his projector in his own study at his or her convenience to examine any book, any document, in an exact replica.

—H. G. Wells, *World Brain,* 1938.

In March 2020, the Covid-19 lockdown finally swept into the United Kingdom. In its wake, in the space of a week, many institutions including my own underwent the kinds of change that would normally take five years or more to bring about. In particular, the sector was forced into a comprehensive reevaluation of online teaching. We were suddenly faced with searching questions of what it is for, as well as what it should be and how it should be done. But in those panicked weeks leading up to, and after, the national lockdown on March 23, 2020, there was little time for anyone to consider these questions in detail, least of all with any kind of historical perspective.

Considering the forced acceleration of change in the spring of 2020 in its wider historical context is valuable. In the United Kingdom, universities have been offering online teaching in one form or another for at least two decades, with the concept of remote teaching stretching back much further. Most notably, remaining with the UK context, the Open University was established in 1969 to offer remote education by correspondence course. The motivation for this, on a relatively small island, was not to enable students to overcome geographical barriers to their education but rather to promote social inclusion and mobility as the country emerged from the post–World War II period (Open University, "Take Your Teaching Online"). The sudden shock of the total move online in March 2020, therefore, fell within a longer historical trajectory, one in which online teaching is only part of the story. In this extended historical period, universities moved from predominantly paper to predominantly electronic communications. The United Kingdom's JANET network connecting campus computing systems was established in 1984, at the time a pioneering system driven by substantial government investment (JISC, "History of the Janet Network"). Since the 1990s, higher education institutions (HEIs) have adopted Virtual Learning Environment (VLE) systems, and digital and/or automated systems for most aspects of administration and governance. And although many studies dismiss the idea of the "digital native" as a myth (e.g., Kirschner and De Bruyckere, "Myths of the Digital Native"), in the fifteen years or so since the inception of so-called Web 2.0, students (and staff) in western HEIs have generally become more digitally connected as social media platforms have taken hold, and digital communication channels have become dominant in social and political discourse. This has changed many important relationships, including HEI members' relationships with their institutions. When considering the disruption of Covid-19, we must remember that the digital space is one that universities and their inhabitants have occupied gradually, incrementally, and cautiously, over a period of decades.

In the "new normal" of the Covid-19 pandemic, however (a phrase that rapidly became hackneyed and overused in media discourse), lectures, seminars, whole modules, and programs were reimagined for the digital world within weeks, if not days, within the capacity that was designed for teaching in the "old normal" world. Despite this, many such changes persisted and continue to challenge the assumptions about any relative benefits and drawbacks of online and in-person teaching. Blended learning, where students will have an option of taking their courses in the virtual and physical worlds, will surely continue to have a role, given the great dependence of the global higher education I sector on academic and student mobility. This sudden, exponential, and enforced occupation of digital space far beyond the frontiers of anything that had gone before should therefore be seen partly as a matter of institutional resilience. After all, the protointernet itself emerged in the 1960s and 1970s in part as a response to the shadow of the Cold War, providing a means of channeling executive command decisions through "distributed networks" that could survive a nuclear attack (Abbate, *Inventing the Internet,* 183). Given that Covid-19 and other pandemics may well recur and that national and global issues continue to dominate, including climate change and—since the pandemic—the cost-of-living crisis, we have a responsibility to our students and to each other to consider how the digital space might help weather such future storms. We must, in other words, seek to ensure that our ongoing occupation of the digital space can sustain as well as survive.

With the benefit of some distance from the pandemic, it is worth taking stock and looking again at some of those bigger questions and what they mean for digital humanities (DH) in general, which I approach below through the particular lens of our work at King's College London. Many in the world of the old normal might have assumed that DH would be naturally placed to embrace these changes, indeed that it already occupied "the digital" in a way that other disciplines did not. Most digital humanists would probably argue that the reality is more nuanced and complex than this. However, I believe that the initial distinction between what we teach versus how we teach it, exposed by the emergency situation of March 2020, remains and indeed holds deeper significance when we consider the digital in our teaching. The digital in the context of the digital humanities in my view means an increased entwinement of digital and nondigital modes of critical discourse, practice, and analysis that include teaching and learning in which frictionless networked contact alters not just how we communicate but how we interact, behave, and think. This is an old idea in the context of the internet's history. Such a blended place is much as the internet geographers Matthew Zook and Mark Graham imagined it in the world of "DigiPlace" back in 2007, as digital mapping platforms emerged: "DigiPlace is not determined and constrained by transcendental structures but exists instead in a fluid and complex state of being, in which agents and structures are interminably enabling and shaping one another" ("Creative Reconstruction of the Internet," 480). The digital, as a space that DH (and other academic disciplines) had to occupy so rapidly, thus blends both form and content, both "what" and "how." A cursory examination of the history of the digital before DigiPlace shows that this dichotomy, so starkly exposed by Covid-19, is even older, being indeed almost contemporaneous with the establishment in the United Kingdom of distance learning in the late 1960s. In 1968, J. C. R. Licklider and Robert Taylor, the U.S. computer scientists and administrators of the ARPA program, noted the following in a paper titled "The Computer as a Communication Device": "Creative, interactive communication requires a plastic or moldable medium that can be modeled, a dynamic medium in which premises will flow into consequences, and above all a common medium that can be contributed to and experimented with by all. Such a medium is at hand—the programmed digital computer. Its presence can change the nature and value of communication even more profoundly than did the printing press and the picture tube, for, as we shall show, a well-programmed computer can provide direct access both to informational resources and to the processes for making use of the resources" (22). When university pedagogy, which we might certainly consider to be an example of "creative, interactive communication," is placed into this context, the "dynamic medium" of the digital must be considered not, in fact, just as a medium, but rather as an environment. And most would accept that since the mid-2000s, the internet has been a conversational networked environment rather than a formal one (Castells, "Network Theory of Power," 782).

Moving from a physical environment to a digital one is therefore a matter of pedagogy, or more precisely of pedagogical environment, and not just a shift from one mode of teaching to another; it follows, then, that moving teaching normally done in person to an online format during a time of emergency is not the same thing as online pedagogy, never mind good online pedagogy (this may be extremely obvious within the DH community, but it perhaps still needs restating). No one—academics, students, management—should expect it to be. The lessons of internet history are clear on this. Once this fundamental truth is acknowledged, a range of important and self-reflective questions about what constitutes good online pedagogy emerge that DH as a field needs to address.

The flurries of discussion about online teaching in the first part of 2020—the relative merits of Discord, Microsoft Teams, Zoom, and institutional VLE platforms—were driven by how we coped with the crisis. The "how" changed (literally) overnight, driven by the need to deliver what had already been promised to students. Despite this, the creativity and innovation of DH was much in evidence. Much of this came through in the roundup of Covid-19 think pieces in *Digital Humanities Now* and other contributions ("Editors' Choice"). There were many stories of compromise, improvisation, imagination, and the challenges of the digitalization of content and delivery. However, taking a wider historical-environmental view of online pedagogy, it becomes clear that the Covid-19 crisis merely accentuated, rather than caused, the distinction between what we teach online (in DH and everywhere else) and how we teach it, while also greatly accelerating the shift between the two. Looking both beyond the immediate and pressing need for digital teaching as a palliative for the institutional problems caused by the sudden immobility of the student population and to the more distant history of the digital, we see that these "how" questions are purely symptomatic.

In the longer term, the question of what we teach online and how this differs from in-person degree programs presents many more fundamental challenges and opportunities. What kinds of learning can best be imparted remotely, how might these be used to meet the specific challenges of graduate study, and how can the digital itself be co-opted into such new forms of learning? It will take time, resources, effort, and imagination beyond the teaching we already do and the efforts that we have all made to salvage our existing teaching tasks.

We can begin by asking if it is even possible to deliver remotely the same learning outcomes for graduates as we do from the lectern. Should we even try? If not, what should we be doing instead? These are fundamental questions that have been bubbling under the surface of DH pedagogy for years. Any current debates in the newer forms of DH embrace the digital as its own theoretical construct. These debates frame the digital as having its own modes of production and interpretation that are separate from printed materials or physical image media. Indeed, this idea permeates much of our teaching and research in the Department of Digital Humanities (DDH) at King's, where one of our core aims remains to build and contribute to the global body of that theory as driven by the humanities (Dunn and Schuster, "General Introduction," 8). It follows that "digital methods" should be seen as a body of methodology distinct from other types of methods, particularly the discursive approaches used by humanities researchers to understand and interpret the human record. If this is true, then we will have to accept that delivering the digital and digital methods online to students means that the fundamental building block of higher education programs, the learning outcome, must be rethought for online delivery. What are learning outcomes for in the digital age, when students are, as part of their everyday lives, increasingly connected with networks of knowledge, information, ways of doing things, cultures, and economies that are fundamentally enabled by the digital?

In the DDH at King's, we offer five master's programs. Hitherto, these have rested relatively comfortably within the standard credit and timetabling structures: generally, they have been delivered as one core module, four elective modules, and an extended personal dissertation research project. Learning outcomes, defined as the skills and knowledge that a student possesses upon completion of a course, are inevitably tied to the types of material we teach within these structures. In the kind of humanities-driven learning of, with, and about the digital that we pursue in the DDH, the origins of such material may lie in the physical world (such as manuscripts, artworks, and photographs) or the digital world (content created purely online). The latter, especially, are of significance for our more professionally facing modules, whose subjects include advertising, digital content, and social media analysis and subjects related to the digital economy. For reasons set out in more detail below, I believe that online teaching, in particular, offers opportunities to question the distinction between these different kinds of material in new ways.

Digital humanities researchers of all kinds need to engage with the ways that the digital changes our interpretive relationship with our material. We have been forced to confront and deconstruct the assertion that "an exact replica" can be easily delivered to any student, anywhere, as in the vision in the quotation from H. G. Wells given at the start of this chapter. The medium in such a world will never be value-free, as it will always have phenomenological significance, forming part of the interpretive process. Of course, digital transmission changes our perception and reception of cultural material. Try writing a tweet with a fountain pen and posting it through the mail or opening a text file in MS Word 95. The digital is a prism through which we see and experience the human record of past and present, not a window. Online teaching needs to embrace this, and this is very much a matter of what as well as how.

Therefore, one challenge for DH's pedagogical theory and practice as it approaches both the how and the what of online learning in the post-Covid-19 world is the need to construct new forms of learning outcome that enable students to embrace that prism: the teaching of digital methods, digital citizenship, and digital ways of being rather than just digital content, as per Wells, as simply an exact replica of what we get in the library or the archive. There is much one could draw on from other DH discourses here: for example, much is made in library and archive studies of the truth that preservation (e.g., the creation of exact replicas of content) is not sustainability, which is the ability to use those replicas in some way. I make no claim that this is a new idea in DH pedagogy, and it is certainly very present in my own department, but it shows that DH has many rich and deep seams to draw on in understanding the key how versus what difference for engaging in both teaching and research online.

There are some areas that I think we need to consider when building a new framework for online teaching in DH. I do not purport to offer any answers here but rather present these as high-level ideas to act as way-markers to help kick off conversations that many of us will be having as the years of the post-pandemic world unfold. No doubt they will be changed, deleted, reorganized, reordered, and added to, but for teaching that approaches the digital in a humanities-driven way—which, for me, is the essence of DH pedagogy—these represent the starting points as I see them.

Participation and Placemaking

As I point out in one of the early lectures of my Maps, Apps and the GeoWeb: Introduction to the Spatial Humanities module at King's College London (a module delivered as ten lectures and seminars, the standard format referred to above), the classroom or lecture hall is a "place" that all present within it contribute to through the medium of presence. It is more than walls, floor, and a ceiling: its function channels Heidegger's Being as *Dasein,* of physical presence. Place is a human construct that we create collectively and socially through processes of actually being there and, as in the world outside the academy, this has been disrupted by the digital. To an extent, pervasive network technologies have collapsed the distinctions between different kinds of places, both geographical and conceptual: public and private, personal and shared, political and social, and even inside and outside. However, the university as a set of physical spaces has proved rather durable. In DH we have—slowly—learned to teach and develop bodies of theory with our students in the framework of "traditional" in-person teaching in the classroom and the lecture hall. Consequently, the act of speaking in, and to, a group in the same physical location is a staple of the traditional seminar. However, for many of our students, physical place has already been collapsed. The channels of social media platforms like Instagram, Twitter, and Snapchat may connect to the physical world through geolocation, but they "exist" aspatially.

More to the point, in the interconnected world, we now have an opportunity to deliver teaching across places, where students physically located in one place can be encouraged to critique and question their own experiences of their environments as mediated by the digital. This is the thinking behind a graduate module I introduced in 2020, *London as a Digital City,* which flexibly and comparatively explores how London differs as a "digital city" from other parts of the world, assuming that the student is located elsewhere and has firsthand experience of inhabiting another place. Thinking critically about the "placelessness" of virtual spaces and the complexity of their connections to emplaced and embodied realities has particular relevance to graduate students, the majority of whom come to King's from a wide range of places across the United Kingdom and the wider world.

Embracing Asynchronous Conversation

The seminar—small-group teaching of students co-located in time and place—is one of the key planks of graduate study in the humanities. Like many in other departments and disciplines at King's, we have embraced the synchronous online seminar, conducted in a virtual chat room with video, and we have found they impose both positive and negative impacts on our teaching. The post-Covid-19 reality means that we need to develop equivalent frameworks for teaching using digital objects outside the time frames of the seminar, for two reasons. First, in common with most research universities in the United Kingdom, many graduate students at King's are not physically present in London and are scattered across multiple time zones. Second, many key tasks related to the analysis of the kinds of digital objects and assets we work with in our teaching—image collections, metadata, and digital maps, among others—are designed to be carried out incrementally and collaboratively. These constraints challenge us to design teaching activities that are unconstrained by the time frame of the seminar and that therefore reflect more creatively the actual working practices for which we are preparing students.

New Kinds of Assessment

Although the essay is as much an artifact of conventional teaching in the humanities as the seminar, the limitations of the essay format for assessing what students have learned and how well they have learned it in DH have long been apparent. While they will also have a role in assessing discursive understanding of core concepts, there is a general assumption across the arts and humanities in the United Kingdom that assessment will always be by essay, unless there is a reason for it to be otherwise. In post-Covid online DH, I would suggest the opposite should be true, especially for online teaching, and that essay-based assessment should have to be justified by the impracticability of shorter, practice-focused forms of evaluation. To follow is an example of one learning outcome of the Maps, Apps and the GeoWeb module described previously: "[The student should] be able to demonstrate knowledge of fundamental web standards for geospatial data, with a primary focus on KML, but with a broader appreciation of how these standards relate to generic frameworks, including most importantly the World Geodectic Data system. They will also be able to discuss the limitations these impose on the expression of information in the digital humanities, and discourses built around it."[1]

This reflects what Cecily Raynor (see chapter 11 in this volume) describes as "in-depth, intense training for students eager to engage with digital methods and critical data science." Before the pandemic, I assumed that this outcome would be assessed discursively by a four-thousand-word essay, structured across four to six examples, or four to six arguments focused on a single case study. There is, however, no reason at all why this assessment could not be broken down instead into four to six web-mounted exercises based on real-world problems centered on humanities materials (in the best of all worlds, students could be given a list of ten or more mini-cases from which to select and then explain the methodological link between them). This would, in any case, get them much closer to the technical core of the problem described. Such a mode of assessment would also be amenable to placeless, asynchronous modes of teaching described above.

The Importance of Open Access and Open Data

The Covid-19 crisis prompted many publishers and content providers—among them Cambridge University Press, Wiley, and Taylor and Francis—to make freely available materials related to coronavirus research that would otherwise have been paid for. This was a welcome, if temporary, development that opened up the opportunity to rethink the importance of open data in the humanities.

In theory, of course, online teaching can continue to be done behind institutional VPNs, by means of subscriptions to services such as Shibboleth and Athens and to individual publishers; as described at the start of this essay, this has been standard practice in the United Kingdom for years anyway, although some of these resources are unavailable to students accessing content from certain regulatory regimes, which is another key factor. Moving toward online teaching must be accompanied by educating students on how to critically assess open data and open resources in the "wild west" of the World Wide Web. Teaching that happens in the online "place" must include methodological skill-building in understanding how the features of that place—datasets, articles inside and outside peer review, formal and informal research outputs, and content produced by other students—function and how they can best be evaluated and navigated.

The human cost of Covid-19 must never be underplayed. According to the WHO's online data dashboard, as of May 2022, 6.27 million people have died of the disease, and it has brought untold disruption to lives, national economies, and all levels of society. However, looking forward, there is much that DH, and especially DH teaching, can learn from its sudden, enforced expansion into the digital realm. Using the longer history that lies behind this sudden traumatic event, I have sought to show here that the what and the how of online teaching are the axes on which all our field's most important considerations need to be plotted. Reconciling them will require resources and imaginative thinking, alongside the wide range of theories, ideas, and resources with which DH has been experimenting already for years.

Above all, I have seen firsthand that it has the skillful and creative people needed to put them into practice.

Note

1. See https://www.kcl.ac.uk/abroad/module-options/module?id=38938234-3d8f -4788-9f12-0a046318ee14 for full course description. Last accessed April 17, 2024.

Bibliography

Abbate, Janet. *Inventing the Internet.* Cambridge, Mass.: MIT Press, 1999.

Castells, Manuel. "A Network Theory of Power." *International Journal of Communication* 5 (2011): 773–87.

Digital Humanities Now. "Editors' Choice: COVID-19 Roundup." March 17, 2020. https:// digitalhumanitiesnow.org/2020/03/editors-choice-covid-19-roundup.

Dunn, Stuart, and Kristen Schuster. "General Introduction." In *The Routledge International Handbook of Research Methods in Digital Humanities,* edited by Kristen Schuster and Stuart Dunn, 1–9. Abingdon, UK: Routledge, 2021.

JISC. "The History of the Janet Network." Janet Network. 2023. Accessed April 17, 2024. https://web.archive.org/web/20230306054833/https://www.jisc.ac.uk/janet/history.

Kirschner, Paul A., and Pedro De Bruyckere. "The Myths of the Digital Native and the Multi-tasker." *Teaching and Teacher Education* 67 (2017): 135–42. https://doi.org/10.1016/j .tate.2017.06.001.

Licklider, J. C. R., and Robert W. Taylor. "The Computer as a Communication Device." *Science and Technology* 76, no. 2 (1968): 21–41.

Open University. "Take Your Teaching Online." Open Learn. 2023. Accessed April 17, 2024. https://www.open.edu/openlearn/education-development/education/take-your -teaching-online/content-section-overview.

Zook, Matthew A., and Mark Graham. "The Creative Reconstruction of the Internet: Google and the Privatization of Cyberspace and DigiPlace." *Geoforum* 38, no. 6 (2007): 1322–43. https://doi.org/10.1016/j.geoforum.2007.05.004.

Teaching Digital Humanities Online

STEPHEN ROBERTSON

Prior to the early months of 2020, online teaching had become a growing presence in university curricula though not yet in digital humanities teaching. Then Covid-19 forced all teaching and learning online, notwithstanding the previous disinterest and opposition of many faculty and the flawed learning management system (LMS) platforms that universities had adopted. Two years later, teaching had fitfully and unevenly moved to mask-to-mask teaching on the way to a return to face-to-face classes. Although the ramifications of those processes are not yet fully known, it is already clear that online teaching will not be returning to the place it occupied in curricula before the pandemic. For all the challenges faculty encountered while teaching, and the struggles students faced while learning, university administrators now have concrete examples of the possibilities online delivery offers as well as its pitfalls. Less cynically, so too do teachers and students. If the experience of teaching online that this essay shares is now more common among educators than before the pandemic, the lessons I learned about how to effectively teach digital humanities still have value as we look to move from a pedagogy patched together as best we could in a crisis to a more reflective and sustainable practice.

My reflections on these challenges come out of my experience as part of a team at the Roy Rosenzweig Center for History and New Media (RRCHNM), a team that collaborated with the Department of History and Art History at George Mason University (GMU) in 2014 to develop an online graduate certificate in public digital humanities.[1] In the U.S. context, a graduate certificate is a credential available to those with an undergraduate degree that involves approximately half the courses of a master's degree and is typically focused on a specific field of study within a discipline.[2] At that time, only a handful of other digital humanities certificates existed in the United States at Michigan State University; University of North Carolina, Chapel Hill; University of California, Los Angeles; University of Nebraska; and Texas Tech University. Only the last was taught online and available to students not already enrolled in graduate programs at the institution, and it was narrowly focused on book history and digital humanities. In the years since the course was launched, the landscape has changed significantly: by 2020, there were around thirty graduate certificates in digital humanities on offer in the United States. However, few of those programs share the features of GMU's program. Where GMU's certificate is open to any qualified student, nineteen (nearly two-thirds) of other certificates are available only to graduate students already enrolled in master's and PhD programs at the institution, part of a trend that locates digital methods outside of disciplinary training and limits engagement with how digital tools and methods are transforming scholarship in disciplines. Whereas all three courses in GMU's certificate are interdisciplinary and designed for the program, almost all the digital humanities certificates include only one or two courses specific to the program, instead relying on elective components drawn from existing offerings in departments. Those courses are often outside the humanities and take no account of humanities sources and questions, leaving certificate students to try to learn in classes designed for a different audience. Only one other certificate, at the University of Iowa, has a focus on public digital humanities, but it is only offered to students already enrolled and is not taught online. There are five online digital humanities certificate programs, but four are taught at small institutions not engaged in high levels of research activity (not R1 schools), and one is available from the University of Missouri School of Information Sciences, which represents one of three graduate certificates offered by information science programs.

The limited number of online digital humanities graduate certificates reflected a widespread skepticism among faculty about online teaching before the pandemic. Many universities had adopted LMS platforms such as Blackboard, Canvas, and Moodle that use discussion boards, quizzes, and video conferencing to provide feedback, facilitate engagement, and deliver content. However, a focus on moving face-to-face courses online, rather than designing courses for the medium of the web, had directed attention to the personal interaction and engagement lost in that shift and made online teaching an unattractive option for faculty. That online courses have been promoted as a vehicle for cost saving and casualization, as tools of the neoliberal university, has frequently served to harden that disinterest into opposition. What remained as the one indisputable benefit of online delivery was access to learning for students unable to participate in face-to-face classes.

In light of this wider context, I argue that what makes the online introductory course I teach as part of GMU's certificate particularly effective in supporting student learning is a focus on iterative, scaffolded activities. To an extent, this approach is an element of digital humanities teaching that involves working with digital tools or programming, regardless of the mode of delivery. However, the course also used this approach in activities focused on assigned readings and content in other media. As those elements are found in courses across the humanities, I suggest that the effectiveness of this scaffolded, iterative approach in digital humanities offers lessons for graduate education more broadly.

The effectiveness of those iterative, scaffolded online learning activities is closely related to the platform used to deliver the course and to the fit of the activities with the needs of specific groups of students. Delivering the introductory course on a custom-built platform built using the content management system Drupal has given me and the staff at RRCHNM with whom I collaborated the scope to develop an approach different from the options provided by an LMS such as Blackboard, Canvas, or Moodle; it also allowed us to use the features of the online environment rather than trying to reproduce a face-to-face teaching experience. The course design works best for students who were working professionals and for non-traditional students who both needed and were equipped to learn independently and asynchronously. A key lesson I took from this as a teacher was the benefit of not allowing the features offered by an LMS to determine how I approached online teaching. However, the limited scope to pursue those principles in graduate education back in 2019 seems likely to be further foreclosed in the post-Covid context. Few, if any, universities give faculty the option or resources to use an online platform of their own, especially after increased investment in LMS platforms to move all teaching online during the pandemic. Similarly, my other key lesson, reinforced by the experience of teaching during the pandemic, about how online learning works best for specific groups of students is also more difficult to apply after the pandemic. At least some of the courses moved online in response to the pandemic are not returning to face-to-face delivery at many universities. In that sense, a central concern for those engaged in online teaching remains consistent both before and after the pandemic: to what extent do the available platforms and curriculum offer the opportunity to design an effective course for students equipped to learn independently and asynchronously?

In my own efforts to reimagine online teaching in designing and teaching, I found that the context of the graduate certificate as a whole shaped the design of the course I taught, a reminder that our teaching needs to be understood in relation to the curricula as well as institutions in which we teach. Extending an existing partnership with Smithsonian Associates, the fifteen-credit graduate certificate includes a six-credit online internship at a Smithsonian institution and three 3-credit asynchronous courses designed by faculty in the Department of History and Art History, which has offered a separate set of graduate digital history courses with a disciplinary focus since the late 1990s as part of its master's and PhD programs.[3] The learning outcomes of these courses reflect the scale of what can be accomplished in a certificate program: a familiarity with the field of digital humanities and how digital tools and media have transformed research, analysis and presentation in the humanities, and a working knowledge of tools, skills, and processes used to produce digital projects. Shrinking this foundation to allow for a more detailed focus on particular software or programming languages can leave students ill-equipped to think computationally about humanities sources and questions, to conceive digital projects, and to have the digital humanities literacy to mediate between technical and nontechnical staff.[4]

Delivering the graduate certificate online aligned with the orientation of graduate coursework at GMU toward working professionals, and online delivery was in response to the desire, expressed by graduate students in history and public history at institutions without such offerings, for access to digital history courses like those offered by the department. What made reimagining online delivery feasible was that staff at RRCHNM had expertise with Drupal, expertise that had been honed in projects creating resources for online teaching, providing professional development for teachers and faculty in teaching with digital tools, and teaching shorter online professional development and recertification courses for K–12 teachers.[5] Our colleagues' ability to use Drupal to build a platform for online teaching as an alternative to an LMS freed us to design activities beyond the elaborate structure of content and assessments of an LMS—an option obviously not available at most institutions. Most of the activities we created at their core involved collecting submissions from students and later displaying those submissions so they could be reconsidered and revised, an approach not explicitly offered in an off-the-shelf LMS at the time.

The online course I developed and teach as part of the certificate is Introduction to Digital Humanities. Courses with such a focus are ubiquitous in digital humanities certificates but can be taught in a variety of ways. My course defines a field, surveys methods and projects, and offers limited hands-on work with a range of tools.[6] As Ryan Cordell insightfully articulates in "How Not to Teach Digital Humanities," digital humanists increasingly reject this approach as too shallow in its treatment of topics and skills and are opting for syllabi more narrowly focused on a particular digital method. However, in the context of the GMU certificate, such breadth makes sense, providing as it does a foundation for students going on to courses in digital public history and digital teaching and learning.[7] I organized the course around the process of developing a digital project, beginning with gathering sources then creating data and metadata; describing that data; using digital tools to visualize, analyze, and present data; and crowdsourcing and promoting digital projects. Students were asked to both analyze case studies and do hands-on work with a variety of off-the-shelf tools and a dataset created for them, which enabled them to extend their understanding of those case studies and how they might use the tools in their own work. They were then asked to choose one tool to use in a digital project, generally working with sources they had encountered in another class or that were part of collections at the institutions where they worked. With guidance from Kelly Schrum and Jennifer Rosenfeld, in designing the course for online delivery I looked to the properties of the online medium and what possibilities they offered rather than simply replicating my existing face-to-face teaching activities. The resulting course was far from the thorough reimagining of online teaching that I called for at the start of this essay, but it illustrated how building a custom platform in Drupal enabled us to harness the procedural and participatory characteristics of the online medium to make the course interactive.

Shaking free of existing approaches in this way is hard work. Our efforts produced a scaffolded series of activities and tutorials that helped students learn a range of unfamiliar concepts and skills and develop computational thinking. The structure of those elements encouraged more engagement with the course material than the "read and take a quiz or post a response" model baked into LMS-based online courses and produced a more systematic critical engagement with the texts for all students than a typical in-class discussion. Students applied readings to examples through processes of categorization, classification, comparison, creation, and reflection. These activities broke down and made concrete ways of thinking and ensured that each student participated and worked through the material. For example, in a module on defining digital humanities, after activities tracing changed definitions of digital humanities and breaking down the components of those definitions, students were given a brief reading on folksonomies and then a set of projects to review and tag with their digital features. They then reviewed TaDiRAH, a taxonomy of digital research activities, and were allowed to revise their tags using that model. In the final activity, they were presented with word clouds of their two sets of tags and asked to reflect on what had changed and why.[8] The response of one student in the 2016 class captured what this approach was able to achieve: "The format of the activities was excellent—they were not things you could breeze through easily, you really needed to think about how each DH project was developed and implemented—and the questions requiring us to compare them all pushed us to think critically." One drawback of this scaffolding, however, is its inflexibility: some students grasped concepts more quickly than others and were frustrated that they had to work through multiple examples in an activity, whereas others reported that they needed that variety and repetition. Nonetheless, the experience of having to scaffold and make visible the learning I aimed to promote made me rethink my reliance on discussion in graduate classes, and it led me to look to include some more structured activities to model and highlight ways of thinking and reflecting.

Tutorials were another approach that worked well when transposed to the online context of this course. The tutorial is a well-established genre in digital humanities education highlighted by ongoing projects such as the *Programming Historian,* which publishes peer-reviewed online tutorials for a range of platforms and programming languages associated with conducting specific tasks, and the exemplary classroom-focused tutorials of UCLA digital humanist Miriam Posner.[9] When our GMU students worked with software, we provided carefully written step-by-step tutorials with embedded, annotated images, which were revised over time to remove ambiguities and errors. This is essentially the same approach taken in many face-to-face digital humanities classes, an element that makes the field particularly amenable to online teaching. The narrow scope of tutorials fits the nature of the skills taught in digital humanities classes, as they focus on concrete, specific research problems rather than generalized, abstract problems. However, in a face-to-face setting, teachers are on hand to troubleshoot in person and can respond relatively quickly, depending on the size of the class and the number of students who experience problems. In an asynchronous online class, troubleshooting via Slack or email generally means a time lag in responding that students can find frustrating (although because I am online far more than is good for me, that time lag is often quite short). Having to wait for help can also encourage students to try to seek solutions themselves, which they rarely do in class, helping them gain the confidence to tap into the opportunities for self-taught digital humanities skills. Students overwhelmingly reported finding the tutorials an effective hands-on means of understanding the digital tools and how they work and of understanding the perspectives offered in the readings and activities.

One major limitation of tutorials is that students can successfully complete one without necessarily understanding what they have done. One way that this might be mitigated is to set up collaborative annotation of the tutorials, which has the flexibility to be a vehicle for providing explanations of what is being done, soliciting explanations from students, and discussing specific issues where they appear. When resources permit, creating video versions of tutorials would improve accessibility, provide the opportunity for more commentary on the instructions, and cater to increasing numbers of students accustomed to platforms such as YouTube and TikTok who express a preference for video. As it is, we addressed the limits of tutorials primarily by having each student complete a project using one of the off-the-shelf tools introduced in the course, which allowed us to assess the limits of what they had learned.

The approach I took in my online course for the GMU graduate certificate worked particularly well for students who were working professionals. Librarians, archivists, teachers, and faculty made up roughly half of the seventy students who enrolled in my course from 2014 to 2019. They came to the course with a sense of what digital humanities is and why it matters to them and the field in which they work; they generally had a project in mind; and they managed their time carefully. Such students reported appreciating how much they learned about exploring and evaluating digital tools in a way that could be directly applied to their work. The other major constituency for the certificate are students enrolled in the master's degree offered by the Department of History and Art History or who recently completed their undergraduate degree; this group generally have a somewhat different experience.[10] Few of those students have any sense of what digital humanities is when they enroll in the course and are frequently following advice that digital humanities will complement their degree or set them up for work in public humanities. Consequently, they are simultaneously being introduced to a humanities field and learning how it is being transformed. The students in the master's program also struggle to balance the mix of active and passive learning inherent to the online certificate program courses and the face-to-face classes they are taking as part of their degree track, and they struggle to dedicate the time needed to complete the scaffolded activities. This group of students is also generally intimidated by digital technology; as a result, they tend to find the course more work than they expected.

At the same time, the students who successfully complete the course report having the foundation for further work in digital humanities, a key learning outcome for the certificate, and they often express this in terms of increased confidence. One student in 2019 reported that the activities allowed them to "gain confidence in our abilities to interact with cool digital platforms," and another in the same class wrote, "I came out of this course with more knowledge than I envisioned and with the courage to continue with the certificate program."

These varied outcomes for online teaching are not unique to digital humanities teaching, of course. Online courses in other fields have often produced good outcomes for working and nontraditional students, both of whom need and are equipped to learn independently and asynchronously. Students mixing face-to-face and online classes and with less background knowledge and confidence have more uneven outcomes. Nonetheless, online courses such as my Introduction to Digital Humanities can be effective in teaching digital humanities by incorporating established formats such as tutorials and building scaffolded, iterative, and reflective inquiry-based activities to develop the ability to think computationally, with the advantage of the flexibility and accessibility that asynchronous teaching offers. Assembled from courses in this form, an online graduate certificate can contribute to a future digital humanities education a foundation that enables students to conceive digital research projects and equips them to identify and gain the skills to analyze their sources and answer their research questions in critically robust ways that demonstrate their adaptability to a rapidly changing world.

Notes

1. For an overview of the course structure, see https://historyarthistory.gmu.edu /digital-public-humanities/dph-courses.

2. A survey of digital humanities programs in 2015 found that most Anglophone programs took the form of certificates and specializations, whereas most European programs were master's degrees. See Sula et al., "Survey of Digital Humanities Programs."

3. For a detailed overview of the George Mason University PhD program's digital history requirements, see https://historyarthistory.gmu.edu/programs/la-phd-hist.

4. Goldstone makes a related point about the limits of what can be achieved in a single course; see Goldstone, "Teaching Quantitative Methods."

5. For the team that developed the Drupal platform, see https://web.archive.org/web /20220617033046/https://rrchnm.org/digital-public-humanities-graduate-certificate/.

6. For a discussion of teaching this kind of survey course, see Selisker, "Digital Humanities Knowledge."

7. This is equally true of the courses in the department's program for PhD students; see Mullen, "Confirmation of Andrew Goldstone."

8. See http://tadirah.dariah.eu/vocab/index.php. For a broader discussion of this approach to online teaching, see Sharpe et al., "How We Learned."

9. The online tutorials are available at https://programminghistorian.org/. For more on Posner's work, see, for example, "Digital Humanities 201" and the discussion of tutorials in Norton, "Making Time."

10. Doctoral students in the Department of History and Art History do not enroll in the certificate because their program includes two required digital history courses and the option to take additional courses to complete a minor field in digital history.

Bibliography

Cordell, Ryan. "How Not to Teach Digital Humanities." In *Debates in the Digital Humanities 2016,* edited by Matthew Gold and Lauren Klein. Minneapolis: University of Minnesota Press, 2016. https://dhdebates.gc.cuny.edu/read/untitled/section/31326090-9c70-4c0a-b2b7-74361582977e#ch36.

Goldstone, Andrew. "Teaching Quantitative Methods: What Makes It Hard (in Literary Studies)." In *Debates in the Digital Humanities 2019,* edited by Matthew Gold and Lauren Klein. Minneapolis: University of Minnesota Press, 2019. https://dhdebates.gc.cuny.edu/read/untitled-f2acf72c-a469-49d8-be35-67f9ac1e3a60/section/620caf9f-08a8-485e-a496-51400296ebcd#ch19.

Mullen, Lincoln. "A Confirmation of Andrew Goldstone on 'Teaching Quantitative Methods.'" February 8, 2017. https://lincolnmullen.com/blog/a-confirmation-of-andrew-goldstone-on-teaching-quantitative-methods/.

Norton, David "Jack." "Making Time: Workflow and Learning Outcomes in DH Assignments." In *Debates in the Digital Humanities 2019,* edited by Matthew Gold and Lauren Klein. Minneapolis: University of Minnesota Press, 2019. https://dhdebates.gc.cuny.edu/read/untitled-f2acf72c-a469-49d8-be35-67f9ac1e3a60/section/f1b1d9a6-974b-46c4-afde-7606bf238fc3#ch25.

Posner, Miriam. "Digital Humanities 201, UCLA—Winter 2019: Tutorials & Guides." Last accessed April 12, 2024. http://miriamposner.com/classes/dh201w19/tutorials-guides/.

Selisker, Scott. "Digital Humanities Knowledge: Reflections on the Introductory Graduate Syllabus." In *Debates in the Digital Humanities 2016,* edited by Matthew Gold and Lauren Klein. Minneapolis: University of Minnesota Press, 2016. https://dhdebates.gc.cuny.edu/read/untitled/section/2328bdb8-b7ea-4931-8258-12e220b3d767#ch17.

Sharpe, Celeste Tường Vy, Nate Sleeter, and Kelly Schrum. "How We Learned to Drop the Quiz: Writing in Online Asynchronous Courses." In *Web Writing: Why and How for Liberal Arts Teaching and Learning,* edited by Jack Dougherty and Tennyson O'Donnell. Ann Arbor: University of Michigan Press, 2014. http://epress.trincoll.edu/webwriting/chapter/sharpe-sleeter-schrum.

Sula, Chris Alen, S. E. Hackney, and Phillip Cunningham. "A Survey of Digital Humanities Programs." *The Journal of Interactive Technology and Pedagogy* 11 (2017). https://jitp.commons.gc.cuny.edu/a-survey-of-digital-humanities-programs/.

PART III

PEDAGOGICAL IMPLICATIONS

Digital Humanities and the Graduate Research Methods Class

LAURA ESTILL

Increasingly, humanities research methods are digital, and using digital resources is not the opposite of traditional humanities research.[1] In 2019 Ted Underwood noted, "It seems increasingly taken for granted that digital media and computational methods can play a role in the humanities" ("Digital Humanities," 96). He concluded his brief reflection by saying, "Now it is just a matter of doing the work and teaching others how to do it" (97). The reality of our current digital research practices needs to be clearly reflected in how we design graduate research methods classes. I contend that graduate students need to learn to "read" digital projects and search interfaces—ideally, early in their graduate programs. "Reading" interfaces and projects involves learning their scope and boundaries, determining how they mediate the knowledge of the present, and establishing how to utilize them ethically and efficiently. Tanya Clement posits that as digital humanists, we need to be explicit about our research methodologies and why and how they matter. Graduate students must learn to apply their rigorous critical skills and information literacy to digital research methodologies, or they will be ineffective at humanities research ("Where Is Methodology in Digital Humanities?").

This chapter is not the first to argue that all humanities students need to learn digital research methods.[2] Indeed, Christine L. Borgman maintains that "graduate school is rather late" to "learn how to use and how to evaluate digital cultural materials" (para. 66). This chapter offers concrete examples of how graduate humanities students can be encouraged to use and assess digital resources. The examples here are taken from an English-department research methods course structured around small weekly assignments, but many of the principles extend beyond literary studies and could be used in other disciplines.[3] In this brief piece, I offer suggested readings and assignments that lead to discussions around three interrelated topics: library catalogs and search engines; databases and bibliographies; and digital humanities projects.

So often when a digital humanities component is included in a course, the question becomes, "But what do you cut to fit in the digital?" In a research methods class, however, the question becomes, "Are we teaching current research practice if we exclude the digital?" The three topics outlined here were incorporated into a literary studies research methods class, but they could apply to other disciplines too. In this class, we covered other nondigital topics such as descriptive and analytic bibliography, textual studies, and manuscript studies; we also covered digital topics such as digital editions, text analysis, and data visualization. The goal of this class was not to have students create digital resources but to learn to use them to undertake different kinds of literary and cultural analyses.

Basic library searching skills are fundamental to humanities research at all levels and need to be taught in undergraduate classes, yet it is important not to assume that graduate students possess these research skills. One way I address the unevenness of students' familiarity and skill with library research is by assigning chapters from Thomas Mann's *Oxford Guide to Library Research* throughout the semester. Texas A&M University, like many institutions, had both an online library catalog and the single search bar library discovery system.[4] Candace Benefiel, the English subject librarian, would join us to discuss the difference between the two searches.[5] Students then wrote a short response comparing the results of two searches about a lesser-known author in their field.

Once students learn some basic skills for how to navigate the library catalog (or unified search solution, as the case may be)—using, for instance, Boolean operators or faceted searching—we turn to the results that are returned from these searches. Students are often surprised to learn that algorithmic biases filter the results they seek, even in their home institution's library catalog. Safiya Noble's *Algorithms of Oppression* and Matthew Reidsma's post on bias in library algorithms both offer clearly written examples of how algorithms can offer problematic search results. Reidsma, for instance, shows how ProQuest previously suggested "hearsay in United States law" when a user looked for "rape in the United States" ("Algorithmic Bias in Library Discovery Systems"). Noble's examples of googling "Black girls" and "Asian girls" continue to offer pornographic and fetishizing results on the first page. To avoid the false "algorithms were problematic but then we fixed them" narrative, I bring in a recent story of algorithmic bias from the news and find a problematic example using Google autocomplete or Google Images to discuss in class.[6] In July 2020, for instance, a Google Image search for "professor" yielded results where the first twenty-five images returned—that is, an entire screen of results—were white males (including one white boy playacting professor); the twenty-sixth image was a woman and the thirty-fifth image was a Black man. Because search results change—and can change depending on who searches them, but that is another teachable moment[7]—it is important to find a current example before each class. Critically assessing search results and their weighting is a fundamental skill for humanities researchers. Having to sift through biased results puts pressure on the researcher; assuming that digital results are impartial leads to biased research.

Many databases and bibliographies give students the impression that they have searched everything, yet determining a database's limitations is pivotal to making sound claims about existing scholarly discourse and crafting arguments that enter confidently into that discourse. An undergraduate might think that searching JSTOR is an adequate research method, but, as Lisa Gitelman points out, "If students or scholars stop with JSTOR—without seeking additional sources or pondering its contents and their limits . . . it becomes the system governing statements" (78). I offer paired sessions on databases and bibliographies of secondary sources:[8] before the first class, students complete a small assignment where they search and compare results from two databases (such as Project MUSE and Literature Criticism Online). Before the second class, students undertake the same search using field-specific bibliographies after reading Graziano's "Retrieval Performance and Indexing Differences in ABELL and MLAIB" as a model for the importance of comparative queries.

For these sessions on databases and bibliographies of scholarship, I assign Gitelman's article, "Searching and Thinking about JSTOR," as well as the entries from James L. Harner's *Literary Research Guide* (LRG) on "Digital Archives" (which in the LRG are JSTOR, Project Muse, and IngentaConnect) and "Database Vendors" (including EBSCO, ProQuest, and Gale, among others). Harner drily notes that "none of [these] vendors provides a remotely adequate explanation of the scope or editorial procedures governing the databases they purvey," which highlights the importance of assessing the scope and content of these sources.[9] As Harner explains, "Serial bibliographies, indexes, and abstracts (print and electronic) that are published or updated at regular intervals are important resources . . . since they guide researchers to the most recent scholarship." Harner criticizes "the unfounded assumption that the presence of such electronic bibliographical behemoths as WorldCat or MLAIB [MLA International Bibliography] and Internet search engines have rendered more specialized bibliographies obsolete."

The main takeaways from the readings, the comparative searching assignments, and the class discussion are first, the importance of field-specific bibliographies and second, a consideration of how digital bibliographies structure the knowledge they present. Perhaps the most striking part of this class is when we undertake to draw a Venn diagram on the board: what are the overlaps among JSTOR, Project MUSE, ProQuest Dissertations, and the MLA *International Bibliography*? As we add circles to the Venn diagram, it becomes clear to students that no digital search is all-encompassing. I also ask students to identify the gaps in coverage in the bibliographies: it is often non-English voices from disparate geographical regions that are silenced (Gitelman, 77).

Learning to question what is privileged and what is marginalized in our searches (of libraries, online, and of bibliographies and databases) leads nicely to a critical analysis of digital humanities projects, with a focus on *what* they cover and *how* they present information.[10] I ask students to do a brief presentation (four minutes plus discussion at the end of class) on a digital resource that is germane to their research. I offer students a list of resources they might consider based on their area of focus but also welcome them to propose others for analysis. The students create presentations and online factsheets to offer their classmates the tl;dr (too long; didn't read) summary to help make the class aware of research projects within and beyond their areas of specialization. In an ideal world, undergraduates will have already learned to assess digital projects in a basic way, using, for instance, the CRAAP test (Currency, Relevance, Authority, Accuracy, Purpose) (Blakeslee). Graduate students need to go beyond asking whether a source is "scholarly" enough; they need what Tara Brabazon calls "critical literacy," which is "an intervention" that involves the "interpretation, critique and analysis" of digital projects and search results (Brabazon, 30). Critical literacy when it comes to digital projects (and all media) is important not only for students who will become digital humanists but also for research across disciplines as well as for fostering better critical thinking beyond the academy.

Because I teach in a literature department, I emphasize that assessing digital projects is a form of critical reading. As Janine Solberg asserts, for the study of history, "the digital tools and structures that increasingly support our research efforts have material and epistemological implications for how we discover, access, and make sense of the past" (Solberg, 54). Indeed, as I have claimed with Andie Silva, "Digital projects need to be considered as arguments: they argue for the importance of the material they present, and they shape the ways users conceptualize and research texts and archives" (Estill and Silva, 131). Digital projects do not just present data; they offer ways of knowing and understanding the data they present.

Thinking critically about search results, scholarly databases, and digital projects might sound like a simple proposition, yet actually grappling with these ideas is in no way easy. To identify omissions in a project's scope, for instance, a graduate student would need to be already adept in a given field of study. Thinking about how a digital project presents materials can mean looking at a site's metadata systems and considering issues of taxonomy and categorization. All too often, digital humanities projects reify problematic notions of race, gender, and canonicity.[11] Neither classification systems, nor metadata, nor quantitative data are neutral.[12] Miriam Posner suggests that to truly "interrogate race, gender, and other structures of power . . . would be much more difficult and fascinating than anything we have previously imagined for the future of DH; in fact, it would require dismantling and rebuilding much of the organizing logic that underlies our work" ("What's Next," 32). Although dismantling and rebuilding digital humanities is beyond the scope of any one course, starting to grasp and then question the "organizing logic" of digital projects is possible but challenging.

Incorporating digital humanities in the graduate research methods class is not about staying abreast of developments in a given subfield, though often new research is shared digitally, and digital projects enable new research and even, as Susan Brown puts it, "new kinds of knowledge" (Brown, para. 14). Rather, bringing digital humanities to bear in the graduate research methods class is about fostering a mode of critical inquiry. A strong humanities research methods class will offer students an understanding of the field and the skills to undertake research using a variety of available techniques. Ultimately, the best graduate research methods classes equip emergent researchers to navigate future digital projects that have not yet been developed.

Notes

I would like to thank Andie Silva, Sarah Potvin, Heidi Craig, Kailin Wright, Manfred Thaller, and Stephen Robertson for their thoughtful feedback on this chapter. I am also grateful to my students for their willingness to explore and learn digital approaches to humanities research.

1. For more on humanist digital scholarship, see Drucker, "Humanistic Theory and Digital Scholarship."

2. See, for instance, Booth and Taddeo, "Changing Nature of the Book" and Locke, "Digital Humanities Pedagogy as Essential Liberal Education."

3. I have had the pleasure of teaching English graduate research methods in my former appointment at Texas A&M University, a large state school. I wrote this chapter while in my position there. For another example of how this graduate research methods class has been taught, see Ives, "Integrating 'Bibliography' with 'Literary Research.'"

4. On how discovery layers change the way we undertake library research, see Lown et al., "How Users Search."

5. In this case, on libcat.tamu.edu (the library catalogue) and library.tamu.edu (the single search discovery layer); we also touched on archon.library.tamu.edu (the special collections search).

6. Stories of algorithmic bias appear regularly. See, for instance, Lapowsky's "Google Autocomplete Still Makes Vile Suggestions" (2018) and Cohn's "Google's Algorithms Discriminate" (2019) for examples.

7. On this topic, see Vaidhyanathan, *Googlization of Everything,* 182–84.

8. When teaching three-hour classes that meet once weekly, I combine these into a single day.

9. The final MLA *Literary Research Guide* is the sixth edition, which was made available only online. The MLA discontinued the website (mlalrg.org) and left a GitHub repository with the files, which Andrew Pilsch transformed and made available here: https://oncomouse.github.io/literary-research-guide/.

10. I use the terms "digital project" and "digital resource" interchangeably here to offer a capacious definition that includes tools, editions, portals, archives, and databases. This capitalizes on the "amorphous" meaning of "digital project" as Price points out in his consideration of how we name and describe digital research; see Price, "Edition, Project, Database, Archive, Thematic Research Collection."

11. See, for instance, Earhart, "Can Information Be Unfettered?"; Mandell, "Gendering Digital Literary History"; and Estill, "Digital Humanities' Shakespeare Problem." Risam exhorts "digital humanities practitioners" to "resist the reinscription of a universal human subject in their scholarship, whether at the level of project design, method, data curation, or algorithm composition," in "What Passes for Human?," 51.

12. See D'Ignazio and Klein, *Data Feminism*. On how humanists approach data and "the inadequacy of data to truly represent reality," see Posner, "Humanities Data."

Bibliography

Blakeslee, Sarah. "The CRAAP Test." *LOEX Quarterly* 31, no. 3 (2004): art. 4. https://commons.emich.edu/loexquarterly/vol31/iss3/4.

Booth, Austin, and Laura Taddeo. "The Changing Nature of the Book: Literary Research, Cultural Studies, and the Digital Age." In *Teaching Literary Research: Challenges in a Changing Environment,* edited by Kathleen A. Johnson and Steven R. Harris, 143–66. Association of College and Research Libraries, 2009.

Borgman, Christine L. "The Digital Future Is Now: A Call to Action for the Humanities." *Digital Humanities Quarterly* 3, no. 4 (2009). https://digitalhumanities.org/dhq/vol/3/4/000077.html.

Brabazon, Tara. *The University of Google: Education in the (Post) Information Age.* Aldershot, UK: Ashgate, 2007.

Brown, Susan. "Survival: Canadian Cultural Scholarship in a Digital Age." *Studies in Canadian Literature / Études en Littérature Canadienne* 42, no. 2 (2018). https://journals.lib.unb.ca/index.php/SCL/article/view/26269.

Clement, Tanya. "Where Is Methodology in Digital Humanities?" In *Debates in the Digital Humanities 2016,* edited by Matthew K. Gold and Lauren F. Klein, 153–75. Minneapolis: University of Minnesota Press, 2016. https://dhdebates.gc.cuny.edu/read/untitled/section/cfa5a92d-0d35–4e3d-b632–856440s39cb1c.

Cohn, Jonathan. "Google's Algorithms Discriminate against Women and People of Colour." The Conversation. April 24, 2019. https://theconversation.com/googles-algorithms-discriminate-against-women-and-people-of-colour-112516.

D'Ignazio, Catherine, and Lauren F. Klein. *Data Feminism.* Minneapolis: University of Minnesota Press, 2020.

Drucker, Johanna. "Humanistic Theory and Digital Scholarship." In *Debates in the Digital Humanities,* edited by Matthew K. Gold, 85–95. Minneapolis: University of Minnesota Press, 2012. https://dhdebates.gc.cuny.edu/read/untitled-88c11800-9446-469b-a3be-3fdb36bfbd1e/section/0b495250-97af-4046-91ff-98b6ea9f83c0.

Earhart, Amy. "Can Information Be Unfettered? Race and the New Digital Humanities Canon." In *Debates in the Digital Humanities,* edited by Matthew K. Gold, 309–32. Minneapolis: University of Minnesota Press, 2012. https://dhdebates.gc.cuny.edu/debates/text/16.

Estill, Laura. "Digital Humanities' Shakespeare Problem." *Humanities* 8, no. 1 (2019): 45. https://doi.org/10.3390/h8010045

Estill, Laura, and Andie Silva. "Storing and Accessing Knowledge: Digital Tools for the Study of Early Modern Drama." In *Shakespeare's Language in Digital Media: Old Words, New Tools,* edited by Janelle Jenstad, Jennifer Roberts-Smith, and Mark Kaethler, 131–43. New York: Routledge, 2018.

Gitelman, Lisa. "Searching and Thinking about JSTOR." *Representations* 127 (2014): 73–82.

Graziano, Vince. "Retrieval Performance and Indexing Differences in ABELL and MLAIB." *Journal of Electronic Resources Librarianship* 24, no. 4 (2012): 268–87.

Harner, James L., and Angela Courtney. *Literary Research Guide.* 6th ed. New York: Modern Language Association, 2014.

Ives, Maura. "Integrating 'Bibliography' with 'Literary Research': A Comprehensive Approach." In *Teaching Bibliography, Textual Criticism, and Book History,* edited by Ann R. Hankins, 117–23. London: Pickering & Chatto, 2006.

Lapowsky, Issie. "Google Autocomplete Still Makes Vile Suggestions." *Wired,* February 12, 2018. https://wired.com/story/google-autocomplete-vile-suggestions/.

Locke, Brandon T. "Digital Humanities Pedagogy as Essential Liberal Education: A Framework for Curriculum Development." *Digital Humanities Quarterly* 11, no. 3 (2017). https://digitalhumanities.org/dhq/vol/11/3/000303.html.

Mandell, Laura. "Gendering Digital Literary History: What Counts for Digital Humanities." In *A New Companion to Digital Humanities,* edited by Susan Schreibman, Raymond G. Siemens, and John Unsworth, 511–23. Malden, Mass.: Wiley-Blackwell, 2015.

Mann, Thomas. *Oxford Guide to Library Research.* 4th ed. Oxford: Oxford University Press, 2015.

Noble, Safiya Umoja. *Algorithms of Oppression: How Search Engines Reinforce Racism.* New York: New York University Press, 2018.

Posner, Miriam. "Humanities Data: A Necessary Contradiction." June 25, 2015. https://miriamposner.com/blog/humanities-data-a-necessary-contradiction/.

Posner, Miriam. "What's Next: The Radical, Unrealized Potential of Digital Humanities." In *Debates in the Digital Humanities 2016,* edited by Matthew K. Gold and Lauren F. Klein, 265–73. Minneapolis: University of Minnesota Press, 2016. https://dhdebates.gc.cuny.edu/read/untitled/section/a22aca14–0eb0–4cc6-a622–6fee9428a357#ch03.

Price, Kenneth. "Edition, Project, Database, Archive, Thematic Research Collection: What's in a Name?" *Digital Humanities Quarterly* 3, no. 3 (2009). http://www.digital humanities.org/dhq/vol/3/3/000053/000053.html

Reidsma, Matthew. "Algorithmic Bias in Library Discovery Systems." March 11, 2016. https://matthew.reidsrow.com/articles/173.

Risam, Roopika. "What Passes for Human? Undermining the Universal Subject in Digital Humanities Praxis." In *Bodies of Information: Intersectional Feminism and the Digital Humanities,* edited by Elizabeth Losh and Jacqueline Wernimont, 39–56. Minneapolis: University of Minneapolis Press, 2018. https://dhdebates.gc.cuny.edu/read

/untitled-4e08b137-aec5-49a4-83c0-38258425f145/section/34d51cdb-2a89-4e4b-9762-bf6461cf0bb7#ch03.

Solberg, Janine. "Googling the Archive: Digital Tools and the Practice of History." *Advances in the History of Rhetoric* 15 (2012): 53–76.

Underwood, Ted. "Digital Humanities as a Semi-Normal Thing." In *Debates in the Digital Humanities 2019,* edited by Matthew K. Gold and Lauren F. Klein, 96–98. Minneapolis: University of Minnesota Press, 2019. http://www.jstor.com/stable/10.5749/j.ctvg251hk.13.

Vaidhyanathan, Siva. *The Googlization of Everything (and Why We Should Worry).* Berkeley: University of California Press, 2016.

Bringing the Digital into the Graduate Classroom
Project-Based Deep Learning in the Digital Humanities

CECILY RAYNOR

The impact of the digital on the humanities is often examined at the level of faculty engagement, scholarship, and ways of defining digital work in the twenty-first century. Meanwhile, the intersection between analog and digital heightens, deepens, and complicates what it means to participate in the academy. What happens when digital engagement becomes a core component of graduate-level pedagogy in the humanities? In this short chapter, I evaluate graduate offerings at the master's level in the digital humanities (DH) at McGill University, reflecting upon our program and its connection to our department, with a particular focus on student projects, skill-building, and tools.[1] Our emphasis on project-based learning provides students a way to strengthen their skillset in computational analysis of humanistic questions, which serves as an opportunity for sustained interaction with tools and skills—a helpful endeavor for those seeking work outside of the academy upon graduation.

The idea of a graduate degree in DH at McGill dates back to 2011 when the late Stéfan Sinclair was hired to spearhead new DH programs through coursework, events, interdepartmental collaboration, and other activities that fell under the broad rubric of digital humanities initiatives.[2] Within the Faculty of Arts, the Department of Languages, Literatures, and Cultures (LLC) became the formal home of digital humanities, with DH faculty spread across departments.[3] More widely, digital humanities initiatives included faculty members from music, religious studies, law, and the libraries. Currently, McGill houses an ad hoc master's degree in digital humanities developed in collaboration between LLC professors—Sinclair, as well as Andrew Piper—and guided forward by Matthew Milner, then assistant director of the Centre for Digital Humanities.[4] The program welcomed its first student in 2016 and has since built its cohorts from two to five on average as of 2022. In terms of positionality, I have been involved in DH programs at McGill since 2015 and served as the graduate program director from 2020 to 2022.

At the departmental level, DH courses are open to students from across the university, with a particularly high concentration from the Department of English.[5] Ad hoc programs at McGill differ from standard graduate programs in that they typically draw from more than one discipline and thus require interdisciplinary committee approval on a candidate-by-candidate basis (remaining true to its Latin etymology "when necessary or as needed"). The program's creation followed several years of discussion on what kind of graduate training and education would best meet an already diverse set of graduate options at McGill. Existing courses were canvassed for their suitability to form the basis of the program, and foundational and capstone courses were added. Digitally inflected graduate research cuts across the department, with students in Italian, Russian, Spanish, and German frequently choosing to pursue topics and methods that come from what would be considered the DH toolbox. One of the advantages of housing a DH program in a department that gathers students from many language homes and geographies is that multidisciplinary and intercultural research is part of its core mandate. Indeed, much of the work that our students and faculty undertake falls outside of the anglophone canon, with a particular attentiveness to decolonizing methods and projects.

In terms of structure, McGill's ad hoc master's in digital humanities is composed of one year of coursework and one year of thesis research. Students take an introductory course that is designed to familiarize them with some of the central practical and theoretical considerations of the field. They can then choose from an array of disciplines, ranging from computer science to anthropology. The courses are organized into five categories: cultural theories, data and text mining, quantitative and computational methods, spatial analysis, and sound and music.[6] In the second year of the program, which is dedicated to thesis work, students collaborate with their advisors to build and pursue their research questions. In recent years, these projects have included using machine learning to examine a corpus of screenplays and test linguistic features and analyzing digitized migrant letters through computational text analysis with a particular attention to sentiment, topics, and social networks. We have benefited from the participation of several students from the Global South, including China and Nepal.

Examples of students' project work show the variety of DH approaches that students can explore in their work. One of our students used Python to apply topic modeling and word embedding analysis (Word2Vec) in her exploration of cultural questions related to historical feminisms. She also carried out data mining and applied a decision-tree classification model to predict the adolescent fertility rate of several countries. This student carried out both projects during her first year of courses, a testament to the fact that project-based learning does not begin during the thesis year but is embedded in the toolkit students acquire in pursuing projects in their classes. In a student survey, this same student cited data mining and Python as essential to her work within data analytics, skills that she is confident will serve her in the private sector job she secured following graduation. Another student, who worked on the aforementioned migrant letter database, has considered pursuing work as a data analyst specializing in computational text analysis, which she envisions undertaking in the private or public sectors. But some DH students would like to stay in the academy; a third student expressed a desire to remain engaged in research upon graduation and investigate issues related to postcolonial DH, artificial intelligence, and tool sustainability.

Among the benefits that flow between both our ad hoc cohort and the humanities graduate community at large is the creation of a culture in which digital methods and research are welcome and increasingly the norm, evidenced by the fact that projects on text mining, web analytics, topic modeling, and metadata analysis are prominent throughout LLC. To cite a few examples, one PhD student in Hispanic studies engaged in digital research web analytics to examine how Latin American audiences and partners of the Biodiversity Heritage Library, an online archive of digitized global literature on biodiversity, engage with historical archives and create content.[7] She mapped the selection and classification of texts using GIS and visualizations in Tableau, while performing topic modeling analyses (with MALLET) to interrogate how concepts of Latin America and biodiversity are constructed. Another PhD student in German studies worked with a dataset from the German National Library to apprehend why certain literary texts are translated over others and whether there might be stylistic or aesthetic consequences to wide-scale translation of German literature that could shape how fiction is written. This student utilized topic modeling and text mining methods including tagging, extraction, and matching to pursue her research questions. Meanwhile, a PhD student in Italian studies completed work on the Italian countercultural collective Wu Ming, including analysis of their online presence and their use of Twitter hashtags for political purposes. Another Hispanic studies student examined a corpus of Ibero-American short films using metadata modeling to better approach the commonalities and characteristics of this cultural database. She drew on text-based information such as tags, paratext, and keyword descriptors in databases and festival programs online to probe nationality, distribution, and impact. Many of these students were first introduced to theoretical frameworks and the application of computational methods to cultural questions in our introductory seminar, and their work speaks to the value of bringing computational mixed methods from the digital humanities to bear upon projects and disciplines across languages and fields of study.

Our experiences in running and establishing the master's program speak directly to the view that engaging in sustained, multiyear digital research allows students to refine their computational skills and that said skills can be primarily acquired during their studies. In line with the scholarship, many students plan to pursue opportunities outside of the academy, in text analytics, archival work, and digital curation jobs in national and international libraries (Opel and Simeone, "The Invisible Work"). These experiences speak directly to some of the pushback experienced when presenting the idea of graduate programs in digital humanities—that is, that there is no clear benefit to longer-term engagement with digital methods and that the marketability of the degree is poor (McCarty, "PhD in Digital Humanities"). Given the shift toward data science, digital archival work, and text analysis in the private and public sectors, we hope to remain dynamic in how we meet students' needs. With this in mind, we are actively creating a one-year master's program that includes two semesters of DH labs and culminates in a summer capstone project. This twelve-month, nonthesis MA will be the center of a concentrated, project-based graduate program that will offer students with varying backgrounds an entry point into using digital tools and data analysis on humanistic research questions. Our nonthesis program will stress supervised, hands-on, collaborative training in a lab setting where students develop knowledge that is then applied to their capstone projects.

In concluding this brief chapter, I would like to return to some core questions and raise others. Many of the case studies I discuss above demonstrate engagement with digitally inflected projects across a semester, a yearlong thesis, or a multiyear dissertation. However, the length of study is but one factor worth examining when looking at DH graduate work. The creation of a shorter, project-based program that focuses on labs and a capstone is one of many modes of in-depth, intense training for students eager to engage with digital methods and critical data science. At the same time, there are challenges at the level of faculty skill building in digital humanities, given the need to supervise and train students around a diverse set of digital tools. Although summer training programs in digital methods including the Digital Humanities Summer Institute and the Digital Humanities Research Institute certainly offer options, it is inevitable that graduate programs in DH need to rely upon many disciplines and colleagues on a project-by-project basis. This is equally important in the area of assessment, as digital projects often require interdisciplinary collaboration to best evaluate their quality at varying intervals. In our engagement with our students and our vision for the future, project-based learning is at the heart of our pedagogy, whether it be in an individual course, a graduate thesis, DH labs, a dissertation, or potential capstone projects. In many ways, our students benefit from the multilingual, varied methodological landscape of our department in that collaboration is not a choice but an obligation of conducting research in an intercultural, multidisciplinary department.

Notes

1. It is vital to recognize the many modes of graduate education in DH that focus on team-based problem solving and connecting digital humanities with community-engaged learning as our new program grows; see Jewell and Lorang, "Teaching Digital Humanities." Although this reflection is on the benefits of project-based learning, community engagement is something that we hope to pursue as we build our DH program.

2. Professor Sinclair passed away on August 6, 2020. His obituary can be found here: https://csdh-schn.org/stefan-sinclair-in-memoriam-2/.

3. Montreal has long been considered a tech hub, with industries including gaming and more recently artificial intelligence gaining prominence.

4. Andrew Piper runs a text lab at McGill (.txtLAB), which allows students from a variety of backgrounds to explore cultural questions through text and data analysis.

5. This is also true of digitally inflected graduate courses across the university.

6. Our core faculty in the LLC have strengths in text and data mining, geospatial research and GIS, and web analytics. Introducing students to computational methods and how to apply these to humanistic questions is at the heart of our program. Programming languages including Python and R are frequently part of our pedagogical toolkit, as is the web stack (Javascript, CSS, HTML) and social media analysis. In more recent years, predictive and prescriptive analytics, machine learning, and artificial intelligence have gained notoriety.

7. Tools referenced in this chapter: (1) SimilarWeb: https://www.similarweb.com/; (2) Alexa: https://www.alexa.com/; (3) Tableau: https://www.tableau.com/; (4) Voyant Tools: https://voyant-tools.org/; (5) MALLET: http://mallet.cs.umass.edu/.

Bibliography

Jewell, Andrew, and Elizabeth Lorang. "Teaching Digital Humanities through a Community-Engaged, Team-Based Pedagogy." Paper presentation, Digital Humanities 2016, Krakow, Poland, 2016. https://digitalcommons.unl.edu/library_talks/128/.

McCarty, Willard. "The PhD in Digital Humanities." In *Digital Humanities Pedagogy: Practices, Principles and Politics,* edited by Brett D. Hirsch, 33–46. Cambridge: Open Book Publishers, 2012. https://doi.org/10.11647/OBP.0024.

Opel, Dawn S., and Michael Simeone. "The Invisible Work of the Digital Humanities Lab: Preparing Graduate Students for Emergent Intellectual and Professional Work." *Digital Humanities Quarterly* 13, no. 2 (2019).

Support, Space, and Strategy
Designing a Developmental Digital Humanities Infrastructure

BRADY KRIEN

On-ramps to Digital Graduate Studies

One of the biggest challenges facing graduate students interested in the digital humanities is that of efficiently *integrating* DH training into their course of graduate study. Many students have few training opportunities and may not be able to serve as an "apprentice" on a large-scale digital project, which, as Geoffrey Rockwell notes, often serves as one of the most direct paths into DH ("Inclusion in the Digital Humanities"). Lisa Spiro similarly points out that students may find that there are few faculty in their department who are able (or willing) to support digital projects ("Opening Up Digital Humanities Education"). As a result, digital training and projects often end up being "extra"—extra courses, extra workshops, or an extra digital component on top of a traditional dissertation—and this can make it difficult for students to fit DH into the course of their graduate education in a cohesive, meaningful, and efficient way. Although these barriers are not insurmountable, they do exacerbate the existing challenges of graduate school and make it more difficult for graduate students to engage with digital methods, get digital training, and use digital tools within their scholarship as Olivia Quintanilla and Jeanelle Horcasitas demonstrate in chapter 15 of this volume. Given the potential power of the tools that DH offers and its ability to cultivate valuable digital skills, all graduate students who wish to should have an opportunity to integrate DH into their courses of study. The ability to understand and leverage these tools will prepare students not only to advance their own scholarship but also, as Cathy Davidson and Bethany Nowviskie both argue, to more effectively participate in and shape the humanities as they evolve in response to the advent of digital technologies (Davidson, "Humanities 2.0"; Nowviskie, "Graduate Training").

Another set of barriers to graduate DH training includes the lack of representation within the digital humanities and the degree to which it prevents DH from being more accessible but also inclusive. Numerous scholars have commented upon the lack of diversity and inclusivity within DH communities. This has included both a lack of racial and gender diversity (who gets to participate in the digital humanities) and a lack of methodological inclusion (what "counts" as the digital humanities).[1] Although efforts are underway to help make DH more inclusive and diverse, including the #TransformDH movement, the lack of inclusion and accessibility within the field is an ongoing challenge at all levels.[2]

One strategy for addressing these shortcomings and making DH training more integrative and accessible is critically examining the experience of graduate students and the way that the traditional structures of graduate education—as well as the particular nature of DH and how it is (or is not) situated within departments, disciplines, and universities—create barriers for graduate students wishing to engage with digital methods and scholarship as the essays in this volume by Sethunya Mokoko, Hoyeol Kim, Sean Weidman, and Sara Mohr and E. L. Mezsaros all attest. In "Cultural Politics, Critique and the Digital Humanities," Higgin argues that "without a robust critical apparatus, DH has and will continue to unwittingly remake the world in its old image. (You know, the one that has a whole bunch of white guys sitting around a highly polished oak table comparing business cards)." Beyond the development of this critical apparatus, changes in policy and practice, including those at the graduate level, can help to reimagine the DH community and ensure that *all* students are able and welcome to integrate digital scholarship into their graduate experience.

One potential pitfall in the efforts to ensure that all graduate students have the opportunity to pursue DH is what Moya Z. Bailey refers to as the " 'add and stir' model of diversity, a practice of sprinkling in more women, people of color, disabled folks and assuming that is enough to change current paradigms" ("All the Digital Humanists Are White"). A more productive alternative is to approach graduate training in DH with a mindset of radical accessibility, focusing on removing barriers and creating opportunities for integration, exploration, and experimentation with digital tools. In other words, in continuing to build academic digital research and teaching infrastructures, it is important to include as many "on-ramps" as possible for graduate students and to make sure they are well marked and (mostly) free of potholes. To that end, I outline three general guiding principles—creating space, providing support, and strategic planning—for restructuring graduate education to more fully serve the needs of graduate students, especially those interested in integrating digital methods into their work. These principles are borne out of my experience in the U.S. academy though they can likely be translated to other contexts as well. I connect these principles with specific practices that can be implemented by individual faculty, programs and departments, or at the collegiate or university level. These concrete strategies are a starting point and can be implemented with a range of resources to ensure that the pursuit of DH training does not, in itself, become a barrier to the timely and successful completion of a graduate program.

Embracing the Digital Village: Toward a Culture of Multiple Mentoring

Mentors really matter in graduate training. Though the role and influence of graduate mentors has received little scholarly attention relative to mentorship in the undergraduate context, both Barbara Lovitts and Chris M. Golde have found ample evidence that mentors have a major impact on graduate student persistence, timeliness (toward degree), and success (Lovitts, *Leaving the Ivory Tower*; Golde, "The Role of the Department and Discipline"). Mentoring is especially important within DH for, as Anderson et al. argue, "Mentoring is perhaps the single most important and sustainable form of training in DH, as students who benefit from these activities will be more likely to share their own expertise in a similar way" ("Student Labour and Training"). Mentoring is thus hugely important in considering the openness and accessibility of DH at the graduate level, but the data suggest that mentoring within doctoral programs in the humanities is inconsistent at best. In a 2006 study by Michael T. Nettles and Catherine M. Millett, 25 percent of humanities graduate students reported that they did not have a mentor, and only 52 percent of students reported that their mentor and their advisor were the same person. The data also point to significant racial disparities in graduate student mentoring relationships, with 76 percent of white graduate students across STEM disciplines (the only ones for which data are listed) reporting having a mentor as compared with only 57 percent of African American students (Nettles and Millett, *Three Magic Letters*, 99). Given the importance of mentoring in the development and retention of graduate students, these statistics suggest that much work remains to be done in developing effective and inclusive mentoring systems, not just within DH or even within the humanities, but across graduate education more generally.

Mentoring deficits can present major challenges to graduate students interested in integrating DH into their training, in large part because of how departments and disciplines tend to be structured. Golde points out that many humanities departments are organized around subfields rather than around methods ("Role of the Department," 679). Spiro has identified the potential for significant misalignment between subfield and methodological expertise of faculty relative to the interests and needs of students that may result from this organizational structure ("Opening Up Digital Humanities Education"). The DH infrastructures on many campuses exist separately from departments with many—like the University of Virginia Scholars' Lab—situated in libraries; others, such as Indiana University Bloomington's Institute for Digital Art & Humanities, function as centralized research centers, and still others operate as their own departments, as in the case of the Emergent Digital Practices program at the University of Denver.[3] Because graduate education tends to be profoundly department-focused, some graduate students may easily find themselves in a department without strong ties to existing DH opportunities. This can lead to situations where students are forced to choose between the subjects and the methods that interest them, unable to find faculty members with expertise in both areas.

One way to address the particular challenges of mentoring graduate students within the digital humanities is to encourage students to work with multiple mentors, connecting them with a range of people who can provide advice and guidance regarding their personal, scholarly, and professional goals. Given the range of mentoring roles, expertise, and time commitments necessary to effectively support graduate digital humanists, it is unrealistic to expect any one faculty member to provide all the mentoring necessary for a graduate student, particularly when that student may be interested in a multiplicity of methodologies, topics, and career pathways. Engaging with multiple mentors allows graduate students to draw upon the expertise of a greater number of people and distributes the labor of mentoring. Many graduate students already connect with multiple mentors, at least informally. In a 2008 study, Walker et al. found that around 80 percent of students in the English and history departments they surveyed reported having two or more mentors, significantly surpassing their colleagues in STEM fields (*Formation of Scholars*, 95). The key changes in practice, then, are consistency and intentionality—helping more students connect with mentoring and connecting students with the appropriate set of mentors. Rather than limiting mentorship to the faculty in a student's home department, mentors can and in many cases should include people outside the department, the faculty, or even the university. Kathleen A. Langan and Ilse Schweitzer VanDonkelaar argue that DH subject librarians are increasingly playing such a role, providing not just technical and methodological support but also academic and professional mentorship to supplement that provided by faculty advisors ("Moderating a Meaningful DH Conversation"). In her study of doctoral mentoring in Library and Information Science programs, Cassidy Sugimoto found that it was common for dissertation committees to have a "methods" person who brings methodological expertise to the committee ("Are You My Mentor?," 8). Amy J. Lueck and Beth Boehm advocate for going further in rethinking the committee approach common in the United States to "reconfigure the dissertation committee as a structure capable of supporting a wide range of future careers both inside and outside of the academy for degree recipients," allowing and even encouraging diverse dissertation committees that would include, where appropriate, members from outside academia ("Beginning at the End," 138). Explicitly guiding students through the process of assembling a committee built around their own needs, methods, and goals can help maximize the scholarly and professional preparation that a student receives during the dissertation process.

The culture of mentoring in the humanities often, as Zhao, Golde, and McCormick argue, constructs the doctoral advisor as the most important person in a graduate student's career; the decision about who that person should be is similarly often described as the most important decision that one makes in graduate school ("More than a Signature"). The choices regarding mentors are indeed important ones; in her study of graduate student mentoring relationships, Lovitts found that graduate students fare better when their mentors are chosen rather than assigned, but encouraging students to connect with multiple mentors can provide them with a broader range of support and guidance (*Leaving the Ivory Tower*, 132–33). Simple changes in practice can help communicate to students that connecting with multiple mentors is not only acceptable but actively encouraged. Building opportunities to connect with mentors into orientation and introduction to graduate studies courses, revising graduate handbooks to encourage students to build multiple mentoring relationships—including with people outside of the department—and hosting informal colloquia or networking events with presentations involving a variety of digital humanities practitioners from across different disciplines all help create opportunities for students to connect with multiple people with a range of DH and professional expertise.

Changes in policy and practice may also help shift graduate training mentalities toward a culture of collaborative mentoring. In line with the suggestions of Lueck and Boehm, working within departments or colleges to change committee composition requirements and allow for dissertation committee members from outside of the faculty or outside of academia can help spur change. This is especially important in the digital humanities where faculty may not be well equipped to mentor graduate students in DH methods, having actively been discouraged from pursuing the "risky" work that would prepare them to do so, but where staff members often have considerable expertise and experience (Nowviskie, "Graduate Training"). Digital humanities librarians can bring especially valuable expertise as they may well have significantly more project management experience than many faculty members and can contribute unique perspectives on goal setting and time management as Alex Wermer-Colan's essay in chapter 22 of this volume attests. L. R. Roberts, Christa M. Tinari, and Raymond Bandlow similarly identify support in these areas as essential components of doctoral mentoring and, depending on the campus and the department, DH subject librarians may be able to provide important additional support in these areas (Roberts et al., "Effective Doctoral Student Mentor"). Even in university contexts where a DH subject librarian is unavailable, seeking out other faculty or staff members, or even those with expertise from other universities, can help round out the dissertation committee and ensure that it is not only able to evaluate the student's work but also support their research and professional goals.

Departments can ensure that students have mentors and are connecting with them by checking in periodically. Zhao, Golde, and McCormick report that it is common practice, in many humanities departments in the United States, to assign students a preliminary faculty advisor with the expectation that they will choose a permanent advisor as they move through their program ("More than a Signature," 264). This approach can foster productive advising and mentoring relationships, particularly as Lovitts has found that assigned permanent advisors are associated both with lower rates of satisfaction and higher rates of attrition among graduate students (*Leaving the Ivory Tower*, 132–33). Small interventions like communicating expectations to students and faculty and checking in with all students in a program (or at least those who are beyond coursework) to ensure they have had a mentoring and advising conversation, in the last year and with at least one faculty member, that touched on their goals and progress toward the degree can go a long way toward ensuring that students do not fall through the cracks of a graduate program.

Although there exist many challenges to both learning digital methods and effectively integrating them into one's graduate training, collaborative and responsive mentoring represents an important first step in making this possible for many students. Embracing the concept of multiple mentoring and drawing widely from the DH community, whether within a program or beyond the bounds of a campus, can help students cultivate what Vicki (Baker) Sweitzer refers to as developmental networks ("Towards a Theory"). This "constellation" of mentors, as Monica C. Higgins and David A Thomas refer to it, can help guide students through the various challenges, including the technical, scholarly, bureaucratic, and cultural challenges, that they face in meaningfully integrating DH into their training ("Constellations and Careers").

Creating Space: Strategies to Support DH Development

Mentors can help provide essential guidance and support for graduate students in the digital humanities, but many students still face significant challenges in carving out space within their degree program to learn to use and implement digital tools. This is a particularly significant obstacle for students who may not have had any prior experience with digital tools and who may need to devote significant time to mastering them. With the exception of a few programs that focus solely on DH or that offer a large number of DH-related classes, DH training for graduate students all too often takes the form of what Nowviskie calls "stop-gap, renegade, extramural, and tacked-on models for methodological training" ("Graduate Training," 127). Such training can involve taking additional courses that may not count toward a student's primary graduate degree or may involve workshops or training sessions that students attend on top of the coursework that they are already completing. At its best, this training may involve working collaboratively on a DH project in a course or as part of an assistantship or additional employment. At its worst, graduate DH training may involve working one's way piecemeal through a series of Coursera or LinkedIn learning courses in the few spare moments a student can steal from their teaching and research (not to mention personal) responsibilities. Such haphazard, jury-rigged training can ultimately prove helpful, but it creates major hurdles for student engagement with DH, piling more work on top of already overworked students and potentially extending their time to degree.[4]

Digital humanities practitioners have long advocated for a reassessment of the ways in which digital scholarship is evaluated and "counted" for the purposes of promotion and tenure.[5] This issue extends to the graduate level, as well as to whether and how digital components of dissertations are evaluated and counted and to how

DH courses fit within degree programs. Although, as Ted Underwood argues in his essay in chapter 29 of this volume, most digital humanists thrive on engagement with other departments or units, courses that students take outside of their own program may not always count toward their degree completion. This can represent a major barrier to students getting the training and developing the skills necessary to successfully utilize digital methods. Having to take another course or courses on top of their existing coursework and obligations is likely not practicable for many students. Some students are even advised to hold off on taking these courses until after they have completed all of their coursework and qualifying exams, only to be told that they then need to focus all of their time and energy on the dissertation. In these situations, it is far too easy for DH training simply to get squeezed out of a student's degree path, perpetually deferred until some future point when they will have the time and space to undertake it. Mentors can help counter this by advising students how and when they might ideally integrate these courses into their degree plan. A more systematic approach would be for programs to reassess how DH coursework counts toward degree completion. In the absence of specific policy changes, however, many departments allow students to petition for courses in other humanities departments to fulfill part of their requirements (e.g., a gender studies class to count toward an English degree). Ensuring that this option is not only available but also *clearly communicated* to students interested in pursuing DH training can go a long way toward ensuring that its very real contributions toward a graduate student's professional and scholarly development are formally recognized as such.

At the pedagogical level, it is important to recognize that DH training of all kinds involves a degree of risk, as both Katherine D. Harris and Nowviskie have observed.[6] For students with little or no previous experience with digital tools, learning them often necessitates accepting not just the frustrations that go along with learning a new tool but also the possibility of failure. There is a learning curve with any new tool and although quietly cussing at one's laptop after receiving an error message for the fifty-eighth time is arguably an unavoidable part of the learning process, risking a failing grade in a course because of a lack of familiarity with Python should not be. The idea that in taking a DH class a student might be assessed on their mastery of ArcGIS to the same extent that they would be assessed on their knowledge of, say, critical theory or historical methods, and thus that it might involve risking one's academic standing or funding, represents a major obstacle to engaging with DH scholarship.

A key part of facilitating engagement with digital tools and scholarship within the classroom is creating low-risk environments for students to learn, explore, and fail productively. One possible strategy for facilitating these environments is to create project-based courses—or to integrate projects into existing courses— that focus on helping students learn and explore the tools that they are using. For examples of this, see Cecily Raynor's essay in chapter 11 of this volume. This pedagogical approach can, as Malte Rehbein and Christiane Fritze note, be particularly effective in classes where many students may have little or no experience with digital tools and much less experience with the specific tools being used in the course ("Hands-On Teaching Digital Humanities"). Other options include opening up the kinds of assignments and work that students can complete and grading the students' work wholly or partly based on their research and exploration process rather than on the degree of development of the final product. Such approaches create spaces for students to experiment within the classroom, allowing them to, as Harris suggests (borrowing from Stephen Ramsay), productively "screw around" or playfully tinker (Harris, "Play, Collaborate, Break, Build, Share," 6). These spaces are, according to Anita Say Chan and Harriett Green, "particularly valuable for humanities instruction, where curricular structure, facilities, and pedagogy are oriented less toward tinkering and lab-like practices than those in science, engineering, and technology" ("Practicing Collaborative Digital Pedagogy"). Exploratory approaches, implemented within some individual classrooms, can help students explore and learn to productively deploy digital tools and help revitalize graduate seminars in line with the recommendations of Peter H. Khost, Debra Rudder Lohe, and Chuck Sweetman, integrating intentional pedagogy that will benefit all students in the course, not just those who are interested in pursuing DH ("Rethinking and Unthinking").

Outside of the classroom, there are larger-scale opportunities that can significantly advance students' DH training and skills. Students might work in an assistantship as part of a team on what Davidson refers to as a "Big Humanities" project, learning from and collaborating with other team members as Laura Crossley, Amanda Regan, and Joshua Casmir Catalano describe in their essay in chapter 13 of this volume (Davidson, "Humanities 2.0," 714). Alternatively, they may hold a DH fellowship and work in a directed way on a collaborative project or in a more open way to pursue their own research and training with the support of DH experts as in the Praxis Program and Digital Humanities Fellowship Program at the University of Virginia Scholar's Lab.[7] My own experience with a DH fellowship at the University of Iowa Digital Scholarship and Publishing Studio provided me with time and the support of a DH librarian to work with tools that I ultimately learned were not the right ones for completing my dissertation project, long before I had to submit and defend my proposal. The key elements of such space-creating opportunities, whatever form they may take, are the same as those for creating a productive DH classroom: a high degree of freedom for creativity and experimentation and sufficient support or guidance to work through challenges when they (inevitably) crop up. Even at institutions where limited resources might not allow for the creation of digital humanities fellowships, collaborations with other DH practitioners, research support offices, graduate colleges, and programs at other institutions can help create opportunities for additional training and practice. As an example of this, a number of consortia, including the Florida Digital Humanities Consortium, the Digital Humanities Collaborative of North Carolina, and the New England Humanities Consortium-Digital Humanities have formed in recent years to support interuniversity networks of DH scholars and practitioners.[8] These and similar efforts can facilitate the creation of spaces for the meaningful learning and experimentation necessary to learn how to effectively utilize digital tools.

Intentional pedagogical practices, internships, and counting courses in other departments can help remove barriers to students' digital training but, as Donna Bussell and Tena Helton's essay in chapter 5 and others in this volume attest, not all students may have access to digital humanities opportunities, either in their own departments or others. For graduate students at universities without specific DH offerings, an even greater degree of departmental flexibility and support may be necessary to ensure that students have adequate opportunities to advance their training. Such efforts could include connecting students to DH practitioners on campus or through DH consortia or networks, allowing students to utilize digital methods in their coursework, or providing support for training opportunities beyond the university such as the Digital Humanities Summer Institute or Digital Humanities Forum, where students can connect with the expertise and training necessary to develop their skills. At institutions with few existing spaces for DH training, helping students locate those spaces beyond the bounds of the institution can enable them to effectively navigate the challenges of getting additional DH training and bring their burgeoning expertise back to campus. In all forms of DH training, but especially at campuses without robust DH infrastructures, developing a coherent plan for when this training can occur is especially important to ensuring that students do not "miss their exits" to the on-ramps of the digital humanities.

On Grad Strategy: Pulling It Together with IDPs

As graduate students work to include digital humanities elements in their graduate training, careful planning can ensure that these elements are integrated as efficiently and seamlessly as possible. This is particularly important for students whose goals might diverge somewhat from the traditional ones pursued by others in their department, that is, if they are contemplating undertaking supplemental training in digital tools, applying for DH fellowships, or petitioning for other courses or experiences to be included in their degree requirements. Knowing in advance about these opportunities and plotting them out with an Individual Development Plan (IDP)—identifying their goals and the steps necessary to achieve them—can make balancing the demands of graduate school a bit easier and even ensure that DH training and scholarship are as well integrated into their degree plan as possible. Individual Development Plans are a means of operationalizing and strategically organizing advice from mentors, planning when to take advantage of experimental spaces and opportunities, and setting both long and short-term research and professional goals.

Though they are gaining popularity in the humanities, IDPs are predominantly used by graduate students in the health sciences, and a description of whether and how IDPs are used has been a required component of National Institutes of Health funding involving graduate students since 2014 to help students and postdocs "to participate successfully in a broad-based and evolving research and research-related economy" (National Institutes of Health, "NOT-OD-14–113"). Though IDPs can make use of a variety of different tools, their core components involve students completing self-assessments and reflections, exploring options and opportunities (both at the university and beyond), setting short- and long-term goals, and planning for accomplishing those goals with the input and guidance of their mentor(s).

Importantly, IDPs provide a framework or roadmap for developmental mentoring meetings and can, as Beronda L. Montgomery suggests, help students strategically cultivate multiple forms of expertise and support ("Mapping a Mentoring Roadmap," 10). Vincent et al. describe a system wherein they hold annual one-on-one meetings between mentor and mentee that accomplish five things: motivate people by celebrating their accomplishments; set short-term and long-term research and career goals; help people make rapid progress by prioritizing projects and identifying barriers; clarify and solidify relationships by giving honest constructive criticism; and clarify expectations in both directions and address any disagreements ("Yearly Planning Meetings," 718). This approach helps mentors explicitly and periodically check in on their students, their progress, and any support that they might need and provides useful feedback to mentees, which helps them structure and achieve their goals. Within a DH context, a student and their mentor might discuss the student's long-term research interests and career goals, the best classes or training experiences to help them achieve those goals, and a map of those experiences to chart the time the student is planning to spend in graduate school.[9]

Although IDPs can initially seem like an extra bureaucratic barrier, and implementing them can involve some resistance, both Vincent et al. and Julie Gould report that they quickly prove their worth as a career planning and development tool, particularly in the context of research training and planning, which is one of the primary benefits that they bring to graduate students who are interested in DH (Gould, "A Plan for Action"). Faculty members and graduate students alike can advocate for the adoption of IDPs as a required part of graduate advising in their home departments, but they can also get started just by creating them. There is a wide variety of templates available online, and students and faculty can find ones that they like and that fit their needs as Crossley, Regan, and Catalano discuss in their contribution to this volume. Mentors can get started by explaining what an IDP is and why it matters and then asking or requiring their mentees to complete one. Grad students can initiate the process by completing an IDP and setting up a meeting with one or more of their mentors to talk about it. The document, which evolves with the graduate student's interests, goals, and needs, is important in itself, but more important is the process—planning, exploring, and facilitating discussions between mentors and mentees. In mapping out students' graduate experiences, IDPs can ensure that students are ready and able to identify and take advantage of the best DH on-ramps for their goals.

As Patrik Svensson argues, DH has become a laboratory for the humanities, one that "is associated with a visionary and forward-looking sentiment and [that] has come to constitute a site for far-reaching discussion about the futures of the field itself as well as the humanities at large" ("Envisioning the Digital Humanities"). As the members of that laboratory imagine the future of both DH and the humanities, it is imperative that they contemplate how best to prepare the humans who will populate that future. There has arguably never been more of a need for digitally literate humanists, scholars who can not only productively utilize digital tools but also critically examine them. Developing methods for ensuring that all humanists have viable pathways into expanding their own digital literacy, whether they are interested in exploring basic tools or mastering Python, is essential to imagining the future of the humanities.

Digital humanities has a major role to play in the future of both the humanities and graduate education, and it requires a correspondingly robust infrastructure. In addition to building new tools and datasets and developing new methods and applications for the range of projects that they work on, the efforts of digital humanists to create additional and more clearly defined onramps to DH can help strengthen the field and make it more accessible and inclusive. The acts of adopting more effective and intentional mentoring practices and policies, implementing pedagogies that create space for experimentation and exploration, and encouraging graduate students to strategically plan a variety of possible futures will not accomplish this on their own. But they are an excellent start.

Notes

1. This is a rich area of scholarship and commentary in the digital humanities. For a discussion of representation within DH communities as it pertains to race see Bailey, "All the Digital Humanists Are White" and McPherson, "Why Are the Digital Humanities So White?" On gender inclusivity in DH, see Nowviskie, "Don't Circle the Wagons." For questions about what kinds of projects qualify as "digital humanities," see Barnett, "Brave Side of Digital Humanities," and on the role of coding in DH practice, see Posner, "Some Things to Think About."

2. Perez, "Lowriding through the Digital Humanities" offers a discussion of the #TransformDH movement and the need for greater engagement between DH and critical theory, and in "Beyond the Margins," Risam discusses the need for a more theoretically informed and intersectional digital humanities.

3. For a description of these organizational units, see University of Virginia Scholars' Lab, "About"; Indiana University Bloomington Institute for Digital Arts and Humanities, "Institute for Digital Arts & Humanities" (https://idah.indiana.edu/); University of Denver

College of Arts, Humanities, and Social Sciences, "Emergent Digital Practices: Creatively Shaping the Future" (https://www.du.edu/ahss/edp/).

4. This last consideration is particularly important when considered in light of financial costs associated with extending time to degree and the potential to run out of funding. The Council of Graduate Schools found that financial support was the leading factor cited by graduate students in degree completion, though humanities students were less likely than their peers in other disciplines to cite this factor (Council of Graduate Schools, *Ph.D. Completion and Attrition*). Obviously, the magnitude of these financial impacts are likely to be significantly exacerbated by the challenges brought on by the Covid-19 pandemic.

5. See, for instance, Purdy and Walker, "Valuing Digital Scholarship"; Nowviskie, "Where Credit Is Due"; and Day et al., "What We Really Value."

6. Harris and Nowviskie explore the risks inherent to pursuing training in digital methods, which may or may not pan out; see Harris, "Play, Collaborate, Break, Build, Share," and Nowviskie, "Graduate Training."

7. A description of the Praxis Program can be found in Nowviskie, "Digital Boot Camp."

8. For information about these confederations, see Florida Digital Humanities Consortium, "About" (https://www.fldh.org/about); New England Digital Humanities Consortium, "Digital Humanities @ NEHC" (https://nehc.edu/digital-humanities/); Digital Humanities Collaborative of North Carolina, "About Us" (https://dhcnc.org/about-us/).

9. It is important to note that graduate students should not be required to share their entire IDP with any or all of their mentors. Some of their goals are likely to be personal and private, and they may not feel comfortable sharing all goals with all mentors.

Bibliography

Anderson, Katrina, Lindsey Bannister, Janey Dodd, Deanna Fong, Michelle Levy, and Lindsey Seatter. "Student Labour and Training in Digital Humanities." *Digital Humanities Quarterly* 10, no. 1 (2016). http://www.digitalhumanities.org/dhq/vol/10/1/000233/000233.html.

Bailey, Moya Z. "All the Digital Humanists Are White, All the Nerds Are Men, but Some of Us Are Brave." *Journal of Digital Humanities* 1, no. 1 (Winter 2011). http://journalofdigitalhumanities.org/1-1/all-the-digital-humanists-are-white-all-the-nerds-are-men-but-some-of-us-are-brave-by-moya-z-bailey/.

Barnett, Fiona M. "The Brave Side of Digital Humanities." *differences* 25, no. 1 (2014): 64–78. https://doi.org/10.1215/10407391-2420003.

Chan, Anita Say, and Harriett Green. "Practicing Collaborative Digital Pedagogy to Foster Digital Literacies in Humanities Classrooms." *Educause Review,* October 13, 2014. https://er.educause.edu/articles/2014/10/practicing-collaborative-digital-pedagogy-to-foster-digital-literacies-in-humanities-classrooms.

Council of Graduate Schools. *Ph.D. Completion and Attrition: Policies and Practices to Promote Student Success.* Washington, D.C.: Council of Graduate Schools, 2010.

Davidson, Cathy. "Humanities 2.0: Promise, Perils, Predictions." *PMLA* 123, no. 3 (2008): 707–17.

Day, Michael, Susan H. Delagrange, Mike Palmquist, Michael A. Pemberton, and Janice R. Walker. "What We Really Value: Redefining Scholarly Engagement in Tenure and Promotion Protocols." *College Composition and Communication* 65, no. 1 (2013): 185–208. http://www.jstor.com/stable/43490813.

Golde, Chris M. "The Role of the Department and Discipline in Doctoral Student Attrition: Lessons from Four Departments." *Journal of Higher Education* 76, no. 6 (2005): 669–700. https://doi.org/10.1080/00221546.2005.11772304.

Gould, Julie. "A Plan for Action." *Nature* 548 (2017): 489–90. https://doi.org/10.1038/nj 7668-489a.

Harris, Katherine D. "Play, Collaborate, Break, Build, Share: 'Screwing Around' in Digital Pedagogy: The Debate to Define Digital Humanities . . . Again." *Polymath* 3, no. 3 (Summer 2013): 1–26.

Higgin, Tanner. "Cultural Politics, Critique and the Digital Humanities." *Tanner Higgin: Gaming the System* (blog), May 25, 2010. https://www.tannerhiggin.com/2010/05/cul tural-politics-critique-and-the-digital-humanities/.

Higgins, Monica C., and David A. Thomas. "Constellations and Careers: Toward Understanding the Effects of Multiple Developmental Relationships." *Journal of Organizational Behavior* 22, no. 3 (2001): 223–47. https://doi.org/10.1002/job.66.

Khost, Peter H., Debra Rudder Lohe, and Chuck Sweetman. "Rethinking and Unthinking the Graduate Seminar." *Pedagogy* 15, no. 1 (2015): 19–30. https://doi.org/10.1215 /15314200-2799132.

Langan, Kathleen A., and Ilse Schweitzer VanDonkelaar. "Moderating a Meaningful DH Conversation for Graduate Students in the Humanities." In *Digital Humanities in the Library: Challenges and Opportunities for Subject Specialists,* edited by Adrianne Hartsell-Gundy, Laura Braunstein, and Liorah Golomb, 19–38. Chicago: Association of College and Research Libraries, 2015.

Lovitts, Barbara E. *Leaving the Ivory Tower: The Causes and Consequences of Departure from Doctoral Study.* Lanham, Md.: Rowman and Littlefield, 2001.

Lueck, Amy J., and Beth Boehm. "Beginning at the End: Reimagining the Dissertation Committee, Reimagining Careers." *Composition Studies* 47, no. 1 (2019): 135–53.

McPherson, Tara. "Why Are the Digital Humanities So White? Or Thinking the Histories of Race and Computation." In *Debates in the Digital Humanities,* edited by Matthew K. Gold, 139–60. Minneapolis: University of Minnesota Press, 2012.

Montgomery, Beronda L. "Mapping a Mentoring Roadmap and Developing a Supportive Network for Strategic Advancement." *SAGE Open* 7, no. 2 (2017): 1–13. https://doi .org/10.1177/2158244017710288.

National Institutes of Health. "NOT-OD-14-113: Revised Policy: Descriptions on the Use of Individual Development Plans (IDPs) for Graduate Students and Postdoctoral Researchers Required in Annual Progress Reports beginning October 1, 2014."

Policy update, National Institute of Health. August 14, 2014. https://grants.nih.gov /grants/guide/notice-files/NOT-OD-14-113.html.

Nettles, Michael T., and Catherine M. Millett. *Three Magic Letters: Getting to Ph.D.* Baltimore: Johns Hopkins University Press, 2006.

Nowviskie, Bethany. "A Digital Boot Camp for Grad Students in the Humanities." *Chronicle of Higher Education,* April 29, 2012, B26–B27. https://www.chronicle.com/article /a-digital-boot-camp-for-grad-students-in-the-humanities/.

Nowviskie, Bethany. "Don't Circle the Wagons." *Bethany Nowviskie* (blog), March 4, 2012. http://nowviskie.org/2012/dont-circle-the-wagons/.

Nowviskie, Bethany. "Graduate Training for a Digital and Public Humanities." In *A New Deal for the Humanities: Liberal Arts and the Future of Public Higher Education,* edited by Gordon Hutner and Feisal G. Mohamed, 115–30. New Brunswick, N.J.: Rutgers University Press, 2016.

Nowviskie, Bethany. "Where Credit Is Due: Preconditions for the Evaluation of Collaborative Digital Scholarship." *Profession* (2011): 169–81. https://www.jstor.org/stable /41714117.

Perez, Annemarie. "Lowriding through the Digital Humanities." In *Disrupting the Digital Humanities,* edited by Dorothy Kim and Jesse Stommel, 143–54. Santa Barbara: Punctum Books, 2018.

Posner, Miriam. "Some Things to Think about Before You Exhort Everyone to Code." February 29, 2012. http://miriamposner.com/blog/some-things-to-think-about-before -you-exhort-everyone-to-code/.

Purdy, James P., and Joyce R. Walker. "Valuing Digital Scholarship: Exploring the Changing Realities of Intellectual Work." *Profession* (2010): 177–95. http://www.jstor.com /stable/41419875.

Rehbein, Malte, and Christiane Fritze. "Hands-On Teaching Digital Humanities: A Didactic Analysis of a Summer School Course on Digital Editing." In *Digital Humanities Pedagogy: Practices, Principles and Politics,* edited by Brett D. Hirsch, 47–78. Cambridge: Open Book Publishers, 2012.

Risam, Roopika. "Beyond the Margins: Intersectionality and the Digital Humanities." *Digital Humanities Quarterly* 9, no. 2 (2015). http://digitalhumanities.org:8081/dhq/vol /9/2/000208/000208.html.

Roberts, L. R., Christa M. Tinari, and Raymond Bandlow. "An Effective Doctoral Student Mentor Wears Many Hats and Asks Many Questions." *International Journal of Doctoral Studies* 14 (2019): 133–59. https://doi.org/10.28945/4195.

Rockwell, Geoffrey. "Inclusion in the Digital Humanities." *philosophi.ca* (blog), September 7, 2011. https://philosophi.ca/pmwiki.php/Main/InclusionInTheDigital Humanities.

Spiro, Lisa. "Opening Up Digital Humanities Education." In *Digital Humanities Pedagogy: Practices, Principles and Politics,* edited by Brett D. Hirsch, 331–63. Cambridge: Open Book Publishers, 2012. http://www.jstor.com/stable/j.ctt5vjtt3.19.

Sugimoto, Cassidy R. "Are You My Mentor? Identifying Mentors and Their Roles in LIS Doctoral Education." *Journal of Education for Library and Information Science* 53, no. 1 (2012): 2–19. http://www.jstor.com/stable/23249093.

Svensson, Patrik. "Envisioning the Digital Humanities." *Digital Humanities Quarterly* 6, no. 1 (2012). http://www.digitalhumanities.org/dhq/vol/6/1/000112/000112.html.

Sweitzer, Vicki (Baker). "Towards a Theory of Doctoral Student Professional Identity Development: A Developmental Networks Approach." *Journal of Higher Education* 80, no. 1 (2009): 1–33. https://doi.org/10.1080/00221546.2009.11772128.

Vincent, Ben J., Clarissa Scholes, Max V. Staller, Zeba Wunderlich, Javier Estrada, Jeehae Park, Meghan D. J. Bragdon, Francheska Lopez Rivera, Kelly M. Biette, and Angela H. DePace. "Yearly Planning Meetings: Individualized Development Plans Aren't Just More Paperwork." *Molecular Cell* 58, no. 5 (June 4, 2015): 718–21. https://doi.org/10.1016/j.molcel.2015.04.025.

Walker, George E., Chris M. Golde, Laura Jones, Andrea Conklin Bueschelm, and Pat Hutchings. *The Formation of Scholars: Rethinking Doctoral Education for the Twenty-First Century.* New York: Jossey-Bass, 2008.

Zhao, Chun-Mei, Chris M. Golde, and Alexander C. McCormick. "More Than a Signature: How Advisor Choice and Advisor Behaviour Affect Doctoral Student Satisfaction." *Journal of Further and Higher Education* 31, no. 3 (2007): 263–81.

Graduate Assistantships in the Digital Humanities
Experiences from the Roy Rosenzweig Center for History and New Media

LAURA CROSSLEY, AMANDA E. REGAN,
AND JOSHUA CASMIR CATALANO

G raduate research assistantships in digital humanities centers can be transformative opportunities for students. They provide hands-on experience and valuable skills, and they often complement coursework. However, contradictions between this work as training and labor present challenges for students and the center or project. Project directors and supervisors must navigate tensions between providing structure and allowing for independence, achieving project deliverables and facilitating meaningful learning, supporting student leadership and respecting competing demands for time and energy, and meeting student needs and abiding by funding limitations. In this chapter, we offer suggestions for structuring graduate student work in the digital humanities based on our experiences as Graduate Research Assistants (GRAs) on grant-funded DH projects at George Mason University's Roy Rosenzweig Center for History and New Media (RRCHNM) between 2013 and 2020.

First, we argue that practicum courses bridging coursework and the assistantship can provide critical support as students are introduced to DH work. To ensure that both specific project demands and the student's broader learning goals are met, we call for students and faculty to design individualized applied learning plans. These plans should outline how the student's work meaningfully contributes to the project and the student's intellectual development; integrate professionalization objectives, including publishing and presenting; and, when possible, accommodate student-initiated projects. We then recommend creating and adhering to job descriptions for graduate assistants that provide for student growth and leadership opportunities while insulating against undue responsibilities and stress. Finally, we argue that flexible work schedules, budget transparency, and opportunities for academic credit can help mitigate the financial and time pressures graduate students face. At the heart of our argument is the conviction that facilitating professionalization and student-driven learning, establishing clear work expectations, and creating supportive work conditions are essential whether managing multiple graduate assistants at a large DH center or one graduate assistant on an individual grant-funded project. We put forward the following practices below as a starting point for achieving these aims and ensuring that the graduate student experience beyond the classroom is pedagogically valuable.

Although RRCHNM is exceptional for its large size and long history, for those reasons it has also provided its graduate assistants a range of experiences with different projects, leadership styles, funding structures, grant cycle stages, and levels of curriculum integration.[1] George Mason University is home to one of the first history PhD programs to require digital coursework. Historically, the history PhD required a two-semester sequence of digital history courses, known as Clio Wired I and II. First developed in 1998 by Roy Rosenzweig himself, the course's name refers to Clio, the muse of history, being "wired" into the internet. As technology and the field of digital history have developed over the years, Clio has gone "wireless," and the content of the course has shifted numerous times, but the name has persisted.[2] When we completed our coursework, the Clio I course introduced students to a range of digital history tools and methodologies, and Clio II provided a deeper dive into computational history through the R programming language.[3] Beyond the Clio sequence, students have had the opportunity to pursue minor fields in digital history and even complete entirely digital dissertations.[4] The program's digital pathways are made possible, in part, by the faculty expertise, assistantships, and grants at RRCHNM, which is affiliated with the history department. Founded in 1992, RRCHNM and its staff have played an important role in the creation and development of Zotero, Omeka, History Matters, and other major projects familiar to DH practitioners. During our time there, RRCHNM relied heavily on grant funding and sometimes offered assistantships to history PhD students through these grants.[5] George Mason University's R1 status also shapes RRCHNM's particular challenges and opportunities, but the principles drawn from our experiences working on grant-funded digital humanities projects are applicable to a variety of institutional contexts.

Balancing Structure and Independence with an Introductory Practicum

Graduate students starting out at a DH center or on a project may have little to no experience on grant-funded projects and bring varying degrees of technological expertise. Project managers must acknowledge the diversity of skill levels and strike a balance between setting students loose to learn on their own and providing guidance and oversight. The digital skills required for a project, such as a programming language or software program, are also usually disconnected from a student's formal coursework, which makes learning on the job essential. Without at least a semblance of structure, graduate students can easily become disillusioned with their assistantship and DH work. It may be difficult for them to see any connection between the assistantship and their larger goal of becoming a humanities scholar. If this occurs, they may see learning digital skills as an annoying hurdle or task to be completed rather than an integral part of becoming a humanities scholar in the digital age.

During our time at RRCHNM, the Digital History Fellowship offered a model for creating structure by building connections between coursework and the graduate assistantship. The fellowship was installed in 2012 and funded by the Office of the Provost. Each year, the award provided two to three new history PhD students with full tuition waivers and a stipend for taking a two-year practicum course at RRCHNM.[6] Similar to a paid internship, students received course credit for their assistantship hours and learning at the center, which counted toward their full-time course load. In the first semester of the fellowship, an RRCHNM faculty member directed students in a module exploring the history of the center and the development of digital history as a field. This was designed to complement and enhance what the fellows learned concurrently in Clio I. Over the next few months, the fellows rotated quickly through the center's active projects, learning the ropes and contributing to appropriate small-scale tasks. In the second semester, fellows were assigned to one or more projects and began to hone the skills associated with that project.[7] During the second year, fellows continued working on center projects, undertaking greater responsibilities.

An introductory practicum is a useful starting point for building a valuable assistantship experience. At its best, the Digital History Fellowship immersed students in the work of RRCHNM and the field more broadly. Fellows walked away with a sampling of the center's diverse projects, the ability to critically engage with digital scholarship, and a foundation of new skills, such as using the command line and GitHub, navigating web servers, and installing development versions of Word-Press. However, this model was time intensive. It placed responsibilities on project directors and managers that did not always align neatly with grant deliverables, amounting to invisible labor that could not be budgeted for directly. Already busy juggling other tasks to meet project outcomes, center staff had to find ways to structure meaningful short-term projects and assignments for fellows at varying skill levels. Often they were highly successful in teaching and guiding junior scholars in the tools and practices in DH. Other times, fellows were left idle without direction.

Despite the unevenness of the experience, we believe the practicum model is worth pursuing as a way to integrate training and pedagogy into DH graduate assistantships. By necessity, a practicum at another institution will look different. To be effective, though, learning objectives need to be laid out specifically and clearly, and they need to be communicated not just to the students but to all faculty and staff involved. Ideally, students should participate in shaping their own learning objectives.[8] Students should have the opportunity to work with and learn from the various faculty, staff, and other graduate students at the center or on a project. However, as exposing inexperienced students to a new project is more likely to create work than offload it, the added labor needs to be recognized and accounted for. At the same time, an introductory practicum helps mold students into more well-rounded DH practitioners who understand their strengths and interests, are able to serve as integral members of a project team, and are ultimately better prepared to pursue their professional goals. Former DH fellows and center GRAs have launched promising careers. It is not a coincidence that many have landed tenure-track jobs and prestigious positions in DH centers, libraries, museums, and archives. In a seemingly ever-worsening humanities job market, the skills learned at RRCHNM have served former graduate students exceptionally well.

Planning for Achieving Project and Learning Goals

A well-structured practicum supported by institutional resources can provide a solid foundation, but as graduate assistants settle into a project, sharpen their skills, and expand their responsibilities, the alignment between the student's pedagogical needs and the researcher's objectives needs to be carefully considered. Project directors must navigate the tensions between achieving project deliverables and facilitating meaningful learning for graduate assistants. Students want and need to do intellectually interesting work that prepares them for their career and research goals. They also need time and opportunity to experiment and learn from failing. But work needs to get done on projects, including rote tasks.

To support student learning while meeting project deliverables, we recommend implementing individualized applied learning plans. Fulfilling the pedagogical responsibilities of a DH center means working with students to build their unique skill sets and facilitate connections to their interests. One helpful mechanism to facilitate student growth is formalizing the broader learning agenda for each student with written plans. In chapter 12 in this volume, Brady Krien calls for Individual Development Plans to ensure that DH training is integrated into a student's degree plan. An applied learning plan would fulfill a similar function within the specific context of a student's work on a grant-funded project. On a regular basis, each graduate student needs to work with project directors to assess skill gaps, with an eye toward the student's career and research goals, and identify opportunities for development.[9] These plans need to delineate how the student's role will facilitate meaningful learning within the scope of the assigned project; what professional development opportunities the student will pursue and what support the directors will provide; and, when possible, how student-initiated projects will fulfill learning gaps.

The primary purpose of an individualized applied learning plan is to ensure that graduate assistants are assigned work that meaningfully contributes to the project and ensure that they understand how the work fits into the larger project and their personal growth. This requires intentional effort from the earliest stages of a project. When planning and writing a grant, it is essential to consider the potential value of the work assigned to graduate students for their own development as scholars, so as to include them not simply in support roles but as full participants in the intellectual process of (re)conceptualizing the project's aims and methods.[10] At many institutions, graduate students cannot be principal investigators on grants. During our time at RRCHNM, individual faculty members made an effort to give graduate students roles such as project manager, outreach coordinator, or managing editor, and, on occasion, bring them into the grant writing process itself. The experience we gained working on these grant-funded projects helped prepare us to write and serve as principal investigators on future grants.

Within the lifecycle of a grant, the point at which a student joins a project determines a large part of their experience, but at all stages of a project, graduate students should be engaging in scholarly interpretation. The grant lifecycle often includes upwards of one year of planning and preparing for an application submission. If funded, the project usually starts three to six months later and lasts from one to three years. Projects are sometimes extended by an additional grant that repeats this cycle. All three of the authors worked on the grant-funded PressForward project at different stages. The PressForward WordPress plugin enables teams of researchers to aggregate and disseminate relevant scholarship. The digital publication *Digital Humanities Now* had long served as a test case for the project. Regan, who joined the team in 2014, came on toward the end of the initial PressForward grant and was involved in writing and planning for the second. Catalano, who joined the team in 2015 in the middle of that grant cycle, focused on software testing, documentation writing, and managing *DHNow*. Crossley, who joined the team in 2017 during the third grant period, also concentrated on software testing and managing *DHNow* as well as outreach work. By fall 2018, Crossley was the only remaining graduate assistant on the project. The earlier stages of the project offered more opportunities to shape the aims of the project and the features of the software. For Crossley, it was also important to meaningfully engage with the intellectual questions around digital open scholarship guiding the project. She pursued this by conducting a critical evaluation of the landscape of digital humanities blogging through quantitative and text analysis of nine years of posts shared on *DHNow*. The center covered travel expenses for her to present this work at a conference. Having the center's support to do this project made working on the final stages of a grant a more fulfilling experience and illustrates that when planning graduate student project work, creating opportunities for intellectual inquiry is valuable, regardless of the project stage. This bears out Kayla Shipp's assertion in chapter 14 in this volume that graduate students' present and future careers are better served by DH work that goes beyond the technical and methodological to the creative and critical. At the beginning of a project, graduate students need not just collect data but can understand and help shape the arguments built into the project's modes of collecting, structuring, and presenting information.[11] Toward the end of a project, they should not just be wrapping up project deliverables but critically assessing the project's achievements, failures, and possible futures.

By engaging in scholarly interpretive practice throughout the project, students are positioned to publish and present on their work. A student learning plan needs to incorporate professionalization goals because fostering professionalization is one critical way that project directors can prioritize pedagogy and treat students as scholars in training rather than employees.[12] As Alison Booth argues in chapter 2 in this volume, graduate training in DH is, ideally, a shared inquiry, with students given opportunities to coauthor and present as part of their work on collaborative projects. It is not enough to encourage students to publish and present. Project directors must take the time to think through and discuss concrete topics and venues with students. Time and expenses should be paid, and it is critical to be realistic about the time investment required by students and directors. Disseminating research can benefit the student and the project, but only if it is integrated into the student's workload and does not become added labor.

Encouraging Student-Driven Learning

Individualized learning plans should acknowledge when a designated project cannot fully meet a student's learning expectations. Many projects require depth rather than breadth in learning and involve applying a narrow set of tools and skills. When this skill set pairs well with the student's interests and career goals, the experience can be empowering. However, if a student feels that the specialized needs for a project do not align with their own objectives, this can create frustration and a sense of missing out on vital career training. When circumstances allow, then, it is worth including opportunities to split time across projects and support student-initiated projects. Splitting a student's time across more than one project can expand the range of experience while providing an opportunity for more students to work on a project. One way RRCHNM maximized the range of experiences was to implement graduate student-initiated projects in academic year 2019–2020. At the start of the year, students partnered in groups of two to four to develop modest year-long project proposals, complete with budgets, which the center faculty reviewed in a mock grant application process. The projects included a software prototype, an Omeka website, and a secondary school curriculum website. As a trial run, working out the kinks was a challenge, and Covid-19 interrupted the completion of projects. But by giving students the freedom to choose their projects and roles within the projects, the experiment was successful in enabling students to fill their own skill and knowledge gaps. Other institutions, such as the Scholars' Lab at the University of Virginia, have experimented with similar programs that facilitate DH training by allowing students to pursue collaborative projects with the support of center staff as part of the Praxis Program, a year-long paid internship for a small group of graduate students to design and build a shared DH project.[13] If student projects or splitting time across grant-funded projects is impossible, flexibility for student-driven learning needs to be created within the scope of an individual project.

In developing a student learning plan, project directors and students should work together to design student-driven subprojects that bring together skill development, learning goals, and project deliverables. At RRCHNM, an example of this model was Regan's development of a custom user management WordPress plugin that could offer administrative and user tools to manage the volunteer editor process for the online publication *DHNow*. After identifying that the registration and scheduling of editors each week required staffing and administrative resources that were unsustainable in the long term, Regan took the initiative to solve this issue. Regan researched possible solutions and determined that she could build a custom plugin to streamline the registration and scheduling process. Once Regan decided on this approach, she worked to identify the skills needed to build such a program and then built a rudimentary proof of concept to present to the project managers. Open to the idea, the project managers asked for a proposal, written in a similar manner to a grant proposal, and used the opportunity to provide mentorship in project development and grant writing skills. After revising the proposal and outlining clear deliverables for the mini-project, Regan led the effort to develop the software, and together with a team of graduate students tested and deployed the software. The resulting plugin for *DHNow* not only led to a more refined user registration process for *DHNow* but also provided Regan with project management, grant writing, and coding skills.

Managing Expectations of Faculty and Student Labor

Prioritizing pedagogy by supporting graduate student learning and professionalization requires supporting the project faculty and staff who train and mentor them. Developing the user management plugin propelled the project and the students' skills forward, but it required staff at RRCHNM to engage in the labor of mentorship, professionalization, and training, which are often undervalued and disincentivized within the context of grant-funded projects, especially for nontenure-track faculty and staff. Because of grant constraints, fully grant-funded staff are not necessarily paid to do this work. And although the best project managers take seriously their responsibility of training and mentoring graduate students, this often adds uncompensated labor to their workload. As Katina Rogers points out in chapter 1 in this volume, mentorship, guidance, and other acts of care are a crucial counterbalance against the emotional challenges of graduate school. Especially because women, faculty of color, and junior faculty perform a disproportionate share of this "invisible labor," expectations of mentorship cannot remain informal and implicit.[14] For tenure-track faculty, departments need to formally recognize and credit the additional labor of graduate assistant professionalization. Course releases for work on projects can help offset this added labor. For non-tenure-track clinical/research professors and staff, graduate mentorship should be formally included in the job description and evaluation process. When possible, we recommend that grant proposals include graduate professionalization hours in their budgets for faculty and staff to incentivize and compensate for quality mentorship.[15] However, because granting agencies in the humanities generally do not allow funding for this kind of work, we recommend prioritizing the use of departmental and center funds to support this labor.

In addition to developing individualized applied learning plans, we recommend implementing job descriptions for graduate assistants. Although job descriptions are generally required for staff, they are not commonly applied to graduate assistantships. Documenting the responsibilities of graduate assistants is necessary to ensure that their expected contributions are not only clearly defined but also remain reasonable for an assistantship position. Just like learning plans, job descriptions need to be reevaluated and updated on a regular basis. It makes sense for graduate assistants who spend a significant amount of time working on a particular project to take on new responsibilities and leadership roles, and graduate assistants often welcome the experience. However, graduate students have competing demands that need to be respected. Students who take on the added labor and responsibility of training and managing their peers do not always receive formal credit or recognition for this work. While it may teach valuable project management and leadership skills, the added responsibility comes with additional stress and no additional financial compensation or funding security. It is often not commensurate with the responsibilities and expectations of graduate assistantships, at least in the humanities. When an individual's role shifts away from being a student and toward that of an employee, this may increase the time to degree and interfere with their overall educational goals. As a graduate student becomes indispensable to a project, they may feel obligated to continue working on it at the expense of other academic and career opportunities. Ideally, students taking on roles beyond the typical expectations of a graduate assistant would be formally recognized for their role and compensated accordingly, but university guidelines constrain the ability of centers, departments, and principal investigators to increase compensation for graduate assistants. This is why job descriptions should be employed to help guide graduate assistants' growth within their roles while guarding against responsibility creep.

Staff turnover presents a particular challenge for maintaining reasonable expectations from graduate assistants, so we also recommend that every project develop a transition plan from the outset of project development. Given the nature of grant-funded work and higher education, turnover is inevitable for longer projects. During our time at RRCHNM, numerous staff and faculty departed for new opportunities. On an individual faculty-led humanities project, the project moves with the faculty member, but in the context of a center, projects might instead stay with the institution's team of project staff. Turnover is understandable and inevitable. Centers and projects should plan for retention and transitions because project turnover can lead to a loss of institutional memory that may place greater demand on a project's senior graduate students. This is especially likely to occur toward the end of a project or on projects that are no longer supported by a grant but continue to be indirectly supported by an institution. A project transition plan can provide for continuity in the management, training, and mentorship of graduate students on the project team and account for graduate student turnover as students graduate and move on to new opportunities. Continuity should receive as much attention in sustainability planning as documentation and project sunsetting.[16] Project transition plans and job descriptions can be useful tools for managing graduate assistant labor on projects while ensuring that graduate assistants can prioritize their own needs and responsibilities as students.

Creating Supportive Work Conditions

Finally, we agree with our colleagues who have highlighted the direct link between funding and the success and well-being of graduate students. As Brandon Walsh has argued, pedagogy extends beyond the classroom to everything faculty do in relation to students, so advocating for better conditions for students involves treating budgets as pedagogical documents.[17] Funding stability and budget transparency are critical, as grant-dependent funding can intensify financial anxiety for students. Funding also influences the collegiality of a program, as limited funding can create unhealthy competition and erode cohort cohesion and cooperation, which is especially important to maintain in collaborative digital humanities work. We recommend keeping funding packages as even as possible throughout different forms of graduate assistantships within a department and, to the extent possible, guaranteeing student funding through hard monies that can be supplemented with grant funds. Although we as graduate assistants at RRCHNM rarely knew if we had a spot on a grant-funded project from year to year, we knew that we at least had a set number of years of funding through another teaching or research assistantship through the department. At a minimum, transparency helps avoid unnecessary conflict and stress. Learning about the budget should not be optional.

The funding limitations of grant-based projects and strict university guidelines make it challenging for digital humanities centers or project teams to address the financial stresses of graduate assistants, but offering flexible schedules and opportunities for course credits can alleviate some of the stresses of an assistantship. Consider how the workload and obligations of a project-based graduate assistantship compare to teaching assistantships in the department. It is worth factoring in if students are required to travel several days a week to a physical location to "clock in," adding to commute time and travel costs. Granting graduate assistants flexibility and control over their work schedules and course loads can help. Depending on the nature of a grant project, some of the expectations for graduate students are analogous to additional academic coursework completed without credit. Due to various funding packages in the history department, some graduate assistants at RRCHNM were required to take nine credit hours per semester plus the twenty-hour assistantship, but those in the Digital History Fellowship detailed above took six credits and had their twenty hours count toward three additional credits. This resulted in uneven funding and educational experiences, problems that could be mitigated by creating a practicum course open to all graduate assistants, with specific learning objectives that can build upon work completed on a project while providing course credit if desired.[18] This would also have the benefit of fostering a closer connection between the graduate curriculum and career training. If practicum courses are not feasible, credit hours could be awarded for methodological or skills training through an independent study.

Our time as GRAs at RRCHNM was an essential part of our training as digital historians. For most graduate students, it takes time and dedication beyond fulfilling the requirements of a degree program to build DH knowledge and skills.[19] Assistantships in DH centers can play a critical role in filling this gap, but only if project and program directors recognize that assigning graduate students to digital projects does not automatically foster their development as DH scholars. Directors should center graduate student education and professionalization by building direct connections between the assistantship and coursework, implementing practicum courses when possible, developing individualized applied learning plans and carving out time for student-initiated projects, assigning work that is not merely preparatory but positions students to engage in scholarly interpretation throughout the life of the project, and integrating student publishing and presentations into the project goals. At the same time, directors should seek to prevent stress and burnout by not overburdening graduate students with leadership responsibilities beyond the scope of an assistantship, granting flexibility in graduate student work schedules, discussing budgets openly and often, and creating options for counting work toward academic credit. To implement these practices, DH programs and project directors require latitude and support, as well as accountability, and, ideally, reliable funding from department heads and administration. They need to see themselves as responsible for professionalizing students into the practice of DH, and departments need to formally recognize and credit this labor. Directors also need to frame the goals of individual projects from a broader perspective. There is a balance to be struck between students completing routine tasks and having the freedom to explore, learn, and fail. If students are too occupied with busywork to step back and see the meaning of their work on a broader level, the center or project risks missing out on new ideas and possibilities. When graduate students are supported, intellectually fulfilled, and trusted to pursue and produce interesting, valuable scholarship, it benefits not only the student but the project, the center, and the future of digital humanities.

Notes

1. The following clarifies the years each contributing author worked at RRCHNM: Amanda Regan, fall 2013 to spring 2018; Joshua Catalano, fall 2015 to spring 2018; and Laura Crossley, fall 2016 to spring 2020. During our time there, eight to twelve history PhD students and candidates were placed as GRAs each year.

2. See Cohen, "Pragmatic as Well as Prescient" for a discussion of the origins of George Mason University's PhD in history as well as the origins of the "Clio Wired" course sequence.

3. The curriculum for the second half of the Clio Wired sequence has changed over the years as the field has evolved. It previously focused on presenting historical information on the web using HTML and CSS.

4. For a discussion of digital dissertations out of history departments, see Sharpe, "Digital Dissertations and the Changing Nature," and Agarwal, "History Dissertation Goes Digital." See also the George Mason University Department for History and Art History's "Digital Dissertation Guidelines."

5. Funding came from various sources during our tenure at RRCHNM. Regan's and Crossley's first two years were funded through the Digital History Fellowship (2013–2015 and 2016–2018, respectively). Catalano's three years were funded through the Presidential Scholarship (a recruitment fellowship funded through the Office for the Provost). Others held GRAs that were sometimes funded by grants or through the history department.

6. Due to the funding cycle of the program, most cohorts received two-year fellowships, but others received one-year fellowships. In our experience, the full two-year fellowship helped create a more immersive introduction to the work of the center and digital history.

7. In previous iterations of the fellowship, the module came at the end of the project rotations. Additionally, project rotations used to last the entire first year, with the main project assignment scheduled to start in the second year.

8. For an example of articulating shared values, common goals, and individual goals within a practicum, see the discussion of the Praxis Program Charter in Nowviskie, "On Capacity and Care."

9. We echo Anderson et al., in "advanc[ing] a model of project management that sees training as an end in itself, distinct from the project's teleology." As they argue, "Training must be a deliberate and planned activity that is formally budgeted and accounted for in the project's timeline, and should be compensated to the same degree as other tasks performed within the project." But student training must also be measured and evaluated as its own goal, separate from progress on project milestones. See Anderson et al., "Student Labour and Training."

10. In surveys of faculty and student researchers on DH projects, Anderson et al. found that "students perceive their work to be less collaborative than faculty researchers, and this is possibly a consequence of the nature of the work given to them." Too often student work is preparatory, undervalued, and "literally 'unseen' because it exists in hidden coding and programming." We believe that project directors should treat and credit student labor as constitutive of, rather than preparation for, the "real" scholarly work of a project. See Anderson et al., "Student Labour and Training."

11. For an example of turning the "seemingly mundane or taken-for-granted work" of data construction into a pedagogical opportunity for digital literacy and critical thinking,

in this case with undergraduates, see Rivard et al., "Building Pedagogy into Project Development."

12. We support the principles outlined in "A Student Collaborators' Bill of Rights," but we agree with Mann that these principles do not go far enough in addressing the hierarchical structures of research relationships. Mann argues for "replacing the collaborative model for working with graduate students [on DH projects] with a pedagogical model." According to Mann, "Conceiving project partnerships as simply collaborative, rather than as more formally structured research relationships, masks some important responsibilities that faculty members owe to their students." Single-authored, peer-reviewed publications remain "the most valued work attached to digital projects," yet the collaborative model, as typically practiced, tends to shut graduate students out of this step. "Paying graduate students to work, but not encouraging them to think and write about their work, creates a disconnect between their labor and their intellectual development," so as part of a pedagogical model, project directors "have a responsibility to help their students publish in the field." See Mann, "Paid to Do."

13. For a discussion of the collaborative model used at the Scholars' Lab, see Nowviskie, "Too Small to Fail"; Walsh, "Praxis and Scale."

14. Numerous scholars have discussed the impact of emotional labor on female, faculty of color, and junior faculty. For example, see Bellas, "Emotional Labor in Academia"; June, "Invisible Labor of Minority Professors"; Tunguz, "In the Eye of the Beholder"; Social Sciences Feminist Network Research Interest Group, "The Burden of Invisible Work in Academia"; and Guarino and Borden, "Faculty Service Loads and Gender."

15. As Opel and Simeone argue, "The graduate students who come to labor in the lab are a visible and direct result of the synergistic forces of funding and institutional shaping rather than consideration for the goals and objectives of graduate education . . . much of that graduate training and education is invisible because it is not tied to these funding models and resultant lab practices." See "The Invisible Work of the Digital Humanities Lab."

16. For more on the importance of planning for turnover, see Nowviskie, "Too Small to Fail."

17. See Brandon Walsh, "Your Budget Is a Question of Pedagogy and Equity" for a discussion of how the economic conditions created by a program directly influence the kinds of people who are able to participate and the kind of work that can be done.

18. Practicum course credits should apply toward degree requirements, and students should not take more practicum credits than can be productively applied to the degree. During our time as fellows, up to six credits from the Digital History Fellowship practicum could count as electives or toward a digital history minor field, but each semester of the practicum counted as a three-credit course, for twelve credits total in a two-year fellowship. With new limits on the number of credits covered by tuition waiver, students felt that they were unable to take enough additional credits to make timely progress on degree requirements. Based on student feedback, the practicum was modified to count just once for three credits.

19. See Brady Krien in chapter 12 in this volume for more on the difficulty of integrating DH training into graduate education.

Bibliography

Agarwal, Kritika. "A History Dissertation Goes Digital." American Historical Association. *Perspectives on History* (blog), August 28, 2017. https://www.historians.org /perspectives-article/a-history-dissertation-goes-digital-september-2017/.

Anderson, Katrina, Lindsey Bannister, Janey Dodd, Deanna Fong, Michelle Levy, and Lindsey Seatter. "Student Labour and Training in Digital Humanities." *Digital Humanities Quarterly* 10, no. 1 (2016). http://www.digitalhumanities.org/dhq/vol/10/1/000233 /000233.html.

Bellas, Marcia L. "Emotional Labor in Academia: The Case of Professors." *The Annals of the American Academy of Political and Social Science* 561, no. 1 (1999): 96–110.

Cohen, Daniel J. "Pragmatic as Well as Prescient: Digital History Education at George Mason University." American Historical Association. *Perspectives on History* (blog), May 1, 2009. https://www.historians.org/perspectives-article/pragmatic-as-well-as-prescient -digital-history-education-at-george-mason-university-may-2009/.

Di Pressi, Haley et al. "A Student Collaborators' Bill of Rights." UCLA Digital Humanities. Accessed July 10, 2020. http://www.cdh.ucla.edu/news-events/a-student-collab orators-bill-of-rights/.

George Mason University Department for History and Art History. "Digital Dissertation Guidelines." Accessed July 10, 2020. https://historyarthistory.gmu.edu/graduate /phd-history/digital-dissertation-guidelines.

Guarino, Cassandra M., and Victor M. H. Borden. "Faculty Service Loads and Gender: Are Women Taking Care of the Academic Family?" *Research in Higher Education* 58, no. 6 (2017): 672–94.

June, Audrey Williams. "The Invisible Labor of Minority Professors." *Chronicle of Higher Education,* November 8, 2015. https://www.chronicle.com/article/The-Invisible -Labor-of/234098.

Mann, Rachel. "Paid to Do but Not to Think: Reevaluating the Role of Graduate Student Collaborators." In *Debates in the Digital Humanities 2019,* ed. Matthew K. Gold and Lauren F. Klein, 268–78. Minneapolis: University of Minnesota Press, 2019.

Nowviskie, Bethany. "On Capacity and Care." *Bethany Nowviskie* (blog), October 4, 2015. http://nowviskie.org/2015/on-capacity-and-care/.

Nowviskie, Bethany. "Too Small to Fail." *Bethany Nowviskie* (blog), October 13, 2012. http://nowviskie.org/2012/too-small-to-fail/.

Opel, Dawn, and Michael Simeone. "The Invisible Work of the Digital Humanities Lab: Preparing Graduate Students for Emergent Intellectual and Professional Work." *Digital Humanities Quarterly* 13, no. 2 (2019). http://www.digitalhumanities.org/dhq/vol /13/2/000421/000421.html.

Rivard, Courtney, Taylor Arnold, and Lauren Tilton. "Building Pedagogy into Project Development: Making Data Construction Visible in Digital Projects." *Digital Humanities Quarterly* 13, no. 2 (2019). http://www.digitalhumanities.org/dhq/vol/13/2 /000419/000419.html.

Sharpe, Celeste Tường Vy. "Digital Dissertations and the Changing Nature of Doctoral Work." American Historical Association. *Perspectives Daily* (blog), April 23, 2019. https://www.historians.org/perspectives-article/digital-dissertations-and-the-changing -nature-of-doctoral-work-april-2019/.

Social Sciences Feminist Network Research Interest Group. "The Burden of Invisible Work in Academia: Social Inequalities and Time Use in Five University Departments." *Humboldt Journal of Social Relations* 39, no. 39 (2017): 228–45.

Tunguz, Sharmin. "In the Eye of the Beholder: Emotional Labor in Academia Varies with Tenure and Gender." *Studies in Higher Education* 41, no. 1 (January 2016): 3–20.

Walsh, Brandon. "Praxis and Scale: On the Virtue of Small." *Brandon Walsh* (blog), June 15, 2018. http://walshbr.com/blog/praxis-and-scale-on-the-virtue-of-small/.

Walsh, Brandon. "Your Budget Is a Question of Pedagogy and Equity." *Scholars' Lab* (blog), April 13, 2020. https://scholarslab.lib.virginia.edu/blog/your-budget-is-a-question-of -pedagogy-and-equity/.

More Than Marketable Skills

Digital Humanities as Creative Space

KAYLA SHIPP

The traditional digital humanist origin story often goes something like the following. At some point a trained humanities scholar finds the methods and tools of their field inadequate for asking the questions they really want answered. They may have questions of frequency and scale: how many times does a word, phrase, or idea appear in a corpus that would take months or years to scan by hand? They may have questions of space and time: how can they chart the variant history of a document such that its constitutive variations are visible all at once or plot geographical locations within a landscape that has changed over time? Eventually, they learn that computing tools are particularly well equipped for parsing questions of frequency, scale, and variation and could potentially allow their research to extend beyond the reach of what raw brain power could reasonably work out or beyond the constraints of a physical page. They then undertake the daunting task of using technical instructions written for an entirely different audience to teach themselves how to use the relevant digital tools and technologies, while still meeting the expectations of their own field. The work feels thrilling and revelatory; it is also frequently isolating and poorly supported.

The current training graduate students receive within a growing number of digital humanities centers, humanities departments, and certificate programs continues to overwhelmingly prioritize learning tools and digital methods and putting them toward analytical ends.[1] Faculty regularly teach current students to approach the work of DH in the way they originally had to, that is, as a collection of tools acquired to amplify their research—as a methodology. Although this methods-centric framing is unsurprising and entirely reasonable given the particular moonlit path many faculty traditionally take to the field, it has the unintended side effect of sentencing new scholars to deal with the same shortcomings of the version of DH through which faculty came, a field with a tendency toward isolated work and infrequent structural support and a self-conscious urge to prove the field's relevance by pushing it toward analysis. In academia broadly, DH's tool-centric branding has led faculty and administrators outside of the field to also push students pragmatically toward tools and methods, stating in various ways, "Do DH work and you will have 'marketable skills' if you want to leave the academy, or you can demonstrate a diverse 'skill set' to hiring committees if you want to remain." In doing so, they inadvertently set students up for potential inefficacy. According to this logic, students who move into nonacademic jobs will have to pit themselves directly against candidates who have dedicated the majority of their time solely to technical training, asking to be judged primarily on their technical ability as if they had done the same. Alternatively, students who remain in academic roles will have to continue splitting their time and commitment between visible and invisible labor—humanities scholarship and the solitary process of tool-learning—demonstrating an ability to divide their work in half while somehow being wholly devoted to each.[2] At this promising moment when DH is increasingly accepted at and formalized within the institutions where graduate training takes place, new digital humanists' present and future careers would be better served by a framing of DH that moves through and beyond methodology to theory and creativity—a framing that traditional humanists understand instinctively and nonacademic environments sorely need.

My introduction to digital humanities work was highly structured for a field that has often evolved informally; I earned my MA in digital humanities from King's College London, the first and oldest digital humanities center in the world (and one of the only places to even get an MADH at the time). My time at King's was enormously instructive and generative and a representative example of the most formalized versions of DH; I was exposed to the breadth of the theoretical questions through which the field originally emerged, and I developed technical competence in various tools to enable me to create my own niche in the field's current work. I came into the program with a background and future in English: I had earned my BA in English and a minor in computer science and deferred my acceptance into Emory University's English PhD program to study at King's. The King's program encouraged me to realize my textual inclinations by exploring the field's gravitation toward archival digitization and formal text analysis through learning the corresponding methods, a process that I found increasingly unexciting and practically frustrating to navigate. The self-taught nature of my professors' own technical instruction meant that their technical knowledge was specific to the projects they had done. Though I received strong encouragement and personal enthusiasm from faculty about my research, it was often up to me to figure out how to make the technology work for my unique purposes.

In studying the early history of the field, I saw a playfulness and curiosity that was not emphasized in my own methods-heavy instruction, which above all pushed me toward tools and analysis—text and otherwise. I think of the "first wave" of digital humanities' critical development as the period when scholars separately found themselves experimenting with what we would now collectively call "digital humanities" work, but at the time could have had any number of labels—projects like the

Index Thomisticus, the Lost Museum interactive game, and the Women Writers' Project. The first wave developed in roughly the second half of the twentieth century and was characterized by a broad interest in using (and building) different technologies and bringing them to bear on the humanistic corpora with which they were previously seen as incompatible.[3] The radical intervention of the first wave was the notion that computers could have anything at all to do with the humanities; its central shortcoming was the diffuse nature of its projects and lack of a unifying language for describing its work.

According to this framework, the second wave of DH development emerged in the early 2000s when the field became more self-conscious, and digital humanists began to attempt to organize their work around central labels and definitions. Digital humanities projects in the second wave were characterized by scholars' interest in furthering the field as such, using a now-familiar collection of tools to reveal and analyze previously obfuscated meaning within humanistic objects. The intervention of the second wave was the premise that DH was capable of being synthesized into a recognizable set of scholarly outputs through a dependable set of practices; its central shortcoming was the fact that by naming itself "digital humanities," its practitioners were asked to expend a significant amount of energy proving the field's relevance in both technological and humanistic spheres, resulting in a standardized tool-centric and analytical definition of what it means to do digital humanities work.

Thanks in large part to their successful institutional struggles for legitimacy, DH practitioners who came to the field through its second wave have been training scholars in a different academic world for some time now—a third wave that more regularly accepts and makes space for DH's academic presence and so has less to prove. "Third wave DH" has the potential to be the product of the best impulses of the first two and can route future waves beyond the problems of the past, but when it frames and defines DH primarily as a methodology, it mis-serves or entirely misses its newest scholars, who are poised to shift DH in their own new directions. These emerging scholars are motivated by what I see as the increasingly expressive theoretical questions of DH scholarship's third wave and are interested in ultimately moving beyond it by asking questions like: What does it *mean* to use a digital publication to provide an interpretation of a text rather than just to provide access or analysis? What does the process of mapping a shifting political boundary teach us not just about the particular geopolitical tensions in a region but about the way that maps themselves can shape those tensions? How can creating an object like a digital text or map explore and express questions such as these? The natural evolution from methods places the third wave's emphasis increasingly on the process of inquiry rather than the product of analysis—on the object a tool creates and how, rather than on the tool itself and the analysis to which it leads—but the structure of much DH framing continues to push students into the past.[4]

In my current post-PhD capacity as the codirector of the Digital Dissertation Scholars Program at Emory University, I have seen related tensions play out repeatedly. Graduate students already interested in DH are often taught that their main offering is in the analysis they contribute, which causes them to shelve more experimental projects that do not fit the expected mold. On a number of occasions, their academic advisors have expressed concern that their students' interest in doing a digital dissertation will distract them from their "scholarly" work, because their only impression of DH output is the development of databases and datasets through the use of complicated tools. I have also seen formally innovative students rule themselves out as digital humanists because they value qualitative work and "are not good at technology"; they do not think of themselves as having analytical questions, so they do not think they are capable of, much less already in the early stages of, "doing DH." Framing third-wave DH through and beyond its methods creates space for these students to explore DH as a theoretical mode of inquiry, looking for ways to use digital tools to theorize and express rather than simply expose and analyze. It allows students to see the movements of the past as foundational bedrock rather than a series of Sisyphean boulders all future digital humanists are destined to forever roll uphill. A DH graduate program framed this way focuses introspectively on the theoretical implications introduced by using any tool. It introduces DH inquiry as the vital work of understanding how different tools do not just parse meaning but create it, focusing broadly on process—experimentation and iteration—and the interpretive objects generated along the way.

As it turns out, the relevance of a field that emphasizes theory, process, and creation is often an even easier sell within humanities departments than methods-heavy DH, at least in my past experience in creating a digital dissertation and current experience consulting on the digital dissertations of other graduate students.[5] I was the first student in the Emory English department to complete a digital dissertation, a project I framed with my committee as equal parts theory and application: a written dissertation of four chapters and four accompanying digital publications. Each chapter addressed different nineteenth-century texts or collections of texts that were unsuccessful as printed editions. I argued that the originals failed in print because the texts were more structurally interactive and expressive than print allowed them to be; in other words, they were digital, and as a result would express themselves better as digital publications. The written chapters gave me space to close-read the texts and present my expansive definition of what it means for any text to be "digital"; the digital publications gave me space to test those theories in application. Between the two, I could both argue for and present *Moby-Dick*'s chaotic content as a linked, nonlinear Choose Your Own Adventure story, the indecisive drafts of Emily Dickinson's envelope poems as a clickable series of interactive objects, the newspaper poems of Frances Watkins Harper as a virtual ephemeral archive, and Walt Whitman's autobiography as a virtual exhibition. Even though (at the time) no English faculty were directly involved with DH work, and no one on my interdisciplinary committee had personal research experience with DH, the feedback I received from them was incredibly valuable. My committee members were able to critique my argument on the grounds of literary theory and make suggestions for what the digital publications should prioritize and demonstrate, all while having no specific knowledge of the practicalities involved in doing so. I was also able to supplement my coding background by bringing in technical experts whenever I hit the limits of my knowledge. I have seen similar situations play out with the Digital Dissertation Scholars Program. Once faculty have been relieved of the expectation that supporting a digital dissertation means having to advise on its technical execution, they frequently dive into their own interpretive suggestions for what the object the student has built can do and mean. Once students have been relieved of the expectation that they should find technical solutions themselves, they regularly shift their energy into collaborative, experimental possibilities for their work.

When framed within a more theoretical and ultimately creative mode, the practicalities of doing DH work take on a deeper pragmatism for students' future careers as well. Learning to use digital tools becomes a necessary and exploratory exercise in what different forms of expression can reveal and create rather than a mechanical process of value primarily for its basic utility. Graduate students are not left trying to solve problems using tools they largely teach themselves, with the goal of finding answers. They are encouraged to approach digital methods with probing curiosity about what layers their tools could reveal and generate instead of seeing them as potential keys to long-standing problems and their future job security. By not deriving the value of their DH work from solitarily laboring over tools and methods in order to prove their mettle, students are empowered to seek the expertise of others in order to fill out their understanding; in academic and nonacademic spheres, students can work collaboratively with the extensively and exclusively trained technical experts rather than seeing themselves as directly in competition with them.

Digital humanities training in the academy should make it clear that the task assigned to graduate students is not to learn to code to solve problems but to become informed critics of the tools used to create any digital object environment. Digital scholarship teaches graduate students that the value they bring to academic and nonacademic spaces is their ability to see the theoretical questions behind any inquiry—to code and build, yes, but also to understand the broader human implications of what they build and how.[6] By creating space for DH to be more than analysis, we also allow it to be a creative space that is always working to become more than the sum of its parts, a place characterized by expression, experimentation, and endless curiosity.

Notes

1. For instance, see Estill's argument for more DH methods training in graduate classrooms in her essay "Digital Humanities and the Graduate Research Methods Class" in chapter 10 in this volume.

2. For a thorough overview of the problem with labor inequity in DH, see Boyles et al., "Precarious Labor." The authors point specifically to academia's lack of accommodation and recognition for the unique and varied demands on DH scholars' time and call for an institutional restructuring that would "demonstrate the institutional and professional value of their labor to audiences who do not find its importance self-evident" (694). Boyles et al. conclude that "if American studies [in particular] is serious about supporting digital humanities work in an ethical and sustainable manner, it should also reflect more broadly on the privileging of certain forms of labor and kinds of laborers in its professional networks and channels of employment and promotion" (698).

3. I have chosen the framework of waves in an effort to *characterize* DH movements over time rather than define them (or the field in general); I have also done so in an attempt to capture key points of internal reckoning, much in the way that other waves of critical theory (feminist, Marxist, etc.) each emerge in response to the one that directly precedes it. My particular framing of DH in waves diverges from a few similar histories of the field in different ways. For instance, in their *Digital Humanities Manifesto,* Schnapp and Presner argue that "the first wave of digital humanities work was quantitative, mobilizing the search and retrieval powers of the database, automating corpus linguistics, stacking hypercards into critical arrays. The second wave is qualitative, interpretive, experiential, emotive, generative in character. It harnesses digital toolkits in the service of the Humanities' core methodological strengths: attention to complexity, medium specificity, historical context, analytical depth, critique and interpretation" (2). However, my experiences have demonstrated a distinct programmatic lack of qualitative emphasis in DH work. On the other hand, Berry characterizes the first wave of DH as one focused on infrastructure, the second wave as one focused on born-digital materials, and suggests the usefulness of a third wave of DH work "concentrated around the underlying *computationality* of the forms held within a computational medium" ("Introduction," 4; emphasis original). While I agree with Berry that there is much fodder for research in a theoretical framework for DH as a field, I disagree that theory is an ultimately useful end in and of itself.

4. Along these lines, in "Data Modeling" Flanders and Jannidis summarize DH's current treatment of the process of inquiry, stating that currently "in digital humanities there seems to be a general understanding that a data model is, like all models, an interpretation of an object, either in real life or in the digital realm. Similarly, most assume that data modeling is primarily a constructive and creative process and that the functions of the digital surrogate determine what aspects have to be modeled" (234).

5. Relatedly, in chapter 25 in this volume, Gorman argues in his contribution to "A Tale of Three Disciplines: Considering the (Digital) Future of the Mid-Doc Fellowship in Graduate Programs" not for mandatory digital history training for graduate students but "for digital history to become a standard (but not mandatory) MA/PhD major concentration and minor field in every history graduate program. Instead of classifying DH only as an elective or even a hobby, departments should provide institutional support for the teaching and practice of DH as a historical specialty. Departments should dedicate the

same resources to DH as to venerable subfields such as public history and documentary text editing."

6. In their contribution to this volume (see chapter 27, "Soft Skills in Hard Places, or Is the Digital Future of Graduate Study in the Humanities outside of the University?"), Edmond et al. illustrate that the moment could not be better for the type of intervention DH scholars are prepared to make, particularly in Europe. They cite a 2018 skills report from the European Council for Doctoral Candidates and Junior Researchers that emphasizes the value of graduate students' " 'cognitive' skills of abstraction and creativity; critical thinking; and analysis and synthesis, as well as the 'research' skills that included interdisciplinarity; open access publishing; and open data management (ibid, 4–5), all of which are central to DH scholarly practice as well." The authors state that "this movement from an implicit definition of transferable digital skills to a more explicit one shows not only an increased recognition of their place within society but also of their place within academe as a whole—and not just for the 'digital' scholar."

Bibliography

Berry, David M., ed. "Introduction." In *Understanding Digital Humanities,* edited by David M. Berry, 1–20. Basingstoke, Hampshire: Palgrave Macmillan, 2012.

Boyles, Christina et al. "Precarious Labor and the Digital Humanities." *American Quarterly* 70, no. 3 (2018): 693–700. https://doi.org/10.1353/aq.2018.0054.

Flanders, Julia, and Fotis Jannidis. "Data Modeling." In *A New Companion to Digital Humanities,* edited by Susan Schreibman, Ray Siemens, and John Unsworth, 229–37. West Sussex, UK: Wiley Blackwell, 2015.

Schnapp, Jeffrey, and Todd Presner. "Digital Humanities Manifesto 2.0." Humanities Blast. Accessed November 19, 2020. http://www.humanitiesblast.com/manifesto/Manifesto _V2.pdf.

PART IV

FORUM ON GRADUATE PATHWAYS

Rewriting Graduate Digital Futures through Mentorship and Multi-institutional Support

OLIVIA QUINTANILLA AND JEANELLE HORCASITAS

As two first-generation university graduates and women of color, we knew navigating our doctoral programs meant using the self-starter mentality we had ever since we stepped into the academy. As we moved from two-year public community colleges (CC) to the four-year California State University (CSU) and University of California (UC) public university systems, we recognized the importance of creating our mentor networks and pursuing and creating opportunities to help us develop digital humanities (DH) skills. We also knew that student success is more likely when multi-institutional support is at play. We reimagined success as graduate students by reformulating the personal and professional growth we sought to achieve beyond the dissertation. As graduate students at UC San Diego, a large public research university, our departments prioritized research-related productivity and discouraged outside interests such as DH in favor of completing the degree by university-required timelines. The pressure to graduate, combined with our alternative plan to gain as much additional training and professional development as possible while part of the UC network, sparked a fire within us to work creatively, critically, and collectively to redesign the (graduate) futures we envisioned for ourselves.

This chapter argues that mentorship and multi-institutional support are necessary for rewriting the graduate digital futures we hope to see. We draw from our experiences developing alternative curricula in addition to our research, teaching, and other job duties; these activities provided us with the tools to learn DH, network with other digital humanists, and share these skills as scholars, educators, and professionals. We discuss how we established an inclusive environment to learn DH skills through multi-institutional support, which we define as collaborations across research universities, state universities, community colleges, and educational organizations. In our case, we worked at the intersections of UC-wide partnerships: UC San Diego, the San Diego Community College District (SDCCD), and San Diego State University.

The future of graduate education we hope to see looks like the recent Integrated Internship Initiative, a partnership with SDCCD and the UC San Diego Division of Arts and Humanities that funds three PhD humanities fellows' professional development through SDCCD and UC San Diego mentorship to support CC and academic administration career exploration. The Division of Arts and Humanities, in partnership with SDCCD, also created the Digital Technology for Collaborative Innovation workshop series, an example of educational institutions working together to promote digital humanities skill development as professional development for UC and CC students, faculty, and staff. These programs effectively inspire underrepresented students to integrate DH and multi-institutional collaborations into their academic journey.

Although the Integrated Internship Initiative is an excellent model for how educational institutions can facilitate funded professional development for graduate students to diversify career options, this initiative only recently launched in 2019 and was unavailable when we were graduate students. We had to act as liaisons across different UC programs and multiple institutions to gain a similar experience to the one the Division of Arts and Humanities is now offering. We worked hard to acquire DH training and establish strong relationships with mentors to pursue diversified career options and CC employment to supplement our department's doctoral program. Still, our DH journey was under the radar and underfunded. The extra work we did to incorporate DH into our graduate training was integral to our development as students, scholars, mentors, and professionals. In hindsight, we wish the opportunities we secured had been formalized options available to all students and supported by our departments, both with funding and encouragement. To follow is a discussion of the professionalization programs and mentoring opportunities we created or sought out to develop a foundation in DH that enhanced our work as researchers, scholars, and instructors, with a particular focus on how our experiences as first-generation women of color in the academy intersected with how we navigated both learning and practicing DH across multiple institutions.

Our approach to DH is intersectional; it often challenges the digital tools themselves and the dominant groups using and writing about them while paying particular attention to who does or does not have access to such resources. Moya Bailey's seminal essay "All the Digital Humanists Are White, All the Nerds Are Men, But Some of Us Are Brave" urged a burgeoning digital humanities field to inform its theory and practice by addressing and including intersectional identities. As Bailey explains, "By centering the lives of women, people of color, and disabled folks, the types of possible conversations in digital humanities shift" (9).

Issues of intersectionality continue to be discussed, such as in the collection of essays in *Bodies of Information: Intersectional Feminism and Digital Humanities*. This work reveals that despite the growing interest and scholarship in digital humanities, representation from women, people of color, and historically underrepresented people is still severely lacking. In the introduction, the editors Jacqueline

Wernimont and Elizabeth Losh reflect upon the 2016 *Los Angeles Review of Books* critique of digital humanities initiatives as neoliberal tools used as a "means for serving the ends of cultural conservatism and political reaction within increasingly corporatized universities and colleges" (2). This critique suggests a "techno-utopianism of digital humanities" that focuses primarily on the "repeating different versions of the solo white male inventor" and excludes "women and people of color as digital humanities innovators" (3). In *Data Feminism,* Catherine D'Ignazio and Lauren Klein "insist on intersectionality" because, as they argue, "Feminism has always been multivocal and multiracial, but the movements' diverse voices have not always been valued equally" (215). The authors attribute their intersectional framing to the work of activists and scholars, particularly Black feminists, who over the past forty years have insisted "on a feminism that is intersectional, meaning it looks to issues of social power related not just to gender, but also to race, class, ability, sexuality, immigrant status and more" (216). These critiques and considerations deeply resonated with us throughout our academic journey. Applying an intersectional feminist lens has shaped the creative ways we pursue digital humanities scholarship and projects that engage our wider communities.

As ethnic studies and literary scholars, we were intrigued by DH as a resource for empowering ourselves and our students to tell their stories in multifaceted ways that contributed new perspectives to the traditional curriculum we studied. Inspired by speculative fiction, world-making, and design-thinking, we perceive DH as providing what we call "speculative tools of knowledge" that serve historically underrepresented communities, especially people of color, with alternative ways of learning, being active knowledge creators, and transforming the society through activism and social justice with digital media. Practicing speculative tools of knowledge in the classroom insists on teaching students how to consider context, a process that D'Ignazio and Klein describe as "understanding the provenance and environment from which the data was collected, as well as working hard to reframe context in data communication"; practicing speculative tools of knowledge in the classroom also engages questions like "whose knowledge about an issue has been subjugated, and how might we begin to recuperate it?" (*Data Feminism,* 172). We argue that these speculative tools of knowledge are best used in practice, particularly in ways that speak to marginalized communities' lived experiences, histories, stories, and socioeconomic conditions.

Digital humanities as a speculative tool of knowledge has encouraged us to center our histories and stories within the dominant narratives of academia. As educators, our work to bring these tools and ideas into the classroom empowers our students to envision themselves as future scholars, world makers, and changemakers. Arguing for the importance of intersectionality in such endeavors, Roopika Risam proposes that it provides "a viable approach to cultural criticism in digital humanities, enabling us to write alternate histories of the field that transcend simplistic 'hack' vs. 'yack' binaries" ("Beyond the Margins," 16). Thus, rewriting these digital futures, histories, and stories is only possible when intersectionality is accepted in the broader academic conversation and field.[1] Moreover, scholars such as Amy E. Earhart explain that it is essential to "center the human experience" and specifically "rethink our working partnership with historically marginalized communities." Earhart further states it is important to recognize historically marginalized communities "stripped of control of their materials over centuries, sometimes by the very institutions that are our employers." The reality is, according to Earhart, that "structures of academia are built on the exploitation of particular groups" ("Can We Trust the University?," para. 12, 18). Because we are part of the small percentage of women of color in the university, we hope to rewrite and reclaim the narrative for ourselves and other historically underrepresented communities. Thus, our positionality as CC alumni and adjunct professors constantly reaffirms our commitment to implementing an intersectional feminism lens into the DH work and pedagogy we use in the classroom, and CC classrooms in particular, as a way to revitalize hidden histories and rethink possibilities for the future.

In one example, we implemented DH in our CC courses by teaching students how to build a digital companion to their final essays on the platform Scalar, a free and open-source authoring platform that allows for multimodal formats such as text video, images, and annotation. This assignment aimed to give students the tools for undertaking basic web design, curating each page with the most impactful and concise information, and complementing the text with relevant media. This example is a compelling illustration of how DH as a speculative tool of knowledge empowered students to be intentional about the narratives they wanted to tell and allowed them to engage creatively with others in an interactive digital space.

Unfortunately, for adjunct professors to integrate this Scalar assignment into the course required additional unpaid labor, resources, and time. Teaching a new platform to students meant making space during class and during and beyond office hours to troubleshoot technical questions. Even though this initiative was fruitful, it often left us feeling burnt out to ensure everyone received the mentoring and training needed. Our expertise in DH and Scalar in particular resulted from our active engagement in online tutorials and occasional DH workshops on campus at UC San Diego, voluntary commitments we made that took away from our doctoral research.

Digital humanities at UC San Diego did not gain momentum until 2014. A Digital Humanities Research Group (DHRG) was created through collaborative efforts with library staff and graduate students, with DH-specific workshops, programs, and community-building activities. These efforts, however, were not supported with funding, and much of the labor required to run the group was unpaid. It was not until 2016 that a digital scholarship librarian was hired. The business need was proven to the university that a full-time staff member was necessary to become more formalized and consistent in its DH goals. Our experiences serving as chairs and committee members for the graduate student association and other institutions that supported DH work helped us identify other internal and external funding sources and help grow our group's membership.

During the first years of the DHRG's existence, we submitted a monthly funding request to the graduate student association to fund coffee and snacks to engage more people across campus. Once funding was approved, we still had to purchase the snacks and coffee with our funds and then get reimbursed afterward. Additional work also fell to us, such as submitting orders, picking up orders, and transporting items to the meeting, all of which were unpaid labor and required us to personally cover some additional costs. This was not a sustainable model, especially for low-income graduate students like ourselves. On the other hand, we significantly enhanced our DH skills, knowledge, and networks. We also learned valuable budgeting and event-organizing skills and earned project management expertise. Although the experience gained in this role was practical for skill-building and networking, the labor and time were taken away from our research and teaching responsibilities.

Much of the work of sustaining the DHRG fell on the digital scholarship librarian, which was difficult because this person also needed to focus on establishing the academic aspects of DH at our institution. Their labor was not consistently recognized either. As Risam and Susan Edwards explain, DH projects and scholarship produced by librarians and students are not always recognized, primarily because of the perception that librarians are "in service" rather than collaborators with other scholars ("Transforming the Landscape," 6–7). As a result, librarians may not be considered DH "experts" compared to faculty who work on these projects, even if the librarians are active collaborators. Moreover, Lisa Brundage, Karen Gregory, and Emily Sherwood explain that despite all this expertise, when one provides some sort of "affective and support labor, the more invisible the effort becomes" ("Working Nine to Five," para. 15). As a result, this perspective becomes the antithesis of the digital humanities to make "scholarship in the humanities more open and public" ("Working Nine to Five," para. 15). Unfortunately, when we left the DHRG to concentrate on finishing our dissertations, the group became less active. In 2020, the digital scholarship librarian left her position with UC San Diego, and as a result, the group lost much of the momentum and community we tried to build over the years. The DHRG was essential in bringing scattered offices, students, staff, and faculty together in a meaningful way to establish some DH community and presence on campus. This example illustrates the immense loss when DH initiatives such as this one are inadequately resourced or supported and shows that despite the great successes of the group, much of the responsibility and labor (and some of the financial support) fell to the graduate students themselves.

In 2019, we participated in a new UC-comprehensive initiative called Humanities Careers in Science History, Policy, and Communication (H-SCHIP). This year-long career development program was created by a group of graduate students at UC Riverside and funded by the UC Humanities Research Institute (UCHRI) to support graduate students interested in developing skills in public pedagogy and DH. Workshops occurred virtually and in person, and when Covid-19 hit, everything was moved online without much disruption. As program organizers, we were in a position to craft our dream DH training program by listening to what the fifteen participants wanted to learn most according to their career aspirations and what they were missing from their home institutions. This model was innovative in that participants did not begin a predesigned program but participated in its cocreation. We reached out to our mentor networks inside and outside academia who could offer DH training to enhance our capacity to tell our dissertation stories in innovative formats and explore DH career possibilities. We created workshops on geographic information systems (GIS) and story maps, coding, text mining, museum exhibition planning through a decolonial lens, open publishing platforms, and more. Additionally, H-SCHIP leveraged our existing UC, CSU, and CC mentor networks to design DH professional development programming for graduate students across the UC system and introduced us to a dozen new mentors who offered their expertise and continued support after the program ended.

Another program we participated in over several years was Humanists@Work (HumWork), a graduate career initiative created by the UCHRI to facilitate graduate student-led initiatives to build the structures and communities necessary to allow PhD students in the humanities and social sciences to feel valued as professionals with diverse career opportunities. HumWork organized biannual workshops that rotated throughout California and fostered a community of doctoral students who shared similar fears and hopes about the transferability of their PhD to nonacademic opportunities, as well as DH-related professional development interests. HumWork paid for travel, food, and accommodations so that we felt treated as professionals rather than students, and the amount was more than for travel grants we typically received from UC San Diego. In our experience as graduate students, when receiving travel grants or funding awards, we had to pay the costs of travel up front (usually on credit cards) and then wait weeks, sometimes even three to eight months, to get repaid. While waiting to be reimbursed, we had to take on additional student loans, accrued interest on our credit cards, and sent weekly emails to administrators to remind them about our repayment. This common reimbursement game created additional stress and feelings of shame stemming from a perception that we were harassing administrators to get repaid on top of managing our regular graduate work.

The HumWork organizers at UCHRI created an important model for supporting graduate student professionalization by creating a budget that prioritized paying stipends for graduate advisory committee members and paying travel grant recipients up front. This approach might not seem like a significant intervention for some, but for us, as low-income, first-generation students and early career researchers, it was a game changer. Without their intentional support model, we would have been unable to attend the workshops and join a community of peers who proved to be so transformational in our journeys. The HumWork workshops brought speakers to teach us about the value of learning digital tools and seeking professionalization training while we completed our degrees. HumWork facilitated our engagement with a peer and professional mentor network that helped us reimagine our potential as scholars and humanists by honoring our interests in pursuing DH training *as* professional development. We served as graduate advisory members for HumWork and brought our newfound DH empowerment to UC San Diego to support our peers.

One final challenge we faced in our DH journey that we want to share is the difficulty of identifying DH mentors, on top of existing struggles to find supportive faculty mentors to champion our evolving career interests. We struggled with imposter syndrome due to being the first in our families to attend college, combined with our shared determination to learn digital skills and pursue careers outside of academia. We stressed about conversations with our mentors because no one discussed digital humanities training, tools, or benefits; moreover, no one was talking about careers outside of a tenure-track position, and graduation requirements, research, and extracurricular campus activities were squeezed into the six-year normative time-to-degree time frame. Serious conversations about mentorship for underrepresented graduate students focused solely on faculty helping students complete their degrees on time according to the institution's expected deadlines. As first-generation women of color, we were regularly asked to volunteer for tasks such as sharing our "diversity" experiences and providing first-gen advice on panels for other students, making recommendations to university administrators through focus groups, meeting and recruiting prospective graduate students, and mentoring undergraduates. With our many professional development interests and our investments in supporting students like ourselves, we realized the normative timeline was not made for graduate students of color and certainly not for those taking advantage of professional growth opportunities or invested in supporting the campus community through diversity labor. We realized that seeking out mentors and a community who could affirm the value of our DH interests and our diverse career interests would be vital in completing our degrees "on time." Our experience suggests that academia, in general, and digital humanities, in particular, do not provide adequate opportunities and pathways for DH mentorship for students of color. The DH programs and mentor networks we became a part of helped us fight through and grow beyond imposter syndrome.

We want our experiences to inform future conversations about graduate programming and budget decisions that will prioritize support for expanded understandings of what graduate student work can be when enhanced by digital tools and digital culture and for ways that graduate work can be transferred outside our programs and beyond the academy. With DH as a speculative tool of knowledge creation and exploration, graduate students from historically underrepresented backgrounds like ours can be empowered to write and share their stories in new ways. They can also serve as the mentors needed to effect actual change in our institutions, especially for those in the most vulnerable categories such as adjuncts who are underpaid and overworked, community college students without access to adequate technological tools or financial support to purchase those tools, and graduate students who are too often forced to choose between focusing solely on their research and exploring other career paths. By committing to multi-institutional partnerships and collaborations that can support existing DH initiatives and programs, as well as those yet to be conceived, graduate digital futures can be rewritten and reimagined in transformative ways that value labor and inclusivity for generations to come.

Note

1. Because intersectionality has not always been recognized as a method within DH, alternatives such as #transformDH have emerged. Risam also argues that this work has been ongoing for some time, even though it has been unrecognized: she points out that women of color, particularly Black women Afrofuturist scholars, were conducting digital humanities research during the 1990s, many years before DH became legitimized in the academy ("Beyond the Margins," 19).

Bibliography

Bailey, Moya Z. "All the Digital Humanists Are White, All the Nerds Are Men, but Some of Us Are Brave." In *Intersectionality in Digital Humanities,* edited by Barbara Bordalejo and Roopika Risam, 9–11. York, UK: Arc Humanities Press, 2019.

Brundage, Lisa, Karen Gregory, and Emily Sherwood. "Working Nine to Five: What a Way to Make an Academic Living?" In *Bodies of Information: Intersectional Feminism and Digital Humanities,* edited by Elizabeth Losh and Jacqueline Wernimont. Minneapolis: University of Minnesota Press, 2018.

Davis, Dannielle. "Mentorship and the Socialization of Underrepresented Minorities into the Professoriate: Examining Varied Influences." *Mentoring & Tutoring: Partnership in Learning.* 16, no. 3 (2008): 278–93.

D'Ignazio, Catherine, and Lauren F. Klein. *Data Feminism.* Cambridge, Mass.: The MIT Press, 2020.

Earhart, Amy E. "Can We Trust the University? Digital Humanities Collaborations with Historically Exploited Cultural Communities." In *Bodies of Information: Intersectional Feminism and the Digital Humanities,* edited by Jacqueline Wernimont and Elizabeth Losh. Minneapolis: University of Minnesota Press, 2018.

Risam, Roopika. "Beyond the Margins: Intersectionality and Digital Humanities." In *Intersectionality in Digital Humanities,* edited by Barbara Bordalejo and Roopika Risam, 13–33. York, UK: Arc Humanities Press, 2019.

Risam, Roopika, and Susan Edwards. "Transforming the Landscape of Labor at Universities through Digital Humanities." In *Digital Humanities, Libraries, and Partnerships:*

A Critical Examination of Labor, Networks, and Community, edited by Kate Joranson and Robin Kear, 3–17. Cambridge, Mass.: Elsevier Science, 2018.

Wernimont, Jacqueline, and Elizabeth Losh. "Introduction." In *Bodies of Information: Intersectional Feminism and the Digital Humanities,* edited by Jacqueline Wernimont and Elizabeth Losh. Minneapolis: University of Minnesota Press, 2018.

The Problem of Intradisciplinarity

SEAN WEIDMAN

Alison Booth and Miriam Posner open the introduction to their Varieties of DH *PMLA* special issue by pondering the locations—discursive, geographic, ideological—of the digital humanities: "It seems inappropriate to call this a burgeoning or nascent field, still less a hot new thing [. . .] yet these clichés feel inescapable as one attempts to describe a field that has yet to coalesce around a set of methods or assumptions" ("Introduction," 9). As their prefatory remarks frame so thoroughly, even admitting its critical parameters are nebulous by design, or that its failure of totalizing definition is partly its benefit, the "digital humanities" is a tremendously messy container that still does not travel all that well, especially among U.S. English departments.[1]

Because this collection has invited us to think about (and through) such travel and its pathways of graduate work in the digital humanities, I want to address an obstacle along the route: in certain circumstances, the debate about DH's definition and its efficacy as a discipline has ended up leveraged against English graduate study in the digital humanities. In U.S. English departments (and, indeed, in many other humanities disciplines in large PhD-granting research institutions), graduate students invested even nominally in digital methods are suspended regularly within the institutional and departmental politics that follow from DH's disciplinary indeterminacy.[2] More specifically, graduate students in English studies who work in DH but attend institutions lacking explicit social infrastructure for DH (e.g., centers, faculty lines, training programs, research support, and funding) may still find themselves caught up in the emergence of the field's intradisciplinarity, in its somehow-still-alienness among long-since accepted approaches in the humanities, particularly in departments that have resisted, or that have been late to adopt, digital approaches to humanistic study. Among other forms of accepted critical work in U.S. English departments, like those organized by period, theory, geography, identity, or various other cultural, social, or political angles of critique and its legacies, DH stands academically in between, with a disciplinary status that varies from university to university and department to department. I aim to point out the effect this inconsistency can have on graduate student futures in U.S. English departments.

Whether the question is of its novelty, its critical value, its sustainable relevance, its masquerade as humanist inquiry, its disguised history of surveillance capitalism and public data accumulation, its complicity in administrative neoliberalization, or its role in American universities' ballooning corporatism, many decision-making faculty and administrators within the humanities seem incredulous of (or at least conflicted about) DH as a discipline and thus as an institutionalizable realm of graduate work.[3] And, to be fair, just as these anxieties have compelling counterarguments, most of them also have merit. The oft-latent forces and investments that legitimize critical areas and modes of study in English have, in close to equal measure, valorized and villainized the digital humanities as both area and mode, so I want to first clarify that I do not mean to claim falsely some sort of critical oppression. The institutional horror stories and embittered denials of feminist critique, queer theory, and critical race studies (and the poststructuralism that preceded them) prove there are far more insidious forms of gatekeeping in U.S. higher education. Resistance to the codification of these approaches shares an oppressive politics of inaccess and inequity, and the stakes of DH's contest for wider disciplinary legitimation are neither of the same degree nor, perhaps, even of the same kind. In some cases, however, it does have similar effects, and despite the volume of critical accounts that assess the split between adopters and nonadopters of DH in U.S. English departments, DH's influence on the everyday politics of English *graduate* study in the U.S. has never been fully addressed.[4]

Let me offer a broad example, which I think many DH graduate students, but especially those unattached to mainstream DH programs, will find familiar. I am a recent PhD graduate in English from a public R1 university that does not explicitly boast a dedicated DH contingent. The English department has an association with a university humanistic research center (which is often DH adjacent), and we have had tremendous digital scholarship librarians; however, we also have departmental faculty deeply suspicious of the rise of DH in humanities departments generally (again, not without good reason). The result of this seesaw of DH support is that to those outside the broad fields of the digital humanities, which in my case included at least a dissertation director, a director of graduate studies, a department head, teaching faculty, and myriad nonspecialist committees and their members, I sometimes dabbled in "the digital humanities," a hazy side-interest that had no real bearing on my graduate work or eventual degree. Drop me around other digital humanists, however, or in the middle of a DH conference, or the Digital Humanities Summer Institute, or any other established arena of DH study and community, and I suddenly work with (among other things) various kinds of computational formalism and digital literary study to explore the styles of twentieth-century literature. To amend the title of Ted Underwood's hopeful state-of-the-field writeup from 2019,

this is "[still only] Digital Humanities as a Semi-Normal Thing" ("Digital Humanities as a Semi-Normal Thing," 96).

After years of conversations with English faculty across the DH spectrum,
I am no longer convinced the above disparity between non-DH and DH scholars
is merely English studies' habitual differentiation of in-group versus out-group, in-
specialty versus out-of-specialty. Whereas the latter's supportive stance acknowledges the already institutionalized, methodological nuance of a field that captures
a certain kind of epistemic authority, more often than not the vague gesturing of
the former is a shoulder shrug toward a nonentity, or, at least, a distinctly foreign,
distinctly non-English research practice. Among U.S. English colleagues and mentors outside of DH and its longstanding institutions, we often simply do "DH" and
so, too, are often simply "DH people." But to those outside of other primary areas
of English studies, for instance—which might entail, for the sake of argument,
early American racial politics, affect, and nineteenth-century settler colonialism—
one often simply does, well, early American racial politics, affect, and nineteenth-
century settler colonialism. The same terminal definitions rarely apply. Although
departmental quirks abound, that institutionalized split between the digitals and
the antidigitals does not seem to exist, or does not exist in the same way, for any
other methodology currently taught in English studies. To be sure, the pro- versus
anti-DH dynamics in some U.S. English departments are particularly strong, and
perhaps few of those experiences apply globally. For those in non-Anglophone or
non-English departments, and especially those studying non-English topics, languages, or contexts, these sorts of administrative and institutional marginalizations
may be doubly familiar. But this limitation of the culture of English studies, or of
what Jacob Richter and Hannah Taylor term in chapter 28 in this volume the discipline's "rhetorical infrastructure," seems to me a significant and often unremarked
difference in the normal social politics of U.S. English departments and their graduate students' professionalization.

After all, laying claim to digital expertise in the humanities can earn the indif-
ference, disinterest, or suspicion of both nondigital and antidigital scholars, a refusal
of critical relevance that digital humanists have normalized in service of playing well
with others. However, in U.S. English programs without specific DH alliances—and,
for me, this is key—the resulting political negotiation (whether departmental, institutional, or disciplinary) often falls squarely and solely upon affected graduate students. Intellectual delineations quickly turn into time-intensive social labors, and
we must always be wary of hidden lines in the sociocritical sand as we pursue our
trendy form of scholarship. As we navigate the administrative contours of earning
an advanced degree, we are also tasked with differentiating the techno-utopian faculty from the mere DH friendlies, the digital nonnatives from the anti-DH scholars, the nondigital media historians from the antidigital media theorists, and on and
on. So polarizing are these splits, in fact, that they introduce their own functional

limitations for graduate work. Opposing views do not generally play well together on our committees, at our organized talks, and in other arenas of our academic training, all of which may require different sorts of approval from those on one side of the DH debate or the other. A project might seem too digital to one and not digital enough to another; a chapter might convincingly deploy computational methods for one but incompatibly for another; a syllabus may look too DH-y or not DH-y enough; and an invited speaker may be too focused on DH's critique or highlight too limitedly its benefit. In departments with no dedicated DH faculty or in-house DH institute, both of which tend to demand an alignment with certain (digitally receptive) scholarly politics, DH-adjacent graduate students must tiptoe carefully, lest our intellectual choices offend or irritate or—worse—foreclose professional futures. As scholars, the ways we are legible to nondigital faculty, mentors, and advisors are also generally nondigital, and the many benefits of joining the digital with the humanities are dismissed when DH, as an investment of our time and critical labors, is weighed always against traditional English graduate training. Collaborate, but not too much; pursue digital skills, but not too many; contribute to digital projects, but not too often. The ideal academic balance looks different at each non-DH English department and program in the United States, but too many seem to agree that the game is zero-sum—that, at some point or another, these scholars-in-training must prove that their forms of scholarship and academic work can look traditional, recognizable, and like they are supposed to.

As a manner of disciplinary reduction, the "DH person" shorthand certainly is not helped by DH's vast critical boundary lines, as Booth and Posner note ("Introduction," 9). But what I want to make clear is that this lax moniker is not always (or ever just) the innocent unfamiliarity or willful naiveté of nonexpertise. It is indicative of erasures of insight, of specialty, and for U.S. English graduate students in particular, of other sorts of mastery-in-training. Once we set foot across the DH fence line, in some ways we can no longer step back over. Our realm of study solidifies, and we cease to be students of anything else. In that moment where our varieties of thinking are presumed and thus concretized, to the DH skeptic, we no longer look like students at all, just looming specters of things most feared: pawns of stagnant thinking; empirical conquerors of nuance; practitioners of misapplied and ill-understood methodologies; a clique of neoliberal quants; apprentices to an invading, corporatizing order; and actors complicit in the ends of a whole discipline.

In the context of DH's intradisciplinary limits at non-DH US institutions, I do not think we fully grasp the effects our crisis-laden moment is having on the intersecting futures of DH and English studies. Under normal circumstances, this oppositional dialectic may have fallen under the umbrella of routine critical squabble. Yet even bearing in mind our discipline's long reliance on the normalcy of crisis, as Travis Bartley stresses in chapter 4 in this volume, these are not normal circumstances. Allying with one side over another, or, as I am suggesting, merely appearing to hold

certain alliances over others, garners many bad-faith assumptions, and U.S. graduate students will find themselves squarely in the fray. Our easy disciplinary stereo-
typing has specific effects for humanities graduate students, as scholars who (lest we
go a day without a reminder) have already chosen fading disciplines, who confront
exponential professional precarity, who face historically depressed markets, who in
the wake of a global pandemic have undergone imminent hiring freezes and search
interruptions, who look toward professional futures under indefinite suspension,
and who enter a realm of market logic that is much worse than usual, and which
was already the worst it had ever been.

Just as these near-constant, proliferating stresses of uncertainty affect graduate
student teaching and research output (directions, topics, load, and pace), so too do
they affect the ways we present, are taught to present, and are asked to present ourselves as scholars. This self-cultivation manifests most commonly in the ways our
job-market preparation, training, and advice demands that we circulate (or do not)
our scholarly likenesses, and there seem to be no shared best practices for applicants
or hiring committees. If, to the non- or anti-DH disciplinary vanguard in many U.S.
English departments, I simply "do DH" and thus am always already (and only) a
"DH person," then what, exactly, do I look like in a job market that variously tight-
ens and expands its desired candidate profiles, in a field that cannot decide whether
or not what I do is worth institutionalizing?

I am really after two claims here: first, that there is an uncareful and unhelpful
confluence of DH methodologies, fields, and scholarly identities; and second, that
this quirk is not really a quirk at all but a disciplinary feature that has turned into a
very real mechanism of power wielded (in U.S. English departments, at least) for the
purposes of disciplinary gatekeeping and which requires regular, unpaid emotional
and social labor from its already thinly stretched graduate students. In some departments, what this boils down to is the handwashing of entire subfields of humanistic
inquiry and English study, simply because that study is taking place through digital approaches that may not *really* belong. And one result of that broad uncare is a
totalizing reduction of scholarly nuance that renders, deliberately, an overly generalized conception of DH as a singular, enigmatic, possibly malevolent entity. In doing
so, U.S. faculty and administrators tend to reify the issue, imagining the place of
this "DH" in the future study of English in unhelpful and vague ways, or not at all.

Of course, it does seem easy to point to a *PMLA* special issue, a university-
backed journal, a new research center, a longstanding national fellowship, or an
internationally renowned graduate program and say, "Relax, DH is here to stay."
What else could "making it" even look like for a subdiscipline of the humanities? If
a humanities student finds he or she wants to study digital methods, why not choose
a program dedicated to such things? Is DH's absence from only certain programs,
departments, or university administrations really all that different than any other
field of study in the humanities? Do all research areas not foster specific departmental alliances, institutional densities, and disciplinary limitations? Does an essay

on the poetics of twentieth-century Caribbean literature not face the same hurdles (or more) to publication and circulation as a DH piece on twentieth-century poetic style? As far as disciplinary gatekeeping is concerned, DH does not exactly have it bad, and as U.S. English students with theoretical access to much deeper networks of funding than our peers, perhaps neither do we (Allington et al., "Neoliberal Tools").

Regardless of the public recognition of our discipline, in non-DH-heavy U.S. English departments, the authorization of both our scholarship and our status as scholars is still up in the air. It is a fact truer still in programs with a high density of faculty (or faculty-in-power) resistant to the sanction of DH as a subdiscipline of English studies, faculty who help determine, for many of the same graduate students, the uneven territories of funding, mentorship, assistantships, teaching assignments, time to degree, and other types of institutional access and support. These alone can represent serious, forgotten, often hidden material effects on graduate students' lives and professional futures, and so too on disciplinary health. So if we are thinking through DH's disciplinary thoroughfares, we should not ignore the dissonant limbo of its intradisciplinarity; it marks an ideological roadblock to which we have long given a wide berth but which at some point may need clearing.

Notes

1. This difficulty is at least one reason that the self-termed academic amphibian Ted Underwood, in his essay in chapter 29 in this volume, "The Life Aquatic: Training Digital Humanists in a School of Information Science," wonders whether the location of the digital humanities should be one shared among humanities and information science departments.

2. Although I cannot address firsthand non-English graduate work, this DH dynamic seems to extend beyond English departments and into other humanities graduate programs; Erin Francisco Opalich et al. attest to this elegantly in their multiperspective writeup in chapter 25 of this collection, "A Tale of Three Disciplines: Considering the (Digital) Future of the Mid-doc Fellowship in Graduate Programs."

3. I list here only the most regular of the DH critiques that circulate among humanities scholars, and though each has many proponents/opponents, here are some of the most popular: The concern about the novelty of the digital is one of Da's best defended claims in "The Computational Case against Computational Literary Studies"; Fish's "Mind Your P's and B's" remains a classic example of DH critique that wonders about the critical value of its methods; the shallow trendiness of DH disciplines, meanwhile, is tracked by Brennan's "Digital-Humanities Bust," which lays out a view opposed by Hunter's "Digital Humanities and 'Critical Theory'"; Golumbia's "Death of a Discipline" attests skeptically to DH's non-humanist contours, whereas Witmore's essay on Latour and the Digital Humanities offers an equally impressive retort; Mangrum wonders about DH's role in data exploitation; both Allington et al. and Kopec investigate DH's "Neoliberal Tools" and the history of its stranglehold on corporatizing university administrations; and Greenspan's "Scandal of Digital Humanities" can be read in response to those lines of thinking.

4. As far as I can tell, until the publication in this volume, there were two notable exceptions: the first is Cordell's "How Not to Teach," which addresses several of the ways the constant self-evaluation and redefinition of DH, as both term and field, produces graduate student resistance to "DH *qua* DH"; the second is Mann's "Paid to Do," which contests (among other things) the tendency of faculty-led DH projects to frame graduate student involvement as collaborative learning rather than as the unpaid labor it tends to be.

Bibliography

Allington, Daniel, Sarah Brouillette, and David Golumbia. "Neoliberal Tools (and Archives): A Political History of Digital Humanities." *Los Angeles Review of Books,* May 1, 2016. https://lareviewofbooks.org/article/neoliberal-tools-archives-political-history-digital-humanities/.

Booth, Alison, and Miriam Posner. "Introduction: The Materials at Hand." *PMLA* 135, no. 1 (2020): 9–22.

Brennan, Timothy. "The Digital-Humanities Bust: After a Decade of Investment and Hype, What Has the Field Accomplished? Not Much." *Chronicle of Higher Education,* October 15, 2017. https://www.chronicle.com/article/the-digital-humanities-bust/.

Cordell, Ryan. "How Not to Teach Digital Humanities." In *Debates in the Digital Humanities 2016,* edited by Matthew K. Gold and Lauren F. Klein. Minneapolis: University of Minnesota Press, 2016. https://dhdebates.gc.cuny.edu/read/untitled/section/31326090-9c70-4c0a-b2b7-74361582977e.

Da, Nan Z. "The Computational Case against Computational Literary Studies." *Critical Inquiry* 45, no. 3 (2019): 601–39.

Fish, Stanley. "Mind Your P's and B's: The Digital Humanities and Interpretation." *New York Times,* January 23, 2012. https://archive.nytimes.com/opinionator.blogs.nytimes.com/2012/01/23/mind-your-ps-and-bs-the-digital-humanities-and-interpretation/

Golumbia, David. "Death of a Discipline." *differences* 25, no. 1 (2014): 156–76.

Greenspan, Brian. "The Scandal of Digital Humanities." In *Debates in the Digital Humanities 2019,* edited by Matthew K. Gold and Lauren F. Klein, 92–95. Minneapolis: University of Minnesota Press, 2019.

Hunter, John. "The Digital Humanities and 'Critical Theory': An Institutional Cautionary Tale." In *Debates in the Digital Humanities 2019,* edited by Matthew K. Gold and Lauren F. Klein, 188–94. Minneapolis: University of Minnesota Press, 2019.

Kopec, Andrew. "The Digital Humanities, Inc.: Literary Criticism and the Fate of a Profession." *PMLA* 131, no. 2 (2016): 324–39.

Mangrum, Benjamin. "Aggregation, Public Criticism, and the History of Reading Big Data." *PMLA* 133, no. 5 (2018): 1207–24.

Mann, Rachel. "Paid to Do but Not to Think: Reevaluating the Role of Graduate Student Collaborators." In *Debates in the Digital Humanities 2019,* edited by Matthew K. Gold and Lauren F. Klein, 268–78. Minneapolis: University of Minnesota Press, 2019.

Underwood, Ted. "Digital Humanities as a Semi-Normal Thing." In *Debates in the Digital Humanities 2019,* edited by Matthew K. Gold and Lauren F. Klein, 96–98. Minneapolis: University of Minnesota Press, 2019.

Witmore, Michael. "Latour, the Digital Humanities, and the Divided Kingdom of Knowledge." *New Literary History* 47, nos. 2–3 (2016): 353–75.

Challenges of Collaboration
*Pursuing Computational Research in a
Humanities Graduate Program*

HOYEOL KIM

R esearch in the digital humanities ranges across a number of fields and implements both qualitative and quantitative methods. As Neilson et al. observe,
however, "Digital humanists cannot claim a shared body of literature or
theory that orients their work" ("Introduction: Research Methods," 6). Rather, the
digital humanities includes the academic outputs of collaboration between "people
with different disciplines, methodological approaches, professional roles, and theoretical inclinations" (Spiro, " 'This Is Why We Fight,' " 16). Similarly, "disciplinary
difference in digital humanities is not a binary" but is rather "a spectrum of emphasis, with varying degrees of interest in methods, tools, and values" (Robertson,
"Differences between Digital Humanities," 291). Collaboration between different
disciplines can make up for the deficiencies of any one particular research method.
Humanities scholars, however, are still accustomed to working alone, which is
very different from working collaboratively in a lab (Giannetti, "Against the
Grain," 259). Humanists, therefore, can clash with practitioners, professionals, and
theorists based in other fields over research methods in the digital humanities (DH)
and over questions such as how computational approaches should be deployed, if
practice should be emphasized over theory, and how workloads should be distributed. As a PhD candidate who holds not a research assistantship under a DH center
or lab but a teaching assistantship in the English department at Texas A&M University, I am pursuing a focus on computational literary studies in my PhD dissertation. But I have found it difficult to collaborate while pursuing computational
research in the humanities due to the different cultures and environments between
departments and institutions, a lack of proper technical support and funding, and
my inability to access a DH lab. In this chapter, I explore the limits of current institutional systems in serving the needs of humanities graduate students pursuing computational literary studies based on my empirical experience as a current graduate

student. I argue for the value of providing graduate students with opportunities to participate in virtual and physical DH labs.

In my PhD dissertation, I mainly draw upon computational research methods using deep learning models for literary analysis. Though I am a humanities graduate student, I deal with a broad range of tasks for my dissertation, from literary analysis to fine-tuning deep learning models and creating deep learning datasets, all of which require extensive time, effort, and funding. In his chapter "The Life Aquatic: Training Digital Humanists in a School of Information Science" in chapter 29 in this volume, Ted Underwood argues that it would be challenging for those who pursue computational research in the humanities to finish their PhD dissertation within five or six years if they had to start from scratch for their digital projects, a statement that applies to my situation. In my dissertation, I deploy deep learning models, namely, the BERT-Base model developed by Google Research and a conditional Generative Adversative Networks (GANs) model, which stems from a GAN model created by Goodfellow et al. ("Generative Adversarial Nets"). Although I use the deep learning models created by others, I have to fine-tune them for each task to tailor them to my research purposes, along with creating my own datasets. As a graduate student who pursues computational research in the humanities but is not a machine learning engineer, my dissertation is highly interdisciplinary; thus, collaboration, which Katherine D. Harris describes as the "lynchpin" that supports "productivity, learning, experimenting, and knowledge acquisition," is key to my research ("Play, Collaborate, Break, Build," 8).

I tentatively identified a coauthor, a PhD candidate in computer science at an R1 university, through one of the communities that I belong to for a project aimed at developing a new deep learning model for sentiment analysis. However, we reached an impasse for several reasons, all of which stemmed from the different systems in place at our respective academic institutions. To develop a deep learning model and run repeated tests on it with cloud services, we needed a research grant, which we did not obtain. According to Jessica Webster's survey on digital collaborations, 10.29 percent of participants answered that their projects "would be more successful with increased funding" ("Digital Collaborations," para. 34), and this was the case for our potential collaboration. Without funding, it is challenging to pursue deep learning projects, especially with colleagues from different institutions. Another difficulty arose when attempting to establish equal workloads between coauthors from different departments. Although one of us considered writing to be a minor task and experiments to be a major task, the other believed that both were equally important. Compared to measuring the workload of experiments, there are difficulties in measuring the workload of writing and research, which can create barriers to receiving credit for one's work. Graban et al. contend that humanities scholars' labors are "often made invisible by the writing, much of their own work disappear[ing] in the redistribution of digital labor," and humanities scholarship can therefore be undervalued during collaboration due to its potentially invisible character ("Introduction: Questioning Collaboration," para. 23, 10). Webster mentions Posner's argument that "information professionals face different workloads than other DH scholars often do, especially those scholars for whom teaching and research is a primary responsibility" ("Digital Collaborations," para. 19). In engineering and computer science, lab research with experiments is a major part of scholars' responsibilities, whereas the absence of lab research in the humanities means that the work of research and teaching tends to be distributed differently. Dissimilarities in both research environments and research methods can give rise to differences in scholars' understandings of the workload that will be expected to complete an academic paper. In other words, epistemological difference is an obstacle to collaboration across fields.

According to Webster's survey on digital collaborations, the number of information professionals who collaborated with graduate students from another institution was only three out of 197 ("Digital Collaborations," para. 27). Although my case is slightly different from her survey question, I assume that graduate students from different institutions face difficulties when attempting to collaborate due to differences in the availability of funding. Graduate students in engineering and computer science are mostly tied to their professors under research assistantships that restrict them from working with other graduate students from other departments or institutions. Collaborations between graduate students in the humanities, engineering, and computer science have the potential to be fruitful combinations yielding outputs that a single scholar could not produce. Without changes to the exclusive collaboration system in the engineering and computer science fields, however, there will continue to be obstacles to collaboration between graduate students from different departments.

Collaboration comes in forms other than teamwork. Participating in discussions with various communities by sharing experiences and suggestions is another way to collaborate. Through community activities, new ideas or solutions to issues can arise. For instance, while working on my project about deep learning-based colorization and sentiment analysis, I often received feedback on online communities from expert users of specific technologies. Stack Overflow, one example of such a community, is a question-and-answer space for both novice and professional developers, and its archives offer some of the best resources for learning coding and fixing bugs. A plethora of questions, however, remain unanswered on its pages, in part because the community is so comprehensive and includes questions about a large number of computer languages, both managed and unmanaged. For this reason, I draw mainly upon three communities: the TensorFlow KR and Computational Humanities Research (CHR) communities to get feedback and technical support for my DH projects and the Pseudo Lab for collaboration.[1] The TensorFlow KR community, which has around fifty-four thousand members on Facebook, consists of a variety of deep learning users, from a high school student who created an automatic recycling system at his school by using deep learning models based on technical support from the community to senior engineers and computer science professors. The community is responsive, passionate, and benevolent: when posting a question about deep learning, it often takes less than thirty minutes to start receiving comments. Most members of the deep learning community, however, are not from the humanities and therefore lack disciplinary knowledge in that area. To make up for this, I also take advantage of the CHR community to get feedback for my DH projects. The CHR has a discussion forum where digital humanists across a range of subfields freely share opinions on DH projects, theory, and coding, and it is a mutually beneficial space where it is possible to get specific feedback and collaborate, participate in ongoing discussions, and share recent information in the field of computational humanities research. Lastly, I have actively participated in the Pseudo Lab by collaboratively writing deep learning tutorials and helping with the implementation of deep learning models as a collaborator. The Pseudo Lab is a virtual nonprofit lab for those who need a space to learn, create, and share knowledge of deep learning. It brings together several groups with varying focuses, such as Kaggle AI competition groups, a study group for deep learning theory, a tutorial group, and a coding group for the implementation of deep learning models based on academic articles. All resources created by the Pseudo Lab are open to the public, including reviews of academic articles, code reviews, and tutorials. The Pseudo Lab is an example of how a virtual lab can act as a valuable space for graduate students who need technical assistance and who wish to work and learn collaboratively.

As a graduate student who pursues computational humanities research, being able to get feedback from professionals and scholars in the field is significant. Not only is feedback from my committee members from the humanities helpful for improving my work in terms of the H (humanities) in DH, but technical advice from my committee member in computer science also validates the D (digital) aspect of my work. Due to the different conventions between departments, however, it is necessary to maintain communication with committee members from outside of the department to avoid misunderstandings. A faculty member who supervises a graduate student in engineering and computer science, for instance, is usually included in the student's paper as a second author by providing feedback or research environments, whereas this is uncommon in the humanities. Understanding how different disciplinary cultures result in differences in funding systems, citation practices, and other important practicalities is key to the relationship between graduate students and faculty members from outside of their departments. It is important to clarify that I am speaking based on my knowledge of one specific PhD system, that of the United States. In some countries, such as the United Kingdom, it is still possible to have a second supervisor from outside of the home department, but it remains uncommon.

Digital humanities centers and specialist DH librarians are another source of support that can provide consultation, instruction for project assistants, and access to potential collaborators. Through DH centers, graduate students and faculty members can access resources and advice for their projects and "develop [the] digital competencies" needed for their work (Fraistat, "Data First," 83). The benefits of DH centers, however, are only available to digital humanists affiliated with institutions that are sufficiently well-resourced to have such initiatives. In addition, getting the right kind of specialist technical support can be challenging. As Bobby Smiley points out, a DH librarian is not "a messianic unicorn" who can support every digital project with robust technical assistance ("From Humanities to Scholarship," 416). Similarly, DH centers are usually not places primarily oriented toward troubleshooting but rather are more likely to be helpful in setting up projects with technical support or funding. For instance, when developing the Victorian400 dataset, a deep learning dataset of nineteenth-century illustrations created for the colorization of black-and-white illustrations, I had difficulty finding experts in computer vision and deep learning datasets at my own institution who could provide feedback on my colorization project (Kim, "*Victorian400*"). Instead, I received technical feedback from my committee member from computer science, from deep learning engineers through my personal networks, and from the online communities mentioned above. I also spent my personal funds to initiate the project on my own device, though this was later supplemented with a project development grant from the Center of Digital Humanities Research (CoDHR) at TAMU and graduate funding from my department so that I could continue the project's development. These project development grants, however, are required to receive assistance from the CoDHR. Without the initially successful prototype of the project, it might have been challenging to secure the grant and funding, in addition to assistance from the CoDHR. Although it is technically possible to get CoDHR funding for a project before starting it, many DH projects do not qualify and require personal funding in the incubation stage, as my project did.

Though a multitude of environmental difficulties exist for graduate students pursuing computational humanities research in the humanities, these obstacles can be mitigated by communicating with a variety of experts in different communities, collaborating with practitioners and professionals outside the academy in addition to scholars, and getting technical and funding support from DH centers and departments. Digital humanities centers and DH institutional programs, such as the Mellon Graduate Program that Erin Francisco Opalich, Daniel Gorman Jr., Madeline Ullrich, and Alexander J. Zawacki introduce in "A Tale of Three Disciplines: Considering the (Digital) Future of the Mid-doc Fellowship in Graduate Programs" in chapter 25 in this volume, are helpful for graduate students pursuing digital projects, but collaboration between individuals is one of the most valuable ways of pursuing interdisciplinary digital work, especially for projects of any significant magnitude. The DH community has organized a supportive system for communication, for instance, with the Association for Computers and the Humanities (ACH) mentorship program and a DH Slack channel, which create opportunities for col-laboration.[2] By contrast, opportunities for collaboration within individual institu-tions such as DH centers and DH mentoring programs are offered to few graduate students. Therefore, having a virtual DH lab across departments and institutions such as the Pseudo Lab is one way to facilitate collaboration on digital projects. In addition, as Gorman et al. point out, it is important to have institutional support from departments for both teaching and practicing DH. More specifically, depart-ments in the humanities might consider whether it is possible to set up a DH lab without a principal investigator, following Amy Earhart's argument that a "neutral laboratory space" is needed to provide a research environment for both students and faculty members, without any initial requirements, which can serve as an unham-pered space for individual and team research projects as well as for collaboration ("Digital Humanities as a Laboratory," 397). It might take time to build an institu-tional system that provides graduate students with a lab space that facilitates collab-oration with students from different institutions, but efforts to improve the system even in small, incremental ways will make it easier for future students to become digital humanists who can freely collaborate with other scholars on digital projects, without being stymied by environmental research restrictions.

Notes

1. More information about each community can be found at the following web-sites: TensorFlow KR, https://www.facebook.com/groups/TensorFlowKR; Computational Humanities Research, https://discourse.computational-humanities-research.org; and Pseudo Lab, https://pseudo-lab.com.

2. Digital Humanities Slack: https://digitalhumanities.slack.com.

Bibliography

Earhart, Amy. "The Digital Humanities as a Laboratory." In *Between Humanities and the Digital,* edited by Patrik Svensson and David Theo Goldberg, 391–400. Cambridge, Mass.: The MIT Press, 2015.

Fraistat, Neil. "Data First: Remodeling the Digital Humanities Center." In *Debates in the Digital Humanities 2019,* edited by Matthew K. Gold and Lauren F. Klein, 83–85. Min-neapolis: University of Minnesota Press, 2019.

Giannetti, Francesca. "Reading for the Challenges of Collaborative Digital Humanities Pedagogy." *College & Undergraduate Libraries* 24, nos. 2–4 (2017): 257–69.

Goodfellow, Ian, Jean Pouget-Abadie, Mehdi Mirza, Bing Xu, David Warde-Farley, Sherjil Ozair, Aaron Courville, and Yoshua Bengio. "Generative Adversarial Nets." Paper presented at Advances in Neural Information Processing Systems, Montréal, Canada, December 8, 2014.

Graban, Tarez Samra et al. "Introduction: Questioning Collaboration, Labor, and Visibility in Digital Humanities Research." *Digital Humanities Quarterly* 13, no. 2 (2019). http://www.digitalhumanities.org/dhq/vol/13/2/000416/000416.html.

Harris, Katherine D. "Play, Collaborate, Break, Build, Share: 'Screwing Around' in Digital Pedagogy." *Polymath: An Interdisciplinary Arts and Sciences Journal* 3, no. 3 (2013): 1–26.

Kim, Hoyeol. "*Victorian400*: Colorizing Victorian Illustrations." *International Journal of Humanities and Arts Computing* 15, nos. 1–2 (2021): 186–202.

Neilson, Tai, lewis levenberg, and David Rheams. "Introduction: Research Methods for the Digital Humanities." In *Research Methods for the Digital Humanities,* edited by lewis levenberg, Tai Neilson, and David Rheams, 1–14. Cham, Switzerland: Palgrave Macmillan, 2018.

Posner, Miriam. "No Half Measures: Overcoming Common Challenges to Doing Digital Humanities in the Library." *Journal of Library Administration* 53, no. 1 (2013): 43–52.

Robertson, Stefan. "The Differences between Digital Humanities and Digital History." In *Debates in Digital Humanities 2016,* edited by Matthew K. Gold and Lauren F. Klein, 289–307. Minneapolis: University of Minnesota Press, 2016.

Smiley, Bobby. "From Humanities to Scholarship: Librarians, Labor, and the Digital." In *Debates in Digital Humanities 2019,* edited by Matthew K. Gold and Lauren F. Klein, 413–19. Minneapolis: University of Minnesota Press, 2019.

Spiro, Lisa. "'This Is Why We Fight': Defining the Values of the Digital Humanities." In *Debates in Digital Humanities,* edited by Matthew K. Gold, 16–35. Minneapolis: University of Minnesota Press, 2012.

Webster, Jessica. "Digital Collaborations: A Survey Analysis of Digital Humanities Partnerships Between Librarians and Other Academics." *Digital Humanities Quarterly* 13, no. 4 (2019). http://www.digitalhumanities.org/dhq/vol/13/4/000441/000441.html.

Triple Consciousness

*A Scatterling Lesotho Native on a PhD Journey
in the American South*

SETHUNYA MOKOKO

I enter this conversation as a graduate student in a transdisciplinary digital rhetoric PhD program in a theoretically oriented department in the American South. My background is highly international in terms of my place of birth, the countries in which I have studied, and the development of my scholarship. In this conversation about the possibilities for graduate study in digital humanities, I present my nontraditional experience of encountering digital graduate learning environments while navigating racial (mis)recognitions, linguistic and cultural complexities, and growing pedagogical awareness. I begin by exploring my first experiences of racialization in the United States, my experience of both double and triple consciousness in American graduate programs, and the effects that these have had on my development as a writer, scholar, and activist.

The English language saved my life when, orphaned at age twelve, I taught myself how to read and write. I used an English dictionary, *National Geographic* magazine, and a Sesotho dictionary, uttering words I hoped would be heard in my forgotten Kingdom of Lesotho, Southern Africa. My village chief recognized my natural ability in English and depended on me to translate to U.S. Peace Corps volunteers. Eventually, this led me to the United States. From the genesis of my arrival, I faced many culture shocks and language barriers and struggled to comprehend my new American identity. Though I had come from a rich cultural background and wholeheartedly knew myself, the conundrum I faced was that while operating in and navigating America, I was constantly being mislabeled and miscategorized.

I arrived in Los Angeles, California, in 2006 and then moved to San Diego with my adoptive mother, whom I met in my village while she was a Peace Corps volunteer. There was a bicycle in the garage, which I was granted permission to ride once I proved that I was capable. When he worked in the South African Dutch (Boer) mines, my father had managed to buy me a bicycle before he died. While riding this bike in the streets of Vista, California, a white man decided to spark a conversation with me. I was fifteen years old, with a wide African smile, and a white woman had just assisted in being the vehicle to my better life in America and had saved my life; thus, my approach to white Americans was one full of joy. The entitled white man, standing amid his yard holding tree pruning scissors and with gloves on, shouted what initiated the first labeling of me in America by uttering, "Hey n__, are you lost?" I pulled the brakes on my bike, unbuckled my helmet, and responded, "No, n__, I am not lost; I am riding my new bicycle." Surprisingly, he got angry. His skin changed color, turning pink around the ears. I had experience with Boers, having grown up during the years of the apartheid regime, and knew they used to beat my people. I thus knew that my exchange with this white man was not as pleasant as I thought. I rode my bicycle home to ask my parent about this encounter. You can imagine how catatonic my adoptive mother became when I asked, "What is a n__?" While still in the village, she had prepared me for what I should expect in America. Unfortunately, during our "So, when we get to America" conversations during supper in the village, she had not versed me well on being called the n-word. This time, however, I was in a particular American town, where my mother had lived the majority of her life but before me did not host an African son. This labeling marked the first moment of my racial consciousness as a Black American and as the Other. My hyperawareness of myself as an outsider had begun.

A decade into my transition to American life, still dealing with my identity as an African, an American, and a scholar and having begun to teach, I took on leadership roles in my city, Long Beach, California. I became a youth mentor and an advisory board member of a nonprofit organization, the California Conference for Equality and Justice, whose mission is to eliminate bias, bigotry, and racism through education, conflict resolution, and advocacy. I facilitated school groups and community groups, making a difference by bringing restorative justice to schools and practicing it in communities. It was during this work that, as an African, American, scholar, and community leader, I dealt with some of the subliminal tensions around labels and identity among Black people in America as they relate to belonging. The African American group that I was leading commented, during their discussion about using the n-word and regarding a critical comment made by Bill Cosby, that I did not fit in. They desired to exile me from the discussion because I was African; they felt I did not have their shared understanding of the word. This was my second time dealing with an identity conflict, yet this time it was delivered by Black people.

In Southern Africa, there exists a word that is similar to the n-word: "kaffir." Unlike the n-word in America, the k-word in South Africa is banned and forbidden to all. Black Africans do not use it between one another, and when used by a Boer to a Black African, it is a crime, punishable in a court of law and physically by the subject being called thus. The court will usually rule in favor of the victim, citing self-defense, if the insulted retaliates physically. My African American group desired to exile me from our racial group discussion because I opposed the use of the n-word among Black Americans—just as I would oppose the use of the k-word in South Africa. For cultural context, the word is best described by Mark Mathabane in *Kaffir Boy: The True Story of a Black Youth's Coming of Age in Apartheid South Africa*. Mathabane powerfully elucidates how much has been written and spoken about the politics of apartheid: the forced removals of Black communities from their ancestral lands, the Influx Control and Pass laws that mandated where Black people could live, work, raise families, and be buried; the migrant labor systems that forced Black men to live apart from their families in the ghettos as the authorities sought to create a so-called white South Africa; and the brutal suppression of the Black majority as it agitated for equal rights. My opposition to the n-word arose because I comprehended its impact but had come from a place where a parallel word was banned and its use was a criminal offense. This experience showed me that though I feel connected to both lands and racial histories, the view of these Black Americans that I am literally both an "African and American" contains within it an ironic misrecognition.

Within my graduate school career, my double consciousness became transmogrified into a triple consciousness. I began navigating my scholarship as an African and an American citizen and as an African scholar as opposed to merely a Black scholar. During the latter stages of my MFA career, while I was teaching a fiction seminar and a rhetoric and composition course, I took a graduate seminar that focused on Black writers. This marked the third time that I was, once again, labeled differently by a white superior; on this occasion, it was a white female professor from the American South, where, as she said, "They do things a bit differently." She assigned the class thirteen books of her choosing, all written by Black writers, because there were only thirteen students in the course. She wrote our names and the title of the book we were to present on. I was the only Black student in the course. Without prior consultation, I was shocked on a rainy Tuesday afternoon to read the sheet of paper, from which I learned which title was assigned to me: "Sethunya— *Our Nig*." I still wonder if this professor failed to recognize the problematic nature of assigning the only Black student in the class a book written by a Black writer, titled with a controversial derogatory label, without prior discussion with me. Her "doing things differently in the South" alluded, it transpired, to her sense of authority. She was dissatisfied with me questioning her choices and taking issue with them.

The Black-authored novel *Our Nig* by Harriet E. Wilson paints a significant picture of what it was like to be Black in a white American world—excluded, alienated, challenged by racial prejudice, targeted, denied rights, and ill-treated. W. E. B. Du Bois's *The Souls of Black Folk* is an excellent text that illuminates this novel and examines the concepts that Wilson was trying to exemplify and challenge. In his book, Du Bois describes the concepts of the veil and double consciousness. Though he sets these terms apart, their meanings and usage are deeply intertwined. Du Bois transmits the struggle of Black people who felt they could not express themselves, something accentuated by a lack of words and the pain they endured. He succinctly explores what it meant to be Black in America during the era of slavery and the civil rights movement and what it meant in the twentieth century. In his articulation of the concept of "the veil," he refers to it in three ways. First, the veil suggests the literal darker skin of Black people, which is a physical demarcation of difference from whiteness. Second, the veil suggests white people's inability to see Black people as "true" Americans. Finally, the veil refers to Black people's lack of clarity in being able to see themselves outside of what white America describes and prescribes for them. Du Bois describes the life-altering moment that every socially aware African American has experienced—the realization that being Black is a problem—and demonstrates this by sharing his own youthful experience of being rejected, due to his skin color, by a white girl whom he liked: "Then it dawned upon me with a certain suddenness that I was different from others; or like [them perhaps] in heart and life and longing, but shut out from their world by a vast veil. I had thereafter no desire to tear down that veil, to creep through; I held all beyond it in common contempt, and lived above it in a region of blue sky and great wandering shadows" (Du Bois, 29). In my experience of triple consciousness, I am not necessarily a problem. Perhaps I may be "extra work" for my white professors who may now have to delve into Sub-Saharan African history and scholarship within and for my work. However, I do, like Du Bois, face the veil that reminds me of how I am not a "true American" and "not fully Black American," which I find ironic, given that the label "African and American" describes me well.

Du Bois makes us comprehend that white people's view of Black people is obstructed by this not-so-invisible veil that hangs between the races. He attests to the fact that although the veil shades the view of both Blacks and whites, Black people have traditionally had a better understanding of whites than the reverse, due to the "two-ness" lived and felt by Black Americans. In other words, upon realizing what being Black in America has meant both historically and in the present, Du Bois argued that Black people have long known how to operate in two Americas— one that is white and one that is Black. This phenomenon intriguingly describes "double consciousness," or the awareness of the two-ness of being an "American and an African American" and the largely unconscious and almost instinctive movement between these two identities, as needed. Using Du Bois's concepts of the veil and "second sight," a vision that yields him no true self-consciousness but lets him see himself through the revelation of another's perspective, we can better comprehend this struggle with identity, fitting in, being accepted, and being treated as true Americans, and more fundamentally human beings. In tracing my own triple consciousness, I have observed how my knowledge and acknowledgment of my "belonging to Africa" can frustrate those in authority.

My triple consciousness is the basis for all I do in my digital rhetoric graduate program. In line with Emanuel Levinas and Toni Morrison's theorizing of the relationship between the self and the Other, I find myself often "othered" within my involvement at my university. I am a Black man, a Black man with locked hair (i.e., dreadlocks), and a Black man with an accent from Africa. When I teach, I embody the roles of the American and the African, something I have come to appreciate through my relationships with students. I am an American and am recognized through that lens because I teach in American institutions and follow the western curriculum with which my students are familiar. However, when I attempt to collaborate in research projects with fellow PhD candidates, I am the Other and set in opposition to favored research topics. Additionally, for example, when I am observed teaching, my teaching philosophy and pedagogical approaches generate caution to some observers because I resist colonial residues and use decolonial rhetoric at an institution that was once a slave plantation. In my capacity as the assistant director of the University Writing Lab, where I am the only PhD candidate employed, I find that some students make appointments with me with preconceived notions, both good and bad. International students schedule their appointments seeing opportunity and abundance in my views because I am the only Black employee at the lab and an international student as well. I have also noticed from reserved attitudes and pondering questions that when white, especially southern, students arrive at the lab, having scheduled appointments with me as the only graduate-level writing consultant, they are at first frustrated. In this case, then, being the Other puts limitations on my positionality. I am a walking digital rhetoric subject on the website of my university. My image, description, and appearance either invites or uninvites others based on their racially and geographically biased judgments.

In addition to my coursework and teaching, I have grounded myself in a solid foundation of literary research and literacy pedagogy, and I have explored the residues of marginalization in the education systems of Southern Africa that survive to this day, long after the plague of apartheid. Committed to remedying this injustice, I joined hands with my past high school students and established a college-level African Book Club. In the African Book Club, I use digital technologies to assist ambitious youth in Lesotho, nurturing their literacy skills and encouraging them to read diverse and challenging texts. I still teach composition and creative writing in Lesotho, using the African Book Club website. Seasonally, I supervise writing contests that enable young African writers to exercise their skills with creative essays that propose sustainable and developmental approaches to benefit the country. Through these digitally mediated efforts, I hold the responsibility of ensuring that while I code-switch from being a Black American scholar, I focus my attention on being an African scholar. From a distance, I continue to support my African people during such catastrophes as the HIV epidemic and the Covid-19 pandemic by providing lifesaving information on proper health and body care, all while dismantling the plague of disinformation that, unfortunately, misguides my people into unhealthy routines or health practices that further endanger their lives. In this work, my triple consciousness persists in the sense that now, during my PhD journey, my people mistake me for a medical doctor who is not arrogant or white and can perform circumcisions and other medical procedures.

My triple consciousness also inflects my PhD work by leading me to police myself in a manner that often exacerbates my anxiety. In the present moment, we are often, as we should be, engaged in conversations regarding racial violence and police brutality. We are now recognizing that in numerous ways, university departments have not directly attended to racism, and key Black authors have not been adequately included in our scholarship. Although I appreciate the dialogue when I converse with peers and professors in academic settings, my embodied experience continues to be that of an outcast. When I participate in groups in which Black bodies are limited, I still find myself limiting what I say in terms of racial discussions. Though I have lived in America now since 2006, my voice is welcomed in academic spaces, but comments continue to be made that remind me that though my skin may be Black, my input is not seen as representing the Black American experience. In a university seminar during a discussion about Ta-Nehisi Coates's essay "Paranoid Style of American Policing," in which he discusses tasering, killing, and beating as forms of "keeping the peace" in communities, I was still asked, "But how is that for Africa?" even though my input came from thirteen years of American citizenship and life as a Black civilian. I speak in a way that polices myself, so as not to cause discomfort to my American-born brothers and sisters.

In my experience as a PhD student, I have found that for some professors, I pose more work for them, because to help me they must first do their homework on African epistemological thought. Although I enjoy and comprehend the value of speaking to the ongoing discourse within western academic fields, my purpose is to also make a difference in the far-off land from which I originate, where there are limited academic opportunities and few who have received the life-changing opportunities from which I benefited. I often find myself struggling with genuflecting to American scholars instead of anchoring myself deeply in the work of researchers outside the United States with the potential to improve the lives of people living in destitute situations across the globe. I write and publish from the position of an African who aims to make a difference in the lives of the forgotten, and I approach situations in America in a manner similar to the way my heroes Nelson Mandela and Bob Marley navigated adversities. However, I teach from the position of an African-and-American. I teach with the sensitivity that if I push the envelope a little too far or outright reject policies and behaviors that echo the institution's past associations with slavery and plantations, I may get booted off campus or perhaps be left out of discussions for disturbing the "peace." I say this because I produced a digital rhetoric piece that pointed out how my institution was misusing its technologies in the guise of advocacy, activism, and social justice, using a staged and carefully choreographed racial justice event on campus as a case study. Following the publication of this multimedia piece, I experienced a backlash from university members, especially alumni with long-established ties to the university and its conflicted racist history. I nevertheless remain hopeful and grateful to be involved in this learning opportunity. My triple consciousness simultaneously puts me in the spotlight and yet provides me with shade and relief.

Bibliography

Coates, Ta-Nehisi. "The Paranoid Style of American Policing." In *Between The World and Me*. New York: Spiegel & Grau, 2015.

Du Bois, W. E. B. "The Veil and Double Consciousness." In *The Souls of Black Folk*. Cambridge, Mass.: Harvard University, 1999.

Mathabane, Mark. *Kaffir Boy: The True Story of a Black Youth's Coming of Age in Apartheid South Africa*. New York: Free Press, 1986.

Wilson, E. Harriet. *Our Nig: Or Sketches from the Life of a Free Black*. New York: Vintage, 2002.

Taking the Reins, Harnessing the Digital
Enabling and Supporting Public Scholarship in Graduate-Level Training

SARA MOHR AND E. L. MESZAROS

D igital tools and methods are not just for analysis and for understanding humanities research in new ways. They can also be harnessed to afford research a reach and scope beyond what has traditionally been available in the humanities.[1] One of the most wide-reaching methods in leveraging digital platforms and increasing reach is public scholarship, defined by diverse modes of creating and circulating knowledge for and with certain publics and communities. An example of this kind of work is apparent in the work of MA students, as described by Maria José Afanador-Llach, and Germán Camilo Martínez Peñaloza in "Digital Futures for the Humanities in Latin America" in chapter 7 of this volume, who used digital tools and methods to create a space for a community in Colombia to share and record their traditional knowledge. Sharing research digitally can be just as much a force for advancing research as doing digital work; however, this is a skill often neglected by graduate programs, many of which already fail to provide their students with sufficient training and guidance in writing. Although the traditional model of academic publishing has changed and many programs are incorporating public scholarship into aspects of hiring and tenure review, graduate programs have yet to update their curricula to provide sufficient training in such areas; as a result, training in public scholarship and digital research has fallen squarely on the shoulders of graduate students who must take on the tasks of training and supplying venues for public scholarship. Reflecting on their work as graduate students at the University of California San Diego, Olivia Quintanilla and Jeanelle Horcasitas's "Rewriting Graduate Digital Futures through Mentorship and Multi-institutional Support" in chapter 15 of this volume describes how this often occurs in practice. Often this means finding our way through the dark together toward an understanding of just how robust a tool digital public scholarship platforms truly are. Providing training in this area and a venue for this work, through whatever means necessary, has become crucial for successful graduate student careers.

How do we recognize the time- and effort-intensive work required to provide training in digital, public scholarship from the top down but still give graduate students the tools they need? One method for training public scholarship outside of an academic–public binary is to allow graduate students to take the reins in their public scholarship education beyond the structures of bureaucratic academia and without any association with the rigors of promotion, tenure, and the job market. Writing for a digital public scholarship venue can also give graduate students clarity about their commitments to specific communities, often ignored and undifferentiated by traditional academic discourse. As Gold and Klein argue, "Now is the time when digital humanists can usefully clarify our commitments to public scholarship, addressing our work not simply to 'the public' but also, as Sheila Brennan has observed, to specific communities and the needs that they, and not we, identify as most pressing" ("Introduction: A DH That Matters").

The following chapter argues for a particular version of student-led public scholarship. At Brown University, a private, research-intensive American university, we implemented a graduate student-run public scholarship blog called *The Ratty*, providing students with training based on the concept of digital publication. Graduate students approach the blog with an idea, and we work with them through multiple rounds of editing to translate or transform that idea into a scholarship directed at and created for the public and using digital methods of presentation, citation, and supplementation. Our goal with this project is not just to provide an outlet for graduate student research but to focus on training. Each participant works with many different editors, focusing on everything from content to copyediting, to readability online and beyond a student's discipline. *The Ratty* also works on training editors to provide this feedback and offers carefully designed workshops for graduate school departments to provide a one-shot guidebook for students on how to start thinking about crafting research for the digital and public spheres.

This initiative grew out of the apparent general absence of available training and mentorship in public scholarship and digital publishing methods. We recognized that such engaged scholarship was important and that our careers, both within and beyond the academy, would be improved by such training. It was no surprise to us that the students most interested in joining *The Ratty* and training in public scholarship belonged primarily to populations that academia has reliably left behind—women and nonbinary students, Black students, students of color, and queer students. In the absence of reliable modeling, mentoring, and teaching in public scholarship, and as faculty and bureaucracy fight about how public scholarship should be viewed for faculty members, these are the students who stepped up to gain their own experience and use their own learning to help guide and train others.

Training in digital public scholarship benefits graduate students even when under-cultivated. Students who leave their graduate programs having engaged in public scholarship often leave with stronger writing skills, favoring clarity and concision over the ability to cite entire historiographies. Moving from an academic venue to a more popular one requires more than just reshaping lecture notes or revising research data (Cox, "Accountability, Public Scholarship, and Library"). Writing for a digital platform means writing differently, if not considerably better, which requires restructuring, rephrasing, and refocusing different aspects of the work.[2] Although discipline-specific language is important for advancing discipline-specific discourse, developing a communication style that translates ideas concisely in the time it takes the average person to scroll through a webpage is an equally important skill (Glass and Vandegrift, "Public Scholarship in Practice"). In confronting the isolated, disciplinary nature of academic writing, offering students pedagogies that ask them to write more concisely for a wider audience is in essence asking them to move beyond the model of the traditional monolithic research paper. Writing for a public digital platform means carefully assessing whom one wants to reach and choosing one's venue accordingly (Meyers, "Public Scholar, Beware"). In turn, students become more reflective about their writing and about the nature of their research.

Considered in terms of impact and reach, harnessing digital tools in graduate education can make research resonate with not only fellow graduate students and faculty but also with a diverse set of publics beyond the walls of academia; in fact, much public scholarship writing does a far better job of fulfilling the mission of educating, advancing ideas, creating an intellectual environment, and bettering the lives of others than projects upheld by a more limited view of scholarly activity (Williams, "Lack of Reward Mechanisms"). Further, students can reach beyond their scholarly communities and connect with readers in hours or days rather than the months or even years required by the traditional scholarship trajectory (Meyers, "Public Scholar, Beware"). The increased pace of these digital tools allows us to engage with time-critical issues and supports conversations through which community input can be readily incorporated and supported.

Public scholarship is also one channel for graduate students to advocate for their disciplines and for themselves in the time after their degree. This form of scholarship arises from an ethical call to engage with the public intellectually and to position ourselves for the future as citizen-scholars in a variety of possible jobs. Institutionalizing public scholarship may lead to greater academic recognition and value, greater exposure, and wider accessibility between academics and the public (Kilty and Crépault, "Institutionalizing Public Scholarship"). As tenure-track jobs become scarcer and graduate students look beyond the ivory tower both during and after their programs, the very survival of academia is predicated on encouraging graduate students to engage in wide-reaching activities that speak to and for the public.

Although students are arriving at graduate programs with increasing levels of interest in and experience with diverse forms of sharing knowledge through writing, recognizing the benefits writing offers to their academic progress and extra-academic jobs, there may be few opportunities in graduate programs for students to further develop these skills (Clark-Taylor et. al., "Modeling, Mentoring, and Pedagogy"). The lack of opportunity not only halts the expansion of skills for these students but also fails to acknowledge the integral role public scholarship plays in crafting doctoral students who can succeed both inside and outside of the academy. Often the work of academic writing is considered crucial preparation for the writing to come in a later academic career. However, engaging students in civic-minded writing asks them to consider their future roles as professionals in a wide variety of contexts and as citizens of the wider community (DelliCarpini, "Coming Down"). Further, the nature of online digital platforms forces students to remain engaged in their work—by responding to comments and publishing follow-up material, for example—in ways that traditional academic venues do not. Therefore, the graduate students influenced by this training receive their degrees as much more civic-minded citizens, aware of the impact their research has on the larger population beyond their academic department.

Given the evidence of student interest in public scholarship, as demonstrated by the creation of platforms by graduate students, and the (nascent) recognition of how it benefits both research and researchers, some faculty have begun the work of incorporating public scholarship into their research or their teaching (Parry, "The New Ph.D."). This is most often conceived of in the form of pedagogy—that is, providing training for students through coursework, lectures, and workshops. However, the additional work required to reconceive classes can be a barrier to the implementation of the traditional pedagogical approach (Cox, "Accountability, Public Scholarship, and Library"). Of course, there are other ways to support developing public scholarship skills. Clark-Taylor et al. argue that establishing collaboration with community partners and embedding these extra-academic relationships within graduate school curricula can cultivate engaged scholarship ("Modeling, Mentoring, and Pedagogy"). Modeling such engaged behavior is a critical component of training for graduate students and has the benefit of being a productive outlet for faculty as well. Additionally, working one-on-one to mentor students in public scholarship is another potential outlet for training.

Methods of mentoring, modeling, and pedagogy seem to be necessary components of graduate student training in public scholarship (Clark-Taylor et al., "Modeling, Mentoring, and Pedagogy"). Yet these methods can be demanding for faculty who are often already overworked and buried under extra-academic demands of service, especially in the cases of the early career researchers and contingent faculty who are more likely to recognize the importance of public scholarship and digital tools. Furthermore, the current setup of the academy that focuses on "publish or perish" in the pursuit of promotion and tenure puts those who do work on public scholarship at risk for their own career advancement, contributing to feelings of isolation within the academy (Kilty and Crépault, "Institutionalizing Public Scholarship").

To lighten the load on faculty, we must change how fellow academics view public scholarship. We must be careful, for example, not to fall into the trap of considering public scholarship as any less academic or well-researched than the traditional form of academic writing. The very definition of public as opposed to other forms of scholarship implies a binary that we do not endorse. As graduate students prepare for life after graduate studies, they are also preparing to enter academic institutions with increasing levels of recognition for public scholarship. Compared with the most lavishly resourced institutions, a significant portion of higher education evaluates faculty publications through a more diverse set of lenses (Bond and Gannon, "Public Writing and the Junior Scholar"). Rather than arguing that op-eds and blog posts are a waste of time, these institutions are beginning to recognize their scope and power. Several graduate degree-granting institutions have served as models in this kind of recognition. Most notably, George Mason University and the University of Nebraska have implemented public scholarship requirements at the institutional level, as Laura Crossly, Amanda Regan, and Joshua Casmir Catalano assert in chapter 13 in this volume. This view, more indicative of a general reception of public scholarship, should be recognized and emulated more widely.

Instead, we are taught about the strict requirements that must be completed to be viable candidates on an increasingly fraught academic job market.[3] "As we internalize these expectations and work to meet them," argue Kilty and Crépault, "our intellectual labour becomes increasingly oriented around the demands of the institution" ("Institutionalizing Public Scholarship," 628). Not only is public scholarship disincentivized as standard scholarship methods are prioritized, but graduate students are trained to therefore place less value on public scholarship, as it does not help them meet the requirements of the academic job market.

The struggle to understand how to "count" public scholarship in tenure files and toward article requirements for doctoral students mimics the early days of the digital humanities (Bond and Gannon, "Public Writing and the Junior Scholar"). For example, how was a traditional, publication-oriented professor on a tenure committee supposed to evaluate a candidate's interactive digital project? In trying to compare digital projects with traditional ones, one ends up misunderstanding both. As a corollary, those who do prioritize public scholarship list their digital works under headings like "other professional activity," categories of a CV that are undervalued by most academic institutions (Kilty and Crépault, "Institutionalizing Public Scholarship," 619). Though their contributions harness digital platforms to disseminate their work far beyond the insular academy, they are working against a system that does not know how to value this work.

There are similar problems with incorporating public scholarship into coursework. When public scholarship is explicitly juxtaposed to academic writing, as is often the case for "public engagement" assignments within a class, we inadvertently reinforce the binary between the two types of writing (Hardy and Milanese, "Teaching Students to Be Public Intellectuals"). This contributes to misunderstanding public writing as somehow "not academic" and public audiences as somehow less intelligent; both are untrue and contribute to poorer public engagement. We must, therefore, incorporate public scholarship in ways that do not only juxtapose it with academic writing, putting the analog at odds with the digital. Luckily, the digital, open-access nature of many modern methods of public scholarship can reduce the amount of work necessary for inclusion within coursework, for both faculty and students: no purchase necessary, no library legwork required—just a hyperlink. Despite this seeming ease, we must be cognizant of the time and effort required to update existing sources and exercises in syllabi. Recognizing this need and supporting the labor required to fill it are integral for enacting this change.

Placing the burden of training on graduate students does mirror some of the issues encountered with asking professors and early career researchers to do this work. Graduate students are often overworked and underpaid (Freeman; Hugo; Linder et al.; Perry; Puri). Asking them to contribute what little free time they have to continued academic activities is morally questionable, no matter what good may come of the endeavor. Moreover, asking them to serve as advisors for themselves and their peers brings up issues of labor and stress that pervade graduate studies and the digital humanities (Boyles et al., "Precarious Labor"). However, working to recognize the value of digital engagement and public scholarship at the faculty level can help graduate programs to recognize the value of graduate-led training and the value of supporting it. Although graduate-led initiatives like *The Ratty* are valuable for students' leadership training, legitimizing its work at the faculty level could shift the narrative around digital engagement and public scholarship.

Looking to the future, higher education needs to expand current thinking and practice to see public scholarship not just as an end for promotion and tenure. Instead, engaged scholarship should be integrated as much as possible into an institution's mission by everyone from professors to the graduate students they train (Franz, "Holistic Model of Engaged Scholarship"). Acceptance of an expanded definition of scholarship necessarily requires the integration of public writing into graduate training (Scarpino, "Some Thoughts on Defining"). At their core, graduate programs are lengthy internships that socialize future academics into the profession. Teaching students to harness and value the digital forms of research dissemination will make research more accessible and produce more civic-minded academics.

Writing this chapter is a luxury that many untenured faculty likely could not afford as a result of the general attitude toward public scholarship and, tacitly or otherwise, taught to graduate students (Williams, "Lack of Reward Mechanisms"). The current disciplinary publishing conventions often dissuade emerging scholars from exploring open publishing options. Although a significant number of journals are being made available online, their openness still does not compare to that of digital public scholarship platforms. Rather than argue that engagement should be valued equally with scholarship, more institutions and graduate training programs need to show that public scholarship *is* research and scholarship (Johnsen, "Public Scholarship"). This notion applies regardless of the form the engagement takes.

Ultimately, training graduate students in public scholarship, whether it comes from faculty or programs or the students themselves, is necessary. Such training prepares us for careers outside of academia and for the majority of academic jobs that are available at institutions that value teaching and outreach (Bond and Gannon, "Public Writing and the Junior Scholar"). But more than just career preparation, training in public scholarship can help make us more engaged students and citizens. We increasingly live in a digital world where our academic and digital personas are becoming more difficult to keep separate. However, being present in academia should not exempt us from being present citizens of the larger digital world.

Notes

1. Academic publication has been traditionally characterized by esoteric research often hidden behind paywalls or institution-specific access. The traditional academic article is therefore not accessible beyond the walls of academia, in terms of understanding content or simply obtaining a copy of the article, nor does it claim to be.

2. By digital platform, we mean to make the distinction between journalistic resources and self-published blogs and the peer-reviewed digital public scholarship platforms currently available. In particular, great examples of this kind of platform are *Contingent Magazine, Lady Science, Nursing Clio*, and the *Journal for the History of Ideas Blog*, among many others. Each of these platforms requires a pitch process followed by an intensive editorial process that imitates the traditional academic peer-review process.

3. Although some programs have adopted more flexible requirements regarding comprehensive or qualifying exams and standards for a specific field, most graduate programs lag behind. In our experience as graduate students and working with graduate students from other institutions, most graduate programs retain the antiquated modes of testing ability and readiness for graduation through rigorous examination, academic journal publishing requirements, submission of book reviews, and the construction of dissertations like books. It is clear that these requirements are aimed at a specific academic career, which is by no means a guaranteed desire or outcome for all graduate students; see Bartram, "Why Everybody Loses."

Bibliography

Bartram, Erin. "Why Everybody Loses When Someone Leaves Academe." *Chronicle of Higher Education,* February 15, 2018. https://www.chronicle.com/article/why-every body-loses-when-someone-leaves-academe/.

Bond, Sarah E., and Kevin Gannon. "Public Writing and the Junior Scholar." *Chronicle of Higher Education,* October 15, 2019. https://www.chronicle.com/article/public-writing -and-the-junior-scholar/.

Boyles, Christina, Ann Cong-Huyen, Carrie Johnston, Jim McGrath, and Amanda Phillips. "Precarious Labor in the Digital Humanities." *American Quarterly* 70, no. 3 (2018): 693–700.

Clark-Taylor, Angela, Molly Sarubbi, Judy Marquez Kiyama, and Stephanie J. Waterman. "Modeling, Mentoring, and Pedagogy: Cultivating Public Scholars." In *Envisioning Public Scholarship for Our Time: Models for Higher Education Researchers,* edited by Adrianna Kezar, Yianna Drivalas, and Joseph A. Kitchen, 179–95. Sterling, Va.: Stylus, 2018.

Cox, Richard J. "Accountability, Public Scholarship, and Library, Information and Archival Science Educators." *Journal of Education for Library and Information Science* 41 (Spring 2000): 94–105.

DelliCarpini, Dominic. "Coming Down from the Ivory Tower: Writing Programs' Role in Advocating Public Scholarship." In *Going Public: What Writing Programs Learn from Engagement,* edited by Shirley K. Rose and Irwin Weiser, 193–215. Boulder: University Press of Colorado, 2010.

Franz, Nancy. "A Holistic Model of Engaged Scholarship: Telling the Story across Higher Education's Missions." *Journal of Higher Education Outreach and Engagement* 13, no. 4 (2009): 31–50.

Freeman, Amy. "The Spaces of Graduate Student Labor: The Times for a New Union." *Antipode: A Radical Journal of Geography* 32, no. 3 (2002): 245–59.

Glass, Erin Rose, and Micah Vandegrift. "Public Scholarship in Practice and Philosophy." Humanities Common. Accessed April 23, 2024. https://hcommons.org/deposits/item/hc:22279/.

Gold, Matthew K., and Lauren F. Klein. "Introduction: A DH That Matters." In *Debates in the Digital Humanities 2019,* edited by Matthew K. Gold and Lauren F. Klein, ix–xiv. Minneapolis: University of Minnesota Press, 2019.

Hardy, Sarah Madsen, and Marisa Milanese. "Teaching Students to Be Public Intellectuals." *Chronicle of Higher Education,* June 29, 2016. https://www.chronicle.com/article/teaching-students-to-be-public-intellectuals/.

Hugo, Kristin. "Graduate Students are Underpaid and Overstressed: Can Academic Unions Change That?" *PBS News Hour,* April 19, 2017. https://www.pbs.org/newshour/science/ph-d-students-underpaid-overstressed-can-academic-unions-change.

Johnsen, Rosemary Erickson. "Public Scholarship: Making the Case." *Modern Language Studies* 45, no. 1 (2015): 8–19.

Kilty, Jennifer M., and Charissa Crépault. "Institutionalizing Public Scholarship: Lessons from Feminism and Symbolic Interactionism." *Symbolic Interaction* 39, no. 4 (2016): 615–33.

Linder, Chris, Stephen John Quaye, Alex C. Lange, Ricky Ericka Roberts, Marvette C. Lacy, and Wilson Kwamogi Okello. "'A Student Should Have the Privilege of Just Being a Student': Student Activism as Labor." *Review of Higher Education Supplement* 42 (2019): 37–62.

Meyers, Helene. "Public Scholar, Beware." *Inside Higher Ed,* April 11, 2019. https://www.insidehighered.com/advice/2019/04/11/risks-and-rewards-engaging-public-scholarship-opinion.

Parry, Marc. "The New Ph.D.: Momentum Grows to Rewrite the Rules of Graduate Train-
    ing." *Chronicle of Higher Education,* February 16, 2020. https://www.chronicle.com
    /article/the-new-ph-d/.

Perry, David M. "How Universities Are Failing Their Grad Students." *The Week,*
    May 19, 2019. https://theweek.com/articles/834111/how-universities-are-failing-grad
    -students.

Puri, Prateek. "The Emotional Toll of Graduate School." *Scientific American Blog,* Jan-
    uary 31, 2019. https://blogs.scientificamerican.com/observations/the-emotional-toll
    -of-graduate-school/.

Scarpino, Philip V. "Some Thoughts on Defining, Evaluating, and Rewarding Public Schol-
    arship." *The Public Historian* 15, no. 2 (1993): 93–105.

Williams, Sierra. "The Lack of Reward Mechanisms for Public Scholarship Severely Lim-
    its the Future of Public Engagement in the Academy." *London School of Economics
    Blog,* April 9, 2014. https://blogs.lse.ac.uk/impactofsocialsciences/2014/04/09/public
    -scholarship-promotion-criteria/.

More Than a Watchword

Sustainability in Digital Humanities Graduate Studies

MARIA K. ALBERTO

From August through December 2019, I was fortunate to be a graduate student fellow at Digital Matters, an emerging digital humanities (DH) initiative at the University of Utah, a large public research university in the American West. The time I spent at Digital Matters impacted my research and thinking in indelible ways, not only boosting my capacity for DH scholarship but also encouraging me to think through what this capacious term actually describes as well as how it relates to my other—arguably more traditional—work, experience, and training as a graduate student in the humanities. Reflecting on this graduate fellowship, which coincided with the third year of my PhD in English and cultural studies (and concluded just months before the Covid-19 pandemic hit the United States), I suggest that sustainability offers several key considerations for graduate work in DH, all gesturing toward the value of ongoing, community-based learning in areas that may otherwise tend to encourage individualistic models of scholarship.

At the same time, "sustainability" itself can run the risk of becoming a simple watchword: that is, summing up purportedly core beliefs without examining or troubling them. With the term sustainability in particular, we can usually tell from its contexts that something of value to the speaker is being described, but what precisely that is and where its value lies are certainly worth interrogating, especially when, as our Digital Matters space initially began, and as I continue in limited scope with this brief chapter, sustainability itself becomes a core belief and concept.

In his thought-provoking essay "After Sustainability," Steve Mentz correctly contends that sustainability itself is in part a narrative. For Mentz, however, such narratives are those of "stasis, an imaginary world in which we can trust that whatever happened yesterday will keep happening tomorrow" (586). He continues: "To be sustainable is to persist in time, unchanged in essence if not details" (586), combatting disorder and disruption in both natural and human-made systems (587). However, although Mentz is often focused on the problems of rigidity and fixedness that attend far too many discussions of ecological sustainability, I identify similar questions or issues as one fortunate outcome of my time at Digital Matters.

Sustainability has been both a founding principle and a guiding theme for Digital Matters as a DH initiative since its inception in 2018, as the organization's website highlights. Unlike Mentz's discussion of sustainability as a never-was ideal of "pastoral stasis" ("After Sustainability," 588), Digital Matters and its staff have considered sustainability a lens through which to "challenge ourselves" to reconsider digital production, as well as the ways in which such processes and their outcomes are often assumed to be—or framed as being—stable, accessible, perpetual, and resource friendly. So, although I diverge from Mentz's comprehensive dismissal of sustainability and others like it, this is not because I dismiss concerns about falsified utopian ideals but more because I have been fortunate to participate in models of academic investigation that utilize sustainability as the framework by which to ask comparable questions.

With each DH project at Digital Matters, including graduate fellowships such as my own, participants are encouraged to remain mindful of the contexts and communities adjacent to their work, as well as the resources that they draw upon and the discourses to which they contribute. For its humanities graduate students in particular, though, Digital Matters moves beyond simply fostering this burgeoning awareness of academic contexts as dynamic spaces that both create and sustain impact. Instead, Digital Matters also represents these values in tangible ways—supporting active or discovery learning, promoting demonstrable outcomes, and working alongside existing communities—that help make DH a vital, dynamic part of graduate work. Here, then, sustainability is no rigid ideal but a productive challenge and a means of reflection on how to "do" DH in ways that resonate especially with those just beginning their work in this area, as many graduate students are.[1]

Thinking in terms of sustainability can urge graduate students to consider the dynamism and impact of their DH work: that is, the exploring, practicing, applying, and integrating that are so critical in this area. How do we explicate a key need for ongoing learning, or use resources ethically and responsibly, or envision DH learning and labor in the context of home disciplines and departments that may or may not include anything else remotely like it?

From a Graduate Student Perspective: Digital Matters as Sustainable DH Initiative

As detailed on its homepage, Digital Matters is a joint venture among several entities across the University of Utah, including the Marriott Library and the Colleges of Humanities, Fine Arts, and Architecture + Planning. Its mission is a "threefold initiative": supporting interdisciplinary DH research, providing a space in which interested parties can gather and learn, and ultimately, linking DH concerns with the interests of broader communities, both academic and non-academic. These objectives are served through a wide range of funding and programming opportunities, including a speaker series, reading groups, workshops on tools and methodologies, and drop-in office hours with interdisciplinary staff, such as the fellowship I received.

Digital Matters director David Roh writes about the driving ethos behind this particular DH initiative. Drawing from his own experience in tech startup culture, Roh voices concerns about DH sometimes (whether inadvertently or not) valuing performativity and novelty at the cost of practical, ongoing usability. These concerns, he notes, have guided his work on Digital Matters, a project then still in its inception. Writing of the nascent Digital Matters, Roh outlines several qualities he considers crucial for such an initiative: a mindful focus on "self-sustaining" projects that are grounded in the appropriate discourses and can advance critical conversations, and where any performativity occurs "in the form of services in humanistic training with faculty and students, as well as outreach to local communities" ("DH Bubble," para. 8). If performativity cannot be avoided entirely, Roh maintains, then at least it should serve some purpose beyond ornamentation.

Not coincidentally, the guiding theme of Digital Matters for the first four years of its existence, 2018–2022, was sustainability. Digital Matters articulates its approach to sustainability as "a challenge . . . designed to prompt us to think about aspects of digital scholarship that we might not otherwise consider," and in particular, how to make DH work accessible beyond the university, how digital objects depend on material components, and what digital works actually "sustain."

From a graduate student perspective, Digital Matters' graduate fellowships offer a persuasive example of this sustainability both in theory and in action. These fellowships, which last a single four-month semester, are short-term but fully funded and intended to replace the fellow's other teaching duties so that they can focus completely on a particular research project. There are also light, DH-focused teaching and service requirements, with fellows being requested to attend Digital Matters events and required to complete two of their own: leading a tool-centered workshop and giving a talk on their project progress. Perhaps most importantly, though, fellows need not have extensive previous experience with DH: instead, the annual application highlights how "applicants should demonstrate interest in OR prior engagement with digital scholarship, broadly conceived." Taken together, these characteristics of the Digital Matters graduate fellowship foster active exploration of and engagement with DH, encouraging graduate students to think about DH in contextualized, ongoing ways that support sustained interest, learning, and scholarship.

Support for Active Learning

In the United States, the rhetoric of active learning, such as "exploring," is most often attached to undergraduate learning, where students are required to take general education classes (also GenEd or gen ed) beyond their area of study and encouraged to switch majors if their goals or interests change. Graduate study, though, tends to be more focused. In the humanities, the most successful graduate school applications are those in which applicants can name specific areas, projects, and even faculty with whom they wish to work, and though there are certainly theory seminars and similar coursework, there is no longer a precise corollary to GenEd classes. Although graduate students in the humanities can certainly explore their interests, this exploration takes place within a specific discipline and then proceeds in a much more focused manner than it would have during the undergraduate program. Although active learning is not necessarily absent, then, the focus on it and the rhetoric of it often are.

Digital humanities, though, almost demands a return to a more active, exploratory style of learning. Graduate students coming to DH from the humanities often (though not always) lack a rigorous background in computation, coding, and similar topics, and as Miriam Posner points out, even seasoned DH practitioners do not always have the same access to learning resources ("Think Talk Make Do," para. 1–2). And although the possession of skills in these areas is not necessarily required to "do" DH, it can certainly help explain how DH tools work, why certain methods yield particular results, and why the foundational concepts of DH often still seem to be in flux. In addition, DH itself is a quicksilver field: texts, methodologies, tools, and scholarship move fast, changing the conversation even as graduate students might still be struggling to acquire their sea legs.

Sustainability thus becomes key in a field that is simultaneously new to many and fast-paced even for those familiar with it. Although necessary and productive, the kinds of active, "discovery" learning that come with exploring new topics or skills as graduate students pursuing DH work should also be balanced to avoid burnout and the sunk cost fallacy.

The Digital Matters graduate fellowship offers a blueprint for this model. During my time there, some of the most beneficial work I did included digging into interdisciplinary scholarship to see whether a game studies approach or a computer science one made more sense for my project and then trying out both types on the gaming bots that I was studying. I also had access to Digital Matters staff who were always happy to share their experience in fields different from mine, offer feedback on my work, and point me in different directions to seek further context. The experience was a combination of the autonomy to try different things and see what worked blended with the time, resources, and support needed to do this.

Demonstrable Outcomes

As mentioned, sustainability in DH entails realizing that even primarily digital work takes place in specific contexts and draws upon resources (often material themselves) that may be scarce, finite, or labor-intensive. This realization in turn necessitates assessing and articulating the value of DH projects: how are they cognizant of the surrounding environment, and how do they make meaningful use of such resources? For graduate students, of course, this may be a particularly complex issue, because the context of their DH work includes home departments and their requirements for earning a degree, but resources may include access to DH tools, other DH practitioners, and the time needed to pursue active, discovery-based learning.

An eye toward outcomes offers one possible way of balancing these questions, but these outcomes do not always have to be fully fledged and finished artifacts. Trevor Owens maintains that "everybody working on a digital humanities project needs to be writing" ("Please Write It Down," para. 3), whether it is to record or reflect upon the work at hand, and this is certainly a tack that graduate students can take. Documenting the active learning process and formalizing thoughts in academic genres can be a means of tying in explorations of new tools, methods, and even questions with the overall DH project and demonstrating how each part of this process is valuable and productive.

Digital Matters emphasizes these sorts of outcomes as an integral part of its graduate fellowship. As visible in the annual application, applicants are asked for a standard CV and cover letter but also for a workshop proposal that successful fellows would lead for the Digital Matters community "on a digital platform, tool, or method." Accepted fellows are also asked to consider what their time at Digital Matters will produce and with which the larger Marriott Library and University of Utah communities can engage. My peer fellows have produced art installations, conference papers, and websites; I have prepared conference talks, book reviews, and shorter scholarly works such as this chapter, with an eye toward reworking my main Digital Matters project as a full article. Along the way, however, we have all been writing, discussing, and reflecting on these projects and how they have changed as we progressed further into the details of certain DH tools, methodologies, and concepts. Digital Matters also encourages such reflection on an ongoing basis. For instance, in 2021 as socially distanced meetings resumed, Digital Matters staff organized a series of brown-bag lunches in which all former fellowship grantees returned to the space and gave informal presentations on how their work has since proceeded.

These requirements of the Digital Matters graduate fellowship encourage graduate students to be aware of how their DH work is dynamic, ongoing, and in constant conversation with its environment, rather than something interesting but isolated from the rest of their graduate school training and experience.

Working with Other Communities

Community is vitally important to graduate students, whether it comes in the form of peers, mentors, resources for mental health and work-life balance, their larger community of inquiry, or their home departments. Community also becomes an important consideration of sustainability because it describes not only a significant element of the environment in which a work is produced but also the group(s) impacted by either the work itself or by the use of resources that it necessitates. Matthew Kirschenbaum characterizes DH similarly as "a social undertaking" ("What Is Digital Humanities," para. 2) built on networks of collaborators and communities, and by this token, DH is most sustainable when it considers questions such as who can use the tools it creates, who can access the work it does, who might benefit by the artifacts it sustains, and who is being included or excluded from its benefits.

Sustainability regarding graduate student work in DH brings these two concerns together even more closely. How do humanities departments take graduate students' move to active, discovery-based learning or react to graduate students taking on different sorts of work than their degrees might traditionally entail? Likewise, how *can* DH initiatives build interdisciplinary community, and how *do* they?

Digital Matters models one possible answer to these important concerns through its graduate student fellowships. As mentioned, these short-term fellowships are fully funded and intended to replace the fellow's other teaching requirements for an entire semester, thus maintaining departmental requirements for work hours and similar administrative concerns. Digital Matters also encourages affiliated graduate students, whether fellows or not, to participate in its own interdisciplinary community through events such as reading groups, workshops, and talks that draw peers and scholars from departments across and beyond the university. Although the initiative itself is a venture from the University of Utah library and specific colleges (Humanities, Fine Arts, and Architecture + Planning), Digital Matters also works closely with programs such as the university's burgeoning Entertainment Arts Engineering program, which is focused on game development and design, and has led the way toward developing the university's first Digital Culture Studies Certificate, which offers applied DH praxis to undergraduate students across majors. Taken together, such features encourage graduate students to consider how DH draws from a diverse range of intellectual communities, as well as how it should add to them.

Sustainability: More Than a Watchword

Circling back to Mentz's concerns about narratives of sustainability and their basis in wistful dreams of safe stasis, I hope that this chapter has offered an alternative option for consideration. As a core value and a central tenet, sustainability need not be either about or founded upon the types of falsified "pastoral nostalgia" that so concern Mentz. Indeed, questioning how sustainability underlies often invisible means of digital production, and in fact, scholarship, can help us build the very practices and systems "to accommodate and even enjoy radical change" that he hopes to see ("After Sustainability," 587).

Thinking of graduate student DH work in terms of sustainability means considering this scholarship as dynamic practice with both impacts upon and responsibilities to its environment. As the DH initiative Digital Matters demonstrates, supporting active learning, thinking toward fledgling outcomes, and working in tandem with existing communities are just some possible ways in which sustainability can be encouraged, but as DH continues to evolve, so too should our thought process on what sustainability entails and how we can practice it. Core values are not meant to exist in stasis.

Note

1. The specific nature of DH work and how it can or should be "done" are of course fraught and well-trod topics and far beyond the scope of my brief chapter here. Among others, see Kirschenbaum, "What Is Digital Humanities?" for a useful introduction to some of the debates surrounding this topic and Cecire, "Introduction: Theory and the Virtues."

Bibliography

Cecire, Natalia. "Introduction: Theory and the Virtues of Digital Humanities." *Journal of Digital Humanities* 1, no. 1 (2011). http://journalofdigitalhumanities.org/1-1/intro duction-theory-and-the-virtues-of-digital-humanities-by-natalia-cecire/.

Kirschenbaum, Matthew. "What Is Digital Humanities and What's It Doing in English Classes?" In *Debates in the Digital Humanities,* edited by Matthew K. Gold. Minneapolis: University of Minnesota Press, 2012. https://dhdebates.gc.cuny.edu/read/untitled -88c11800-9446-469b-a3be-3fdb36bfbd1e/section/f5640d43-b8eb-4d49-bc4b-eb31 a16f3d06#ch01.

Mentz, Steve. "After Sustainability." *PMLA/Publications of the Modern Language Association of America* 127, no. 3 (2012): 586–92. https://doi:10.1632/pmla.2012.127.3.586.

Owens, Trevor. "Please Write It Down: Design and Research in Digital Humanities." *Journal of Digital Humanities* 1, no. 1 (2011). http://journalofdigitalhumanities.org/1-1/please -write-it-down-by-trevor-owens/.

Posner, Miriam. "Think Talk Make Do: Power and the Digital Humanities." *Journal of the Digital Humanities* 1, no. 2 (2012). http://journalofdigitalhumanities.org/1-2/think -talk-make-do-power-and-the-digital-humanities-by-miriam-posner/.

Roh, David. "The DH Bubble: Startup Logic, Sustainability, Performativity." In *Debates in the Digital Humanities 2019,* edited by Matthew Gold and Lauren Klein. Minneapolis: University of Minnesota Press, 2019. https://dhdebates.gc.cuny.edu/read/untitled -f2acf72c-a469-49d8-be35-67f9ac1e3a60/section/b5b9516b-e736-4d23-bf5c-7426e 7a9de2d.

Academia Is a Dice Roll

AGNIESZKA BACKMAN, QUINN DOMBROWSKI,
SABRINA T. GRIMBERG, AND MELISSA A. HOSEK

During winter 2020, Stanford University's Division of Literatures, Cultures, and Languages offered a course titled Project Management and Ethical Collaboration for Humanists, which was taught by Quinn Dombrowski. This course took an innovative approach to project management pedagogy by dedicating half of each class period to a tabletop role-playing game, the DH RPG, based on a single, overarching scenario of a faculty member collaborating with people in various institutional roles (including undergraduate and graduate students, librarians, and a postdoctoral student) on a new digital humanities project.[1] Although the articulated learning outcome of the course was to develop project management skills, playing a simulation of academia had powerful consequences for the students' bigger-picture understanding of how, when, and for whom academia works—and where it fails. In this chapter, we reflect on what we learned through the simulation as students and the instructor of the course, and we consider the value of incorporating similar activities into the graduate school curriculum more broadly.

Game Mechanics

The details of the RPG scenario are discussed below, but some significant aspects of the game's mechanics are worth mentioning upfront. This is not the first game, or even the first RPG, created to simulate digital humanities work. Gregory Lord, Angel David Nieves, and Janet Simons's DHQuest, a game developed at Hamilton College, included both a pen-and-paper and a web-based adaptation of an RPG with what Rehn describes as "challenging quests that included finding time, funding, staffing power, institutional support, credibility, and networks. We couldn't win the game unless we had a bank with all of these resources" ("Developing a Model"). Similarly, DH Unplugged, a card game created by students enrolled in the academic year 2018–2019 Introduction to Digital Humanities cohort at Carleton University, involves amassing resources to accomplish projects.[2] Our DH RPG takes a different approach, centering gameplay on the choices of individuals and their relationships to others rather than resource acquisition and combination.

For the DH RPG, students were required to construct a character belonging to an institutional position that differed from their real-life role. The characters of the assistant professor/project director, postdoctoral fellows, graduate students, librarians, and undergraduate students in the simulation were thus played by individuals who had to learn about and imagine what it would be like to occupy that position in a DH collaboration. This was an intentional aspect of the game design intended to cultivate empathy among players. As part of character creation, players designed their characters by allocating skill points. All skills were organized into five groups: disciplinary (e.g., language knowledge, writing good prose), technical (everything from citation management and Word formatting to programming), management (managing oneself, others, work, and time), interpersonal (e.g., empathy, deceit, charisma), and personal (hobbies, relationships, and everything else). Faculty and senior staff characters had more skill points to allocate as part of character creation to reflect their greater experience and knowledge, but senior faculty characters automatically had a penalty levied against the skills of empathy, listening, managing people, and self-control unless they spent skill points to counteract the penalty resulting from spending many years with tenure.

During a turn, players decided how their character would allocate time (measured in twenty "activity points") over the course of one month. Some characters faced different in-game constraints based on their life circumstances; for example, a librarian with young children had fewer activity points available each month, and a noncitizen character had to spend a certain number of activity points struggling with visa issues. Players could freely choose how they spent their activity points, just as people make decisions about how to spend their time. However, if a character decided to undertake an activity that required skill for a successful outcome, the player would have to roll one or more dice. The number of dice available for a task depended on the character's skill level (e.g., a graduate student might roll three, six-sided dice for a language translation task, which would almost certainly guarantee a higher score and better outcome than an undergraduate rolling a single six-sided die). Every roll included one differently colored "randomness die." If the player rolled a 1 on the randomness die (even if that player rolled higher numbers on additional dice), the player then had to roll a twenty-sided die. The outcome of this D20 roll was always something unexpected for the character: something good for a high roll, bad for a low roll, or ambiguous for midrange numbers. The frequent appearance of the randomness die and its responsibility for everything from a graduate student language instructor losing students' midterms to one of those language students winning a fellowship, made evident and consequential the fact that sometimes "stuff happens" through no fault (or merit) of one's own and that effort and skill do not guarantee success.

Vocational Awe

One narrative that the DH RPG confronted is vocational awe, which Ettarh defines as "beliefs that libraries as institutions are inherently good and sacred, and therefore beyond critique" ("Vocational Awe and Librarianship"). Libraries are treated as safe and sacred spaces; librarians are portrayed as the defenders of freedom of access and intellectual freedom and as educators of the public. Often being a librarian is not framed as a job but as a calling, requiring sacrifice from the individual for a higher purpose. Vocational awe has been described explicitly for libraries and librarianship and cannot be co-opted wholesale, but the two professions share structural similarities: the defense of intellectual freedom, the focus on teaching and developing minds for a better society, the awe-inspiring buildings of the most lauded institutions, and the expectations of people to overwork and be underemployed or underpaid for the chance of a professional position. Awe of the institution and the concept of scholarship is at the core of academia.[3]

The paucity of tenure-track jobs disincentivizes scholars with precarious employment (including those occupying pretenure positions) from critiquing the system lest they be labeled as troublemakers and shut out. For newly tenured faculty, vocational awe may collide with a sense of survivor's guilt vis-a-vis peers who have been pushed out of academia, but there are significant social pressures against scholars "lucky" or "talented" enough to secure tenure speaking poorly of the system from which they benefited. As such, vocational awe is more than a sense of pride that surrounds and imbues an institution; in academia, just as in libraries, it shapes the organization of labor as well as expectations for going above and beyond in one's role. Inevitably, this impacts the formation and expectation of working relationships. Through confronting the narrative of vocational awe, our class sought to dismantle the assumptions that can lead to uneven and unfair working partnerships.

The vocational awe of the academy was examined from different angles in the class. Participants played a role they did not hold in real life—a grad student playing the project director and a librarian playing an undergraduate student. Particularly for students, this shifted focus from the potential academic dream path to one of the many possible jobs a student might have in the future: academic, alt-ac, or outside the academy. In the fictional DH project, students were all collaborators with important contributions. Who did basic data entry and who did research was not exclusively tied to the character's role, exemplifying how the traditional academic path does not have to be the only one with scholarly opportunities. The game mechanic of activity points was effective in undermining the frequent overwork inspired by vocational awe, as activity points applied to all activities in the character's life, including work, romantic partners, commutes, recreational activities, and Netflix. A player could always choose to sacrifice sleep or mental health to write or work more, but the explicit tallying of points and automatic lowering of skill level as a result of insufficient sleep showed the toll that such actions have in a way the complexities of real life can hide. Whether or not the effects of the game carried over to the students' real lives, the students tended to act with compassion and care toward their characters, even when the characters were under the pressure of deadlines, almost always allocating at least a few activity points toward relaxation. Viewing the entire working collaboration and its impact upon their character from a "bird's eye view" (which a role-playing game imparts to its players) thus allowed students to critically observe the toll of vocational awe and, at least hypothetically, devise ways to confront and mitigate its impacts.

The game mechanic of acquiring training also challenged vocational awe: it is not sacrifice or genius that ensures success but more likely the acquisition of skills. Project management is especially important in bigger projects, including many DH projects, which pose the added difficulty of collaborators with different backgrounds and skill sets that may make it more difficult to bring the project to a successful conclusion. For several of the students involved, this simulation was their first DH project; having gone through it once will help them see alternative solutions to challenges in future projects, as they have had the chance to make mistakes and see good practices in action.

Social Ecology of the Academy

Although DH workshops often aim to instruct learners in specific research methods and tools, the DH RPG brought attention to the facilities, services, and individuals that are indispensable to the completion of a project, providing a much-needed perspective on the social ecology of the university. The class began by looking at the variety of "character types" that could be drawn upon to build a research team with the skills and labor power to complete a large project. Then, through course readings (e.g., Alpert-Abrams et al., "Postdoctoral Laborers' Bill of Rights"; Mann, "Paid to Do but Not to Think") and discussions, students confronted the reality about how working relationships among collaborators are often shaped by power imbalances and conflicts of interest. The hypothetical world of the game allowed students to see "firsthand" how differences in power, status, and resources shaped behavior throughout the project. For example, when the project director felt concerned about her ability to meet project deadlines, she used her "charisma" skill to persuade an otherwise hesitant student to help digitize texts.[4] Students then witnessed the arrangements and compromises the student character had to make to accommodate the PI. The game thus served as a laboratory where students practiced navigating such working relationships and could observe the consequences of their decisions. The spirit of the game was to act in good faith and with consideration for others; one routine assignment was for the students to write up how their character was feeling about the project and the group at the end of that turn of gameplay and then consider it from another character's point of view. This pushed students to explore fairer, more compassionate modes of interaction. As such, the class simultaneously critiqued the conditions of problematic working relationships and practiced methods to foster a healthier work environment for all in academia.

A good portion of the course was dedicated to learning about the nonfaculty members of the university like IT specialists and librarians who serve as key partners on DH projects. Framed within the context of seeking potential research collaborators, as well as possible career paths, students learned about the various types of projects that IT specialists and librarians undertake in their departments. Offering a range of perspectives from data management to sustaining born-digital projects, students gained an appreciation for how these collaborators can transform a project's execution plan for the better. Recognizing librarians and IT specialists as valuable but busy collaborators impressed upon students the importance of organized project management and clear communication. The class thus located DH as occupying a relatively central node within the social ecology of the university, a position that underscores the value of training humanists in ethical leadership and management skills.

One of the major organizational structures in DH is the research team, but there are few opportunities for graduate students to grapple with the challenges of creating and working with one without facing high stakes. How do you create a research team? And how do people interact within it? For scholars engaging with DH for the first time, these can be intimidating questions, but an RPG-style class is uniquely positioned to address them. A project simulation allows students to grasp important aspects of the potential and the complexities of assembling a research team of participants outside one's discipline. Combined with reflexive readings and discussions, students' experience playing the DH RPG afforded them a wider view of the university than they typically would encounter, exploring matters such as who makes decisions, how funding is allocated, and how these factors ultimately impact one's research team. The class thus positioned future researchers to have greater environmental mastery within the university, but the nature of the class also emphasized the importance of viewing collaborations as opportunities to build fair, functioning, and productive networks, ventures that will help improve the overall working culture of the academy.

Broadening Career Paths

A powerful outcome of the course was that, almost inevitably, it led to a broadening of students' career paths. Because students were required to choose a character type that differed from their "real-life" role, the simulation served as an opportunity to better understand the tasks and responsibilities associated with positions with which they were unfamiliar. Furthermore, it allowed students to become aware of how each of those roles interacts with one another; in particular, it provided them with a lay of the land of positions within universities and led the class to engage in open and honest conversations about the pivotal role of hierarchy and power in

forging relationships, the diverging attitudes to project collaboration, and best practices for bringing a DH project to fruition.

The DH RPG also fostered self-reflection. The scarcity of academic jobs and
fierce competition for the few available positions, combined with the vocational awe
that is pervasive in academia, perpetuate the idea that if a PhD student or postdoc
is among the few lucky ones to land a tenure-track job, they must take it, regardless
of the location, type of school, teaching load, and salary. Although there are narrow
margins for negotiation, the overarching message is that landing an academic job is
an absolute godsend, being ecstatic is the only appropriate reaction to it, and accepting the job offer is the only possible response. In contrast to this mentality, the DH
RPG pushed students to explore an approach that factored in their characters' priorities, hobbies, and overall personal contexts in their answers to how much work
their characters could put into the fictional DH project for that month. Extrapolat-
ing this attitude to career exploration, the simulation showed students that individual priorities, social and financial context, and even personal preferences not only
can but should play an integral part in the decision of what type of job they seek.

Another valuable lesson from the introspection encouraged by the simulation
was that dedicating time and effort to improving or diversifying one's skills has real
consequences. Each character began the DH RPG with a certain level of expertise
for each skill, which depended on their character type. These skill levels were not
static, however; it was possible to "level up" and obtain additional points for a given
skill. Specifying clear leveling up rules instilled in students the message that dedicating time and effort to learning and training leads to visible improvement and to
the opening up of new possibilities. In this light, it becomes worthwhile to invest
time in developing their skills, regardless of whether or not those skills are valued
in graduate education.

What effect might it have on the academy if training in project management, and,
more significantly, ethical collaboration, were a mandatory prerequisite to applying for a grant or holding an administrative role from undergraduate advisor to
the dean? Simulations such as the DH RPG have the potential to take the difficult
decisions typically presented in training workshops and make them both personal
and consequential. Although a systemic overhaul of the training expectations of
the university would be a massive and difficult undertaking, the incorporation of
role-playing games into the undergraduate and graduate classroom is a more man-
ageable feat and within reach of individual instructors or program administrators
(e.g., see Katina Rogers in chapter 1 of this volume). Given a moderate degree of
freedom in course planning, instructors of DH courses are well-positioned to create
a space for grappling with hard questions about the academy, careers, and priorities.
Ultimately, the most important methods to learn in grad school do not involve text
analysis, visualization, or mapping; they are grounded in how to relate to people in
different positions and with different constraints and through those relationships

how to reach an understanding about what a meaningful career might look like for each of us, regardless of where that career is situated within or beyond the academy.

Notes

1. The rulebook, character sheets, example scenarios, and other materials for the DH RPG are available at https://dhrpg.github.io/. The syllabus for DLCL 205 is available at https://github.com/quinnanya/dlcl205.

2. The materials for this game are available at https://playdhcu5000.github.io/dh -unplugged/.

3. As an example, at the end of the PhD graduation ceremony at one author's European alma mater, after the cannon shots the conferrer said (roughly translated from Latin, of course): "May your scholarly insight also in the future be a credit to yourselves, your university, your country and a benefit to humankind."

4. The gamification of rote data tasks like OCR, as commonly found on crowdsourcing sites like Zooniverse, could be seen as a real-world attempt to incentivize participation in the absence of a personal connection with a PI that can provide a more powerful motivational lever.

Bibliography

Alpert-Abrams, Hannah, Heather Froehlich, Amanda Henrichs, Jim McGrath, and Kim Martin, eds. "Postdoctoral Laborers' Bill of Rights." Humanities Commons. April 9, 2019. http://dx.doi.org/10.17613/7fz6-ra81.

Ettarh, Fobazi. "Vocational Awe and Librarianship: The Lie We Tell Ourselves." In The Library With the Lead Pipe. January 10, 2018. http://www.inthelibrarywiththelead pipe.org/2018/vocational-awe/.

Lord, Gregory, Angel David Nieves, and Janet Simons. "DHQuest." Last updated 2015. https://web.archive.org/web/20160306214611/http://dhquest.com/.

Mann, Rachel. "Paid to Do but Not to Think: Reevaluating the Role of Graduate Student Collaborators." In Debates in the Digital Humanities 2019, edited by Matthew K. Gold and Lauren F. Klein, 268–78. Minneapolis: University of Minnesota Press, 2019.

Rehn, Andrea. "Developing a Model: Highlights from DHSI 2015" Whittier College DigLibArts. June 12, 2015. http://diglibarts.whittier.edu/developing-a-model-high lights-from-dhsi-2015/.

On the Periphery
Decentering Graduate Pedagogy in Libraries
and Digital Scholarship Centers

ALEX WERMER-COLAN

Despite the stark economic reality for graduate education in the humanities and social sciences today, curricula and programming for master's
and doctoral studies at research universities in the United States still tend
to treat pedagogical, administrative, and technical skills as subordinate to specialized knowledge for disciplinary scholarship. Even if graduate programs increasingly
promote interdisciplinary methodologies, they all too often socialize students into
a sense of professional success bound by traditional academic career paths. The
aspects of doctoral training most pertinent to postgraduate work, meanwhile, are
often delegated to peripheral centers beyond the confines of departmental programs.

My postdoctoral experience in one such peripheral center, Temple University
Libraries' Digital Scholarship Center (now known as the Loretta C. Duckworth
Scholars Studio), persuaded me of the potential for libraries and other interdepartmental centers to provide unique types of support for humanities and social science
graduate students looking to experiment with new methods and approaches. These
peripheral spaces and their often marginal programming, especially when focused
on digital methods, can present new opportunities for students to contribute to
interdisciplinary projects while learning unfamiliar theories, techniques, and skills.
This multifaceted graduate training proves applicable not just to students' disciplinary research but to a wide range of career paths in library science, education, data
engineering, software development, journalism, publishing, marketing, administration, nonprofit activism, and social justice organizing. While working in this
"peripheral center" alongside generous and inventive librarians and archivists, professors and instructors, technicians and developers, and undergraduate and graduate students, I have been inspired by recent scholarship on digital pedagogy and
design approaches that foreground labor and process to forge inclusive spaces for
diverse disciplinary perspectives and methodological approaches.[1]

In this brief chapter, I reflect on lessons learned during two projects developed out of my postdoctoral research between 2018 and 2020 in a large public university's main academic library and its evolving spaces for collaborative, process-based, pedagogically-oriented research. The first project involved working with doctoral students in media studies, communication studies, information science, and political science to web scrape YouTube comment threads about broadcast news videos from 2018–20 that spectacularized Trump's mythic wall on the United States–Mexico border. The second project involved students from fields as different as marketing and art history, focusing on a holistic approach to the data life cycle through the digitization and curation of science fiction books from Temple Libraries' special collections. Both projects' openness to students' process-based output (selecting materials for digitization, curating datasets, testing software, developing code, discussing use cases, running workshops, and publishing tutorials and scholarship) offers models for those seeking to address the fragmented nature of the graduate experience by bridging disparate departments and centers for research and teaching.

Nearly every digital project I have advised or coordinated at Temple and beyond has required supporting faculty and students from wide-ranging disciplines engaged with the problem of transforming real-world phenomena into data that is amenable to computational modeling and visualization. Depending on their disciplinary background and training, students (and faculty) bring different, and often opposing, questions and approaches to this principal challenge. Early in our exploratory discussions for the web scraping YouTube project, the students' theoretical frameworks and methodological leanings often seemed to conflict, not least because their disciplinary training rarely introduced jargon and theories from foreign fields and frameworks. The participating students came from social science fields with concentrations in new media and communication technologies, but they did not possess a shared theoretical background from foundational perspectives like the Frankfurt School, semiotics and structuralism, or recent work in critical algorithm studies and cultural analytics. Students likewise had received minimal prior exposure or organized training in the digital methods (web scraping and text mining) necessary for robust empirical research bridging qualitative and quantitative modes of analyzing new media.

Many graduate students from across the disciplines came to Temple University Libraries' Digital Scholarship Center precisely in search of these unfamiliar theories and methods, often expressing wonder and excitement to discover what is available beyond the parameters of their department. With this in mind, I sought to devise collaborative projects for graduate students to work on without predetermined hypotheses or methodologies. Through the iterative process of exploring the source material and experimenting with software for data harvesting and analysis and through discussion of what interests we shared, what complementary skills we could offer, what time and energy was available to us, and what we wanted to learn by the end of the project, we homed in on the most relevant theoretical frameworks, hermeneutic approaches, and digital methods for exploring our multifaceted research questions.

When students from different disciplines engage in informal working groups and collaborative, exploratory digital projects, the friction between their perspectives can become surprisingly generative, especially for thinking through what is lost in translation when multimodal, participatory platforms like YouTube or mass-market books of the "paperback revolution" are interpreted as data points for statistical analysis. At this early stage of the science fiction digitization project, graduate students had the opportunity to learn hands-on the intricacies of translating scanned images of books into machine-readable text through optical character recognition, testing the affordances of automated and manual methods for correcting errors and improving the quality of digitized texts. The difficulties of transforming such data brought into relief the problems of labor endemic to most digital projects, as students frequently serve as siloed research assistants and are rarely given proper attribution or invited into project management decisions.

Like the web scraping project, the science fiction digitization project was devised so that each student could work on each part of the project, learning every aspect of both the data life cycle and the cultural import of these underrepresented literary works. Each student received opportunities and encouragement to pursue their own research born out of the collaborative project, with history students studying digital mapping of alternate history narratives, art students exploring machine learning and augmented reality for remediating old book covers, and marketing and law students thinking through the curation of proprietary data for researchers. By foregrounding the labor involved in wrangling data for analysis, students were put in a position to take agency in the design and scope of the collaborative project and make decisions to sacrifice scan quality for the sake of developing a representative corpus at scale. Along the way, students gained the confidence to critique large-scale studies that hid the labor behind their data.

The challenges provoked by these digital projects consistently went beyond the discipline-specific demands of the students' graduate programs in ways that benefited their dissertation research, their growth as scholars, teachers, and technical practitioners, and their hopes and plans for their professional futures. The pedagogical approach integral to such collaborative, cross-disciplinary research involves more than just allowing students to take an active role in establishing the project's research goals and methodological approaches. Such pedagogical strategies also require teaching digital literacy by foregrounding the unlearning of mastery and the importance of being open to making mistakes and having patience for troubleshooting.

For graduate students trained in scholarly research through reading secondary sources, mining archives, and conducting fieldwork, there is something almost uncanny about learning the necessary practice in digital scholarship of debugging technological issues. The process of finding appropriate software for solving problems, searching online for the solutions to error messages, perusing insular discussion forums, and fixing infrastructure that seems irrelevant to the task at hand can prove frustrating for students burdened by imposter syndrome and a fear of failure. A collaborative, playful approach to solving these granular problems, along with the support net of technicians and instructors found in peripheral centers for digital pedagogy and research, can prove crucial to guiding students toward a suitable mindset and workflow for innovative work in the humanities and social sciences today.

At peripheral centers for interdisciplinary research with emerging technologies, collaborative digital projects also offer valuable opportunities for graduate students to make tangible contributions to wider social problems beyond the scope of their graduate programs' explicit demands and implicit leanings. Such peripheral centers, especially in libraries and related digital scholarship centers, are positioned to leverage disciplinary approaches and technological innovation for responding to pressing crises, be it disaster relief through projects like the "mapathon" for Puerto Rico organized at over one hundred digital scholarship centers after Hurricane Maria in 2017, or media studies projects that can analyze, as we sought to do, the spectacle of Trump's wall on YouTube. Collaborative projects such as the Nimble Tents Toolkit and SUCHO (Saving Ukrainian Cultural Heritage Online) that deploy peripheral institutional resources and emerging methods for rapid-response relief offer an underexplored model for decentering the traditional goals of academic work toward practical purposes. Peripheral infrastructures, and the faculty, staff, and students who build and run their services, can open spaces in higher education for students to critique technologies' embedded biases and reverse engineer hardware and software toward the analytical task of ideology critique and the restorative work of remedying social inequality in its myriad forms.

It remains difficult to generalize about the problems facing higher education in the coming years, but the failure of colleges and universities to adapt to the Covid-19 pandemic is not unrelated to the resistance within departmental structures to ensuring graduate training remains relevant to the changing nature of the job market. In the twenty-first century, peripheral, extradepartmental centers for research and teaching, especially those focused on integrating emerging technologies into academic work, have offered uniquely fertile soil for developing alternative scholarly and pedagogical approaches. These varied centers and labs can prove relatively agile at pivoting in the face of constant flux, attuned to the demands of nonacademic industries and careers and suited to nourishing graduate students seeking interdisciplinary, collaborative, and multifaceted learning opportunities.

Now more than ever, academic administrators, directors, and professors in traditional departments have an opportunity to take stock and learn from these institutions and initiatives. Doing so, however, may require changing funding priorities and organizational models, bringing lessons from the periphery into the center, and decentering what has been taken for granted in graduate training for too long. Such change will likewise necessitate that academic departments, especially in their expectations for tenure and promotion, call into question the inexorable dichotomy between teaching and research, and find ways to make the two sides of academic work synergistic: researching through the process of teaching and teaching through the research process.

As it becomes increasingly necessary for education professionals to rethink what counts as essential in a new economic reality, academia's hope lies in pedagogical models too long neglected as marginal, exemplified by alt-ac forms of mentorship and by active-learning, project-based initiatives outside traditional curricula. Graduate programs can no longer afford to hold onto apprenticeship models for outdated career paths; teachers cannot succeed by adopting pedagogical strategies that too often replicate students in their own images. Process-based, pedagogically oriented research, geared toward social justice issues and coordinated at the institutional periphery, offers a promising way forward. These models uniquely foster the kinds of collaborative knowledge production that can justify the humanities to the public, orient students toward a collective vision of alternate futures, and contribute to an academic system that treats its workers equitably while offering its students a diversity of rewarding and sustainable career paths.

Note

1. The scholarly field on digital pedagogy is rich and diffuse, with many perspectives to consider and models to follow. Graduate programs at institutions like the University of Maryland's Institute for Technology in the Humanities, University of Virginia Scholars' Lab, and Columbia University's XP Methods group have greatly influenced my thinking. Nowviskie's writing on speculative futures, as well as the discourse she helped create about alternative academic career paths, Rogers' *Putting the Humanities PhD to Work*, and wide-ranging essays on collaborative scholarship, such as Rawson's and Muñoz's "Towards Collaborative Models," provide crucial background to this essay. This loose field of theory and practice draws inspiration from such disparate institutional critiques as Fitzpatrick's *Generous Thinking*, McPherson's *Feminist in a Software Lab*, Ahmed's *On Being Included*, and Risam's *New Digital Worlds*. Relatively recent initiatives, such as Alex Gil's Nimble Tents Toolkit (https://nimbletents.github.io) and the large-scale, collaborative web archiving SUCHO project (https://www.sucho.org), have built on the lessons learned from institutional experiments in the digital humanities in order to respond to immediate crises. Few influenced me more than the Visionary Futures Collective (https://visionary-futures-collective.github.io), a collaborative group of alt-ac and precarious academics that came together at the start of the pandemic to work across institutions to critique and offer alternatives to academia's endgame during a time of great upheaval.

Bibliography

Ahmed, Sara. *On Being Included: Racism and Diversity in Institutional Life.* Durham, N.C.: Duke University Press, 2012.

Fitzpatrick, Kathleen. *Generous Thinking: A Radical Approach to Saving the University.* Baltimore: Johns Hopkins University Press: 2019.

McPherson, Tara. *Feminist in a Software Lab: Difference and Design.* Cambridge, Mass.: Harvard University Press, 2018.

Nowviskie, Bethany. "A Skunk in the Library." June 28, 2011. https://nowviskie.org/2011/a-skunk-in-the-library/.

Rawson, Katie, and Trevor Muñoz. "Towards Collaborative Models of Digital Scholarship." Paper presented at the Digital Library Federation, October 17, 2018.

Risam, Roopika. *New Digital Worlds: Postcolonial Digital Humanities in Theory, Praxis, and Pedagogy.* Evanston, Ill.: Northwestern University Press, 2018.

Rogers, Katina. *Putting the Humanities PhD to Work.* Durham, N.C.: Duke University Press, 2020.

PART V

INFRASTRUCTURES AND INSTITUTIONS

Graduate Students and Project Management
A Humanities Perspective

NATALIA ERMOLAEV, REBECCA MUNSON,
AND MEREDITH MARTIN

Department X invites applications for a tenure-track assistant professor with a specialization in 19th-century French and Francophone literatures/cultures and expertise in Digital Humanities beginning August 2020. The successful candidate will be expected to teach four courses per year and play a key role in program development and interdisciplinary collaboration with scholars in Digital Humanities within and beyond Department X.

When a humanities job posting asks for digital humanities expertise, the expectations for the position often exceed those of the conventional faculty role. Being the "DH person" will mean that in addition to research and teaching, the new hire will also serve as an administrator, consultant, grant writer, negotiator, mediator, and team builder. Though not every position explicitly bundles these responsibilities, they are implied; this range of activities is always necessary for the project-based, collaborative, interdisciplinary, and cross-professional nature of digital humanities work.

These responsibilities are familiar to anyone with a career in digital humanities, whether faculty, librarian, digital archivist, or staff at a digital humanities or digital scholarship center. Many of these skills can be gained through experience in project management, but few of us have significant exposure or sufficient (or any) training before we take on these roles.[1] It would be an enormous benefit to students at all levels of graduate study if digital humanities centers and programs offered substantive training in project management.

Comprehensive and thoughtful project management experience at the graduate level can have manifold benefits for young scholars about to embark on job searches, whether for traditional academic positions or for other opportunities. Working as a project manager on a digital humanities project provides exposure to collaborative research practices and technology development, both of which can significantly broaden a student's career path but are also rare in conventional humanities programs. Project management teaches an organizational scaffolding that can be applied to a student's research process and help them be better scholars. Moreover, project management work can provide a challenge to the hierarchical power structures that define the culture and practices of academia, elevating the work of students, junior or contingent faculty, and staff. By empowering graduate students to be project managers, they gain skills, experience, and the ethical lens to prepare them for success in a variety of settings, propel their careers, and possibly produce better humanities research and better technologies. The transferable professional skills and confidence graduate students gain through project management experience will be all the more relevant and desirable in a higher education landscape that adapts to a post-pandemic world.

Since the launch of the Center for Digital Humanities at Princeton (CDH) in 2014, teaching graduate students the art and science of project management has been a cornerstone of our graduate program.[2] Although we have always been committed to mentoring graduate students for both traditional academic and alternative career paths, the increased urgency of the Covid-era job market has encouraged us to dedicate more resources to both research mentorship (primarily via our graduate fellows program) and professional development through fellowship positions with administrative components including the Project Management Fellowship. Although this essay focuses on our experience with graduate student project managers, it is worth noting that, for the CDH, project management itself is situated at the heart of a larger goal of changing the way the academy views and supports graduate study as a whole.

This chapter argues that project management in the digital humanities gives students a meaningful grounding in three core concepts: process, contingency, and collaboration. Our position is based on experience as project management mentors, as career placement officers in departments, and as project managers ourselves. In our work with graduate students, we provide formal training with a holistic approach that covers specific tools and techniques, foregrounds the importance of procedure and process, and emphasizes the social and ethical function of project management. As we describe below, our starting point is a critical approach to project management, one that has a distinctly humanistic orientation that is self-reflexive and contextual and that recognizes the project manager's role in organizing the intellectual, ethical, and social infrastructure of a project.

A Critical Approach

At the CDH, Project Management Fellowships are attached to specific projects, most of which are proposed by faculty members and chosen as collaborations by the CDH under the auspices of a Research Partnership Grant. Unlike some of our other fellowship opportunities, which run on an open application model, graduate student project managers are typically nominated by the faculty member for their specialist knowledge or based on a previous project. The term of the fellowship is one calendar year, though the fellowship itself is broken into two halves (and two payments) to allow for a midyear assessment of whether all parties involved are happy for the student to continue in this role. To date, all graduate student project managers have been from humanities PhD programs, and only some have come to the position with experience in digital humanities.

A member of the CDH staff serves as the project management mentor. After the graduate student's nomination, the staff member interviews the graduate student candidate and discusses the responsibilities of the role, ensuring that the candidate is aware of—and excited by—project management as a practice. Faculty motivation for nominating students typically has to do with academic subject awareness; the CDH interview ensures informed consent, and often generates enthusiasm, on the part of the applicant for taking on the administrative side of the role. If all goes well, the graduate student initiates a project manager position with work on the charter.

The charter is a foundational document that describes the rationale, goals, plan of work, resources needed, terms and conditions, and outcomes of a CDH project.[3] Charters are written by core members of a project team in a series of approximately five meetings occurring over the course of a month. The planning process is intensive and collaborative and requires substantial input from everyone on a team. Charters serve as formalized agreements among all team members on such crucial questions as scope, technical design, infrastructural needs, and success criteria. The charter process is the team's first opportunity to establish a team ethos as well as infrastructure to sustain the project over its life cycle. The graduate student project manager shadows their CDH mentor and helps run this series of crucial meetings.

At the same time, the project manager attends a multiday orientation also attended by graduate students working on other CDH projects. This is the first opportunity to create community and connection and where key concepts, themes, and problems are introduced to the cohort of new project managers. Discussions continue throughout the year in the project managers group, which meets monthly. Coordinated by a CDH mentor who assigns short readings and structured discussion topics, the project managers group is the primary space in which disciplinary self-reflection occurs and where project managers can ask questions and candidly share the challenges they face. The number of graduate student project managers at any given time varies because it is linked to the number of active CDH projects. We also open this group to CDH postdoctoral fellows, who attend as mentors, because they are established digital humanities researchers, and as students, because they want to learn more about project management as a discipline.

We are acutely aware that what falls under the term "project management" is often seen as the necessary busy work that is adjacent to the "real" academic endeavors of research or to the creative technical work of software development. Furthermore, the emotional labor involved in negotiating the various unequal power structures in which all academic projects take place—power structures in which graduate students typically occupy the lowest position—results in an enormous amount of unrecognized, invisible labor. In our documentation and labor practices, we empower graduate project managers to value and trust their own instincts while recognizing that raising difficult questions with faculty leads, who are often their dissertation directors as well, may be impractical. The CDH project management mentor and the peers in the cohort are key resources for negotiating this difficult emotional territory. The CDH mentor may, when necessary, escalate issues to the faculty member or serve as the mediator between team members.

The project managers group is where students are first introduced to the concept of critical project management. It is not always clear to students, or even to many established digital humanities researchers, that by becoming a project manager they enter a new field of study with its own literature, practices, and debates. This is often obscured by the highly functionalist application of project management in today's corporate and industry settings. Even though project management is recognized as central to the success of DH projects, especially those that are larger-scale or multi-institutional, there has been little evolution in the way the digital humanities community frames project management guidance and practice.[4] Although many resources are truly helpful in aiding scholars through the project life cycle, they tend to cast project management as little more than a set of best practices, templates, and tools; put simply, project management is viewed as not much more than the necessary scaffolding for efficiency and success.[5] And because of this focus on control and outcomes, project management can easily be undervalued, misunderstood, or blamed for project failures. The project manager is frequently isolated as the sole individual responsible for project organization and administration—bureaucratic work considered beyond the scope of the team as a collective. At its most cynical, project management practices are viewed disdainfully as managerial technologies that prove corporate culture's encroachment into higher education.

Seeking a corrective, we follow the Critical Project Studies movement led by organizational studies scholars Svetlana Cicmil and Damian Hodgson, who urge a reorientation toward the intellectual foundations of project management and the deep social and contextual nature of projects.[6] Bringing project management into dialogue with Jürgen Habermas and Michel Foucault, Cicmil and Hodgson remind us that because projects are "social phenomena that are not neutral, but socially constructed in the interactions among people," managing them entails navigating complex social and cultural forces ("Introduction," 15). They give the project manager, and the project team more generally, agency as cocreators in the project reality. For Cicmil and Hodgson, the urge to universalize project management through standardized terminology, tools, and metrics decontextualizes and even dehumanizes a project by shutting down alternative visions or trajectories and a multiplicity of voices (13). A flattened view of project management can have ethical implications as well. Because projects both perform and inscribe the power asymmetries present in our societies, the project managers must show awareness of—and when necessary and possible create alternatives to—models in which tools are used unreflectively for observation, measure, and control. We agree with Cicmil and Hodgson's position that project success must be defined beyond just time, cost, and quality performance to include aspects such as the environment, health and safety, and ethics, which imposes a more human-centered or humanistic orientation to the overall project.

Introducing this critical approach to novice project managers creates a powerful foundation that helps graduate students link the theoretical and practical, the humanistic and the technical, and the individual and the collective. This conceptual starting point empowers the project managers by raising their understanding of the complexity and impact of their roles, and it fosters an environment of equity and respect on the project team from the start.

Process

As suggested above, the critical approach to project management informs the way that graduate students learn about the tools, workflows, and systems that are part of digital humanities work. Among the most valuable experiences they gain through their project management fellowship is close involvement with our software development team. They become familiar with our process, designed by our lead developer and iteratively modified in collaboration with members of the development and design team. The term "process" in software engineering refers to the set of work phases applied to designing and building a software product and encompasses the workflows, systems, and tools and how they connect and relate to each other.

At the CDH, graduate students are exposed to Agile software development in action and see the value of clear articulation of methods, steps, and goals. They learn the value of team planning, iteration, and retrospectives. They create workflows for collaborative tasks such as transcribing letters or tagging images. The importance of a documentation strategy when working with teams quickly becomes clear to project managers, who can apply this experience to any collaborative endeavor. Graduate student project managers also gain significant experience in the technical aspects of the project. They participate in the design and development process by writing user stories, testing features, and performing user experience testing. They manage and track complex workflows that span scholarly, technical, and social priorities. They become fluent in the approaches employed by the development and design team and serve as translators of the project's technical aspects to the broader community of peers and scholars.

We also aim for graduate student project managers to see process from an epistemological angle. Borrowing ideas developed by economic geographers Gernot Grabher and Oliver Ibert, we discuss how tools, workflows, and systems help constitute the "project ecology," the relational space and site of exchanges that enable the articulation of new knowledge. In "Project Ecologies: A Contextual View on Temporary Organizations," Grabher and Ibert provide useful notions of "cumulative" and "disruptive" project ecologies: cumulative projects are typified by corporate software development teams where modularization and easy replicability are key, whereas disruptive project ecologies are "organized around the imperative of originality," as in many academic environments (178). Because the digital humanities project ecology is the space in which the modular, iterative mode meets with the disruptive ecology of creativity-driven professions, it is particularly important to recognize how a project management process must be able to adapt to this dynamic knowledge-building environment.

By focusing on process as essential to knowledge production, graduate students are taught to make their choices transparent and how to balance planning, implementation, iteration, and reflection. This is a practice that can be broadly generalized and applied in other collaborative endeavors or in independent research such as dissertation writing.

Contingency

One of the main lessons learned in project management for digital humanities is to accept uncertainty—to imagine and be prepared for multiple outcomes. At the same time that much of a project manager's task revolves around keeping the organizational structure intact, we push back against an overemphasis on what is known as the "iron triangle" of project management: budget, scope, and schedule. Openness to course correction is a key aspect of our approach. In digital humanities, project management must be a dialectical process, demanding that its practitioner toggle between the real and the preferable and balance the ideal with the pragmatic. In the early years of CDH project development, when our approach was more "waterfall," each charter for our year-long grants would include elaborate work plans and timelines and Gantt charts. And each year, we struggled to reach deadlines and milestones and often felt disappointment (shared by our faculty collaborators) that we could not reach the goals we set out to accomplish.

Our failures to stay "on track" were not due to incompetence or negligence. Nearly every time we "fell behind," it was due to unexpected scholarly or technical discoveries that forced us to reorient our thinking. This is the precise nature of digital humanities work; the material we work with is far more complex, interesting, and unexpected than we imagine at the outset. Our goal is not only to complete a particular deliverable but to explore and learn and cocreate something new. As important as it is to stay within scope and budget and to respect timelines, it is just as important to establish an ethos of collective flexibility based on intellectual goals coupled with the project team's social and ethical priorities.

In the CDH's latest iteration of project charters, we have eschewed timelines and work plans for a more agile approach.[7] We now provide a "road map," which assigns some chronological guidelines to major milestones, but we have built in time and space for uncertainty and modification. The project manager must learn to balance keeping a team on track, bound to certain time and resource constraints, with the need to discern and accept new directions.

This acknowledgment of multiple paths and undiscovered outcomes must be the approach that today's graduate students in the humanities navigate through their own learning and career paths. The pressure to complete the PhD and to succeed in an ever more competitive and diminishing job market means that young scholars must practice the kind of awareness and honest self-reflection that can accept, or even embrace, new alternatives.

Collaboration

Project management is intrinsically tied to the central innovation of digital humanities, which is the collaborative partnerships among interdisciplinary and cross-professional teams of professors, graduate students, undergraduates, librarians, developers, designers, and communications professionals. Digital humanities practitioners know that establishing a truly collaborative environment among such diverse teams is a challenge. The structures of academia have, by and large, not yet changed in ways that validate and recognize collaborative research in the humanities as scholarship.[8] Bringing together teams surfaces the complex labor landscape that operates in academia, which includes the balance of power between tenured and junior or contingent faculty, the divide between "service"-oriented academic professions versus those dedicated to research, the absence of consistent guidelines for attribution and compensation of student labor, and the role of institutional support from university administration.

At the CDH, we create project charters that model collaboration. The charter engenders a dialogic environment that we view not primarily as a contract or formalization of outcomes and responsibilities, although these are included, but as an active space where project members create a team dynamic with a shared commitment to intellectual, ethical, social, and sometimes political values. By articulating the project's commitment to a set of values, charters thus necessitate the negotiation of such topics as equity and fair labor, accountability, adaptability, accessibility, sustainability, and community practices. Charters are continuously referred to throughout the project life cycle and amended as necessary to document major changes, one way that charters acknowledge the constant renegotiation of outcomes that characterizes digital humanities work.

The emphasis on discussion and revision allows for the incorporation of many voices and creates a cohesive network of relationships among newly assembled project team members. We see this as a key ethical intervention of the CDH project process, which helps transform and enable, however subtly, new intellectual, social, and cultural dynamics to take root in the academic context.

The foundations and practices of a relational model for project management have, in our experience, led to successful projects and successful graduate students who have found careers both in and beyond academia. We are committed to working with graduate students to reflect critically and define success broadly; not all of our graduate student project managers practice "digital humanities" in their scholarship even in its broadest sense, but they all understand, intimately, how these projects work. When knowledge is itself an outcome, the imperative exists to develop a process that allows for flexibility and uncertainty; this is a subtle way we aim to make the CDH a space of discovery and community for graduate students across the university. No academic work happens in a vacuum. We want our students to foreground the relationships and institutional structures that influence their work, along with their ethical implications. By rethinking project management for digital humanities with our graduate student fellows, we have arrived at a theoretical perspective better suited to the spirit of humanist inquiry to which we are all committed.

Notes

1. In her "Curatorial Statement," included in the MLA Digital Pedagogy in the Humanities guide, Siemens explains, "With its associated methods, tools, and techniques, project management provides a way to coordinate people, tasks and resources." Siemens further adopts the Association for Project Management's definition of project management: "Simply stated, though complicated in practice, project management is 'the application of processes, methods, knowledge, skills and experience to achieve the project objectives.'" See Siemens, "Curatorial Statement."

2. For information about the CDH Project Management Fellowship program, see https://cdh.princeton.edu/engage/graduate-students/project-management-fellowship/.

3. For information on the charter process and published CDH project, see https://cdh.princeton.edu/research/project-management/charters/.

4. Useful project management workshops and "how to" trainings are offered regularly at summer digital humanities institutes, such as the University of Victoria's Digital Humanities Summer Institute (DHSI), the European Summer School at Leipzig, and the Humanities Intensive Learning and Teaching. Panels at digital humanities conferences have been a welcome space for more creative and critical approaches to project management; see especially Ermolaev et al., "Project Management for the Digital Humanities" and the Project Management in the Humanities conferences at DHSI.

5. The most useful and comprehensive resource for hands-on project management in digital humanities remains DevDH, available at https://devdh.org/ and created in 2013 by Jennifer Guiliano of Indiana University Indianapolis (IU Indianapolis) and Simon

Appleford of Creighton University. Another excellent resource is the Project Management collection curated by Siemens for MLA's 2020 *Digital Pedagogy in the Humanities: Concepts, Models, and Experiments*. For resources aimed specifically at graduate students, see Storti and Lestock, "Project Management."

      6. In particular, see the volume of essays edited by Cicmil and Hodgson, *Making Projects Critical*.

      7. CDH charters and charter process were revised in summer 2020.

      8. As Grabher and Ibert define disruptive project ecologies, the entrenchment of distinct professional personae means that "interactions within the team are, comparatively speaking, more strongly shaped by antagonistic professional identities than by the joint project task." See Grabher and Ibert, "Project Ecologies," 180.

Bibliography

Cicmil, Svetlana, and Damian Hodgson. "Introduction." In *Making Projects Critical*, edited by Damian Hodgson and Svetlana Cicmil, 1–21. New York: Palgrave Macmillan, 2006.

Ermolaev, Natalia, Rebecca Munson, Xinyi Li, Lynne Siemens, Ray Siemens, Micki Kaufman and Jason Boyd. "Project Management for the Digital Humanities." Panel presented at DH 2018, Mexico City, June 21, 2018. https://dh2018.adho.org/en/project-management-for-the-digital-humanities/.

Grabher, Gernot, and Oliver Ibert. "Project Ecologies: A Contextual View on Temporary Organizations." In *The Oxford Handbook of Project Management*, edited by Peter W. G. Morris, Jeff Pinto, and Jonas Söderlund, 175–98. New York: Oxford University Press, 2011.

Hodgson, Damian, and Svetlana Cicmil, eds. *Making Projects Critical*. New York: Palgrave Macmillan, 2006.

Siemens, Lynne. "Curatorial Statement." Humanities Commons. Accessed February 15, 2022. https://digitalpedagogy.hcommons.org/keyword/Project-Management.

Storti, Sarah, and Brooke Lestock. "Project Management." Praxis Program, Scholars' Lab. Accessed February 15, 2022. http://praxis.scholarslab.org/resources/project-management/.

Notes toward the Advantages of an Agile Digital Humanities Graduate Program

HEATHER RICHARDS-RISSETTO AND ADRIAN S. WISNICKI

This chapter contends that an agile curricular approach to digital humanities graduate programs, such as the one in place at the University of Nebraska-Lincoln (UNL), offers unique opportunities for fostering an effective DH graduate education, especially when the agile approach is paired with a supportive institutional environment.[1] A fixed approach focuses on a defined curriculum where students follow one or more common tracks through year-to-year course offerings. By contrast, an agile curriculum offers students a menu of curricular options that varies year to year based on instructor interests and allows students to select courses based on personal preference and their own research interests.[2] In considering the pros of an agile approach, we use the context of the UNL graduate certificate to examine three main areas that are foundational to an education in the digital humanities: interdisciplinarity, an adaptive development ethos, and community embedding.[3] Our reflection on these three areas underscores their value to an agile curricular approach and reveals that the collective educational experience in such a context has the potential to shift the focus of student investigation from the classroom to real-world applications of acquired DH critical thinking strategies, knowledge, and skills.

Interdisciplinarity

An agile DH curricular program cannot exist in a vacuum. Rather, the program's overarching institutional contexts, including the kind of direct and indirect support that the program might be able to provide to faculty and students as well as to the institution's DH community in general, play a key role in enabling its success.[4] Within DH, and academia more generally, questions about the tension between teaching students technical skills versus critical thinking persist (e.g., Clement, "Multiliteracies in the Undergraduate"; Hirsch, *Digital Humanities Pedagogy*; Mahony and Pierazzo, "Teaching Skills"; Sula et al., "Survey of Digital Humanities Programs"). For example, is one skill set more important than the other?[5] Does the relevance depend on a student's future career goals? And, importantly, how can we ideally reach a balance between these two skill sets, that is, between technical skills and critical thinking skills? We contend that to effectively tackle such questions, an agile DH program benefits considerably when it can draw its faculty from a range of disciplines and when it has the support of an interdisciplinary set of departments (Svensson, "Landscape of Digital Humanities").[6] Such widespread support signals to students in the program (and to those in the university community as a whole) that DH practice can address research questions that extend beyond any one discipline or area of academic inquiry. The widespread support underscores the broader value of the program. The chance for students to work with faculty in multiple disciplines also creates opportunities to gain a firsthand understanding of the value of such interdisciplinarity. Students may find that a chance to shape discourse in other fields is invigorating or discover that questions raised from other disciplinary perspectives can reshape their own disciplinary priorities; they may even come to privilege arguments that resonate in multiple fields at once. Ultimately, these diverse opportunities support and extend the fundamental points made by the application of an agile curriculum within the program itself, as both require a dynamic and multifaceted approach to DH practice.[7]

The Graduate Certificate Program in Digital Humanities at UNL bears out these points. Over the last decade, UNL has used individual and cluster hires to build its strengths in interdisciplinary DH while promoting solid working relationships among DH faculty and between DH faculty and DH-oriented librarians and programmers at the university's Center for Digital Research in the Humanities (CDRH).[8] Graduate certificate courses are offered in anthropology, art history, art theory and practice, classics and religious studies, English, history, and modern languages.[9] Graduate students take two required graduate courses—one in DH readings, the other a DH practicum—which provide strong foundations in DH-based critical thinking as well as the opportunity to develop technical skills in a DH project.[10] Faculty members from different disciplines rotate teaching these two core courses so students are exposed to readings and projects that typically might be considered outside the students' disciplines. These strategies and steps have ensured that students in the DH program have a vibrant, overarching environment in which to grow as scholars and multiple opportunities to appreciate, engage in, and benefit from interdisciplinary work in the digital humanities. Such interdisciplinarity goes hand-in-hand with the agile curricular approach and helps extend it in ways that might not otherwise be possible.

Adaptive Development Ethos

Any DH program relies on developing unique skills not necessarily foundational to a given student's discipline. These skills might include coding, data management, project management, budget building, grant writing, and ethics. However, just as important are more intangible skills: an experimental, creative, and playful attitude; the ability to think critically about and rigorously question digitally inflected worlds; and the potential for successful collaboration with individuals at multiple hierarchical levels. An agile DH curriculum, because it asks students to be flexible and to experiment by its very nature, has the potential to nurture such skills among students in ways more effective than a fixed curricular approach. For example, students majoring in English, journalism and mass communications, modern languages, and other areas often take Digital Heritage Tools, a DH elective. For many, this class is their first exposure to cultural heritage using theoretical and methodological perspectives grounded in anthropology. Students often collaborate on weekly labs and semester projects and bring with them individual interests as well as academic and extracurricular experiences that shape their labs and projects. Some students have strong technical skills, others deeper theoretical training, and as such, labs and projects typically ask students to step outside their comfort zones to experiment not only with new technologies but also with new concepts. Indeed, an agile DH program more readily allows for immediate adaptation to current local and global circumstances because students have the flexibility to experiment in nontraditional arenas and to do so with a broad range of faculty, staff, and students as well as with communities outside of academia. Although some might see the lack of formal structure to a DH program as problematic or at least not geared to help solidify the future of humanities in academia, we contend that such agility is a strength (Pannapacker, "No More Digitally Challenged"; Walzer, "Digital Humanities").

UNL nurtures an adaptive development ethos among students by leveraging the total curricular experience at both the undergraduate and graduate levels. The long duration of this curricular experience enables students to evolve their DH skills over time while tackling important research questions at different levels of sophistication. Additionally, the fact that UNL offers both an undergraduate minor and a graduate certificate, each with a wide range of course options, allows for greater flexibility with regard to tailoring the curricular path based on students' interests while balancing requirements that provide a solid DH foundation in technical and project skills alongside critical thinking.[11] UNL also offers split undergrad-grad courses that bring together students who might otherwise not normally interact in the classroom. These courses emphasize discussion and teamwork-led development with collaborators (i.e., other students) at different stages in their educational careers.[12] Together, these curricular contexts compel students to work in multiple registers and to apply—in critically-inflected ways—the kind of intellectual agility that is also foundational to the layout of the curriculum as a whole.

Community Embedding

Finally, an agile DH curriculum has the potential to best capitalize upon its embeddedness within the given institutional DH community. In fact, the program's agility itself plays a central role in this process by creating opportunities for students, faculty, and staff working in DH to come together, while evolving their shared interests through various activities and initiatives. These might include regular meetings, focused learning initiatives, or public events; students will have recurrent chances to contribute to faculty-led research, pursue research in guided extra-curricular contexts, and/or take part in major national and international DH conferences. The collective quality of such efforts, in turn, provides the occasion for and, indeed, justifies wider institutional investment. The given institution may set aside dedicated funds or create awards to recognize the accomplishments of DH practitioners. Likewise, units on campus, such as departments or centers, might sponsor relevant DH events or other activities. As a whole, the activities in their diversity extend and support the notions of agility that are foundational to the curriculum.

At UNL, the DH community has organized numerous initiatives and events. These include "DH Afternoons," where faculty and students present their research to the local DH community; an annual DH Forum that brings together junior and senior interdisciplinary scholars from outside and within UNL to present on and discuss a common theme; an annual "Digital Scholarship Incubator" fellowship program (now discontinued) that promoted student-led digital research; and the recent "Uncommon DH Critic" series, which brings leading critics to campus for a combination of public lectures and smaller faculty-student gatherings. These initiatives have ensured that the DH community remains highly visible on campus and beyond and, over time, have both drawn and repeatedly rewarded ongoing institutional investment in DH at UNL.[13] These events and initiatives, moreover, introduce students to DH practice in a diverse range of contexts, thereby underscoring the wide applicability of DH and demonstrating the many different ways in which their skills, as learned through the program, might be deployed professionally.[14] In other words, the diverse range of activities makes an implicit argument for the wider professional value of the agility that simultaneously serves as the core of the program.

An agile DH curriculum has the potential to benefit its students considerably more than a fixed curriculum, a point especially valid when factors such as interdisciplinarity, an adaptive development ethos, and integration into the university community work to reinforce the core components of the program itself (Spiro, "Opening up Digital Humanities Education"). In doing so, the agile digital humanities curriculum, such as that in place at UNL, underscores the value of DH research strategies for addressing new and existing questions in one's own discipline and in other disciplines. The program educates students in critical modes of thinking associated with DH practice, especially by highlighting the opportunities for collaboration and intellectual growth created in working across various hierarchical divides. Finally, the program both draws DH practitioners together and creates a focal point for wider institutional interest and investment. Ultimately, therefore, the agile DH program, especially when supported and reinforced along the lines of interdisciplinarity, adaptive development ethos, and community embeddedness, most effectively professionalizes students because the program places student endeavors in wider interdisciplinary contexts, highlights the value of cross-hierarchical collaboration, and transforms "textbook" learning into knowledge that can have a meaningful impact in shaping the wider world.[15]

Notes

1. In using the term "agile," we have in mind a concept different than that usually associated with the term in the context of software development (e.g., Beck et al.). As elaborated further in this chapter, we use the term "agile" to describe a type of curriculum that centers on the concept of flexibility in terms of the courses that are offered, when the given courses are offered, fewer core course requirements, and the parameters of the coursework foundation that students build through the curriculum as a whole. In this model, courses tend to be defined in more abstract terms (e.g., Advanced Topics in the Digital Humanities), so that instructors are free to design course content within a set of minimal guidelines, and students can take courses not only to meet their needs and interests but also in a way that responds to the priorities of their professional development in graduate school over time.

2. Of course, courses offered do not always align neatly with student interests. However, an agile curriculum, such as the one sketched here, has the potential to address this concern in different ways. For instance, some degree of misalignment between course offerings and student majors can be a goal of the program, with a general curricular expectation that students should take diverse courses outside their comfort zone (e.g., major) as a way of expanding and diversifying professional horizons. Alternately, as in the case of UNL, students might also have the opportunity to substitute courses from outside the DH curriculum, provided those courses have a substantial and relevant digital component, or even to substitute relevant DH-focused experiences, such as summer internships, in place of courses from the DH curriculum. In such cases, provided that student expectations were set at the outset of the program, students would be able to plan ahead and prepare and, indeed, might even be motivated to pursue opportunities they might not otherwise consider.

3. Details about the DH certificate are found on the UNL dedicated page: https://www.unl.edu/dhcert/.

4. We discuss this point at greater length later in the chapter.

5. We believe that the advantages of agile DH curricula come to the fore in the context of such questions because the agile curriculum, due to its inherent flexibility, will provide students with options to consider this question and others like it from multiple perspectives, none of which is necessarily privileged from the overall curricular standpoint. It is also worth noting that UNL itself does not have a specific, overarching strategy for addressing such questions either at the level of advising or at the course level. Rather UNL's DH curriculum relies implicitly on the variety of DH courses and opportunities put in front of students during their tenure at the university in order to, de facto, position students to consider such questions from multiple perspectives.

6. At UNL, the DH curriculum at both the graduate and undergraduate levels is not located within a specific department or associated with a specific disciplinary degree or set of degrees; instead, it brings together the course offerings (and faculty and students) of units across the College of Arts and Sciences. As a result, students in the program have multiple options for staging curricular trajectories by, for instance, developing a more general knowledge of DH based on an interdisciplinary set of courses or by becoming more specialized by taking a predominance of courses in a single discipline.

7. The authors of the present article cannot speak with any authority about other university contexts, but at UNL the students that an instructor encounters in any given DH course will—as a general rule—have widely differing levels of DH experience (both technical and critical). This is partly because there is no required sequence in which students need take DH courses and because the wide variety of extracurricular DH experiences available at UNL regularly give different students different degrees and kinds of DH training. Because of the interdisciplinary nature of the DH program, students will also not necessarily be grounded in the given instructor's discipline. As a result, in offering DH courses at UNL faculty must be prepared to accommodate such variety, so courses often seek to begin from a baseline level in terms of content and methodology that thus helps level the playing field and get students on the same page, so to speak. In the case of split undergraduate/graduate DH courses, expectations and assignments for graduate students are more challenging.

8. As has been implied in this chapter up to this point, UNL does not have a dedicated DH department. Rather, faculty from different disciplines are hired into their own departments but also associated with UNL's DH community and, more specifically, with the Center for Digital Research in the Humanities (CDRH) as DH "faculty fellows" and "associates" (terms which, respectively, imply increased and reduced levels of affiliation). Although the nature of this relationship has recently started evolving to a more open and inclusive model that brings together a variety of DH-interested faculty at UNL, the two authors of the present essay were hired at an earlier point, and so their positions as CDRH faculty fellows were formally written into their contracts and defined by an MoU between the authors, their respective departments, and the CDRH. This MoU, inter alia, helped establish the fact that the authors' DH-oriented research, teaching, and service would be properly acknowledged as part of their tenure and promotion. In terms of the DH presence in UNL classrooms more generally, it is worth noting that DH-oriented faculty will teach courses in DH and in their own disciplines *and* that these latter courses may or may not include DH components, based on instructor preference. DH faculty often collaborate with DH staff from the CDRH in the context of grant-funded work, where a percentage of the time of DH staff, for instance, may be written into grants and where, at a general level, DH staff may oversee the overall development of funded faculty DH projects both during the time of the grant-funded work and afterward.

9. In general, DH courses at UNL are not offered through a given department unless that department has at least one DH-oriented faculty member.

10. UNL faculty do not have an overarching way of defining foundational DH skills. Rather, each DH faculty member in each DH course tries to nurture in students the key

skills that are deemed most important from a specific perspective or disciplinary grounding. At UNL, students are required to complete four graduate DH courses to receive the DH graduate certificate. Other than the milestones and final outcomes built into individual courses, there is no final milestone for the certificate as a whole and, as a result, student DH work is assessed on a course-by-course basis. Once students complete four required DH courses, they are automatically eligible for the certificate. Defining a meaningful DH graduate education in the context of taking these four courses, therefore, ultimately falls to the participating students. As a result, in selecting courses to take, students will consult their own interests and speak with faculty in relevant disciplines; as needed, they will also speak with the DH program coordinator, though this last named individual—in our experiences of having served in the position—more often takes the role of helping students clear basic administrative hurdles rather than advising on courses to take.

11. In contrast to the graduate certificate (see footnote 10), UNL's undergraduate DH minor requires students to take six courses. These courses range from entry-level offerings such as Being Human in the Digital Age and Introduction to Digital Humanities to more advanced practical and theoretical courses such as Digital Heritage Tools and Theorizing the Digital. Students can also take the split-level DH courses cited earlier.

12. According to Sula et al.'s survey of DH programs from Australia, Canada, Ireland, the UK, and the U.S., most programs are located within English departments, and only 36 percent offer undergraduate options. Furthermore, only 14 percent of those offer both undergraduate and graduate DH programs. We did not investigate whether undergraduates and graduate students have options to take courses together.

13. Over time, institutional investment in DH research has taken a number of forms, much of it centered on the CDRH, which based on the 2016 CDRH self-study (unpublished) and the 2020 CDRH Strategic Plan (https://cdrh.unl.edu/cdrh-strategic-objectives) has impacted campus in a fashion that radiates outward. The most important of such forms of investment include Programs of Excellence (PoE) funds that support the following positions at the CDRH: 1 FTE, associate professor of English; 1 FTE, metadata encoding specialist; 1.75 FTE, programmer/analyst II; 0.4 FTE, digital development manager and designer; and stipends for the co-directors. Additionally, PoE funds "also support the CDRH graduate fellows, large equipment purchases, such as high production and large format scanners, GPS survey equipment, and servers. In addition, PoE funding is used for Center faculty and staff travel to conferences or workshops, printing, and some supplies." The university libraries, in turn, provide a match to PoE funds via the following salaries: 0.6 FTE digital development manager and designer and 4.5 FTE faculty lines. The libraries also "provide 3200 square feet of space in the Center itself, hourly wages for undergraduate student assistants, supplies, equipment, continuing education funds and travel dollars for Libraries faculty and sometimes staff." Finally, the College of Arts and Sciences "matches PoE funds with salaries for 9.5 faculty lines and provides some travel support for these individuals," and departments with DH faculty "fund personal computers and laptops for these individuals."

14. There is no single, overarching, coordinated way through which DH students learn about how they can apply the skills they gain through their training at UNL in various professional contexts. Rather, the various on-campus DH activities, initiatives, and opportunities implicitly demonstrate this through sheer variety.

15. By "cross-hierarchical collaboration," the authors of the present essay mean that the nature of UNL's DH program depends on students at different levels (within and among the undergraduate and graduate levels) working with one another.

Bibliography

Beck, Kent, Mike Beedle, Arie van Bennekum, et al. *Manifesto for Agile Software Development.* 2001. Accessed April 22, 2024, http://agilemanifesto.org/.

Bonds, Leigh, E. "Listening in on the Conversations: An Overview of Digital Humanities Pedagogy." *The CEA Critic* 76, no. 2 (July 2014): 147–57. https://muse.jhu.edu/article/550519/pdf.

Clement, Tanya. "Multiliteracies in the Undergraduate Digital Humanities Curriculum." In *Digital Humanities Pedagogy: Practices, Principles and Politics,* edited by Brett D. Hirsch, 365–88. Cambridge: Open Book Publishers, 2012. http://www.openbookpublishers.com/product/161/digital-humanities-pedagogy–practices–principles-and-politics.

Hirsch, Brett, ed. *Digital Humanities Pedagogy: Practices, Principles and Politics.* Cambridge: Open Book Publishers, 2012. https://www.openbookpublishers.com/books/10.11647/obp.0024.

Mahony, Simon, and Elena Pierazzo. "Teaching Skills or Teaching Methodology?" In *Digital Humanities Pedagogy: Practices, Principles and Politics,* edited by Brett D. Hirsch, 215–25. Cambridge: Open Book Publishers, 2012. https://library.oapen.org/bitstream/handle/20.500.12657/30295/646740.pdf?sequence=1&isAllowed=y.

Pannapacker, William. "No More Digitally Challenged Liberal Arts Majors." *Chronicle of Higher Education,* November 18, 2013. https://www.chronicle.com/article/no-more-digitally-challenged-liberal-arts-majors/.

Spiro, Lisa. "Opening up Digital Humanities Education." In *Digital Humanities Pedagogy: Practices, Principles and Politics,* edited by Brett D. Hirsch, 331–63. Cambridge: Open Book Publishers, 2012. https://library.oapen.org/bitstream/handle/20.500.12657/30295/646740.pdf?sequence=1&isAllowed=y.

Sula, Chris Alen, S. E. Hackney, and Phillip Cunningham. "A Survey of Digital Humanities Programs." *Journal of Interactive Technology and Pedagogy* 11 (2017). https://jitp.commons.gc.cuny.edu/a-survey-of-digital-humanities-programs/.

Svensson, Patrik. "The Landscape of Digital Humanities." *Digital Humanities Quarterly* 4, no. 1 (Summer 2010). http://digitalhumanities.org/dhq/vol/4/1/000080/000080.html.

Walzer, Luke. "Digital Humanities and the 'Ugly Stepchildren' of American Higher Education." In *Debates in the Digital Humanities,* edited by Matthew K. Gold, 335–49. Minneapolis: University Of Minnesota Press, 2012. http://dhdebates.gc.cuny.edu/debates/text/33.

A Tale of Three Disciplines

Considering the (Digital) Future of the Mid-doc Fellowship in Graduate Programs

ERIN FRANCISCO OPALICH, DANIEL GORMAN JR., MADELINE ULLRICH, AND ALEXANDER J. ZAWACKI

I n the fall of 2014, a cohort of four PhD students formed under a pilot fellowship program at the University of Rochester, in the Mellon Foundation Graduate Program in the Digital Humanities.[1] Together, these students shared a unique two-year journey, exploring both theory and practice related to digital technologies as well as technology's evolving relationship to their own disciplines in English, history, philosophy, and visual and cultural studies. Former Mellon fellow Eitan Freedenberg, a graduate student in the visual and cultural studies program, described the Mellon program as having "a cautious approach to the field of digital humanities. Never veering entirely toward evangelism or skepticism . . . we were encouraged . . . to see both the potentials and pitfalls of DH research and praxis."[2] Freedenberg's assessment of the Mellon digital humanities program rings true with a recent cohort of fellows. This chapter, written by the Mellon digital humanities fellows active in the 2019 to 2021 session, assesses the program's impact on graduate student research, career goals, and collaborations with university faculty and staff and makes recommendations for the program's future.

The original grant of $1 million from the Andrew W. Mellon Foundation that funded the first iteration of the Mellon Digital Humanities Fellowship was renewed in 2019 and runs as a significant mid-doc program at the University of Rochester, providing humanities PhD students with a variety of training opportunities in digital technologies, enabling fellows to incorporate digital techniques into their dissertation research and teaching, and intern on faculty members' ongoing DH projects. (The program has since been renamed the Meliora Digital & Interdisciplinary Graduate Fellowship, as it is no longer funded by the Andrew W. Mellon Foundation.) Students who participate in the Mellon program are not required to have prior training or familiarity with the tools of digital humanists. As a mid-doc fellowship, geared toward PhD students in their third year and beyond, the intention of the program is to train PhD students who have enthusiasm for learning digital humanities methodologies and practices, as well as to successfully integrate the digital humanities into graduate projects.

Hailing from three different disciplines, our experiences with the Mellon graduate program and digital humanities initiatives at the University of Rochester have been wide and varied. They have reshaped the ways in which we think about and implement digital tools and methods in our own research and how we conceptualize and engage with our respective disciplines. Our involvement in the Mellon program has taught us much about the nature of graduate-level work and training through digital humanities frameworks, especially how such frameworks shape a graduate program's curriculum and pedagogy and where such frameworks remain absent.

In this chapter, we explore how the digital humanities address and complement research questions unique to our particular fields while encouraging interdisciplinarity and collaboration. We reflect on both the challenges and advantages of the Mellon program structure as it currently stands and how the program may inform revised training initiatives and projects in our home disciplines. We also explore a series of questions regarding both digital humanities as a means of scholarly inquiry more broadly and also the impact of Mellon grant programs specifically: how might every student in our various programs benefit from grant-funded methodological training and tools? How could feedback from alumni change the fellowship or our graduate programs? Where have our alumni found themselves after degree completion, and in what ways are their career paths related to their Mellon experiences, if at all?

Finally, although we envision humanities graduate programs as receptive to many of the lessons imparted by digital humanities practices, we also acknowledge resistance to such methods. Though the digital humanities have in recent years achieved an institutionalized status, many departments remain ambivalent, or even averse, to the incorporation of digital skills and theoretical frameworks. We imagine such resistance to be especially visible at the level of graduate study, where experimental study and research are often sacrificed to maintain unspoken disciplinary "rules" and "standards" that are especially valued by hiring committees, and where faculty have expressed concerns over the impact of digital humanities initiatives on issues such as exam preparation and time to degree completion. Our case studies consider this difficult side of digital humanities, in particular, the challenges we and our fellow program alumni have faced individually, programmatically, and institutionally in taking up the Mellon fellowship. All in all, the narrative provided by our case studies—through personal experience, interviews, and project excerpts—sheds light on the digital futures of mid-doc fellowships in graduate research programs.

—*Erin Francisco Opalich*

English and Digital Humanities

One primary goal of the Mellon Digital Humanities Fellowship at the University of Rochester is to provide graduate students with the tools, training, and time to investigate the potential for incorporating the digital humanities into their dissertations. In addition to discussing a range of DH literature at weekly meetings, fellows participate in ongoing digital projects at the university across different fields: the William Blake Archive in English, for example, or the Digital Elmina initiative in history.[3] Mellon fellows are also given funding to attend conferences and workshops, both domestic and international, and are further encouraged to study digital tools and techniques (e.g., TEI, coding skills). Of course, not all fellows will ultimately include a digital element in their final dissertation projects, but the option to do so becomes available through the program's DH training, in both theory and practice.

Those who choose to produce a DH-influenced dissertation quickly face an obstacle all too familiar to DH scholars: hiring and promotion committees, by and large, simply do not accord digital projects the same gravity as "traditional" scholarly work. Anke Finger argues that a continuing lack of shared assessment standards for digital scholarly work within departments makes the digital dissertation a particularly risky endeavor for students ("Gutenberg Galaxy," 67). Thus born-digital dissertation projects remain rare, and when they do occur, they are often accompanied by a standard written dissertation. The unfortunate result of this is that adding a digital component to a dissertation generally means undertaking a considerable amount of additional labor on top of a program's traditional degree requirements.

An example will illustrate. Former Mellon fellow Helen Davies, now an assistant professor of digital humanities at the University of Colorado, Colorado Springs, was a long-term member of the Lazarus Project, a DH laboratory affiliated with the English department at the University of Rochester.[4] This initiative uses digital multispectral imaging and statistical software to recover damaged or illegible cultural heritage objects, one of which—the fourteenth-century Vercelli Mappamundi—became the subject of Davies's dissertation.[5] The map's poor state of preservation meant that it had seen little scholarly study, and the only critical edition was erroneous in many of its readings. Through countless hours of computer processing, Davies restored the vast majority of the map to legibility and, using the Pelagios platform, built an interactive digital critical edition (Davies and Zawacki, "Collaboration and Annotation"). This was a labor-intensive project, requiring knowledge of digital imaging, various pieces of statistical software, material chemistry, manuscript production methods, and at least one dead language. But this work had to be accompanied by a 187-page literary-historical analysis of the recovered map. The latter alone would be dissertation material at any university; the addition of the digital element effectively added a great deal more labor than is required for many traditional dissertations.

This example is in no way intended as a slight against the University of Rochester or Davies's dissertation committee. Indeed, Rochester is particularly DH friendly. It plays host to, among others, the abovementioned Lazarus Project, helmed by associate professor of English and textual science, Gregory Heyworth; the Middle English Text Series, a longtime recipient of National Endowment for the Humanities grants for its free digital editions of medieval texts; and the William Blake Archive, one of the first digital humanities projects, which was coedited by former University of Rochester Mellon graduate program director, the late Morris Eaves. The University of Rochester is thus at the forefront, and is particularly supportive, of DH work. Few committees would likely be comfortable with a candidate's dissertation consisting solely, or even largely, of a born-digital project and rightly so: such a dissertation is liable to harm the newly minted PhDs on the job market. Joseph Raben, writing at the launch of *Digital Humanities Quarterly* (*DHQ*) some thirteen years ago, outlined a problem that clearly remains with us today: "Appearance in electronic media is not as highly regarded by the gatekeepers of tenure and promotion as the traditional hard-bound book and the article offprint" ("Tenure, Promotion and Digital Publication," para. 2). The result is a catch-22: born-digital dissertations are likely to negatively stand out owing to their rarity, which in turn will discourage candidates from attempting (and committees from permitting) them, keeping them rare. Although the ensuing success of *DHQ* and other online journals has ameliorated this situation to some degree, the humanities nevertheless remain saddled with a predilection for traditional publishing models.

The problem here illustrated is one that cuts across disciplinary and institutional boundaries. The potential for digital technologies like multispectral imaging to add entirely new texts to the literary and cultural canon is of obvious value to scholars, and yet the "mere" recovery and publication of those texts—as time intensive as such recovery and effort is—is undervalued within the academy. This state of affairs harms the scholars who perform such recovery, of course, but it also harms the humanities as a whole by implicitly disincentivizing the kind of research that might broaden the extant corpus of texts. Surely no one would dispute the value of such work, yet hiring and tenure committees by all accounts remain oriented on a fundamental level toward traditional publications. The scholars behind even groundbreaking efforts like the Archimedes Palimpsest project, which recovered several lost works by Archimedes and the orator Hyperides, did not settle for merely making their work available online but published several books and articles through more traditional channels.[6] These projects stand in for the problem of digital endeavors as a whole; as Rachel Mann laments, "While DH projects are increasingly seen as scholarly in their own right, they often do not count as scholarship" but rather as steps toward the inevitable (usually single-authored) article or monograph ("Paid to Do but Not to Think," 268).

Mellon fellows are released from their normal teaching duties to free up time for them to expand their skill set and assist with various DH projects. But the fact that this is necessary points to a recurring issue in the digital humanities, namely, its time-intensive nature. In addition to the standard and increasingly onerous demands placed upon graduate students (completing coursework, presenting at conferences, learning various languages, and publishing original research), those interested in the digital humanities, or those hoping to make themselves market-able on an increasingly bleak job market, must invest additional time in learning coding languages, digital platforms, and emergent technologies alongside the time required simply to participate in DH projects. And, as noted above and elsewhere, those projects are not granted the same esteem as traditional publications or schol-arly endeavors and so must serve as a supplement to (not a replacement for) the lat-ter. Finally, unfinished projects—those that, for whatever reason, do not successfully culminate in a public website or app—are valued even less. Graduate students must thus rely on a combination of discernment and sheer luck in deciding which DH projects to cast their lot with, as many projects do not culminate in the kind of pol-ished products that can be easily evaluated by hiring committees. Despite increas-ing advocacy and proposed models for evaluation and departmental support for the digital dissertation, as evidenced by the many voices represented in Kuhn and Finger's recent anthology, many remain hesitant to pursue these projects because they may be viewed as a lesser version of the traditional nondigital dissertation (see Finger and Kuhn, eds.). To put it rather cynically, the ultimate deliverable is the line on one's curriculum vitae, and despite regular calls for change in academic pub-lications, the general perception remains that tenure and hiring committees have not moved past valuing the single-author publication far above collaborations and born-digital initiatives.

—*Alex Zawacki*

History and Digital Humanities

When asked to reflect on his Rochester Mellon fellowship, historian Camden Burd emphasized the program's impact on his research: "Without the digital humanities fellowship[,] I wouldn't have had the time and resources to really learn data man-agement and GIS mapping. Those two elements helped to organize my research and more convincingly prove the central argument of my dissertation and current manuscript project."[7] Serenity Sutherland notes the fellowship's positive influence on her career: "The Mellon Fellowship allowed me to transfer my skills earned in the History PhD to be successful as an expert of digital media, thereby broadening my career potential to include jobs in Communication Studies that called for digital media experts. I'm not sure if I would hold a tenure track job now at all if it weren't for the Mellon Fellowship."[8]

Only eight Rochester historians have held Mellon Fellowships since 2014: Burd, Sutherland, James Rankine, Daniel Gorman Jr., Ania Michas, Alice Wynd, Josie

Bready, and Marissa Crannell-Ash. By contrast, the Rochester history department has between twenty and thirty graduate students at any given time, producing four to five PhDs per year. The Mellon mid-doc fellowship model siloes digital humanities resources in a small number of trainees. Even if the fellowship's workshops or training sessions are open to the public, the emphasis remains on the fellows as opposed to the community. As Katina Rogers notes in *Putting the Humanities PhD to Work,* "Small extracurricular programs . . . can only reach a limited number of people, making it difficult to achieve true institutional or cultural change. For lasting reform, it will be important to incorporate elements of this type of professional and methodological training into the structure of departments themselves" (74).

Integrating digital approaches into graduate programs, so that all students and not only fellows can access digital training, is an equitable solution for the long term. A program like the Mellon fellowship is enormously helpful for an institution in the short term, but it offers a temporary rather than permanent solution for graduate education. In this section, we address the larger disciplinary context for digital history and propose strategies for adding digital history to graduate programs. These strategies are also applicable to other humanities disciplines.

The need for long-term digital history training is a pressing one. The American Historical Association (AHA) has made digital training, broadly defined, a central part of its career diversity initiative, as reflected by the organization's list of "The Career Diversity Five Skills": "1. Communication, in a variety of media and to a variety of audiences. 2. Collaboration, especially with people who might not share your worldview. 3. Quantitative literacy: a basic ability to understand and communicate information presented in quantitative form, i.e., understanding that numbers tell a story the same way words, images, and artifacts do. 4. Intellectual self-confidence: the ability to work beyond subject matter expertise, to be nimble and imaginative in projects and plans. 5. Digital literacy: a basic familiarity with digital tools and platforms."[9]

By positioning digital literacy and quantitative literacy as essential skills for the 2010s to 2020s, the AHA gave its seal of approval to digital history approaches. Simultaneously, the career diversity initiative acknowledged the reality that PhD students must look beyond the tenure track for employment. As AHA administrator Dylan Ruediger noted in 2020, that year's AHA jobs report showed the "ongoing sluggishness of academic hiring." Nonetheless, Ruediger continued, "The academic job market is one among many: It has no monopoly on interesting, remunerative careers that make good use of historical expertise" ("2020 AHA Jobs Report").

The AHA Five Skills project began after Rochester launched its Mellon program, however. In a 2020 email to the author, Sutherland noted, "The Mellon Fellowship helped me because it focused on diversifying my skills as an interdisciplinary scholar—rather than simply making me a better scholar in the specific field of history. In my case, the AHA has nothing to do with it, as their guidelines came out well after the Mellon grant at UR started, and so I obviously did not pursue the grant because the AHA suggested I should seek digital literacy in my professional development." Lest we read too much into the Mellon Foundation funding digital humanities fellowships before the AHA launched its career diversity salvo, it does echo Zawacki's observation that academic disciplines change more slowly than individual practitioners. If history organizations and departments are intentional about introducing digital history to graduate students, then they will position students to pursue a range of careers while also expanding their skill sets.

Entirely separate from the career-oriented defense of digital history, historians are making the case that digital history is here to stay as a legitimate field of study that students and faculty should consider relevant to graduate education. Notably, "Digital History and Argument," a collaborative white paper from 2017 crafted by the Arguing with Digital History Working Group of the Roy Rosenzweig Center for History and New Media, endorsed the full inclusion of digital projects within historiographic discourse.[10] Like specialists in other historical fields, digital historians should explicate their methodologies, "elaborat[ing] how they found their sources, and cit[ing] the digital version of a source if that is what they read, elaborat[ing] how they analyzed those sources, and highlight[ing] any ethical issues associated with the digital source" (13). The same group noted with concern that "the incorporation of this [new digital] work into historiographic conversations produced in books and journals has been limited" (2). In other words, mastering technology alone is insufficient to make digital history part of the academic history profession. Rather, historians must treat digital projects comparably to articles and monographs: "Digital public history should be brought into the historiographical conversation by having it reviewed in scholarly journals. This would be more visible as contributions to specific historical fields by not putting those reviews in a separate digital history or public history section" (9).[11]

The shift toward normalizing digital history as simply history, instead of its own special category, moves slowly, with the implementation of this goal uneven and equivocal. The *Journal of American History* began to review history websites in 2001, but these reviews remain in a distinct section, formally labeled "Digital History Reviews" since 2013.[12] The AHA created its own digital history working group and released peer review recommendations in 2015, but the *American Historical Review,* the organization's flagship journal, still has limited digital history content.[13] Special coverage of digital history in issues from 2016 onward, along with the recurring Digital Resources/Digital Primary Sources section, has continued the pattern of cordoning off digital history from the regular article and book review sections.[14] At the level of undergraduate and graduate education, history professors can help further this shift by assigning digital history projects alongside monographs and articles as course readings. Additionally, when students write sample reviews as a course assignment, professors can give students options such as reviewing digital projects on their own or in conjunction with history publications in other media.

As organizational support for digital history grows and scholarly rationales for the field multiply, the next step is institutionalization—the integration of digital history into college history departments' research and strategic planning as well as teaching. The University of Rochester history department has created substantial digital history resources separate from the Mellon fellowship. Multiple graduate-level digital history courses have run in the past decade.[15] Graduate students contribute to the department's ongoing DH projects such as the Seward Family Digital Archive, Digital Elmina, Virtual St. George's, and Hear UR.[16] Additionally, Michael Jarvis has begun to offer digital history as a PhD major field.[17] Digital history is there for Rochester graduate students to explore, regardless of Mellon participation. It is our hope that this model of departmental training proliferates instead of universities relying on externally funded fellowships to finance digital humanities training.

Mandatory digital history training for graduate students does not seem advisable. If career flexibility for historians is the goal, then students should have more, not less, flexibility in planning their courses of study. An undergraduate headed to law school and a graduate student seeking a consulting or government career may not see the relevance of digital history practices to their future work. It is worth saying, "That is okay." Yet the importance of digital fluency in the current job market is clear. The Covid-19 pandemic rendered us dependent on cloud storage, teleconferencing, and learning management systems. The path forward, in our view, is for digital history to become a standard, fully supported, but not required, concentration in graduate programs. Instead of classifying digital history as an elective or hobby, teach digital history as an academic specialty and accept digital historiography as genuine scholarship. Dedicate equal resources to digital history as to venerable subfields like public history and documentary text editing. Convey to students that digital history is a legitimate pursuit and a potential springboard for future employment while giving students freedom to shape their academic paths.

We noted above the importance of digital training as career preparation and the need to teach digital projects as historical scholarship. To follow are further steps we recommend for history and other humanities departments: first, although hiring faculty members with digital history or humanities training is important, expecting professors to be adept at every form of digital humanities—coding, mapping, virtual reality, and web design—is unrealistic. An early-career professor juggling courses, administrative work, and research (not to mention family responsibilities) cannot be expected to learn, much less be an expert in, every technology. Nor is it equitable to hire a single professor to be "the DH person" for the whole department. A better approach is to hire multiple professors who have shown a consistent commitment in their work to at least one form of digital technology. Newly minted PhDs who have interned on long-term digital projects or produced dissertations with strong digital components fall into this category. By offering positions to such PhD graduates, departments will help to solve the catch-22 Zawacki described in this chapter. Digital history is integral to the future of the historical profession, but it must be integrated into a department's labor force without putting burdensome expectations on any single employee.

Second, institutions must support current professors who wish to train in digital history or digital humanities and integrate new approaches into their courses. Given the explosion of in-house workshops about online and hybrid teaching since the Covid-19 pandemic began, one could argue that this is happening already. Our hope is that universities post-Covid will put workshops on digital humanities technology into the rotation of teaching workshops alongside the standard sessions on MyCourses, Zoom, and so on. History and other humanities faculty should petition their institutions' deans and teaching support offices to offer such training.

Finally, if the discipline of history is serious about envisioning itself as a digital one, departments should offer students a range of academic options for digital history education, including seminars, for-credit internships, and independent studies or capstone projects with tutorial-style training; in chapter 24 in this volume, Heather Richards-Rissetto and Adrian S. Wisnicki endorse this approach for humanities programs of all kinds. At the University of Rochester, these options have taken the form of graduate seminars that build on the Seward and Virtual St. George's projects, PhD reading courses in digital and public history, and the recently created internship option that allows students to work on digital or public history projects instead of teaching.[18] By offering students digital history training and the freedom to explore it as much (or little) as they wish, departments can maximize students' choices while revamping the graduate curriculum.

—*Daniel Gorman Jr.*

Visual and Cultural Studies and Digital Humanities

Unlike the neighboring humanities departments of English and history, the graduate program in visual and cultural studies at the University of Rochester (VCS) has faced larger issues integrating the digital humanities into graduate study. This is not due to a lack of enthusiasm toward the Mellon fellowship on the part of VCS students. Like the graduate students in history, VCS students also struggle with integrating digital humanities into dissertation projects due to an institutional lack of training from the outset, an issue that could be remedied by providing introductory coursework in digital humanities (an effective strategy for this graduate program specifically, as students in VCS often do not settle on a topic or field of study until coursework is completed). Like their humanities student counterparts, VCS students share the awareness that born-digital projects are, as mentioned by Zawacki in this chapter, still considered inadequate for the academic job market, in which traditional publishing models remain the basic criteria for securing a tenure-track position. However, the biggest deterrent for VCS students seems to lie not necessarily in a dearth of institutional support for digital humanities or anxiety toward a dwindling job market, though these obviously remain key issues. Rather, the study of visual culture, at least at the University of Rochester, seems to be at odds with the digital humanities, despite the disciplines' shared dissatisfaction with traditional humanities approaches.

When the Graduate Program in Visual and Cultural Studies was founded in 1989, it was largely with the intent of troubling the traditional study of visual objects in more established fields such as art history, film studies, and anthropology. Though the program is housed in the Department of Art and Art History, VCS is simultaneously indebted to and in conflict with the very field of art history. The ambivalent nature of the program's foundation is perhaps best described in the words of VCS professor, the late Douglas Crimp, who described visual culture as "a certain intellectual formation within postmodernism [that] fractures the discipline of art history in such a way that we get a new formation of knowledge to which we give the name visual studies. This is a formation that is not a logical development of art history but rather a deconstruction of art history, or a replacement of art history with an intellectual formation that is broader, has different purposes, and has different methodological approaches" (Dikovitskaya, *Visual Culture*, 133). W. J. T. Mitchell posits a similar definition of visual culture, defining it as an active practice that "commits one at the outset to a set of hypotheses that need to be tested—for example, that vision is (as we say) a cultural construction, that it is learned and cultivated, not simply given by nature" ("Showing, Seeing," 166). In other words, "visual culture" is embedded with the understanding of expanding visual fields beyond disciplinary boundaries; it is less a field or discipline than a methodological approach to visual objects. Calling it a discipline or field, in fact, seems to undo much of its mission, which aims to remain open in theory and practice to a variety of potential objects, approaches, and methods.

The digital humanities could be considered one of the many "methodological approaches" that Crimp referred to in his definition of visual culture; for example, if digital works or practices were previously excluded from more traditional art history or film studies programs, perhaps the practice of visual culture would be more open to methods such as data analysis and visualization. Yet VCS students remain wary of using digital humanities tools as such, at least in ways that heavily impact or transform dissertation research and in turn their career goals. Before exploring exactly why this may be the case, it is useful to turn to some concrete examples.

When speaking to alumni from the Mellon program, one VCS student who has since graduated and one in the midst of completing the dissertation, a common denominator stood out: the digital humanities has served less as an influence in theoretical methods and more as a practical tool for complementing dissertation research.[19] Mellon and VCS alumnus Christopher Patrello, currently the assistant curator of anthropology at the Denver Museum of Nature and Science, shared his experience of how the Mellon fellowship shaped his dissertation research:

Digital Humanities shaped my dissertation in modest ways. I used many more graphs and data visualizations than I would have without the Mellon fellowship. The most elaborate of which was created using Gephi, an open-source social network data visualization software. I used it to create a "citational matrix" that traced the intertextual and interpersonal connections between anthropological texts that discuss Northwest Coast ritual performances, known commonly as potlatches. This was mostly influenced by Franco Moretti and his approach to textual analysis. That being said, none of this really transformed the scope of my dissertation, but simply provided an added layer of interpretive tools to demonstrate my argument.[20]

Another VCS alum, Julia Tulke, currently an assistant teaching professor in the Institute for the Liberal Arts at Emory University, noted in 2020 how her training in digital humanities has helped her, especially during times of great constraint related to the recent Covid-19 pandemic:

> While my participation in the DH fellowship did not explicitly shape my dissertation research, it provided me with a broad repertoire of tools and practices that have resurfaced in certain aspects of my work, at times in unexpected ways. The present moment is a salient example: I am currently conducting ethnographic fieldwork for my dissertation in the city of Athens, Greece, a process that has been severely disrupted by the effects of the COVID-19 pandemic. As the face-to-face methodologies that I would usually rely on, such as interviews and participant observation, have become practically and politically impossible, I have (re)turned to my training in the digital humanities to find innovative ways of gathering and processing data.[21]

It should be said that when students use digital humanities tools in these ways—ways that assisted with research yet did not shape the overall dissertation—it is still a win, so to speak, and it is, in fact, the most realistic outcome given that the Mellon program does not require that students entering the fellowship have experience with digital humanities training or tools. And yet integration, at least at the level that the Mellon Foundation likely intended, seems to be only marginal; as both VCS participants mentioned, the fellowship did not "shape" or "transform" their dissertations. The question then remains: why is this the case?

Besides the practical reasons strongly emphasized in this chapter's sections regarding the disciplines of history and English, one could argue that the digital humanities also presents a hermeneutic dilemma to many humanities graduate students, a problem the art historian Claire Bishop has aptly defined as "a reduction of cultural complexity to metrics" (Drucker and Bishop, "Conversation on Digital Art History," 325). In other words, if the goal of the digital humanities is to bring quantitative modes of analysis to the fore, with the implication that what is quantifiable is somehow more accurate or "better," would this not seem incompatible with the very discipline of visual culture, a field whose raison d'être is to bypass such modes of interpretation in the first place, as represented by the more traditional field of art history? Certainly. VCS students are not blindly devoted to visual culture, at least not enough to resist new and exciting models of interpretation. Yet the similarity of these graduate students' experiences (and my own), as well as those VCS students who have more informally shared their experiences with digital humanities, is striking in both their suspicion toward digital humanities and their resulting cursory use of digital humanities in dissertation projects.

The media studies scholar Jason Mittell addresses this very feeling of suspicion in his own exploration of videographic criticism. Like the graduate students quoted above, he likens the process of using digital humanities tools to enhance, not replace, qualitative and interpretative findings as a "critical rhetoric" and a potential "methodology" in and of themselves, where "videographic criticism can loop the extremes of this spectrum between scientific quantification and artistic poeticization together, creating works that transform films and media into new objects that are both data-driven abstractions and aesthetically expressive" ("Videographic Criticism," 230).

Mittell's use of videographic criticism to expand the notion of both the digital humanities and visual culture is a positive example of how the Mellon Fellowship and the VCS program might work in harmony. However, within his analysis, Mittell points to a problematic terrain that seems to haunt the humanities: the battle over quantitative analysis (what might be considered digital humanities) and verbal narrative (more traditional humanities practices). Although the digital humanities, as Mittell rightly points out, does not actually mean an erasure of subjective interpretation, it perhaps appears that way to practitioners of visual culture, and in particular to graduate students who are often still learning their own disciplines and are more subject to being disciplined *by* their fields of study. Though graduate students are often the greatest and most enthusiastic innovators, this spirit is often stifled by a variety of forces, institutional and otherwise.

This leads to the second and final "why," and I conclude with a point that is hardly original, yet worth revisiting here: this suspicion elucidated above extends beyond the level of interpretative practices to how the humanities has been instrumentalized within the neoliberalization of the university, a process graduate students are well aware of as they are faced with the crushing weight of neoliberal mindset via professionalization workshops and a dwindling academic job market. Although a number of recent essays point out what the digital humanities and neoliberalism mean for scholarly interpretation, faculty hiring, and institutional funding, few scholars take into account how these forces unevenly affect the graduate students who not only operate within these austerity measures with more precarity and less agency than their faculty counterparts but often do so with more finesse out of a necessity to survive (Greenspan, "Scandal of Digital Humanities"; Allington et al., "Neoliberal Tools"). The weight of neoliberal late capitalism is inextricably linked to how VCS graduate students read, write, and interpret, as humanities students are often asked to make their work "matter" to decision-making entities of the university (a body whose decisions almost solely rely on the cost-benefit model of the corporate capitalist world) and if not the university, then in industry. The visual theorist Johanna Drucker makes this connection, noting, "The familiar line of criticism against digital humanities is that computational processing is reductive because it performs statistical analyses on complex artifacts (by contrast to the good or neutral availability of digitized materials in online repositories) and that because it is statistical it is necessarily an instrument of neoliberalism" (Drucker and Bishop, "Conversation on Digital Art History," 321). Drucker's argument is that this need not be the case, but when students of visual culture are asked to justify their work with criteria dictated not by their own field's standards and practices but by capitalist standards—and when DH is often provided as the salve to make humanities research more "interesting," "edgy," and "marketable"—then the association of the digital humanities with neoliberalism by many visual culturalists, especially in a field that has built itself upon the critique of capitalism, is unsurprising.

Moving forward, the question becomes not how the digital humanities might be useful to the VCS student but how, as Mittell suggests, the digital humanities might complement the questions visual culture graduate students are already asking, as well as how it might allow these early career scholars, often responsible for bringing new methodologies into the fold, to ask new questions. There are a number of practical ways to implement this strategy, the first being earlier, hands-on training with tools and technologies that might help ask new questions. At the moment, Mellon fellows are given a broad sense of the different tools available to digital humanists, yet if the program really wants to see the university's students produce digital humanities dissertations, the training must be targeted toward specific research questions and goals, and room must be made for such training to be more intensive and sustainable. Opportunities such as the University of Victoria's Digital Humanities Summer Institute are an example of such extensive training that Mellon might emulate, yet the question of their lasting impact on PhD students, faced with ever-growing responsibilities during the academic year, should be noted.

Additionally, although a mid-doc fellowship of this kind is a unique opportunity afforded to very few, part of the limitation in such an opportunity seems to lie in the fact that the fellowship is ill-timed, at least if it is expected to make a noticeable impact on a given dissertation. In other words, the fellowship seemingly provides too little, too late in the game for many PhD students. Because of the restrictions caused by limited stipends across the board for humanities students, not to mention administrative pressures placed upon students to complete the dissertation as quickly as possible (known as time to degree), most students are forced to sacrifice learning new digital humanities technologies and methods to complete the dissertation requirements put forth not only by their departments and programs but also by the standards set on the academic job market. In short, though the digital humanities pose many benefits and the potential to transform a humanities PhD student's research, methodologies, and academic practices, it first must transform the broken system inherent to the neoliberal university. All the data in the world could not accomplish that task.

—*Madeline Ullrich*

Although the digital humanities signals a wealth of opportunities for graduate students—from tools to enhance research and more clearly elaborate upon and articulate arguments, to diversifying their skill sets amid a dire job market—the promises of DH are only as significant and practical as academic culture at large allows them to be. The Mellon graduate program has fostered a great deal of important collaborative and interdisciplinary work; however, the neoliberal university largely encourages this type of work without equal access to supporting resources or equal recognition for the labor contained therein. If DH is to retain a role in graduate-level training and work, and if it is to be fully recognized for the intellectual labor it requires, then feedback from alumni of programs like Mellon is essential to determining the future of DH in universities' graduate programs.

The University of Rochester, as part of its Mellon Foundation agreement, pledged to sustain DH training once the original fellowship ended in 2024. The Mellon fellowship was meant to be a bridging program that would end with the University of Rochester supporting its own DH program in perpetuity. So far, the university appears to be making good on its promise by refashioning Mellon into the Meliora Fellowship. We believe the university should honor its agreement with the Mellon Foundation through either a permanent DH certificate or DH tracks within individual humanities departments. Such initiatives would enable all interested humanities graduate students, and not only a running cohort of eight Mellon or Meliora fellows, to integrate DH into their education. In addition to a certificate program or DH tracks, DH frameworks could further shape graduate life via digital or public humanities internships, such as a graduate-level version of Rochester's Humanities at Work undergraduate internship program (although a funding source equivalent to the Mellon Foundation grant supporting that program needs to be identified).[22]

What the Mellon Program has taught us is that DH is not a silver bullet for the ailments of contemporary humanities programs, but its role is nevertheless fundamental to the future of academic training. The field of DH connects contemporary audiences to humanities research, and it integrates a humanistic perspective into conversations surrounding how digital frameworks inform research within and beyond our academic disciplines. Former Mellon fellow and historian Jim Rankine puts it this way:

My initial posture going in was that it was imperative to bring the digital into humanities, but after my tenure I found myself equally, if not more convinced that it was essential to bring the humanities into the digital. In many ways the friction that often emerges from attempting to adapt digital tools to humanistic pursuits highlights the extent to which these technologies have emerged without any real humanist input or consideration. Seeing how humanists from across the disciplinary spectrum brought not just their skills and perspectives to bear, but rapidly developed and continue to develop ideas about how digital humanities must embody a set of humanist ideas, ethics, and values has been heartening and inspiring. Where before I might have argued primarily for more injection of digital tools and concepts into humanist disciplines, I find now that we must be promoting more of a genuine exchange and cross-pollination that enhances both sides of the equation.[23]

As Rankine suggests, the role of digital humanists, whether they are graduate students in training or faculty leading DH programs and projects, is to continuously shape digital landscapes through critique, theory, and practice. Our work in DH may not be the key to transforming the neoliberal university, but it serves as an important example of how academic structures may be defined and redefined by the people working critically and reflectively within them.

Notes

1. The authors wish to thank the following individuals for their contributions and feedback: the late Morris Eaves, Michael Jarvis, James Rankine, Emily Sherwood, Julia Tulke, University of Rochester; Gabriel Hankins, Clemson University; Camden Burd, Eastern Illinois University; Anouk Lang, University of Edinburgh; Simon Appleford, Creighton University; Serenity S. Sutherland, SUNY Oswego; Helen Davies, University of Colorado, Colorado Springs; Christopher Patrello, Denver Art Museum.

2. For more detailed information, review the University of Rochester Mellon Graduate Program in the Digital Humanities Informational Packet at https://dhfellows.digital scholar.rochester.edu/about-the-mellon-fellowship/.

3. The Blake Archive is available at www.blakearchive.org. The original Digital Elmina website went offline as of January 2022, but the Internet Archive captured the site on August 10, 2018, at https://web.archive.org/web/20180810104928/https://digitalelmina.org/. The new Digital Elmina website is again located at https://digitalelmina.org/ as of April 7, 2024.

4. As a DH laboratory, the Lazarus Project plays an important pedagogical role. Director Gregory Heyworth, alongside frequent collaborators from the Rochester Institute of Technology such as professor of imaging science Roger Easton, train graduate students, who in turn train and educate other graduate and undergraduate students alike. For a look at how these educational functions can go unseen or undervalued, see Opel and Simeone, "Invisible Work."

5. Davies's "Translating Space," remains unpublished.

6. The multispectral image data is freely available at www.archimedespalimpsest. org. For a critical overview of the project, see Netz et al., *The Archimedes Palimpsest*. See also Easton and Noel, "Infinite Possibilities," https://www.jstor.org/stable/20721527, and Easton et al., "Ten Years of Lessons," https://www.semanticscholar.org/paper/Ten-Years-of -Lessons-from-Imaging-of-the-Archimedes-Easton-Christens-Barry/21886489f896e35 b7281c26315b05d21c93649df.

7. Burd expressed this in a personal email to Gorman on June 22, 2020.

8. Sutherland expressed this in a personal email to Gorman on June 22, 2020. Also, see Sutherland's contribution in chapter 32 in this volume, "Remediating Digital Humanities Graduate Training."

9. "The Career Diversity Five Skills," a list of recommended transferrable skills for all historians in the twenty-first-century job market, is part of the American Historical Association's online career resource guide. "The Career Diversity Five Skills," edited by Lindsey Martin, American Historical Association, accessed January 19, 2022, https:// web.archive.org/web/20220119190658/https://www.historians.org/jobs-and-professional -development/career-resources/five-skills.

10. "Digital History and Argument" is a 2017 white paper edited by Stephen Robertson and Lincoln Mullen and available here: https://web.archive.org/web/20220119191809 /https://rrchnm.org/argument-white-paper/, https://web.archive.org/web/20210820063938 /https://rrchnm.org/wordpress/wp-content/uploads/2017/11/digital-history-and-argu ment.RRCHNM.pdf.

11. Cameron Blevins has noted, however, that a risk of comparing digital projects to print historiography is that a historian might "evaluate digital projects in terms of what the reviewer *wants* them to be (a traditional academic monograph) rather than what they *are* (an online exhibit, research tool, pedagogical resource, etc.)" (emphasis in original). See Blevins, "The New Wave of Review."

12. Survey the available digital history reviews in the *Journal of American History* submissions section here: https://web.archive.org/web/20210323015741/https://jah.oah .org/submit/digital-history-reviews/.

13. See Ayers et. al, "Guidelines for the Professional Evaluation," https://web.archive .org/web/20220119194809/https://www.historians.org/teaching-and-learning/digital -history-resources/evaluation-of-digital-scholarship-in-history/guidelines-for-the-pro fessional-evaluation-of-digital-scholarship-by-historians.

14. The journal's special digital history features include "AHR Exchange [section]"; Scully, "Thematic Digital History Archives"; and "Doing History in a Digital Age [section]."

15. To view descriptions of Rochester's graduate (400-level) digital history courses from 2016 to 2020, consult the Course Description/Course Schedule (CDCS) database, Prior Fall 2020 Environment Version 1.5, University of Rochester, last modified 2022, accessed January 19, 2022, https://cdcs204.ur.rochester.edu/Default.aspx. For courses from Fall 2020 onward, consult the CDCS database, Production Environment Version 2.1, University of Rochester, last modified 2022, accessed January 19, 2022, https://cdcs.ur.rochester.edu/.

16. See "Digital Elmina," University of Rochester and University of Ghana, https://web.archive.org/web/20180810104928/https://digitalelmina.org/; Thomas P. Slaughter et al., "Seward Family Digital Archive," https://sewardproject.org/; "Virtual St. George's [Summary]," https://web.archive.org/web/20220119214839/https://dslab.lib.rochester.edu/virtual-st-georges/; Thomas Fleischman et al., "Hear UR," https://web.archive.org/web/20220119214857/https://hearurpodcast.wixsite.com/hearur.

17. For a profile on Jarvis and his contributions to varied course offerings, visit the University of Rochester Department of History at https://web.archive.org/web/20200616165033/http://www.sas.rochester.edu/his/people/faculty/jarvis_michael/index.html.

18. The revised department handbook reads: "If [students] did not teach or have an internship in the fourth year, they normally teach a one-semester course of their own devising . . . or complete a semester-long or academic-year internship with a digital humanities project, in object-based learning, community-based teaching, or in an archive or museum, in which case they will register for up to five internship credit-hours (HIS 494 or 494P) per semester for the academic year. The internship will include a formal written contract outlining duties, goals, and learning outcomes signed by the student, a resident supervisor in the program or institution where the student will be interning, and the faculty supervisor (a regular member of the UR History Department faculty) who will assign the student a grade." See "PhD Program Handbook of Policies and Procedures," University of Rochester Department of History, last modified June 16, 2020, https://web.archive.org/web/20201121231315/https://www.sas.rochester.edu/his/assets/pdf/graduate-program-handbook.pdf.

19. Students in the VCS program were contacted via email to share their experiences about the Mellon fellowship, including how the fellowship positively or negatively impacted their graduate study experience and their experience on the job market (when applicable).

20. Christopher Patrello related this retrospective in a personal email to Madeline Ullrich on June 23, 2020.

21. Julia Tulke related this perspective in a personal email to Madeline Ullrich on July 7, 2020.

22. For additional detail on the undergraduate internship opportunity labeled Humanities for Life Internship, visit the University of Rochester Humanities Center at https://web.archive.org/web/20200623203118/https://www.sas.rochester.edu/humanities/students/internship.html.

23. James Rankine expressed this in a personal email to Gorman on June 29, 2020.

Bibliography

"AHR Exchange: Reviewing Digital History." *American Historical Review* 121, no. 1. (February 2016): 140–86.

Allington, Daniel, Sarah Brouillette, and David Golumbia. "Neoliberal Tools (and Archives): A Political History of Digital Humanities." *Los Angeles Review of Books,*

May 1, 2016. https://lareviewofbooks.org/article/neoliberal-tools-archives-political-history-digital-humanities/.

Ayers, Edward, David Bell, Peter Bol, Timothy Burke, Seth Denbo, James Gregory, Claire Potter, Janice Reiff, and Kathryn Tomasek. "Guidelines for the Professional Evaluation of Digital Scholarship by Historians." White paper, American Historical Association, June 2015. Accessed January 19, 2022. https://web.archive.org/web/20220119194809/https://www.historians.org/teaching-and-learning/digital-history-resources/evaluation-of-digital-scholarship-in-history/guidelines-for-the-professional-evaluation-of-digital-scholarship-by-historians.

Blevins, Cameron. "The New Wave of Review." March 7, 2016. Accessed January 19, 2022. https://web.archive.org/web/20220119193347/http://www.cameronblevins.org/posts/the-new-wave-of-review/.

"The Career Diversity Five Skills." Edited by Lindsey Martin. American Historical Association. Accessed January 19, 2022. https://web.archive.org/web/20220119190658/https://www.historians.org/jobs-and-professional-development/career-resources/five-skills.

Davies, Helen. "Translating Space: The Vercelli Mappamundi and Visual Pedagogy." PhD diss., University of Rochester, 2020. http://hdl.handle.net/1802/35854.

Davies, Helen, and Alexander J. Zawacki. "Collaboration and Annotation: Pelagios, Recogito, and Multispectral Imaging of Cultural Heritage Objects." *EuropeanaTech Insight* 12 (2019). https://pro.europeana.eu/page/issue-12-pelagios#collaboration-and-annotation-pelagios-recogito-and-multispectral-imaging-of-cultural-heritage-objects.

"Digital History Reviews." *American Historical Review* 125, no. 2 (April 2020): 579.

Dikovitskaya, Margarita. *Visual Culture: The Study of the Visual after the Cultural Turn.* Cambridge, Mass.: The MIT Press, 2005.

"Doing History in a Digital Age: AHR Review Roundtable." *American Historical Review* 125, no. 4 (October 2020): 1337–49.

Drucker, Johanna, and Claire Bishop. "A Conversation on Digital Art History." In *Debates in the Digital Humanities 2019,* edited by Matthew K. Gold and Lauren F. Klein, 321–34. Minneapolis: University of Minnesota Press, 2019.

Easton, Roger L., William A. Christens-Barry, and Keith T. Knox. "Ten Years of Lessons from Imaging of the Archimedes Palimpsest." *Commentationes Humanaram Literarum* 129 (2011): 5–34.

Easton, Roger L., and William Noel. "Infinite Possibilities: Ten Years of Study of the Archimedes Palimpsest." *Proceedings of the American Philosophical Society* 154, no. 1 (2010): 50–76.

Finger, Anke. "The Gutenberg Galaxy Will Be Pixelated or How to Think of Digital Scholarship as The Present: An Advisor's Perspective." In *Shaping the Digital Dissertation: Knowledge Production in the Arts and Humanities,* edited by Anke Finger and Virginia Kuhn, 64–81. Cambridge: Open Book Publishers, 2021. https://doi.org/10.11647/OBP.0239.05.

Finger, Anke, and Virginia Kuhn, eds. *Shaping the Digital Dissertation: Knowledge Production in the Arts and Humanities.* Cambridge: Open Book Publishers, 2021 https://doi.org/10.11647/OBP.0239.

Greenspan, Brian. "The Scandal of Digital Humanities." In *Debates in the Digital Humanities 2019,* edited by Matthew K. Gold and Lauren F. Klein, 92–95. Minneapolis: University of Minnesota Press, 2019.

Mann, Rachel. "Paid to Do but Not to Think: Reevaluating the Role of Graduate Student Collaborators." In *Debates in the Digital Humanities 2019,* edited by Matthew K. Gold and Lauren F. Klein, 268–78. Minneapolis: University of Minnesota Press, 2019. https://dhdebates.gc.cuny.edu/read/untitled-f2acf72c-a469-49d8-be35-67f9ac1e3a60/section/ea501a60-dd3c-4c22-a942-3d890c3a1e72.

Mitchell, W. J. T. "Showing Seeing: A Critique of Visual Culture." *Journal of Visual Culture* 1, no. 2 (August 2002): 165–81.

Mittell, Jason. "Videographic Criticism as a Digital Humanities Method." In *Debates in the Digital Humanities 2019,* edited by Matthew K. Gold and Lauren F. Klein, 224–42. Minneapolis: University of Minnesota Press, 2019.

Netz, Reviel, William Noel, Natalie Tchernetska, and Nigel Wilson, eds. *The Archimedes Palimpsest.* Vol. 2. New York: Cambridge University Press, for the Walters Art Museum, 2011.

Opel, Dawn, and Michael Simeone. "The Invisible Work of the Digital Humanities Lab: Preparing Graduate Students for Emergent Intellectual and Professional Work." *Digital Humanities Quarterly* 13, no. 2 (2019). https://www.digitalhumanities.org/dhq/vol/13/2/000421/000421.html.

Raben, Joseph. "Tenure, Promotion and Digital Publication." *Digital Humanities Quarterly* 1, no. 1 (2007). https://www.digitalhumanities.org/dhqdev/vol/1/1/000006/000006.html.

Rogers, Katina L. *Putting the Humanities PhD to Work: Thriving in and beyond the Classroom.* Durham, N.C.: Duke University Press, 2020.

Ruediger, Dylan. "The 2020 AHA Jobs Report: New History PhDs Awarded Continue to Decline as Academic Job Market Remains Flat." *Perspectives on History.* February 12, 2020. Accessed January 19, 2022. https://web.archive.org/web/20220119191130/https://www.historians.org/ahajobsreport2020.

Scully, Eileen. "Thematic Digital History Archives and Their Wicked Problems: China, America and the Pacific." *American Historical Review* 122, no. 1 (February 2017): 115–22.

Bridging the Gaps in and by Teaching

Transdisciplinary and Transpractical Approaches to Graduate
Studies in the Digital Humanities at the University of Stuttgart

GABRIEL VIEHHAUSER, MALTE GÄCKLE-HECKELEN,

CLAUS-MICHAEL SCHLESINGER, AND PEGGY BOCKWINKEL

D igital humanities is a transdisciplinary field that requires extensive interdisciplinary work and understanding. Digital humanities is transdisciplinary insofar as computational methods and approaches can be adapted to a large set of research questions. At the same time, this adaptation necessitates an interdisciplinary understanding that stretches from the negotiation of epistemological premises to everyday academic practice. It is common knowledge that in DH, interdisciplinary work often needs to focus on bringing together the "digital" and the "humanities." However, in student and research teams that bring together different backgrounds, other disciplinary differences and intersections also come into play.

These different research disciplines have different methodological approaches, research objects, and standards for validation that are negotiated in more or less institutionalized communities. However, as Pickering notes, disciplines differ in these more theoretical aspects and in their practice in that research is conducted in everyday work. To offer a few examples, in traditional literary studies (at least in the German tradition), it is common to read out fully formulated typescripts at conferences, which seems to be regarded as a flaw in computer science. In computational linguistics, a Latex template is normally used for the layout of a paper, whereas humanists tend to use WYSIWYG editors. Also, although things have been changing in recent years, humanities disciplines' mainstreams used to be more skeptical toward online sources, whereas in disciplines nearer to computer science, it is an indispensable practice to use platforms like Stack Overflow. The practices of citation, collaboration, validation, and many other aspects vary widely.

This "how" in most cases does not show up in theory or methods textbooks. It is tacit knowledge and domain-specific knowledge at that. The digital humanities certainly have their own practices, for example, shorter publication rhythms, a focus on teamwork, and an emphasis on experimentation, but the practices inherent to each collaborator's background need to be considered in interdisciplinary projects. Reed, though not directly talking about practical aspects, recognizes this when lamenting that project management skills in DH are considered "soft" and in competition with "harder" skills like programming or literature analysis. A lack of project management skills in DH curricula can lead to graduates being ill-prepared for project-oriented work or institutional ecosystems that require direct involvement in this field, as Natalia Ermolaev, Rebecca Munson, and Meredith Martin explain in chapter 23 in this volume. Similarly, it should be regarded as a core competence in more specific DH work to be able to work with different and complementary practical approaches. This practical aspect is not only relevant for research but also for teaching: our students bring a great deal of tacit, practical knowledge with them when they enter our master's program.

Letting Collaboration Be the Teacher

At the University of Stuttgart, the master's program for digital humanities is centered around the department of digital humanities, which is part of the Institute for Literary Studies. Because Stuttgart also has a longstanding tradition in computational linguistics, textual analytics is a strong focus. Nonetheless, our master's program is open to all kinds of humanities BA graduates. Students have backgrounds in linguistics, history, literature, art history, sociology, and communication; to cover a wider disciplinary spectrum that reflects these backgrounds, we add courses offered by other departments, mostly humanities and computer science, to our DH curriculum. However, for a variety of reasons, it is not always possible to integrate a spectrum as differentiated as would be desirable for our students. For example, sometimes courses require elaborate prior knowledge, and sometimes departments simply do not focus enough on digital methods to provide adequate courses. In chapter 24 in this volume, Heather Richards-Rissetto and Adrian Wisnicki describe similar problems and propose agile DH curricula suited to the needs of students, fostering independence and necessitating experimentation.

The DH program at the University of Stuttgart addresses the need for developing skills necessary for project-oriented interdisciplinary collaboration through project-oriented seminars, or project seminars, as they are called in the curriculum. Placed in the curriculum right after a first semester that is intended to give a broad, yet input-intensive overview of concepts and methods in the field, the project seminar releases that richness of information into research- or application-driven student projects to let students experience how to use this knowledge from start to finish. For the seminars, we split the cohort into small groups of three to four students, each of whom deals with a different topic. Topics, broad research questions, and pertaining context are provided by professors and research staff who act as teachers and facilitators for each group. Students rank the top projects on which they want to work and are then grouped according to their preferences but without overcrowding any specific group.

Digital humanities programs in Germany are focused on graduate education and on providing digital skills for undergraduates who bring backgrounds in the humanities. These programs often have different focal points due to the highly varied nature of local digital humanities scholarship and the individual traditions of humanities computing: some might emphasize the humanities and computer science skills necessary for building digital editions, some might focus more on natural language processing (as is the case in Stuttgart), and some place attention on reflections on digital practice. Most often, these programs are the result of institutional collaboration between the computer science and humanities departments, though sometimes courses are primarily offered through a dedicated department.

Within this framework, some of the programs in Germany offer courses that cover the organization of team-based DH projects. However, seminars explicitly aiming at the practical, team-based DH project are not the norm. If they are offered, this often happens in the form of seasonal electives, not as an integral part of the curriculum.

In our experience, depending on contacts with cultural institutions like archives and museums and on the interdepartmental collaboration at the university level, it is sometimes difficult to find a sufficient number of projects that also offer enough variety for students' very specific backgrounds. For instance, as our questionnaire has shown (see Evaluation section to follow), students with backgrounds in disciplines like art history, which are not easily mapped to the most common DH tasks, sometimes do not feel as represented in the project offerings.

To cover a wider disciplinary spectrum than can be offered by the department itself, we invite colleagues from other faculties and external partners from local institutions in the cultural heritage sector to provide real-world research problems from their domain that are suited to digital approaches. In the past, this has led to seminars that dealt with a variety of topics like propaganda detection in newspaper articles, virtual collections in the Stuttgart Kunstmuseum, a network visualization of historical sources from the Regesta Imperii, or reflections on gender bias in data mining, to name but a few.

Conceptualization and project management are an explicit part of the learning experience. Although most courses do not teach any specific strategy for project management, workflows, or methods, groups are tasked with elements of self-organization and project management, which are communicated as part of the grading scheme at the start of the seminar. Self-organization and management also include the definition of goals and outcomes under the guidance of a supervisor, identification of the necessary means to achieve these goals, and regular assessments of (temporary) outcomes through group presentations and discussions in the small seminar group and in the larger group of all project seminars. This aspect of project management is part of the reflective project documentation—the written part of the graded semester work. The final event of this process is a poster slam and poster session, held at the welcome event for new first-year students.

Students must find answers to many questions: should we use project management software like Trello? Versioning or no versioning? How frequently should we meet? How should we coordinate between meetings? How should we document the process? Last but not least, the group defines and redefines its goals based on the time frame, necessary steps and skills, and the projected outcome. For example, in a project on network analysis and a dataset on the connections of narrative tropes on tvtropes.com, students quickly noticed they lacked some of the necessary expertise in network analysis. Thus, the group tried to find a more appropriate research question for their skill level and differentiated tasks into small work packages (e.g., data cleaning, report writing, and presentation). The resulting, independently defined analysis could only cover a small section of the dataset and was therefore limited in its informative value, but it yielded more confidence in the claims they could make. This does not mean that projects are pure exercises in project planning. Research is the main goal, with a realistic impression of research processes.

Evaluation

To relate past and present participants' broader experiences to our own, we devised a questionnaire based on the standard learning outcome evaluation questionnaires at the University of Stuttgart. We used additional items with custom, more detailed questions. The questionnaire was then distributed to all previous and current project seminar participants. Thirty-five students and alumni filled out the questionnaire. Because regular evaluation is limited to seminars with a group size of five or more, our project seminars do not participate in the usual university evaluation cycles. Thus, our evaluation did not focus on the learning outcomes of single groups but on the overall experience of students with the seminar format. Some of the answers came as no surprise, but others certainly did.

Among the least surprising findings were the pairings of project categories and student backgrounds. The majority of respondents chose a project that had some aspects of their background field incorporated. Students with backgrounds in history chose projects that were more about building digital editions and historical databases. Students with a background in linguistics or literature chose projects that featured elements of computational text analysis, building classifiers, or reflecting text generators.

A minority of the students did not participate in a project close to their background. A rather unexpected finding was that although there were very mixed groups overall, in terms of disciplinary background and experience with digital methods, most respondents did not think this negatively impacted their experience; most students found that they were able to learn from the practices of their colleagues and vice versa. However, this was not true for all participants: for the groups with mixed backgrounds, roughly half (thirteen participants) indicated that they perceived their group to be moderately mixed with regard to background. The other half (fifteen participants) indicated that they had strongly mixed backgrounds. The participants with moderately mixed groups all seemed to have a favorable experience when it came to mapping their past education to that of their colleagues, but three participants from strongly mixed groups indicated a negative experience. Far from being a trend, this still highlights the possibility that some of the students might have had problems in environments where it proved difficult to establish common ground.

We suspect that many groups do have to initially "get an idea" of what a digital humanities project would actually entail. At this point in the curriculum, students only have a broad overview in mind and no idea of how different DH projects, or projects in computer science, statistics, or web development, for that matter, are actually organized. Often, project members do not even know what is possible with the algorithms and frameworks proposed in the initial project description.

Just like it is for many first-time DH researchers from the humanities or computer science, the frame of reference for these project seminar participants is often limited to the practices and expectations of their backgrounds. Within the constraints of DH-specific practices of publication rhythms, presentation styles, and usual work modes, how the research actually comes together and how it is produced, argued, and presented varies with the interdisciplinary multiplicity that often makes up a project. We try to emulate this with the project seminar that lets students work out the collaborative "how" for themselves in a safe environment by offering complex, research, or application-focused projects to be completed over a semester and finalized by reflective written documentation and poster presentations at the end.

Speaking from our own experience, many of the final project presentations are excellent, especially given the short time frame, and most are unique, out-of-the-box approaches to their respective subjects. To get to this point, the groups have to find a way to play to the strengths of their members, without working in different directions. Our questionnaire showed that, indeed, interdisciplinarity was not perceived to be an obstacle on the path to reaching this goal. But this experience was not the same for all participants. The focus on project organization was partly perceived as being too implicit. Self-organization and project management techniques need to be taken into account with discussions about collaboration and different work modes. A closer dialogue with students, based on our evaluation, might uncover more detailed areas of improvement. Though focused on various infrastructures in a program and the practices they can generate, Jacob Richter and Hannah Taylor's contribution in chapter 28 in this volume also emphasizes the way that reflective "consideration of material, discursive, and rhetorical infrastructures," and reflections of practices in a teaching and research environment in general, are vital for consolidating them. The contribution by Ermolaev, Munson, and Martin even explicitly relates a need for teaching critical project management skills, so as to enable future DH project managers to see possible reproductions of bias due to certain ways of project organization. Digital humanities curricula in general must remain agile to be able to react to the rapidly changing ecosystems in the DH landscape, as Richards-Rissetto and Wisnicki make clear.

As Ted Underwood notes in chapter 29 in this volume, having students experience other disciplinary cultures (in this case, information science) can be beneficial and prepare them for a multiplicity of research environments and requirements. Given the experience we had with our project seminar, we agree. The strengths perceived in DH, like interdisciplinary communication and, by consequence, reflection, do permeate to teaching. The trans-practical intersections between disciplines offer synergies that are important for the challenges of the often entirely new research questions that can be built in the digital humanities.

Bibliography

Pickering, Andrew. "From Science as Knowledge to Science as Practice." In *Science as Practice and Culture,* edited by Andrew Pickering, 1–26. Chicago: University of Chicago Press, 1992.

Reed, Ashley. "Managing an Established Digital Humanities Project: Principles and Practices from the Twentieth Year of the William Blake Archive." *Digital Humanities Quarterly* 8, no. 1 (2014). http://www.digitalhumanities.org/dhq/vol/8/1/000174/000174 .html.

Soft Skills in Hard Places, or Is the Digital Future of Graduate Study in the Humanities outside of the University?

JENNIFER EDMOND, VICKY GARNETT, AND TOMA TASOVAC

The digital humanities shows a systemic tendency toward disruption: of methodologies, of disciplines, of epistemic cultures, and, indeed, of training paradigms. Much of the focus in respect to this last element, however, has been framed according to the somewhat narrow context of the undergraduate experience. This research generally references, explicitly or tacitly, the classroom context within a formalized curriculum, pursuing themes such as how the library supports and underpins in-classroom learning (e.g., Varner, "Library Instruction for Digital Humanities Pedagogy"; Fay and Nyhan, "Webbs on the Web"; Burns, "Role of the Information Professional"; Hartsell-Gundy et al., *Digital Humanities in the Library*); specific tools or services (e.g., Barber, "Digital Storytelling"; Saum-Pascual, "Teaching Electronic Literature"; Bellamy, "The Sound of Many Hands Clapping"); or reflection on the purpose and motivations of digital humanities pedagogy (e.g., Cordell, "How Not to Teach"; Ives, "Digital Humanities Pedagogy"; Fyfe, "Mid-Sized Digital Pedagogy"). Within this chapter, we argue that certainly within Europe, there is strong scope for collaboration with those bodies offering nonclassroom-based learning experiences for early career researchers, specifically the European Research Infrastructures. In making this argument, we will draw in particular on writings about DH pedagogy including those by Paul Fyfe and by Geoffrey Rockwell and Stéfan Sinclair, both of which point toward a more student-led and experiential digital humanities pedagogy focused on modes of what the latter work describes as professional acculturation (Fyfe, "Mid-Sized Digital Pedagogy"; Rockwell and Sinclair, "Acculturation and the Digital").

Over the same period in which this corpus of metaresearch into digital humanities skills transmission has emerged, research infrastructures in Europe have also seen a growing shift in their stance regarding training. This was in part driven by European research policy imperatives that placed increasing emphasis on a research infrastructure's need to foster the development of the right people with the right skills (ESFRI, "Long Term Sustainability"; European Commission, "Sustainable European Research Infrastructure"), as well as by a recognition that specialized facilities could not simply expect informed and empowered users to appear. At the same time, researchers came to take up posts in a facilitating or enabling capacity within research infrastructures, changing the culture from the bottom up (Edmond, "Are Para-Academic Career Paths"). For the digital humanities, the Digital Research Infrastructure for the Arts and Humanities (DARIAH) has established itself as a landmark within the European context in this respect, moving beyond the long-standing, narrow training paradigm focused almost exclusively on the skills needed to work with tools a research infrastructure had themselves built or offered (Edmond et al., "PARTHENOS D7.1 Initial Training Plan"). DARIAH has sought to ensure the provision of opportunities that both methodologically and conceptually support a range of learning pathways, including those followed by self-learners and those seeking or pursuing postgraduate training.

Research infrastructures are not universities. But they are knowledge spaces that can—because of the way they are built and implemented—extend and complement traditional offerings in formal university programs. This conviction is rooted not only in the developments we see in research infrastructures but also in the fundamental questions universities are facing about whether their curricular and organizational models can adequately respond to the needs of the twenty-first-century workforce (Moravec, *Emerging Education Futures*; Aoun, *Robot-Proof*). Although we do not believe that education should be discussed in purely instrumental terms, we see the ongoing debates as an opportunity to reflect on the potential of digital humanities pedagogy, and the agile role research infrastructures play in it, to lead the way in developing and disseminating future-proof transferable skills.

This chapter explores different ways in which research infrastructures are, independently and in cooperation with higher education institutions, taking an increasingly active role in the formation of early career researchers. Additionally, we provide suggestions on future directions in this area, including recommendations on how to build stronger and formalized relationships between research infrastructures and higher education institutions. Furthermore, based on DARIAH's decade of engagement across multiple projects and forms of intervention, this chapter provides an overview of different types of pedagogical initiatives with the aim of assessing the challenges of digital humanities pedagogy and the role research infrastructures can play in addressing those challenges. It also highlights the pedagogical potential of research infrastructures such as DARIAH to contribute to the development of digital humanities skills outside the university classroom. We begin with an introduction to DARIAH and its place within the context of the digital humanities pedagogical landscape. We then move on to discuss the role DARIAH has played through major European projects and initiatives to develop and enhance nonclassroom-based interventions in training and pedagogical practice before finally providing recommendations for strategies for successful collaborations between research infrastructures and higher education institutions.

What Is DARIAH?

Although research infrastructures enjoy a long history in forms such as libraries and laboratories, DARIAH is part of a specifically European and specifically contemporary branch of this tradition. DARIAH's formation was sanctioned by its 2006 inclusion in the first road map for the European Strategy Forum for Research Infrastructures (ESFRI). This document that laid out an integrated plan for the enhancement and coordination of Europe's facilities, data, collections, instrumentation, and other specialized assets for the advancement of research and innovation. DARIAH was legally constituted in 2014 as a European Research Infrastructure Consortium (or ERIC, as they are commonly known throughout Europe), a specific legal entity established by the European Commission, as a research infrastructure specifically serving arts and humanities. Today, the transnational DARIAH network works across over 230 institutions from more than twenty member countries throughout Europe, facilitating the integration, creation, sharing, and reuse of tools, data, and knowledge. For a general introduction to DARIAH and the notion of infrastructures as knowledge spaces, see Edmond et al. 2020.

As per the DARIAH Strategic Plan 2019–2026, DARIAH organizes its work around four key pillars: building a "marketplace" for the exchange of tools and services; enabling transnational collaboration by supporting working groups and regional hubs; extending bridges between research policy and communities of practice, and consolidating access to training and education.[1] This last pillar in particular acknowledges DARIAH's commitment and key role in the development and support of pedagogy within higher education and beyond, although in practice, DARIAH's commitment to the formation of young researchers stretches across all of its activities, as will be discussed in more detail below.

Challenges of Digital Humanities Pedagogy

As we continue to develop our understanding of what it means to teach the digital humanities, we need also to reconsider the utility, responsibility, and potential contributions of actors other than universities in this process and how we integrate them into recognized learning pathways. The experiences of integrating research infrastructures show the ways in which doing so will allow us to invent new frameworks for the teaching and learning of the digital humanities. For example, the integration of research infrastructures can enable peer learning, identified as the most desirable and effective way digital humanities skills are transferred (Antonijevic, *Amongst Digital Humanists*). Yet this peer-instructed approach is not without its challenges, as it draws upon the time resources of an academic, which, as Antonjevic notes, is a scholar's most precious resource. Where peer-instructed learning is not an option, often it is the institutional library that steps in to deliver more formal training, but initiating these types of workshops often results in disappointment; instead, word-of-mouth is typically one of the main ways in which scholars at all career stages learn about new techniques and developments in their field (Antonijevic, *Amongst Digital Humanists*; Garnett and Papaki, "Case Studies in Communities").

The integration of research infrastructures into formal teaching programs will enable students to see beyond narrow institutional perspectives in the development of resources, possibly contributing to a reduction in the creation of resources that are not properly imagined for reuse by others. For example, Brett Hirsch refers to what he calls the "bracketed" status of the topic of his work: "By 'bracketing' I refer to the almost systematic relegation of the word 'teaching' (or its synonyms) to the status of afterthought, tacked-on to a statement about the digital humanities after the word 'research'" (*Digital Humanities Pedagogy*, 5). Matthew Gold's assessment of the state of the field at that time was similar: "The digital humanities, as a field, would benefit from a more direct engagement with issues of teaching and learning than it has exhibited thus far" ("Looking for Whitman," 153). Although some further work has appeared since that time, the phenomenon that Hirsch observes—in which the ways that digital humanities knowledge is transmitted takes a subsidiary role to that of how it is created—does appear still to be the case. In addition, to the extent that it has been theorized, work on digital humanities pedagogy has tended to be strongly tied to the classroom experience: how to embed the digital into the traditional humanities teaching experience, what tools to use (or not), and how to balance between theoretical understanding and active participation. This may seem a banal observation or at best a recognition of something natural and expected, but we should remember that a classroom experience, no matter how well-constructed, exists within a particular social and institutional framework: students, seeking knowledge, experience, or qualification; one or more instructors, with mastery of a body of knowledge; and, usually, institutional or curricular boundaries, those "hidden histories" of disciplinary communities as well as the embodiments of a "political vision" (Terras, "Disciplined," 13; Simon, cited in Hirsch, *Digital Humanities Pedagogy*, 27). These restrictions can fly in the face of the stated aim of many of the pedagogical experiments described in the literature to "reconfigur[e] the academic journey itself" (Saklofske et al., "They Have Come," 323).

Perhaps most importantly, the integration of research infrastructures will allow students to experience alternative environments for the use and production of digital humanities resources, building not just their skills but their networks and expanding their imaginations for how they might use these skills in the future. Incorporating contexts such as research infrastructures into digital humanities pedagogy can therefore go beyond the call that "the sage must step off the stage and circulate in real and virtual realms" to a new theater of learning in which many students circulate with many teachers, working together to deliver something in the wider context of infrastructure provision (Saklofske et al., "They Have Come," 319). Under such a vision, learning will focus not just on digital humanities or even on a discipline in which a student or researcher seeks to use digital humanities methodologies, a distinction already made by Ryan Cordell, but also on how these practices engage interdependent communities with intersecting concerns ("How Not to Teach"). As Diane Jakacki stated in her keynote talk at the Canadian Society for Digital Humanities/ Société Canadienne des Humanités Numériques (CSDH/SCHN) 2016 conference in Calgary, the traditional model of having a single instructor (perhaps accompanied by a teaching assistant) does not work for digital humanities courses and needs to change to reflect the complementary skillsets that different experts can bring through an evolving model that allows work to expand ("How We Teach?").

In the years since the appearance of works by Hirsch and Gold dedicated to digital humanities pedagogy, additional work has naturally appeared with a few strong organizing themes dominating. The first of these is the role of libraries in the teaching of digital humanities and the development of appropriate approaches and pedagogies to underpin this (e.g., Varner, "Library Instruction for Digital Humanities Pedagogy"; Fay and Nyhan, "Webbs on the Web"; Burns, "Role of the Information Professional"; Hartsell-Gundy et al., *Digital Humanities in the Library*). Another cluster within the work focuses on how to develop pedagogies around specific tools, disciplines, or approaches such as digital storytelling, electronic literature, or Virtual Research Environments (Barber, "Digital Storytelling"; Saum-Pascual, "Teaching Electronic Literature"; Bellamy, "Sound of Many Hands"). A third interesting set of convergent perspectives appears around the question of how to teach digital humanities without letting it become an end in itself and without losing the essentials of teaching (e.g., Cordell, "How Not to Teach"; Ives, "Digital Humanities Pedagogy"). One of the most interesting examples within this cohort is Paul Fyfe's essay "Mid-Sized Digital Pedagogy," which, by reflecting on the range of pedagogical spaces between massive open online courses (MOOCs) and "sequestered learning" comes out strongly in favor of a number of methods by which to foster student-led, and, in particular, experiential approaches to learning.

In taking this focus, Fyfe's work echoes earlier work by Rockwell and Sinclair, which has particular resonance for the question of how research infrastructures might play an expanded role in digital humanities education and training. Rockwell, who had previously observed that in the digital humanities, "there are few formal ways that people can train" ("Inclusion in the Digital Humanities"), makes a significant contribution, with his coauthor, to breaking down this barrier in "Acculturation and the Digital Humanities Community." As Rockwell and Sinclair describe, the challenge of digital humanities pedagogy and the rethinking of teaching needs to begin at the most fundamental level: "One can think through a digital humanities curriculum in three ways. One can ask what should be the intellectual content of a program and parse it up into courses; one can imagine the skills taught in a program and ensure that they are covered; or one can ensure that the acculturation and professionalization that takes place in the learning community is relevant to the students" (178). From the research infrastructure perspective, of most interest is this third path, because, as Rockwell and Sinclair assert, digital humanists typically "work in interdisciplinary teams, apply digital practices to the humanities, manage projects or collaborate in the management, explain technology and build community," tasks that are more a matter of practice, or more about the how rather than the what ("Acculturation and the Digital Humanities Community," 182). These are very much the kinds of approaches that are best viewed as a cultural transmission of values and practices, rather than one of skills. Rockwell and Sinclair focus on how students can engage with real teams and real projects, but the initiatives they describe do still give the impression of being constrained by the traditional formal classroom model.

In response to these trends, research infrastructures such as DARIAH have taken on an important role in addressing the challenges to digital humanities pedagogy, particularly as they pertain to an emerging understanding of those aspects of acculturation that in other venues are referred to under the rubric of generic or transferable skills. How the increasing importance of transferable skills has been applied in higher educational training, and how research infrastructures are ideally placed to address this, is discussed in the following sections.

Digital Transferable Skills for Early Career Researchers

If the future of higher education is indeed "flexibility," if we agree that we need to encourage "multi-skilled profiles" and "multi-contextual learning practices," and if we recognize the educational challenges of "knowmad society," we need to seriously consider the role that digital humanities pedagogy, in general, and research infrastructures such as DARIAH, in particular, can play in providing twenty-first-century skills and competencies (Zimpher, "Future of Higher Education"; Cobo, "Skills and Competencies," 59; Moravec, *Knowmad Society*).

Part of the answer to this question lies in the recent increase in focus on generic and transferable skills in postgraduate education. Although this focus was rooted in a broad skillset related to research disciplines, the focus later shifted toward explicitly recognizing digital skills across all disciplines. Within its 2018 Skills Report, for example, Eurodoc specifically mentioned skills relating to "digital" competencies but also more humanistic traits such as the "cognitive" skills of abstraction and creativity, critical thinking, and analysis and synthesis, as well as meta-level research skills including interdisciplinarity, open access publishing, and open data management (Weber et al., "Identifying and Documenting," 4–5). All of these areas are central to digital humanities scholarly practice and key characteristics of the work conducted by European research infrastructures such as DARIAH. Policy recommendations surrounding the teaching of digital transferable skills in Europe should be seen against the backdrop of similar moves elsewhere. The U.S.-based National

Science Foundation highlighted, as part of its 10 Big Ideas project, the importance of exploring and investing in the "future of work" with four connected research themes: building the human-technology partnership, augmenting human performance, illuminating the sociotechnological landscape, and fostering lifelong learning (Rockwell, "Inclusion in the Digital Humanities").

Moving from strict disciplinary conceptualizations of postgraduate training can challenge institutions structured according to those very disciplines. Recognizing the role that nonacademic institutions such as research infrastructures, often interdisciplinary and multi-institutional in nature as they are, can play in the development of those key skills is therefore advantageous. Approaching these challenges from outside the established structures and hierarchies that give strength to the higher education institution opens opportunities for new kinds of players building upon different conceptual foundations. For the digital humanities, research infrastructures have been one such smaller and less formal, but well-focused, group providing such a response.

Research Infrastructures and Digital Humanities Training in the Humanities

Training and education were not, however, at the strategic forefront of research infrastructures from the very beginning. Some reasons for this lie in the relationships between universities (as organizations delivering teaching and research) and other forms of research performing organizations (RPO) including research infrastructures, a differentiation that is distinct in some countries such as France or Italy and not a consideration at all in others such as the United Kingdom and Ireland. As this model has given rise to a perception that education and accreditation of early career researchers is a role for educational institutions only, research infrastructures seldom possess the kinds of specialized procedures, staff, resources, and expertise to deliver formal educational programs. Indeed, it is the lack of this layer that most distinctly differentiates activities of the research infrastructures, and many other forms of RPO, from those of the more familiar academic context.

This gap can be seen in a number of the practices of research infrastructures. A 2016 survey of user needs assessments undertaken by research infrastructure and research infrastructure projects addressed the skills development needs of their users or potential users and came to the following conclusion: "The most striking observation is that research infrastructure projects seldom strategise or theorise explicitly about their training interventions, and how they interact with the wider environment of digital humanities" (Edmond et al., "PARTHENOS D7.1 Initial Training Plan"). In fact, with one exception (that of the explicitly training-focused #dariahTeach project described below), the many research infrastructures and research infrastructure projects surveyed would, despite explicitly featuring training activities in their workplans and communications, focus almost exclusively on a definition of skills that reached only as far as an awareness of the specific tools the research infrastructure was either developing, deploying, or both. Any further bridging or boundary competencies that might have been relevant seemed to fall out of consideration. The situation is further complicated by the fact that researchers, and in particular postgraduate students, are often not equipped with the expertise to recognize gaps in their own knowledge and determine how they might seek ways to close those gaps, particularly as the model of face-to-face training, either as part of a long-term degree course or a shorter summer-to-winter school approach, is seen as the optimal choice over online or long-distance learning (Wissik et al., "Teaching Digital Humanities").

As these organizations consolidate and their role in the research ecosystem becomes better understood, policies and practices are beginning to shift. Research infrastructures are rapidly becoming aware not only of the kinds of knowledge they create but also of the distinct learning opportunities they can offer, along the lines of the idea of acculturation discussed previously in this chapter. The drivers for this shift are many and include both internal and external as well as top-down and bottom-up impulses. For example, from the perspective of the European Commission, increasing emphasis within the consideration of the sustainability of research infrastructures is being placed upon the need to have the right people with the right skills in the right places at the right time (ESFRI, "Long Term Sustainability"; European Commission, "Sustainable European Research Infrastructures"). Furthermore, as these very researchers come to take up posts in a facilitating or enabling capacity within research infrastructures, the career paths and perceptions they introduce regarding the researcher-infrastructure relationship have begun to change attitudes from within (Edmond, "Are Para-Academic Career Paths"). This shift in priorities also leverages the research infrastructures' emphasis on the mobility of people and ideas, in particular in niche areas. In total, these many forces are fostering a growing awareness among research infrastructures of the importance of developing and sustaining human capital.

A number of the specific responses that have emerged from humanities-focused research infrastructures due to the need to foster skills development at a higher level than previously are discussed below. But it is important to clarify that for all of their increased commitment to making the acquisition of skills accessible for new cohorts of scholars, the research infrastructures still do not engage in formal certification of these skills, for the reasons outlined above. Many researchers are adequately served by this differentiated landscape and do indeed simply want to understand their tools in order to carry out their analyses, but others might see the wide variety of opportunities within digital humanities as more integral to their career paths and curricula vitae. For these individuals, a pathway that could combine research infrastructure-based knowledge and skills and formal accreditation would perhaps be more attractive.

We do not think that DARIAH or any research infrastructure for that matter should reinvent itself as a university. We do believe, however, that an increased and more systematic collaboration between higher education institutions and research infrastructures should be explored because they can offer different modalities of embedded learning that are practically impossible to achieve following traditional curricula in university classrooms and because universities—with their enormous cultural capital—would be well positioned to stimulate new mechanisms and practices of learning.

DARIAH's Pedagogical Interventions

If the defining aspect of the university training setting is the focused interaction of the classroom, research infrastructures similarly utilize their key capabilities to support training by providing platforms, registries, and other forms of asynchronous, learner-driven (or train-the-trainers-focused) access to resources. This trajectory can be mapped through time via the development of four distinct resources: the Course Registry, DARIAH Teach, the PARTHENOS Training Suite, and DARIAH Campus.

Emerging originally from a DARIAH working group and further developing through collaboration with CLARIN ERIC Consortium, the Digital Humanities Course Registry (DHCR) addressed a need for greater visibility of digital humanities training activities beyond an individual's typical network at a university level (see Sahle et al., "Digitale Geisteswissenschaften"; Thaller, "Towards a Reference Curriculum"; Wissik et al., "Teaching Digital Humanities").[2] The DHCR began as a simple spreadsheet in German to become a multilingual, web-based interactive map featuring contributions from members of the two research infrastructure communities. It has thus become a key port of call, particularly relevant in the context of this chapter for students who want to undertake some manner of formal training in digital humanities and for course providers who want to promote their course internationally (Wissik et al., "Teaching Digital Humanities"). The DHCR further champions findability through a catalog of courses that is both filtered and searchable. Those courses that are included must have a balance between a humanities and digital or computational content. Quality control is assured through national moderators within CLARIN and DARIAH member countries, who also ensure the DHCR is kept current.

The DHCR may not be in itself a location for training, but it represents a significant enhancement to the findability of training options provided through formal means, such as universities, or through established and long-running workshops or summer-to-winter school programs. It also highlights what can be achieved through collaboration at a pan-European level, such as the two research infrastructures we find in CLARIN and DARIAH, beyond the formal higher education framework. It represents an intervention unique to the strengths of a research infrastructure, where the creation and maintenance of registries are an essential form of intervention these organizations are uniquely able to deliver openly and sustainably.

Elsewhere within the DARIAH ecosystem, the first innovation toward the production of training materials emerged from a growing awareness that although many educational programs were beginning to include digital methods, few institutions had the staff and resources to offer expertise in the full range of current methods and approaches. #dariahTeach, a full Moodle-based environment for digital humanities courses and workshops, is designed for use and reuse in university courses so as to enhance student access to advanced methods, strengthen alliances between institutions, and foster innovative teaching and learning practices (Schreibman et al., "#dariahTeach").[3] It was developed with sharing, reuse, and localization (in terms of language and examples) as key design objectives, balancing a role as a support for instructors with one as a locus for self-study.

As such, #dariahTeach "courses" (with proposed five and ten ECTS equivalents[4]) and smaller "workshops" (without ECTS points attached to them) are designed at the intersections of theory and practice and provide ample opportunities for students to develop fundamental skills necessary to create, implement, and engage with scholarly digital objects (e.g., textual, audio, video, 2D, and 3D). At the same time, the offerings are designed to contribute to the development of critical thinking about areas such as digital preservation and the exploitation and transformation of cultural heritage as a vital educational goal in a pluralistic, reflective society.

The strength of #dariahTeach was in its close mapping to the higher education curriculum; however, this left a gap. As mentioned, traditional conceptualizations of training in research infrastructures often did not stretch beyond the specific tooling that they themselves hosted. The formal educational toolkit, however, tended to focus on applications of technology to specific humanities contexts. These parallel developments left a space between them that did not necessarily allow expertise from one context to easily flow to the other, a gap particularly felt in the transfer of skills from educational to professional contexts in the research infrastructures. DARIAH therefore launched the development of the PARTHENOS (Pooling Activities, Resources and Tools for Heritage E-research Networking, Optimization and Synergies) Training Suite to serve researchers, content specialists in Cultural Heritage Institutions, technical developers and computer scientists, and managers of institutions and projects.[5]

The PARTHENOS Training Suite applied an approach different from #dariahTeach, focusing less on enhancing ECTS-linked courses or on skills traditionally taught in digital humanities university courses, but rather on issues more specific to the infrastructural frame of reference, such as challenges of management and collaboration, open data management, ontologies, and citizen science. The materials included in the modules were designed so that they did not necessarily need to be undertaken as a whole, but rather sections or materials such as slideshows, lecture videos, or shorter videos could be used for self-study or reused by trainers within their own courses without modification if required.

By 2019, the Research Infrastructure educational toolkit emerging out of DARIAH's work had proven its utility but had become in some ways a victim of its own success, with users not necessarily understanding the different strengths of the multiple platforms or being able to move easily between them. Therefore, DARIAH-Campus was launched as both a discovery framework (in that it compiles and provides links to existing training materials that can be searched via the DARIAH-Campus website) and a hosting platform for DARIAH and DARIAH-affiliated offerings in training and education.[6] The goal of DARIAH-Campus is to widen access to open, inclusive, high-quality learning materials that aim to enhance creativity, skills, technology, and knowledge in the digitally enabled arts and humanities.

All four of these training and education outputs from DARIAH provide a means for course providers in higher education institutions to integrate research infrastructure outputs into their formal training programs with minimal work on their part. They also, however, offer introductory pathways for students inside or outside of formal education to hone their skills following a different development paradigm shaped by the ethos of research infrastructures rather than those of higher education.

Getting beyond the Data: Training Events

Platforms and registries are key assets that research infrastructures can and do use to address the needs of early career researchers, before and after the completion of the PhD, but they are by no means the only ones. Such relatively blunt instruments can perhaps be seen as mapping onto those aspects of a formal degree program that curate and deliver a preselected, clearly defined set of skills. But one of the most essential modes by which confidence and competence in any field are established is at the interface where teaching becomes mentoring and when instruction becomes the cocreation of knowledge. This dynamic, personalized form of exchange becomes ever more important as an individual begins to establish an independent research career and trajectory, where their own expertise begins to emerge, and in some ways perhaps even to eclipse the specific areas in which a specific institutional team may have direct expertise.

An EDUCAUSE survey from 2019 found that 73 percent of surveyed faculty members from 118 U.S. institutions preferred "completely" face-to-face teaching environments (Galanek et al., "ECAR Study of Faculty," 7). Among student respondents, the numbers were similar, with 70 percent saying they preferred mostly or completely face-to-face learning. This should come as no surprise: humans crave social interaction. While the experiences of the global Covid-19 pandemic have perhaps made us more savvy about how and when virtual and asynchronous teaching modalities can be effectively used, the experience of forced distance has also made the benefits of presence all the more keenly felt. Digital technologies can facilitate communication, but they cannot completely replace the need for and the benefits of nonmediated physical presence.

That is why DARIAH does not focus only on producing and disseminating virtual learning opportunities and organizes two different kinds of face-to-face training measures: those addressing specific communities and those addressing specific topics. It also supports access to face-to-face training more generally, for example, by providing financial assistance to existing training events such as the European Summer University Culture and Technology at the University of Leipzig or the Helsinki Digital Humanities Hackathon.[7]

Events for specific communities offer an opportunity for intensive work on topics relevant to a particular academic discipline. The DARIAH Working Group Lexical Resources, for instance, runs the Lexical Data Masterclass, a hands-on training measure for twenty to twenty-five young scholars interested in learning about methods and techniques for the creation, management, and use of digital lexical data.[8] The weeklong masterclasses cover a wide range of topics from general models for lexical content and Text Encoding Initiative (TEI)-based representation of lexical data to managing digital lexica as online resources and working efficiently with XML editors. The participants are given a chance to attend different sessions and consult one-on-one with experts on their own dictionary projects.

Events DARIAH organizes and promotes on general topics that are of interest to wider scholarly audiences include data management, open science, and research infrastructures. For instance, in December 2019, DARIAH organized a winter school on shaping new approaches to data management in arts and humanities at the Faculty of Social and Human Sciences of the NOVA University in Lisbon. The event provided an opportunity for arts and humanities scholars, librarians, and research managers to learn how to maximize the potential of their scholarly resources and take practical steps in opening their research in ethically and legally responsible ways; the focus was on topics such as optimal implementation of FAIR (that is Findable, Accessible, Interoperable, Reusable) data in the arts and humanities, issues around ethics, Intellectual Property Rights and licensing, data and software citation practices, open research notebooks, and innovative publishing practices (DARIAH-Campus, "Winter School").

Lifelong Learning, Digital Humanities, and Research Infrastructure Approaches: Transnational Access Fellowships

In addition to providing both asynchronous and synchronous training in the traditional scope and sense, research infrastructures also promote a number of modes of engagement that build on the engaged scholarship model proposed and tested by Patricia Hswe and her collaborators, which "seeks to complement classroom-based learning with out-of-classroom experiences–as a means to explore an alternative pedagogical approach to digital scholarship" ("Tale of Two Internships," 3).

Although many master's and PhD programs based in universities would similarly seek to promote internships and other forms of researcher mobility as a complement to institution-based aspects of their programs, European research infrastructures benefit from a long-established and discipline-neutral tradition unique to their own context and sphere of activity, a mechanism known as the Transnational Access (TNA) Fellowships. The duration and nature of these fellowships can vary from program to program and person to person, but in general, they would see a researcher from one country spending a period of weeks or months with a research infrastructure team.

TNA fellowships have been a part of how the function and added value of European research infrastructures have been conceptualized and funded for at least two decades. As with so many other aspects of the European research infrastructure landscape, however, this element of the generic research infrastructure model was systematized as of 2006 with the launch of the ESFRI roadmap, even if the importance of mobility and skills as elements of research infrastructure development and operations was not at the forefront of that document. More instructive in this sense is how TNA was conceptualized in some of the specific calls aimed at funding the development of research infrastructures. The 2016–2017 calls, produced in 2015, for example, stated, "The strongest impact of an integrating activity is expected typically to arise from a focus on networking, standardisation and establishing a common access procedure for trans-national and/or virtual access provision."[9] This only tells part of the story, however, as this document also makes clear the origins of transnational access in the conceptualization of the research infrastructure as a place or large assembly of instrumentation researchers would need to move to access, or sensitive personal data that could not be securely shared virtually. The research infrastructures in development at that time for the arts and humanities research community were therefore called upon to reinvent this model on the basis of specialist access to largely tacit knowledge or expertise, to labs and teams of people, rather than solely to the immovable objects of research infrastructure.

Two forerunner projects in this respect that were related to DARIAH were the European Holocaust Research Infrastructure (EHRI) and the Collaborative European Digital Archival Research Infrastructure (CENDARI), both of which had to reimagine TNA in order to make it a process that could be truly beneficial for the communities of historians those projects served. In its first phase of development, EHRI, despite its strong focus on facilitating access to memory institutions holding Holocaust records, would use TNA to spearhead the approach they referred to as "a technical infrastructure, a human network" (Uiterwaal et al., "PARTHENOS D7.4 Report," 45). This approach was taken even further by CENDARI, for whom the community aspect of the fellowships was quickly recognized to be paramount. All in all, the program hosted twenty-eight fellows, all of whom were early career researchers, some working on PhDs, others having completed in the past five years.[10] This was in itself an interesting result, as the call for applications for the fellowships stated that preference would be given to early career researchers but did not exclude senior researchers.

A 2019 assessment of TNA across five different EU research infrastructure projects reveals much about the reasons behind this appeal and the mechanisms that allowed access to the research infrastructures to become an unparalleled context for developing skills and competencies. A total of eighty-six former fellows were surveyed, of which sixty-eight rated their experience to have been excellent (8–10 points on a 10-point scale). Among the highlighted elements were having "designated time" to pursue their work and having access to "instructors of the highest quality" (Uiterwaal et al., "PARTHENOS D7.4 Report"). The assessment also made clear that many researchers felt that they were afforded opportunities to develop their work through time spent in a research infrastructure context that they otherwise would not have had. The spread of answers to a survey question about curricular embedding makes clear the much greater spread of responses (see Figure 27.1).

One respondent actually qualified their answer in a way that threw into sharp relief the different perspectives represented by their experiences: "My answers above are not stellar but that's not the TNA programme's fault, it's rather a lack of interest in my research area from my own university." Also interesting is the fact that almost 60 percent of fellows surveyed felt that they had learned or experienced something valuable that they had not expected (see Figure 27.2).

Things discovered "by chance" or in an "unplanned" manner ultimately framed many of the most valuable development opportunities these scholars experienced as a result of their placements. This aspect of the learning fostered by TNA underscores the value a research infrastructure with a wide network of partners can bring to the skills development of a young, or indeed mid-or advanced-career researcher. Harnessing their unique structure, organizations like DARIAH can provide unique, situated, tailored learning to suit a wide variety of needs.

Learning by Doing: Participation as Pedagogy

The continuum from the generic model embodied in training materials and training schools through to fellowships and other forms of short-term placement points onward to opportunities that research infrastructures facilitate. These are even more removed from the standard conceptualization of a postgraduate curriculum but can still be seen as ways in which postgraduates and early career researchers can build their skills, competencies, and ultimately their careers via research infrastructures. Although the TNA programs may represent a highly effective, co-constructed form of mentoring and informal training, they still maintain a certain knowledge hierarchy between the host and the visiting researcher. But DARIAH is also a place where the work and learning of postgraduates and early career researchers are deeply integrated into the day-to-day activities of the infrastructure. This can be seen from the perspective of a wide variety of facets of the organization, of which we would like

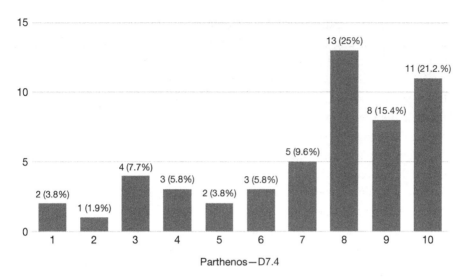

Figure 27.1. Spread of answers to survey question about curricular embedding, where 10 = "excellent." Uiterwaal et al., PARTHENOS D7.4 Report, 2018.

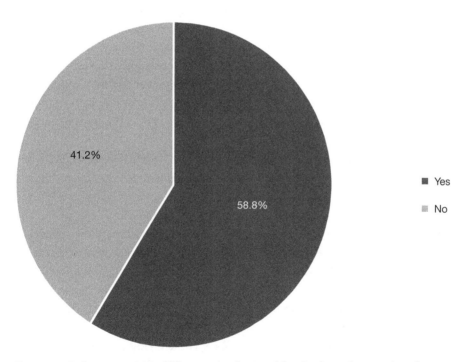

Figure 27.2. In this survey 58.8% of fellows surveyed reported that they learned or experienced something valuable that they had not unexpected. Uiterwaal et al., PARTHENOS D7.4 Report, 2018.

to highlight four. First, DARIAH events are highly inclusive and attract a large percentage of young researchers. DARIAH's community basis, which is stable from year to year, and methodological focus are often easier for researchers just establishing their networks to penetrate. This is true in particular when a large DARIAH event is held in cooperation with a local institute, as this makes for an excellent opportunity for that local group to participate in a major meeting without barriers of travel costs.

Many networks and organizations hold events, however, and it is the integration of these events with other mechanisms that make them such a powerful place to build skills and careers for young researchers. One of the strands of activity at every DARIAH annual event includes the meetings of many of DARIAH's twenty-plus working groups. In an infrastructural context, these working groups provide an opportunity for an ad hoc group of researchers sharing similar goals to establish themselves under the DARIAH umbrella to build components and resolve barriers together. From a DARIAH perspective, they are a "non-competitive, non time-limited, lightweight, transnational mechanism" designed to "encourage the exchange and sharing among groups" (Edmond et al., "Springing the Floor," 225), and this lack of excess formality in the mechanism has the effect of also making them very open. Many working groups, such as the Working Group for Community Engagement and the Working Group for Research Data Management, have been either founded or passed on to the leadership or co-leadership of early career researchers, often PhD students, who find the empowerment they can aspire to within the DARIAH structure gives them a visible and relevant platform to build skills related to research leadership, team management, and the agreement of and practical delivery against a working group's shared vision.

Working groups are one of the four pillars of DARIAH's 2019–2026 Strategic Plan and not the only one where we can see early career researchers building their profiles through an intensive engagement with the research infrastructure. For example, DARIAH's policy work is largely focused on the delivery of open science within the arts and humanities, an area in which it is typically those researchers only starting their careers who are the strongest and most eloquent advocates for change. They make up a majority of the participants in workshops on this topic and are regularly featured through, for example, the infrastructures' blogging competition (Hswe et al., "Tale of Two Internships") and features on best practice (such as Tóth-Czifra, "Open Scholar Stars"). They also form a strong contingent now in the editorial team of the OpenMethods metablog (which had been established with a strong bias toward more senior scholars before DARIAH took it over in 2018). This leadership element from the grassroots has proven essential for DARIAH's success as both a community and a research infrastructure, and it is no surprise that through these many engagement mechanisms, DARIAH has become not only a recognized source for building a skills base, but also for crafting a career in what might be seen as a parallel development in Europe to the North American "alternate academy" (Edmond, "Are Para-Academic Career Paths").

Taking the challenges of digital humanities pedagogy and the experiences of the initiatives discussed above into consideration, a vision begins to emerge of a training ecosystem for digital humanities in which research students and early career researchers can develop their skills according to a model that harnesses the strengths of both the higher education institution and research infrastructure contexts. In this future vision, research infrastructures and higher education institutions will establish active educational partnership networks to validate new approaches to the skills needs of humanities students and researchers, looking beyond the frame of what is currently available in the context of formal educational programs. These networks would jointly explore curricular models and internship opportunities to enable the fluid exchange of knowledge and students between formal educational programs and the applied contexts of the research infrastructure. Furthermore, these networks would formalize and embed both awareness of and reuse modalities for the training content that research infrastructures produce and assemble. Work within both #dariahTeach and PARTHENOS confirmed a demand for reusable content that allows course providers to integrate the materials as they see fit within university programs. Research infrastructures might further this by developing a systematic approach to monitoring the use of any training materials by course instructors, and feeding this back into their development, instigating a culture in which educational materials are not just shared but quality-assured and, indeed, rewarded.

Research infrastructures can support higher education institutes by continuing to create and maintain essential filtering and contextualizing layers for training materials to coordinate and enhance open educational resources while ensuring that these resources are appropriate for use in a structured higher education curriculum context. Within DARIAH, the recent development of DARIAH-Campus, which aims to "capture and consolidate" DARIAH training materials, will assist with this aim by making the materials more discoverable, higher quality, more user-friendly, and increasingly reusable. At the same time, higher education institutions can come to view the research infrastructures as partners not just in research but teaching, feeding back experiences and requirements, and seeking unforeseen synergies and unexpected outcomes. The transformation of the DARIAH-Campus Event Capturer template into an experimental overlay journal for young researchers participating in face-to-face training events was one such unexpected outcome of a DARIAH workshop with educators, and more collaborative work can only lead to further such mutual benefit (Université de Neuchâtel, "Sharing the Experience").

Research infrastructures, while stable, do not remain static. Because of their scale, complexity, and proximity to changes in policy and technology, they present a set of opportunities and constraints different from those found in higher education institutions. Their flexible nature, transnational focus, and ability to conduct discipline-sensitive foresight and to foster not just research-led but research-facing training should become an essential complement to how we see postgraduate training in the twenty-first century, especially in such hybrid, interdisciplinary, and technologically enabled fields as the digital humanities. DARIAH is laying the groundwork for just such an innovation, for the good of its users, its members, and its institutional partners. More than anything, though, this transformation of education will see our students better informed, prepared, and grounded for research and work, a truly worthy goal in a context where the potential reach and contribution of the humanities is all too often misunderstood.

Notes

1. The "DARIAH Strategic Plan 2019–2026" was published in 2019, providing a seven-year plan for DARIAH and identifying key areas for development. This document is available from https://www.dariah.eu/wp-content/uploads/2019/08/Strategic-Plan_2019 -2026.pdf, accessed April 22, 2024.

2. Digital Humanities Course Registry (DHCR). https://dhcr.clarin-dariah.eu/, accessed April 18, 2024.

3. #dariahTeach (https://teach.dariah.eu) was launched in March 2017 as part of an Erasmus+ funded project.

4. The European Credit Transfer and Accumulation System, otherwise known as ECTS, is a system whereby credits are awarded based on the amount of student effort measured in time. For example, 1 ECTS is the equivalent of 25–30 hours of student effort. This includes time spent in lectures and seminars as well as self-directed learning. A short course that claims 5 ECTS is around 125–150 hours of student effort.

5. The PARTHENOS Training Suite (https://training.parthenos-project.eu/).

6. DARIAH Campus (https://campus.dariah.eu) is a discovery platform and hosting framework for free, open online training and learning resources in the digital humanities from the DARIAH community and beyond.

7. The European Summer School in Digital Humanities is held annually, running for approximately two weeks. It has been running since 2009 and was originally devised by Elisabeth Burr at the University of Leipzig ("European Summer University Culture and Technology," https://esu.culintec.de). It has since been taken over by Babeş-Bolyai University in Cluj-Napoca (https://web.archive.org/web/20240305005019/https://esu-ct.con ference.ubbcluj.ro/, accessed April 18, 2024). The University of Helsinki's annual Digital Humanities Hackathon, meanwhile, has been running since 2015 (https://www.helsinki .fi/en/digital-humanities/helsinki-digital-humanities-hackathon).

8. The first Lexical Data Masterclass took place in Berlin in 2017. For an overview of student projects, see https://digilex.hypotheses.org/386, accessed April 22, 2024.

The second iteration took place in 2018, and an overview of student projects is available at https://digilex.hypotheses.org/551, accessed April 22, 2024. The third iteration, which was planned for spring 2020, was canceled due to the Covid-19 pandemic.

9. This quote was taken from the European Commission's call for TNA fellowships, 2016–19. Unfortunately, as this was a funding call, the documentation that this quote was taken from is no longer available from the European Commission's website.

10. A full assessment of this program can be found in Collaborative European Digital Archive Infrastructure, "CENDARI Project Deliverable," http://www.cendari .eu/sites/default/files/CENDARI_D3.2%20-%20Access%20Outcomes%20Report _Final.pdf.

Bibliography

Antonijevic, Smiljana. *Amongst Digital Humanists: An Ethnographic Study of Digital Knowledge Production.* New York: Palgrave McMillan, 2015. https://www.palgrave .com/gp/book/9781137484178.

Aoun, Joseph E. *Robot-Proof: Higher Education in the Age of Artificial Intelligence.* Cambridge, Mass.: The MIT Press, 2017.

Barber, John F. "Digital Storytelling: New Opportunities for Humanities Scholarship and Pedagogy." *Cogent Arts & Humanities* 3, no. 1 (2016). https://doi.org/10.1080/23311983 .2016.1181037.

Bellamy, Craig. "The Sound of Many Hands Clapping: Teaching the Digital Humanities through Virtual Research Environment (VREs)." *Digital Humanities Quarterly* 6, no. 2 (2012): 1–17.

Borek, Luise, Jody Perkins, Christof Schöch, and Quinn Dombrowski. "TaDiRAH: A Case Study in Pragmatic Classification." *Digital Humanities Quarterly* 10, no. 1 (2016).

Burns, Jane A. "Role of the Information Professional in the Development and Promotion of Digital Humanities Content for Research, Teaching, and Learning in the Modern Academic Library: An Irish Case Study." *New Review of Academic Librarianship* 22, nos. 2–3 (2016): 238–48. https://doi.org/10.1080/13614533.2016.1191520.

Cobo, Cristóbal. "Skills and Competencies for Knowmadic Workers." In *Knowmad Society,* edited by John W. Moravec, 57–85. Minneapolis: Education Futures, 2013.

Cordell, Ryan. "How Not to Teach Digital Humanities." In *Debates in the Digital Humanities 2016,* edited by Matthew K. Gold, 459–74. Minneapolis: University of Minnesota Press, 2016.

DARIAH-Campus. "Winter School: Shaping New Approaches to Data Management in Arts and Humanities." Accessed May 11, 2021. https://web.archive.org/web/20210 511084045/https://campus.dariah.eu/resource/ws2019.

Drude, Sebastian, Sara Di Giorgio, Paola Ronzino, Petra Links, Annelies van Nispen, Karolien Verbrugge, Emiliano Degl'Innocenti, Jenny Oltersdorf, Juliane Stiller, and Claus Spiecker. "PARTHENOS D2.1 Report on User Requirements." Zenodo. October 20, 2016. https://doi.org/10.5281/zenodo.2204561.

Edmond, Jennifer. "Are Para-Academic Career Paths about People or Places? Reflections on Infrastructure as the European Alt-Ac." *Debates in the Digital Humanities 2019,* edited by Matthew K. Gold and Lauren F. Klein, 389–98. Minneapolis: University of Minnesota Press, 2019.

Edmond, Jennifer, Frank Fischer, Laurent Romary, and Toma Tasovac. "Springing the Floor for a Different Kind of Dance: Building DARIAH as a Twenty-First-Century Research Infrastructure for the Arts and Humanities." In *Digital Technology and the Practices of Humanities Research,* edited by Jennifer Edmond, 207–34. Cambridge: Open Book Publishers, 2020. https://doi.org/10.11647/OBP.0192.

Edmond, Jennifer, Vicky Garnett, Elisabeth Burr, Stefanie Läpke, Jenny Oltersdorf, and Helen Goulis. "PARTHENOS D7.1 Initial Training Plan." Zenodo. June 7, 2016. https://doi.org/10.5281/zenodo.2575380.

ESFRI. "Long Term Sustainability of Research Infrastructures." ESFRI Scripta Series, Vol 2. October 2018. Accessed April 18, 2024. https://www.esfri.eu/esfri-scripta-series.

European Commission. "Sustainable European Research Infrastructures: A Call for Action." European Commission, staff working document. Last updated Oct 10, 2017. https://publications.europa.eu/en/publication-detail/-/publication/16ab984e-b543-11e7-837e-01aa75ed71a1/language-en.

Fay, Ed, and Julianne Nyhan. "Webbs on the Web: Libraries, Digital Humanities and Collaboration." *Library Review* 64, nos. 1–2 (2015): 118–34.

Fyfe, Paul. "Mid-Sized Digital Pedagogy." In *Debates in the Digital Humanities 2016,* edited by Matthew K. Gold, 104–17. Minneapolis: University of Minnesota Press, 2016.

Galanek, Joseph D, and Dana C Gierdowski. 2019. "ECAR Study of Faculty and Information Technology, 2019." Accessed April 22, 2024, https://library.educause.edu/-/media/files/library/2019/12/facultystudy2019.pdf.

Garnett, Vicky, and Eliza Papaki. "Case Studies in Communities of Sociolinguistics and Environmental Humanities Scholars." In *Routledge International Handbook of Research Methods in Digital Humanities,* edited by Kristen Schuster and Stuart Dunn, 239–60. London: Routledge, 2021.

Gold, Matthew K. "Looking for Whitman: A Multi-Campus Experiment in Digital Pedagogy." In *Digital Humanities Pedagogy: Practices, Principles and Politics,* edited by Brett D. Hirsch, 151–76. Cambridge: Open Book Publishers, 2012.

Hartsell-Gundy, Arianne, Laura Braunstein, and Liorah Golomb. *Digital Humanities in the Library: Challenges and Opportunities for Subject Specialists.* Chicago: Association of College and Research Libraries, 2015.

Hirsch, Brett D. *Digital Humanities Pedagogy: Practices, Principles and Politics.* Cambridge: Open Book Publishers, 2012.

Hswe, Patricia, Tara LaLonde, Kate Miffitt, James O'Sullivan, Sarah Pickle, Nathan Piekielek, Heather Ross, and Albert Rozo. "A Tale of Two Internships: Developing Digital Skills through Engaged Scholarship." *Digital Humanities Quarterly* 11, no. 3 (2017): 1–9.

Irish Universities Association. "IUA Graduate Skills Statement Brochure 2015." Policy Statement, Dublin Irish Universities Association. June 9, 2015. http://www.iua.ie/pub lications/iua-graduate-skills-statement-brochure-2015/.

Ives, Maura. "Digital Humanities Pedagogy: Hitting the Wall and Bouncing Back." *CEA Critic* 76, no. 2 (2014): 221–24. https://doi.org/10.1353/cea.2014.0016.

Jakacki, Diane. "How We Teach? Digital Humanities Pedagogy in an Imperfect World." Keynote address, Canadian Society for Digital Humanities /Société Canadienne des Humanités Numériques Annual Conference. Calgary, June 5, 2016. https://web.archive .org/web/20211129165441/http://dianejakacki.net/how-we-teach-digital-humanities -pedagogy-in-an-imperfect-world/.

Moravec, John W., ed. *Emerging Education Futures: Experiences and Visions from the Field.* Minneapolis: Education Futures, 2020.

Moravec, John W., ed. *Knowmad Society.* Minneapolis: Education Futures, 2013. https:// educationfutures.com/storage/app/media/documents/KnowmadSociety.pdf.

Rockwell, Geoffrey. "Inclusion in the Digital Humanities." philosophi.ca. June 28, 2010. https://philosophi.ca/pmwiki.php/Main/InclusionInTheDigitalHumanities.

Rockwell, Geoffrey, and Stéfan Sinclair. "Acculturation and the Digital Humanities Community." In *Digital Humanities Pedagogy: Practices, Principles and Politics,* edited by Brett D. Hirsch, 177–211. Cambridge: Open Book Publishers, 2012. https://doi .org/10.7939/R37D2QM72.

Sahle, Patrick, Johanna Puhle, and Lisa Rau. "Digitale Geisteswissenschaften." November 2011, Accessed April 22, 2021. https://web.archive.org/web/20210422012911/https:// cceh.uni-koeln.de/Dokumente/BroschuereWeb.pdf.

Saklofske, Jon, Estelle Clements, and Richard Cunningham. "They Have Come, Why Won't We Build It? On the Digital Future of the Humanities." In *Digital Humanities Pedagogy: Practices, Principles and Politics,* edited by Brett D. Hirsch, 311–30. Cambridge: Open Book Publishers, 2012.

Saum-Pascual, Alex. "Teaching Electronic Literature as Digital Humanities: A Proposal." *Digital Humanities Quarterly* 11, no. 3 (2017). https://www.digitalhumanities.org/dhq /vol/11/3/000314/000314.html.

Schreibman, Susan, Agiatis Benardou, Claire Clivaz, Matej Durco, Marianne Ping Huang, Eliza Papaki, Stef Scagliola, Toma Tasovac, and Tanja Wissik. "#dariahTeach: Online Teaching, MOOCs and Beyond." Abstract. Digital Humanities 2016, Jagiellonian University, Kraków, Poland, July 11–16, 2016. https://dh2016 .adho.org/abstracts/292.

Terras, Melissa. "Disciplined: Using Educational Studies to Analyse 'Humanities Computing.'" *Literary & Linguistic Computing* 21, no. 2 (2006): 229–46.

Thaller, Manfred. "Towards a Reference Curriculum for the Digital Humanities." Abstract. Digital Humanities 2012, University of Hamburg, Hamburg, Germany, July 16–20, 2012. http://www.dh2012.uni-hamburg.de/conference/programme/abstracts/towards-a -reference-curriculum-for-the-digital-humanities.1.html.

Tóth-Czifra, Erzsébet. "Open Scholar Stars Interview Series: Interview with Dr. James L. Smith." DARIAH-Open: Hypotheses. September 2, 2019. https://dariahopen.hypoth eses.org/608.

Uiterwaal, Frank, Jennifer Edmond, and Mikel Sanz. "PARTHENOS D7.4 Report on the Assessment of Transnational Access Activities in Participating Projects." Zenodo. October 31, 2018. https://doi.org/10.5281/zenodo.2551489.

Université de Neuchâtel. "Sharing the Experience: Workflows for the Digital Humanities." Dariah Campus. December 2019. Accessed April 18, 2024. https://campus.dariah .eu/resource/events/sharing-the-experience-workflows-for-the-digital-humanities.

Varner, Stewart. "Library Instruction for Digital Humanities Pedagogy in Undergraduate Classes." In *Laying the Foundation: Digital Humanities in Academic Libraries,* edited by John W. White and Heather Gilbert, 205–22. West Lafayette, Ind.: Purdue University Press, 2016. https://doi.org/10.2307/j.ctt163t7kq.14.

Weber, Charlotte Teresa, Melania Borit, Fabien Canolle, Eva Hnatkova, Gareth O'Neill, Davide Pacitti, and Filomena Parada. "Identifying and Documenting Transferable Skills and Competences to Enhance Early Career Researchers Employability and Competitiveness." Zenodo. October 1, 2018. https://doi.org/10.5281/zenodo.1299178.

Wissik, Tanja, Jennifer Edmond, Frank Fischer, Franciska de Jong, Stefania Scagliola, Andrea Scharnhorst, Hendrik Schmeer, Walter Scholger, and Leon Wessels. "Teaching Digital Humanities Around the World: An Infrastructural Approach to a Community-Driven DH Course Registry." HAL Open Science. June 3, 2020. https://hal.archives-ouvertes .fr/hal-02500871.

Zimpher, Nancy L. "The Future of Higher Education Is Flexibility." *New York Academy of Sciences.* Accessed April 18, 2024. https://web.archive.org/web/20240418171049 /https://www.nyas.org/ideas-insights/blog/the-future-of-higher-education-is -flexibility/.

Embracing Hybrid Infrastructures

JACOB D. RICHTER AND HANNAH TAYLOR

Questions of emerging technologies loom pervasively over the possibilities for digital graduate study in the humanities of the twenty-first century. Increasingly, graduate learning occurs in networked digital environments, requiring program stakeholders to interact through, with, and alongside technological infrastructures. Infrastructures are building blocks that humans live, work, and act alongside and as such are crucial for both communicating information as well as for articulating cultural values (Guldi, "Scholarly Infrastructure as Critical Argument"). Critical infrastructure studies commonly approaches infrastructure with particular attention to ethnography (Edwards, "Infrastructure and Modernity"; Neumann and Star, "Making Infrastructure"), media (Blanchette, "Material History of Bits"; Parks, "Media Infrastructures and Affect"; Holt and Vonderau, "Where the Internet Lives"), race and ethnicity (Leker and MacDonald Gibson, "Relationship Between Race and Community"; Nemser, *Infrastructures of Race*), science and technology studies (Strebel et al., *Repair Work Ethnographies*; Latour, "On Technical Mediation"), feminism (Wilson, "Infrastructure of Intimacy"; Verhoeven, "As Luck Would Have It"), and digital humanities (Anderson, "What are Research Infrastructures?"; Benardou et al., *Cultural Heritage Infrastructures*; Smithies, *Digital Humanities,* 113–51; see also Critical Infrastructures Studies.org, "Approaches to Infrastructure Studies"). But infrastructures play other understated roles in human actions: they enable practices and hone collective sensibilities, orientations, and attunements among groups of interconnected people. Infrastructures, in so many words, will not only need to adapt to the humanities of the coming decades but will actively help influence and design what the humanities of the future will be.

This chapter imagines material, discursive, and rhetorical infrastructures as not only important considerations for the future of graduate education in the humanities but also as vital sites for meaningful innovation, evolution, and intervention in how humanities classrooms, curricula, and pedagogies are envisioned in the twenty-first century. Positioning hybridity across infrastructures as a means of expanding learning and connection possibilities for humanities graduate programs, we aim to offer active focus on collective sensibilities and orientations that are honed through practices enabled by infrastructures. Material infrastructures such as emerging technologies enable and contribute in a fundamental way to the formation of collective practices, sensibilities, and orientations. As many students, teachers, and program administrators can attest to, however, putting tools in someone's hands without an accompanying plan or strategy rarely results in the achievement of desired outcomes (Losh, *War on Learning*). This chapter offers a heuristic of embracing hybrid infrastructures as one possible strategy that humanities programs of the near future might employ to better nurture practices, sensibilities, and orientations enabled by infrastructures, rather than focusing on the infrastructures themselves.

We offer these thoughts from a particular grounding within digital graduate study in the humanities. As students in the transdisciplinary and geographically dispersed Rhetorics, Communication, and Information Design (RCID) program at Clemson University, our insights are informed by our experiences completing PhDs in situations nearly always dependent upon hybrid infrastructures, especially those facilitated by the internet. Much of what this chapter extends is directly informed by our experiences in the RCID PhD program, which embraces hybrid infrastructures in numerous important ways, as students are dispersed around the continental United States and frequently connect online. As such, program stakeholders nearly always rely upon networked technologies as crucial cultural-technological infrastructures in their efforts to facilitate networked learning to build program cultures and to pluralize how graduate study in the humanities is experienced.

Material, Discursive, and Rhetorical Infrastructures

Infrastructures are relational, ecological, epistemic, mundane, and never neutral (Star, "Ethnography of Infrastructure"; Star and Ruhleder, "Steps Toward an Ecology of Infrastructure"). Infrastructures are most commonly considered in their material manifestations, primarily associated with near-invisible arrangements of roads, bridges, telephone lines, or fiber optic cables that are most readily visible when they break down (Star, "Ethnography of Infrastructure," 380). Within a humanities education framework, material needs of particular programs range from appropriate technologies enabling interpersonal connections (such as email), synchronous meetings (such as video calling technologies), collaborative learning platforms (such as educational technology tools or social learning platforms), and even particular classroom setups and arrangements. Infrastructures facilitating the material, financial, and connectivity needs of evolving humanities graduate programs are typically what publics most readily identify with the term infrastructure. We suggest, however, that humanities programs look beyond purely material infrastructures and envision infrastructures along other, equally important axes.

A successful infrastructure for humanities education must extend beyond the material to encompass discursive and rhetorical dimensions (Boyle, *Rhetoric as a*

Posthuman Practice). Infrastructure, as Bowker and Star posit in *Sorting Things Out,* can refer to a set of practices that we live through, without necessarily understanding who built or controls those practices (319). Similarly, Danielle Nicole DeVoss, Ellen Cushman, and Jeffrey T. Grabill describe infrastructure as the "taken-for-granted, often invisible, institutional structure" that is implicit for most stakeholders in an organization, including the policies and practices in place ("Infrastructure and Composing," 19). These definitions of the term align with what Read and Frith call discursive infrastructures (Read, "Infrastructural Function"; Frith, "Technical Standards").

Discursive infrastructures are characterized by documents such as organizational plans, procedures, technical standards, and design schemes. Read argues that particular forms of writing function as infrastructures, helping to enable and shape collective actions, focusing on how broad, inclusive definitions of infrastructure can facilitate relationships and alliance brokering ("Infrastructural Function," 14). Discursive infrastructures help condition the human experience, especially as boundaries between virtual and physical space grow more and more porous when interacting alongside emerging technologies (Dourish and Bell, "Infrastructure of Experience").

The discursive infrastructures that support, enable, and shape graduate humanities programs—the program handbooks, plans of study, course descriptions, thesis and dissertation requirements, mentoring routines, extracurricular organizations, email lists, social media groups, and awards and honors—work to organize human action, shape collective practices, standardize operations and activities, and provide an architecture for cooperative, mutually beneficial relationship formation. Assembling a successful humanities graduate program is about far more than collecting material infrastructures and coordinating their use with discursive infrastructures, however. Humanities graduate programs, we argue, benefit on a deeper level from consideration of rhetorical infrastructures.

Rhetorical Infrastructures and Graduate Humanities Education

Rhetorical infrastructures refer to a somewhat abstract, but impactful, assembly of collective sensibilities, values, habits, attitudes, conventions, aptitudes, pedagogies, and attunements that are honed through shared practice across a program's networks. Rhetorical infrastructures leverage the human within the infrastructural system and provide understated pathways for organizations to coalesce, evolve, conflict, transform, adapt, and persist in unified bonds and alliances. A rhetorical infrastructure might be a common warm-up or wrap-up discussion strategy shared across the curriculum, a program-wide commitment to practicing collaboration on research and publications, or even an expectation that students further along in the program mentor and assist newer students. We assert that consideration of material, discursive, and rhetorical infrastructures constitutes a hybrid infrastructure that considers the intersections of humans, technologies, practices, procedures, standards, sensibilities, and material constraints to more holistically orient collective practices at an organization-wide level. If graduate humanities programs focus narrowly on only singular elements of their infrastructures, they risk neglecting attention to the potentially generative intersections of those already hybrid infrastructures.

Material infrastructures, such as particular interconnected technological set-ups, help nurture, condition, and cultivate rhetorical sensibilities that, over time and repetition, grow into sustained infrastructures that programmatic stakeholders draw on and leverage. As emerging digital technologies become more embedded as fundamental components of evolving and innovating humanities graduate programs, the rhetorical sensibilities accompanying them become more worthy of attention and more important to foreground, and they become easier to ignore. Technologies, or material infrastructures, need not be present, in active use, or even plugged in, to enact deep-rooted and ingrained influence on collective habits, orientations, and behaviors (Boyle et al., "Digital"). We argue that technologies and infrastructures themselves are far less compelling and integral for emerging humanities graduate programs to consider compared to the practices, sensibilities, orientations, affects, and modes of being that those technologies cultivate.

For instance, the Covid-19 pandemic forced many in higher education to adopt emerging technologies such as the popular video calling platform Zoom into their everyday practice (Supiano "Why Is Zoom So Exhausting?"; Hogan and Sathy, "8 Ways to Be More Inclusive"; Flaherty, "Synchronous Instruction"). Many students and instructors have commented on how simple adoption of the novel technology did not provide the educational results they were hoping for (Pulsipher, "Beyond Zoom U"). In at least some cases, the successful adoption of the material infrastructure of the Zoom platform may not have been matched by the successful cultivation of rhetorical infrastructures necessary to make the educational experience over the video call an entirely positive one for students. Platforms such as Zoom are material infrastructures, but they induce rhetorical sensibilities in the collective dynamic developed among their users. As more students and program stakeholders express dissatisfaction with the so-called Zoom University, it may help to consider the rhetorical infrastructures in place surrounding those emerging technologies (Lorenz et al., "We Live in Zoom Now").

Adoption of a material infrastructure such as Zoom benefits from the conscious, active development of a rhetorical infrastructure as well. For instance, rather than simply running a lecture through the video calling platform, an instructor might split the class into small breakout rooms using an affordance of the video technology to nurture smaller, more active group dynamics among the classroom population. Additionally, the course instructor might provide active, deliberate guidance on what small breakout group discussions could or should be characterized by, including guidance on the content of the small group conversation but also the tone, the procedure, the available technological affordances, and the discussion's end goal. The instructor might even provide tips to "break the ice" in a small breakout group session and provide discussion guidelines to nurture sensibilities toward, say, collaboration and creativity. Realizing that many students are unfamiliar with not only the video calling technology but also with the format, organization, configuration, and schemes of the course, the instructor might benefit from foregrounding rhetorical infrastructures—collective sensibilities, habits, and orientations formed through practice—as valuable resources for the course or program to mobilize in generative, fruitful ways.

Possible Futures: Embracing Hybrid Infrastructures in Digital Graduate Education

To outline the value of embracing hybrid infrastructures for digital graduate education in the twenty-first century, we offer three orienting principles that can be used programmatically and pedagogically to more strategically build interactions with technological, hybrid infrastructures.

First, when negotiating the infrastructural structures, values, and priorities of future graduate humanities programs, remembering the human as an orienting principle offers a flexible but robust heuristic that helps foreground the ethical, equitable, and socially just implications of cultural-technological infrastructures. Infrastructures—material, discursive, and rhetorical—are only as useful in graduate education as their human stakeholders deem them to be. Additionally, remembering the human can help program administrators and stakeholders conceptualize how their infrastructures serve particular groups of people, including orienting attention to concerns of social injustice, inclusivity, and equity. Graduate humanities programs should consider what their infrastructures do to reinforce existing power structures, privilege some viewpoints over others, and enable particular cultural practices and undermine others. These sensibilities, built up over time, practice, and repetition, evolve into important rhetorical infrastructures that program members cultivate through practice and then codify, communicate, and leverage for later guidance.

Second, an orienting value of holistic attention to infrastructures offers graduate humanities programs the opportunity to gauge the interplay between the material, discursive, and rhetorical infrastructures in which their programs engage. A graduate program giving holistic attention to infrastructures might involve active reflection on how infrastructures in use help shape program culture, how those infrastructures serve students and other stakeholders, and what could be done differently to better orient program practice toward core program values. On a practical level, this might involve active reflection and self-assessment, leading to the addition of additional technological infrastructure such as Otter.ai add-ons to automatically add captions to Zoom calls, which moves program practice closer to program values such as inclusivity. Holistic attention to infrastructures, after a process of self-assessment and self-interrogation on the part of the program, allows the program to calibrate informed responses and adaptions if desired outcomes are not being adequately worked toward. Considering infrastructure not as equipment for everyday use and functioning but as collective practice and as collective capacities and aptitudes allows programs to ensure flexibility, hybridity, and resilience are not merely buzzwords but practiced actions of benefit to involved students, instructors, and administrators.

Lastly, active consideration of documenting rhetorical infrastructures in the context of graduate humanities programs helps ensure that rhetorical infrastructures are not fleeting, temporary additions to a humanities graduate program, but that they can be replicated, sustained, and benefited from in a variety of forms. Documenting rhetorical infrastructures, which might take the form of codified, formalized practices outlined in document form for program-wide adherence and observance, can convey important values, sensibilities, and principles to the diverse array of individuals forming a program. Most graduate programs utilize a centralized, formalized program handbook or guide for students and administrators to reference, which already serves implicitly to orient values, principles, and standards on a program-wide basis. A "values and goals" statement calibrated toward infrastructures can go a long way toward conveying to students, instructors, and administrators what programs value about how their infrastructures are used for discussion, collaboration, research production, and teaching, especially when these practices are undertaken in novel forms using emerging technologies. Graduate programs documenting rhetorical infrastructures can generate strategy documents for effectively engaging technology, more deliberately engaging intentional discussion strategies, systemically connecting disparate elements of the program, and building collaboration opportunities across programmatic structures in an intentional, active process. They might assemble a program repository as discursive infrastructure for stakeholders with collaborative, comprehensive exam advice, best practices for program teaching in the program, or recommendations from program alums on professionalism and post-PhD life. Documenting rhetorical infrastructures can help communicate valued knowledge to new students and instructors and orient the guiding principles for research, teaching, and collaboration as programs transition to increasingly hybrid futures.

Putting digital tools in the hands of humanities programs rarely translates to pedagogical success on its own but benefits greatly from further consideration of the cultures, practices, and learning environments enabled by those technologies (Losh, *War on Learning*). We argue that the humanities of the digital future would do well to focus on the practices, sensibilities, orientations, and attunements formed between students, communication forms, and technological structures that are enabled by digital technologies, rather than focusing primarily on the technologies themselves. In embracing hybrid infrastructures, graduate humanities programs can begin to conceptualize technological infrastructures based on the practices and sensibilities they nurture, in addition to the affordances they might provide.

Bibliography

Anderson, Sheila. "What Are Research Infrastructures?" *International Journal of Humanities and Arts Computing* 7, nos. 1–2 (2013): 4–23. https://doi.org/10.3366/ijhac.2013.0078.

"Approaches to Infrastructure Studies: A Critical Infrastructure Studies Primer." Critical Infrastructures Studies. Last updated March 26, 2022. https://cistudies.org/critical -infrastructure-studies-primer/.

Benardou, Agiatis, Erik Champion, Costis Dallas, and Lorna M. Hughes. *Cultural Heritage Infrastructures in Digital Humanities.* London: Routledge, 2018.

Blanchette, Jean-François. "A Material History of Bits." *Journal of the American Society for Information Science and Technology* 62, no. 6 (2011): 1042–57. https://doi.org/10 .1002/asi.21542.

Bowker, Geoffrey, and Susan Leigh Star. *Sorting Things Out: Classification and Its Conse- quences.* Cambridge, Mass.: The MIT Press, 1999.

Boyle, Casey. *Rhetoric as a Posthuman Practice.* Columbus: Ohio State University Press, 2018.

Boyle, Casey, James J. Brown Jr., and Steph Ceraso. "The Digital: Rhetoric Behind and beyond the Screen." *Rhetoric Society Quarterly* 48, no. 3 (2018): 251–59. https://doi .org/10.1080/02773945.2018.1454187.

DeVoss, Dànielle Nicole, Ellen Cushman, and Jeffrey T. Grabill. "Infrastructure and Com- posing: The When of New-Media Writing." *College Composition and Communica- tion* 57, no. 1 (2005): 14–44. https://www.jstor.org/stable/30037897.

Dourish, Paul, and Genevieve Bell. "The Infrastructure of Experience and the Experience of Infrastructure: Meaning and Structure in Everyday Encounters with Space." *Envi- ronment and Planning B: Planning and Design* 34, no. 3 (2007): 414–30. https://doi .org/10.1068/b32035t.

Edwards, Paul N. "Infrastructure and Modernity: Force, Time, and Social Organization in the History of Sociotechnical Systems." In *Modernity and Technology,* 185–225. Cam- bridge, Mass.: The MIT Press, 2003.

Flaherty, Colleen. "Synchronous Instruction Is Hot Right Now, but Is It Sustainable?" *Inside Higher Ed,* April 29, 2020. https://www.insidehighered.com/news/2020/04/29 /synchronous-instruction-hot-right-now-it-sustainable.

Frith, Jordan. "Technical Standards and a Theory of Writing as Infrastructure." *Written Communication* 37, no. 3 (2020): 401–27. https://doi.org/10.1177/0741088320916553.

Guldi, Jo. "Scholarly Infrastructure as Critical Argument: Nine Principles in a Preliminary Survey of the Bibliographic and Critical Values Expressed by Scholarly Web-Portals for Visualizing Data." *Digital Humanities Quarterly* 14, no. 3 (2020). http://www.digital humanities.org/dhq/vol/14/3/000463/000463.html.

Hogan, Kelly A., and Viji V. Sathy. "8 Ways to Be More Inclusive in Your Zoom Teaching." *Chronicle of Higher Education,* April 7, 2020. https://www.chronicle.com/article/8-Ways-to-Be-More-Inclusive-in/248460.

Holt, Jennifer, and Patrick Vonderau. "'Where the Internet Lives': Data Centers as Cloud Infrastructure." In *Signal Traffic: Critical Studies of Media Infrastructures,* edited by Lisa Parks and Nicole Starosielski, 71–93. Carbondale: University of Illinois Press, 2015.

Latour, Bruno. "On Technical Mediation: Philosophy, Sociology, Genealogy." *Common Knowledge* 3, no. 2 (1994): 29–64.

Leker, Hannah Gordon, and Gibson J. MacDonald. "Relationship between Race and Community Water and Sewer Service in North Carolina, USA." *PLOS ONE* 13, no. 3 (2018). https://doi.org/10.1371/journal.pone.0193225.

Lorenz, Taylor, Erin Griffith, and Mike Isaac. "We Live in Zoom Now." *New York Times,* March 17, 2020. https://www.nytimes.com/2020/03/17/style/zoom-parties-coronavirus-memes.html.

Losh, Elizabeth. *The War on Learning: Gaining Ground in the Digital University.* Cambridge, Mass.: The MIT Press, 2014.

Nemser, Daniel. *Infrastructures of Race: Concentration and Biopolitics in Colonial Mexico.* Austin: University of Texas Press, 2017.

Neumann, Laura J., and Susan Leigh Star. "Making Infrastructure: The Dream of a Common Language." *Proceedings of the Fourth Biennial Participatory Design Conference 1996,* edited by Jeanette Blomberg, Finn Kensing, and Elizabeth Dykstra-Erickson, 231–40. Cambridge, Mass., 1996.

Parks, Lisa. "Media Infrastructures and Affect." *Flow Journal* (May 2014). https://www.flowjournal.org/2014/05/media-infrastructures-and-affect/.

Plantin, Jean-Christophe, Carl Lagoze, Paul N. Edwards, and Christian Sandvig. "Infrastructure Studies Meet Platform Studies in the Age of Google and Facebook." *New Media and Society* 20, no. 1 (2018): 293–310. https://doi.org/10.1177/1461444816661553.

Pulsipher, Scott. "Beyond Zoom U: The Online Learning Experience Students Want." *Forbes,* June 23, 2020. https://www.forbes.com/sites/scottpulsipher/2020/06/23/beyond-zoom-u-the-online-learning-experience-students-want/.

Read, Sarah. "The Infrastructural Function: A Relational Theory of Infrastructure for Writing Studies." *Journal of Business and Technical Communication* 33, no. 3 (2019): 233–67. https://doi.org/10.1177/1050651919834980.

Smithies, James. *The Digital Humanities and the Digital Modern.* London: Palgrave McMillan, 2017. https://www.palgrave.com/us/book/9781137499431.

Star, Susan Leigh. "The Ethnography of Infrastructure." *American Behavioral Scientist,* 43, no. 3 (1999): 377–91. https://doi.org/10.1177/00027649921955326.

Star, Susan Leigh, and Karen Ruhleder. "Steps toward an Ecology of Infrastructure: Design and Access for Large Information Spaces." *Information Systems Research* 7, no.1 (1996): 111–34. https://doi.org/10.1287/isre.7.1.111.

Strebel, Ignaiz, Alan Bovet, and Phillipe Sormani, eds. *Repair Work Ethnographies: Revisiting Breakdown, Relocating Materiality.* London: Palgrave McMillan, 2018.

Supiano, Beckie. "Why Is Zoom So Exhausting?" *Chronicle of Higher Education,* April 23, 2020. https://www.chronicle.com/article/why-is-zoom-so-exhausting/.

Verhoeven, Deb. "As Luck Would Have It: Serendipity and Solace in Digital Research Infrastructure." *Feminist Media Histories* 2, no.1 (2016): 7–28. https://doi.org/10.1525/fmh.2016.2.1.7.

Wilson, Ara. "The Infrastructure of Intimacy." *Signs* 41, no. 2 (2016): 247–80.

PART VI

DISCIPLINARY CONTEXTS AND TRANSLATIONS

The Life Aquatic
Training Digital Humanists in a School of Information Science

TED UNDERWOOD

L ike digital humanists, amphibians lead divided lives. Most breathe air but can only reproduce in water. Some species resolve this tension by organizing their lives around a pilgrimage from one environment to the other. After toads find a pond to spawn in, their descendants spend part of their lives swimming before growing legs and lungs and climbing back into the air. But there are also other solutions. Certain species of aquatic frogs spend their entire life cycle in water, rising to the surface periodically to breathe.

Most digital humanists spend most of their lives in a humanities department; like toads (so to speak), we are basically at home on that ground. But to create new digital humanists, we also need other environments. A graduate student or assistant professor who wants to become a digital humanist often has to spend some time swimming around in another field to gain experience with digital media or computational methods before returning to the home discipline. At least, this seems to be the informal backstory behind many careers. Systematizing that metamorphic life cycle as a formal plan of graduate education remains a bit challenging.

I probably do not have to describe the challenges in detail because they have been explored in other essays. In chapter 6 of the present volume, Manfred Thaller's reflections on "digital Groundhog Day" trace a long history of (mostly failed) attempts to institutionalize graduate training in digital humanities dating back to the 1970s. My own attempts failed, about one decade ago, in ways that closely resemble the story Andrew Goldstone tells in "Teaching Quantitative Methods: What Makes it Hard (in Literary Studies)." Like Goldstone, I started by trying to squeeze all aspects of DH into one graduate seminar in an English department. It seems insane now, but in 2012, there were many reasons to try to pack everything in. Above all, I could not assume that an English department would contain a large population of students committed to taking multiple DH courses. So any course I designed would need to be pitched for students new to the field and perhaps wary of it. In that context, it seemed to make sense to offer a general overview of DH, focused on theoretical debate with a light introduction to data analysis along the way.

Like Goldstone, I found that this sort of course struggled to achieve its stated goals. I think I provided a decent overview of theoretical debate, but I basically failed to prepare students to understand or evaluate the computational side of DH. Computational analysis is simply not something that can be taught well in a single course and certainly not "along the way" in a course where it competes with other topics. In 2012, it perhaps seemed plausible to address computation casually because conversations about DH pedagogy were then framing the computational part of the discipline as a collection of user-friendly "tools." But as others have since pointed out, the tool metaphor was misleading (Tenen, "Blunt Instrumentalism"). Even if we skip coding and teach students to use GUIs, students will need to evaluate the results their GUIs produce. That means learning statistics. Because I could not squeeze a semester of statistics into the margins of a course on the theoretical debate in DH, my course was not really putting students in a position to critically evaluate computational research. Certainly, it was not teaching them how to do it on their own.

I now realize that getting students to the point where they can do computational research requires at least three or four semesters. Students need a semester or two of programming, a course in statistics, and perhaps a capstone course where they learn to apply these methods to the unstructured data and slippery historical questions that typify the humanities. And this still only gets them up to speed in one aspect of DH. For full preparation as a digital humanist, separate courses might be needed on topics like digital preservation and digital scholarly communication. If I had been warned about this in 2012, my answer would have been a sigh. I did not know how to make any of that possible inside an English department curriculum.

Like amphibians, digital humanists have evolved a variety of ways to address a constitutive tension between different environments. We can incorporate aspects of other subjects in the humanities, or we can build an interdisciplinary program, combining courses from several departments. Many of the contributions to this volume explain how to make those models work. But at my own university, there was another option. Just two blocks from the English department, the School of Information Sciences was already offering courses in programming, statistics, data ethics, book history, and a half-dozen other topics relevant to DH. Just as importantly, the value of those courses was clear in the context of information science: graduate students who invested in preparation for computational work would not feel isolated by a risky, controversial choice. (For a graduate student's perspective on the tensions confronting DH students in English departments, see Sean Weidman's contribution in chapter 16 in this volume.)

Because there seemed to be no point in duplicating an institution that already worked well, I asked whether it was possible to move half of my job into information science. The figure later became 75 percent. I have continued to teach courses in English, but most of my graduate training is now done in information science, and I train students mostly for jobs in that discipline. In other words, I changed my disciplinary identity, so that it would be possible to reproduce without a long meta-morphic pilgrimage, and I became an aquatic frog.

Changing disciplines felt like a risky move in 2016, but I am increasingly grate-ful I had the opportunity. At the School of Information Sciences, I found collabo-rators from a wide range of disciplinary backgrounds and an institution that was committed to helping students turn a mixture of humanistic and technical interests into a career. In 2012, I could say that DH added value to an English major, but my promises probably didn't sound confident because they weren't. Now it is easy to point to students who have gone on to work as librarians, research data engineers, or professors of information science. I work in a context where those career paths are familiar: the faculty and staff of the school know how to support them.

I am now sure that a school of information science can be a good place to train digital humanists. But the purpose of this chapter is not to convince anyone to make the same choice. That would be absurd because few of us really have a choice. The institutional options for digital humanists at a given college or university are con-strained by local history. At most institutions, schools of information science do not even exist. One does exist at the University of Illinois Urbana-Champaign (UIUC) because we are a large public research university. But information science is rarely found at smaller private universities and colleges.

So I am not advocating for a mass migration to information science. Most dig-ital humanists will continue to work in other disciplines. I just want to describe the way DH training works in my discipline to enlarge our sense of the field's diversity. Information science is different from the core humanities departments that dom-inate conversation about digital humanities. As a result, I often hear claims about the necessary shape of graduate study that sound to me unconsciously parochial. "It would be unrealistic to expect students to do X," for instance, when I know a con-text where X is already the norm.

First, a bit of historical background. Many programs in information science have roots in libraries. My school was founded in 1893 to staff the multiplying librar-ies of the midwestern and western United States. It remained a school of "library science" for most of the twentieth century.[1] But the rise of information technology in the 1960s posed a challenge and an opportunity for a discipline centered on the management of paper codices. Questions about library organization now clearly overlapped with the new field of information retrieval. By the 1970s, many library schools were adding "Information Science" to their name or simply adopting the latter phrase (Olson and Grudin, "The Information School Phenomenon"). The iSchools movement, which crystallized at the beginning of the twenty-first century, explicitly aimed to harmonize the social ideals and service tradition of librarianship with a broader educational mission that prepares students to manage and analyze information in the private sector as well.

The task of theoretically justifying this synthesis has produced a great deal of discussion (Bawden and Robinson, *Introduction to Information Science*, 37–60; Zhang and Benjamin, "Understanding Information Related Fields"). My task here is not to prove the unity of information science but simply to observe that it is in practice a diverse tradition. Some observers describe the discipline as a social science, but large parts of it could just as easily be called "humanistic" or "computational" (Cibangu, "Information Science as a Social Science"). At UIUC, for instance, the study of children's literature is centered in the iSchool at the Center for Children's Books. But I also have colleagues who teach computational subjects like text mining and bibliometrics. Between those two poles, the center of the institution is occupied by social-scientific research, especially on the social implications of information technology. Because information technology has had ample social implications lately, it is unsurprising that several leading public intellectuals have worked in iSchools (Zeynep Tufekci) or were trained there (Safiya Umoja Noble).

I have already confessed that my immediate motive for moving into a new discipline was a recognition that at UIUC, the computational part of DH graduate training would inevitably be centered in the iSchool. Because my own work is computational, that was decisive. But many other aspects of digital humanities are an equally good fit for information science. Questions about access to cultural heritage, and about the ethical and political risks of new technologies, for instance, are central to the mission of an iSchool. More broadly, Marcia Bates has argued that information science is a "meta-science" ("Invisible Substrate," 1043). Like librarians themselves, information scientists try to understand how other academic fields do their work, and they try to help them do it better. Reflection of this kind has long been central to DH, and several early DH pioneers spent part of their careers at iSchools (see Drucker, *Graphesis;* Renear et al., "Refining our Notion"; Unsworth, "Scholarly Primitives").

There are also pragmatic reasons why the collaborative culture of a (largely) social-scientific field can be a congenial place to train digital humanists. For one thing, it addresses the awkward problem that DH projects are usually too big to make good dissertations. If a student had to build everything themselves—as is the norm in English—their six years could easily be up before they even had a corpus to study. In information science, by contrast, it is normal for many chapters to emerge from coauthored articles. The dissertation is still fundamentally an individual project, but it can use the ongoing collective work of a lab as a starting point that saves the author from having to reinvent every wheel.

On the other hand, I want to acknowledge that information science does not excel at all aspects of DH graduate training. There are important things—even central things—we cannot provide. The humanities differ from the social sciences, after all, partly by insisting on the specificity of historical and cultural contexts. Social scientists *can* limit their inquiries to a particular nation or period, but many social science disciplines perceive that sort of specificity as a constraint, whereas in the humanities, it is often the whole point. If this conception of the humanities is embraced, it will be clear that digital humanities can never become a purely methodological project. It is inseparably bound up with the specificity of languages, periods, and cultures.

Although many students and faculty in information science have acquired that sort of knowledge, it is not usually the mission of the school to transmit it. We do not teach courses in, say, Chinese history or nineteenth-century British poetry. To be sure, there are exceptions to the rule. Many iSchools have domain expertise in children's literature, for instance, because libraries have historically been central to its transmission. The history of science and technology is another place where iSchools often develop domain knowledge. But these are special cases. Usually our contribution lies in methodological reflection rather than historical specificity. This is appropriate because most of the graduate students we serve are master's students who will get jobs as librarians or data scientists—in other words, as reflective experts in method who contribute across a wide range of domains.

We also teach undergraduates and doctoral students. But the emblematic doctoral thesis in information science is expected to advance understanding at a higher level of generality than the typical history or English dissertation. It may explain how other disciplines organize knowledge, or illuminate the social implications of technology, or show how new algorithms can be applied more effectively. It is possible to do those things while contributing to historical understanding of a particular cultural context. But students who want to make that sort of historical contribution would be well advised to build a network in a second discipline as well, presenting at its conferences, publishing in its venues, and connecting with mentors who can provide an informed critique of their domain-specific argument.

In short, I see no way for graduate education in DH to avoid interdisciplinarity. Graduate students studying DH in a humanities department will probably need to venture out into computer science, statistics, or quantitative social science if they want to use computational methods, or even critique them effectively. By the same token, students in a computational or social science discipline (like information science) will only fully understand the humanistic dimension of DH if they pause at some point in their careers to develop deep understanding of a particular historical context. Aspiring digital humanists will always need both kinds of training. But they still usually have to choose one department as an institutional home, and the choice is consequential because different parts of the scholarly life cycle become easier or harder in different locations.

That is why I introduced this chapter with a stretched zoological metaphor. There is no right way to be an amphibian or a digital humanist. The problems created by a complex life cycle are resolved in reality by ecological diversification, not by finding a single correct answer. At the same time, I want to be candid about the reasons why computational humanists, in particular, need information science as one possible option. Fitting computational training into a humanities degree program remains a Sisyphean task. Digital humanists have been trying to do it for decades, but it is not the path of least resistance for anyone, so there is a recurring temptation to abbreviate, downplay, or outsource the computational part of the training, as Thaller's story about Groundhog Day makes clear. That may change eventually. But in the 2020s, I think computational humanists need to be able to point to other institutional worlds. We will not know what this project can be until we see it unfold in an institutional context where local incentives encourage full exploration of its challenges. For computational DH to seem worth all the hard work it requires, it especially needs to be clear how computational training opens new opportunities for students. That becomes easy to explain when DH is integrated into a larger curriculum where data curation, information policy, and data science have a central place.

So I expect graduate training in digital humanities to flourish not only in humanities departments but in information science (and perhaps in computer science as well; see Benjamin Charles Germain Lee's intriguing report in chapter 30 in this volume). Training humanists in departments that have "science" in their names may create tension, but I think this tension is constructive. A version of DH fully captured by social science might lose its grounding in cultural specificity. A version fully contained by humanities departments might have difficulty sustaining methodological ambitions that do not seem to fit yet in the humanities curriculum. But the excitement of DH comes from a struggle to unite those two goals: maximally deep domain expertise and maximally adventurous methodological exploration. One way to guarantee that this dialectic remains lively is to keep the field divided across several disciplinary niches. Diversification will make the whole ecosystem stronger.

Note

1. See the "Our History" section of the UIUC School of Information Sciences web page, accessed July 29, 2020. https://ischool.illinois.edu/our-school/history.

Bibliography

Bates, Marcia. "The Invisible Substrate of Information Science." *Journal of the American Society for Information Science* 50 (1999): 1043–50.

Bawden, David, and Lyn Robinson. *Introduction to Information Science.* Chicago: Neal-Schuman, 2012.

Cibangu, Sylvain K. "Information Science as a Social Science." *Information Research* 15, no. 3 (2010).

Drucker, Johanna. *Graphesis: Visual Forms of Knowledge Production.* Cambridge, Mass.: Harvard University Press, 2014.

Goldstone, Andrew. "Teaching Quantitative Methods: What Makes It Hard (in Literary Studies)." In *Debates in the Digital Humanities 2019,* edited by Matthew K. Gold and

Lauren Klein. Minneapolis: University of Minnesota Press, 2019. https://dhdebates.gc
.cuny.edu/read/untitled-f2acf72c-a469-49d8-be35-67f9ac1e3a60/section/620caf9f
-08a8-485e-a496-51400296ebcd.

Olson, Gary M., and Jonathan Grudin. "The Information School Phenomenon." *Interactions:
New Visions of Human-Computer Interaction* 16, no. 2 (2009): 15–19.

Renear, Allen H., Elli Mylonas, and David G. Durand. "Refining Our Notion of What
Text Really Is: The Problem of Overlapping Hierarchies." In *Research in Humanities
Computing 4,* edited by Susan Hockey and Nancy Ide. Oxford: Oxford University
Press, 1996.

Tenen, Denis. "Blunt Instrumentalism: On Tools and Methods." In *Debates in the Digital
Humanities 2016,* edited by Matthew K. Gold and Lauren F. Klein. Minneapolis:
University of Minnesota Press, 2016. https://dhdebates.gc.cuny.edu/read/untitled
/section/09605ba7-ca68-473d-b5a4-c58528f42619.

Unsworth, J. *Scholarly Primitives: What Methods Do Humanities Researchers Have in Common, and How Might Our Tools Reflect This?* Symposium on Humanities Computing: Formal Methods, Experimental Practice, sponsored by King's College, London,
May 13, 2000. http://www.iath.virginia.edu/~jmu2m/Kings.5-00/primitives.html.

Zhang, Ping, and Robert I. Benjamin. "Understanding Information Related Fields:
A Conceptual Framework." *Journal of the American Society for Information Science
and Technology* 58 (2007): 1934–47.

Computer Science Research and Digital Humanities Questions

BENJAMIN CHARLES GERMAIN LEE

omputer science research and pedagogy occupy essential roles in the digital humanities, informing the methodologies and tools utilized by researchers and the digital systems and interfaces built by them. Although the digital humanities are canonically situated within humanities departments in the context of graduate study, I explore the possibilities for the digital humanities as a rich discipline for graduate research within computer science. In this chapter, I also draw on my experiences of pursuing digital humanities research in the context of graduate study as a PhD student in computer science and engineering at the University of Washington, a large research-intensive public university in the United States.

Methodological advances in computer science in their many manifestations continually shape the contours of research within the digital humanities, as well as our understanding of the discipline itself. Consider, for example, the deep learning revolution of the past decade within computer science and how it has reverberated through the landscape of digital humanities research. Deep learning has reframed how digital humanities scholars study modalities as far ranging as text corpora, photograph collections, television shows, audio recordings, and born-digital artifacts (Arnold and Tilton, "Distant Viewing"; Underwood et al., "Transformation of Gender"; Wevers and Smits, "Visual Digital Turn"). Within the libraries, archives, and museums community, optical character recognition has already transformed how scholars interact with digitized textual sources, and applications of machine learning and artificial intelligence continue to show great promise for digital content stewardship and content discovery (LC Labs and Digital Strategy Directorate, "Machine Learning + Libraries"; Padilla, "Responsible Operations"; Lorang et al., "Digital Libraries"; Cordell, "Machine Learning + Libraries"). Likewise, novel affordances from research in human-computer interaction (HCI), data visualization, and human-in-the-loop computing—considered subfields of computer science at my home institution—inform how digital humanities practitioners design and implement projects as far ranging as volunteer crowdsourcing platforms, public humanities exhibits, and interactive visualizations. User testing methodologies from HCI provide roadmaps for iteratively refining these digital humanities systems and interfaces. Lastly, computer science research at the intersection of artificial intelligence and HCI informs how exploratory search interfaces and recommender systems can better support digital content discovery. The digital humanities as a discipline is thus in constant conversation with computer science.

How, then, do the digital humanities relate to graduate study in computer science? I posit that grounding computer science graduate study in the digital humanities benefits not only the graduate students but also the fields of scholarship writ large. For graduate students in computer science, the digital humanities present the opportunity to study novel computer science ideas, algorithms, and affordances in practice, as well as to foster interdisciplinary collaborations and critically engage with the ethical implications of their work as demanded by proper digital humanities research. Conversely, graduate study in computer science has the potential to contribute emerging computational methodologies to digital humanities research, thereby widening the possibilities for humanistic inquiry with digital sources in both character and scale.

Let me unpack both of these provocations, beginning with the benefits to graduate students in computer science. Graduate research within machine learning, artificial intelligence, computer vision, natural language processing, human-in-the-loop computing, HCI, and visualization often involves deploying systems with novel algorithms, interfaces, or affordances and studying user activity via in-person and online user evaluations. For example, when studying a new recommendation algorithm or interface for content discovery, a computer science researcher may conduct a user study to answer questions that include the following: are users able to find more content of interest with the new algorithm or interface? Does the new algorithm or interface lead to increased user satisfaction? Does the user have more control over the new system? To deploy systems with large user bases, graduate students in computer science often partner with for-profit technology companies or test systems with crowd workers using platforms such as Amazon's Mechanical Turk. Even when deployed with the intent of improving user experience and adhering to the principles of user-centered design, these large-scale deployments come at the expense of enmeshing computer science graduate research within the profit motives, invasive tracking, and exploitative labor practices of surveillance capitalism (Hara et al., "Data-Driven Analysis"; Zuboff, *Age of Surveillance Capitalism*).

Digital humanities projects have the potential to provide similar benefits for computer science graduate students while freeing the research itself from the profit structures and ethical complications inherent to computer science research in the context of for-profit industry. Indeed, concrete questions surrounding searching, visualizing, and semantifying digital collections, coupled with dedicated user groups, make collaborations with digital humanities practitioners and cultural heritage institutions a fruitful path for computer science graduate research. For example, volunteer crowdsourcing initiatives being launched across the world by digital humanities and cultural heritage practitioners have been overwhelmingly successful, routinely engaging many thousands of volunteers. These initiatives produce significant amounts of metadata, from transcriptions of entire collections to many thousands of bounding box annotations of visual content on historic newspaper pages (Ferriter, "Introducing Beyond Words").[1] However, as Trevor Owens argues, "Far better than being an instrument for generating data that we can use to get our collections more used, [crowdsourcing] is actually the single greatest advancement in getting people using and interacting with our collections" ("Crowdsourcing Cultural Heritage"). For computer science graduate students studying human-in-the-loop machine learning, partnering with these crowdsourcing initiatives thus represents a fantastic opportunity to study computer science questions of interest—from improving crowd workflows to understanding feedback mechanisms between humans and algorithms—while contributing to projects that play essential roles in engaging the public with cultural heritage collections. In addition, the datasets derived from these crowdsourcing initiatives provide high-quality sources of ethically collected training and evaluation data for graduate students researching topics as far-ranging as handwriting recognition and speech-to-text conversion.[2] For graduate students studying search user interfaces, large-scale digital collections are ideal for studying how diverse user bases with authentic motivations explore and make sense of large volumes of data (Muralidharan, "Designing an Exploratory Text"). For graduate students seeking hands-on experience with project management, the digital humanities have much to offer, as described in chapter 23 in this volume, "Graduate Students and Project Management: A Humanities Perspective" by Meredith Martin, Natalia Ermolaev, and Rebecca Munson. The digital humanities as a field is grappling with its own systemic shortcomings surrounding the datafication of people, neocolonial thought, and the perpetuation of inequality, as well as its dependence on big tech for computing infrastructure (Noble, "Toward a Critical Black Digital Humanities"; Bartley, "Executing the Crisis: The University beyond Austerity," chapter 4 in this volume). However, graduate research with the digital humanities and cultural heritage is nonetheless better positioned than industry-tied computer science research to foreground the interests of end users and communities.

Indeed, there is already a strong precedent of digital humanities research being carried out by computer scientists at the graduate level and beyond. Consider the work of Aditi Muralidharan, who developed WordSeer, an exploratory text analysis tool with application to literary analysis in collaboration with Marti Hearst ("Designing an Exploratory Text"); Laure Thompson, Xanda Schofield, and David Mimno, who have all advanced research on topic models and latent variable models while focusing on cultural heritage data (Thompson and Mimno, "Authorless Topic Models"; Schofield et al., "Quantifying the Effects"; Mimno and Blei, "Bayesian Checking for Topic Models"); David Bamman, who has pursued a number of empirical questions surrounding natural language processing in relation to the humanities with a specific focus on literature (Bamman et al., "Bayesian Mixed Effects Model"); and David Smith, whose research in natural language processing has spanned a range of directions, from OCR correction to modeling text reuse (Dong and Smith, "Multi-Input Attention"; Smith et al., "Detecting and Modeling"). All of these computer scientists incorporated the digital humanities into their graduate studies, and their highly varied research reveals how capacious this liminal space can be.

Collaborations between computer science graduate students and digital humanities practitioners not only foster interdisciplinary modes of thinking but also present manifold opportunities to marry graduate study in computer science with critical inquiry into the sociotechnical implications of research in the field. How do machine learning systems and classification taxonomies perpetuate racist and colonial oppression (Bowker and Star, *Sorting Things Out*; Noble, *Algorithms of Oppression*)? What are the consequences of reducing individuals and their experiences to data points (D'Ignazio and Klein, *Data Feminism*)? How might visualizations aestheticize and oversimplify difficult histories (Presner, "Ethics of the Algorithm")? In accordance with the rich tradition of privacy-preserving librarianship, how might computationally informed digital humanities projects illustrate the capacity for large-scale user evaluations that emphasize privacy and autonomy? Because questions such as these are intrinsic to the modes of thinking encouraged by research in the digital humanities, the digital humanities have the potential to occupy a rich pedagogical role within computer science graduate study as well, which often suffers from little or no formal training in ethics, critical data studies, and science and technology studies.

Let me now turn to how graduate study in computer science can in turn benefit the digital humanities. As articulated earlier in this chapter, the methods of humanistic inquiry employed by digital humanities practitioners are inevitably informed by emerging methodologies in computer science. Research questions in the digital humanities are often formulated with a specific computational methodology in mind. An alternative to this paradigm is one in which digital humanities research questions are formulated in conjunction with computer scientists who can offer insight into methodological approaches otherwise inaccessible to those without graduate education in computer science or an adjacent field.[3] Computer science graduate study thus presents a capacious opportunity for projecting emerging computer science methodologies back into the digital humanities via collaboration.

In the context of my research as a PhD student in computer science and engineering at the University of Washington, I partnered with the Library of Congress as part of the Library's Innovator in Residence program to carry out a project that I named Newspaper Navigator. The goal of the project is to reimagine how the American public explores the Chronicling America database of sixteen million pages of digitized historic American newspapers (Lee, "Compounded Mediation").[4] In particular, the Newspaper Navigator project consists of two phases: extracting visual content including photographs, illustrations, maps, comics, editorial cartoons, headlines, and advertisements using machine learning techniques to produce the Newspaper Navigator dataset and subsequently building a search platform for users to explore the extracted visual content in the dataset (Lee et al., "Newspaper Navigator Dataset"; Lee and Weld, "Newspaper Navigator"). Within the capacity of my dissertation, Newspaper Navigator enabled me to study a range of computer science research questions in machine learning, artificial intelligence, and human-computer interaction, from information extraction to human-AI interaction. Within its capacity as a digital humanities project, Newspaper Navigator facilitates scholarship in the humanities by not only providing new affordances for searching and discovering visual content in historic newspapers but also widening the methodological possibilities for studying the visual content and exploring the sociotechnical implications of applying machine learning to cultural heritage data. Such possibilities include analyzing newspaper reproduction patterns of photographs, studying editorial practices as inferred from newspaper layout structures, and analyzing newspaper titles for which no reliable optical character recognition exists.

Partnering with the Library of Congress afforded me the opportunity to bridge my computer science graduate studies with my interest in the digital humanities and explore interdisciplinary questions as they relate to both computer science and the humanities. Indeed, Newspaper Navigator is only possible due to the collaboration with and input from a range of digital humanities and cultural heritage practitioners, including the LC Labs team at the Library of Congress; the National Digital Newspaper Program; IT design and development personnel at the Library of Congress; and my PhD advisor at the University of Washington, Professor Daniel Weld. Moreover, as a computer science project, Newspaper Navigator would not exist without the rich genealogy of public domain digital humanities projects at the Library of Congress, including not only Chronicling America but also the Beyond Words crowdsourcing initiative, which I utilized as a training dataset for the visual content recognition model.

I offer my personal experience with Newspaper Navigator as one example of how the digital humanities and graduate study in computer science can exist in symbiosis. Indeed, as digital humanities research and pedagogy continue to evolve within the university, computer science is well-situated, positioned to play an increasingly central role for graduate study across programs. Foregrounding computer science in this context fosters interdisciplinarity and benefits graduate students not only in humanities departments but also in computer science departments.

Notes

1. For examples of transcription projects, see the Library of Congress's By the People, Zooniverse, Smithsonian's Digital Volunteers, and the New York Public Library's What's on the Menu? and Emigrant Cities projects.

2. For an example, see the New York Public Library's Oral History Project and Transcript Editor.

3. An exemplary project that has explored this liminal space for collaboration is the Viral Texts project led by Cordell and Smith at Northeastern University; see Cordell and Smith, *Viral Texts*.

4. The Chronicling America database is a product of the National Digital Newspaper Program, a partnership between the Library of Congress and the National Endowment for the Humanities to digitize historic American newspapers.

Bibliography

Arnold, Taylor, and Lauren Tilton. "Distant Viewing: Analyzing Large Visual Corpora." *Digital Scholarship in the Humanities* 34, no. 1 (2019): i3-i16. https://doi.org/10.1093/digitalsh/fqz013.

Bamman, David, Ted Underwood, and Noah Smith. "A Bayesian Mixed Effects Model of Literary Character." In *Proceedings of the 52nd Annual Meeting of the Association for Computational Linguistics,* 370–79. Association for Computational Linguistics, 2014. http://acl2014.org/acl2014/P14-1/pdf/P14-1035.pdf.

Bowker, Geoffrey, and Susan Star. *Sorting Things Out: Classification and Its Consequences.* Cambridge, Mass.: The MIT Press, 2000.

Cordell, Ryan. "Machine Learning + Libraries: A Report on the State of the Field." LC Labs, Library of Congress. July 14, 2020. https://labs.loc.gov/static/labs/work/reports/Cordell-LOC-ML-report.pdf.

Cordell, Ryan, and David Smith. "Viral Texts: Mapping Networks of Reprinting in 19th-Century Newspapers and Magazines." Accessed January 12, 2022. http://viraltexts.org.

D'Ignazio, Catherine, and Lauren Klein. *Data Feminism.* Cambridge, Mass.: The MIT Press, 2020.

Dong, R., and Smith, D. "Multi-Input Attention for Unsupervised OCR Correction." In *Proceedings of the 56th Annual Meeting of the Association for Computational Linguistics,* 2363–72. Melbourne: Association for Computational Linguistics, 2018. https://www.aclweb.org/anthology/P18-1220.

Ferriter, Meghan. "Introducing Beyond Words." *The Signal* (blog), September 28, 2017. https://blogs.loc.gov/thesignal/2017/09/introducing-beyond-words/.

Hara, Kotaro, Abigail Adams, Kristy Milland, Saiph Savage, Chris Callison-Burch, and Jeffrey Bigham. "A Data-Driven Analysis of Workers' Earnings on Amazon Mechanical Turk." In *Proceedings of the 2018 CHI Conference on Human Factors in Computing Systems,* 1–14. New York: Association for Computing Machinery, 2018. https://doi.org/10.1145/3173574.3174023.

Jakeway, Eileen, Lauren Algee, Laurie Allen, Meghan Ferriter, Jaime Mears, Abigail Potter, and Kate Zwaard. "Machine Learning + Libraries Summit Event Summary." LC Labs and Digital Strategy Directorate, Library of Congress. February 13, 2020. https://labs.loc.gov/static/labs/meta/ML-Event-Summary-Final-2020-02-13.pdf.

Lee, Benjamin. "Compounded Mediation: A Data Archaeology of the Newspaper Navigator Dataset." *Digital Humanities Quarterly* 15, no. 4 (2021). http://digitalhumanities.org/dhq/vol/15/4/000578/000578.html.

Lee, Benjamin, Jaime Mears, Eileen Jakeway, Meghan Ferriter, Chris Adams, Nathan Yarasavage, Deborah Thomas, Kate Zwaard, and Daniel Weld. "The Newspaper Navigator Dataset: Extracting and Analyzing Visual Content from 16 Million Historic Newspaper Pages in Chronicling America." In *Proceedings of the 29th ACM International Conference on Information and Knowledge Management,* 3055–62. New York: Association for Computing Machinery, 2020. https://doi.org/10.1145/3340531.3412767.

Lee, Benjamin, and Daniel Weld. "Newspaper Navigator: Open Faceted Search for 1.5 Million Images." In *Adjunct Publication of the 33rd Annual ACM Symposium on User Interface Software and Technology,* 120–22. New York: Association for Computing Machinery, 2020. https://dl.acm.org/doi/10.1145/3379350.3416143.

Lorang, Elizabeth, Leen-Kiat Soh, Yi Liu, and Chulwoo Pack. "Digital Libraries, Intelligent Data Analytics, and Augmented Description: A Demonstration Project." University of Nebraska-Lincoln Faculty Publications. Digital Commons. January 10, 2020. https://digitalcommons.unl.edu/libraryscience/396/.

Mimno, David, and David Blei. "Bayesian Checking for Topic Models." In *Proceedings of the Conference on Empirical Methods in Natural Language Processing,* 227–37. New York: Association for Computational Linguistics, 2011. https://dl.acm.org/doi/10.5555/2145432.2145459.

Muralidharan, Aditi. "Designing an Exploratory Text Analysis Tool for Humanities and Social Sciences Research." PhD diss., University of California, Berkeley, 2013. https://www2.eecs.berkeley.edu/Pubs/TechRpts/2013/EECS-2013-203.pdf.

Noble, Safiya. *Algorithms of Oppression: How Search Engines Reinforce Racism.* New York: New York University Press, 2018.

Noble, Safiya. "Toward a Critical Black Digital Humanities." In *Debates in the Digital Humanities 2019,* edited by Matthew Gold and Lauren Klein. Minneapolis: University of Minnesota Press, 2019. https://doi.org/10.5749/j.ctvg251hk.

Owens, Trevor. "Crowdsourcing Cultural Heritage: The Objectives Are Upside Down." March 10, 2012. Accessed July 10, 2020. http://www.trevorowens.org/2012/03/crowdsourcing-cultural-heritage-the-objectives-are-upside-down/.

Padilla, Thomas. *Responsible Operations: Data Science, Machine Learning, and AI in Libraries.* Dublin: OCLC Research, 2019. https://doi.org/10.25333/xk7z-9g97.

Presner, Todd. "The Ethics of the Algorithm: Close and Distant Listening to the Shoah Foundation Visual History Archive." In *Probing the Ethics of Holocaust Culture,* edited by Claudio Fogu, Wolf Kansteiner, and Todd Presner, 175–202. Cambridge, Mass.: Harvard University Press, 2016.

Schofield, Alexandra, Laure Thompson, and David Mimno. "Quantifying the Effects of Text Duplication on Semantic Models." In *Proceedings of the 2017 Conference on Empirical Methods in Natural Language Processing,* edited by Martha Palmer, Rebecca

Hwa, and Sebastian Riedel, 2737–47. Stroudsburg, Pa.: Association for Computational Linguistics, 2017, http://dx.doi.org/10.18653/v1/D17-1290.

Smith, David, Ryan Cordell, Elizabeth Dillon, Nick Stramp, and John Wilkerson. "Detecting and Modeling Local Text Reuse." In *Proceedings of the 14th ACM/IEEE-CS Joint Conference on Digital Libraries,* 183–92. Piscataway, N.J.: IEEE Press, 2014. https://dl.acm.org/doi/10.5555/2740769.2740800.

Thompson, Laure, and David Mimno. "Authorless Topic Models: Biasing Models Away from Known Structure." In *Proceedings of the 27th International Conference on Computational Linguistics,* edited by Emily M. Bender, Leon Derczynski, and Pierre Isabelle, 3903–14. Santa Fe, N.Mex.: Association for Computational Linguistics, 2018. https://www.aclweb.org/anthology/C18-1329/.

Underwood, Ted, David Bamman, and Sabrina Lee. "The Transformation of Gender in English-Language Fiction." *Cultural Analytics* 3, no. 2 (2018): 1–25. https://culturalanalytics.org/article/11035.

Wevers, Melvin, and Thomas Smits. "The Visual Digital Turn: Using Neural Networks to Study Historical Images." *Digital Scholarship in the Humanities* 35, no. 1 (2019): 194–207. https://doi.org/10.1093/llc/fqy085.

Zuboff, Shoshana. *The Age of Surveillance Capitalism: The Fight for a Human Future at the New Frontier of Power.* New York: PublicAffairs, 2019.

Realizing New Models of Historical Scholarship
Envisioning a Discipline-Based Digital History Doctoral Program

JOSHUA CASMIR CATALANO, PAMELA E. MACK,
AND DOUGLAS SEEFELDT

Historians are in the process of learning how to construct scholarly arguments using digital tools and experimenting with new means to convey historical analysis in digital forms, a type of scholarly communication that Abby Smith Rumsey has labeled "new-model scholarly communication" ("New-Model Scholarly Communication"). We contend that digital history graduate programs should be the place where that exploration is centered for our discipline, where we can develop new ways to use digital tools to analyze texts, images, and sounds. Rather than learning from computer science or geography courses or on-the-job grant-funded projects, digital history graduate students should learn as part of their disciplinary curriculum how to compile data, conduct spatial analysis, and create visualizations in the context of historical research questions. Professors and graduate students working together in digital history seminars can provide models of what argument-driven digital historical scholarship looks like and how users might apprehend and interact with it.[1] Such a program reimagines the substance as well as some of the forms of scholarly research and communication in our profession. The discipline of history has been slow to move digital methods from the margins; it is time to center it and see what can result.[2]

The Digital Past

Historians have been experimenting and innovating with digital tools from the era of punch cards and magnetic tape to the internet and the World Wide Web (Ayers, "Doing Scholarship on the Web"). Digital historians have also been predicting the transformation of the field for more than two decades, but the majority of students and professors who participate in history doctoral programs do not incorporate digital methods in their research or publications. Historians have been slow to reenvision the field, though there has been a wide range of creative exploration near the margins.[3] As Ben Schmidt pointed out in his 2019 American Historical Association presentation, "The path that digital historians built in the decades of the 1990s and 2000s while avoiding the shadow of cliometrics was a far more interesting one; unlike English-department digital humanities of the period, it had no motive to make history more 'scientific,' and instead found ways to make historical practice live on computers and—increasingly—online" ("Two Volumes"). The most visible of the digital history projects from the 1990s and 2000s were collections of sources often intended primarily for classroom use.[4] Despite Schmidt's praise for early digital history projects, we underscore Stephen Robertson's forewarning that although there is a growing recognition that digital tools are a part of the historian's craft, it "does not mean that most historians have explored what can be done with digital tools, are equipped to do so, or are even convinced that those tools have anything to offer their own research and teaching" ("The Differences between Digital").[5]

The incorporation of digital history into the profession and the establishment of standards has been a slow process. It was not until June 2015 that the AHA published its "Guidelines for the Professional Evaluation of Digital Scholarship in History" (it is worth noting that the Modern Language Association first approved its original guidelines in May 2000).[6] The reward systems in history departments, from merit to tenure, have made change difficult. Individual digital history faculty and their projects have shown what is possible; the next step is to solidify digital history's place in the profession.

The Case for a Digital History Doctoral Program

Creating a digital history doctoral degree program instead of a digital humanities degree or certificate presents new opportunities. The doctoral program we envision centers digital history within the discipline rather than requiring graduate students to fit their digital training—largely acquired elsewhere—into their "traditional" doctoral program. When digital history is an add-on, students may of course take the initiative to seek and acquire training from other areas, but they often find that they lack a community in which to use those skills to think like historians. It has been our experience that history graduate students who acquire their training in digital humanities centers or from interdisciplinary coursework often find that they are in the minority and research agendas from other disciplines are prioritized. Although a doctoral program in digital history will certainly welcome interdisciplinary collaboration, the focus of a digital history doctoral program allows for discipline-specific questions and concerns to be the driving forces behind both teaching and research.[7] This creates an environment where historians and their students who are using digital methods enjoy a community of colleagues working in their own discipline with whom they explore similar questions and employ shared research methods (Paju, Oiva, and Fridlund, "Digital and Distant Histories").

Such a program differs from those currently offered in the United States. The history doctoral program at George Mason University (GMU) is the closest to a formal digital history doctoral program. Although many of GMU's graduates continue to pursue a career training path similar to those at other institutions, including assisting faculty with undergraduate courses, all of its doctoral students complete a six-credit sequence in digital history coursework.[8] Some students have the opportunity to undertake additional digital history training at the Roy Rosenzweig Center for History and New Media (RRCHNM) or to complete more advanced coursework as part of a digital history minor field. A few innovative students have even published digital dissertations. But a significant number of students in the PhD program do not use digital history beyond the two required courses.

Other programs offer interdisciplinary graduate certificates.[9] For example, since 2014, the University of Nebraska-Lincoln (UNL) has offered a Digital Humanities Graduate Certificate Program that is open to graduate students currently enrolled in several graduate degree programs or as a standalone (nondegree) post-baccalaureate certification. The program is shared between several programs, including anthropology, art, art history and design, classics and religious studies, English, history, modern languages, and the University Libraries via the Center for Digital Research in the Humanities (CDRH). Students complete twelve credit hours, including two required courses: Digital Humanities Practicum and Interdisciplinary Reading Seminar in Digital Humanities. Because the contributing disciplines are so varied, the seminar's emphasis is necessarily broader than one focused on a single discipline.[10] Although this "agile" approach, as Heather Richards-Rissetto and Adrian Wisnicki advocate for in chapter 24 in this volume, has proven its value for digital humanities training broadly, and especially at the undergraduate level, it has not resulted in the transformative disciplinary change promised by digital history (Blevins, "Digital History's Perpetual Future Tense").

Without direct history department support, most digital training relies upon rare opportunities for students to work on grant-funded projects most often housed in digital humanities centers that receive support from a combination of gifts, grants, and limited institutional hard money.[11] While acknowledging its obvious hands-on training benefits, it is important to note that this center-focused model is not designed to provide comprehensive discipline-based graduate training in digital scholarship, nor does it necessarily foster original student research.[12] Frankly, it must also be recognized that over the course of two-plus decades, this model has not led to the full integration of digital history into history doctoral programs and meaningful progress toward the long-promised transformation of the discipline (Ayers, "Does Digital Scholarship Have a Future?"). Furthermore, unlike GMU, UNL, or the University of Virginia, most of the 158 U.S. institutions that grant doctoral degrees in history do not have a substantial digital history or digital humanities center around which much of the digital training takes place.[13] Recently, much of the innovative work in digital history has been created by those who were not trained through hands-on experience at a center. One reason for this is that digital history is no longer an expensive, proprietary tool-driven endeavor only available through a center. Teaching digital historical practice instead of a tool-based approach centers the myriad new ways of conceiving, developing, and interpreting historical research questions. Therefore, we argue that it is necessary to integrate digital history into the disciplinary graduate curriculum.

Curricular Considerations

As digital history transforms the discipline, doctoral education must also change. As Roy Rosenzweig predicted almost two decades ago, historians researching the late twentieth and twenty-first centuries will need to grapple with an abundance of sources, many of which are preserved in only digital format(s) ("Scarcity or Abundance?"). In addition to such emerging challenges related to contemporary sources, historians, archivists, and other specialists have demonstrated how advances in archival procedures and digital access are already changing what historians study and what sources we use to form historical interpretations, regardless of the time period.[14] Having the ability to design a new doctoral program from the ground up in response to these challenges permits the department to be intentional about its structure and funding. A program conceived and developed out of the needs and interests of a discipline can hopefully avoid some of the institutional support problems experienced by previous digital humanities initiatives. This organic development can engender the stronger financial commitment and campus buy-in that Bussell and Helton identify as being crucial for a program's success.[15]

This kind of program makes digital history a second major field in conversation with the student's specialty in history. It also allows for centering the conversation between digital historiography and methodology and traditional historiography and methodology. Here we are building upon the framework pioneered at GMU by expanding the core curriculum. The required digital component of the curriculum we advocate comprises six courses: two required courses in digital history methods, a digital historiography course, a digital research seminar, and two elective courses (spatial, textual, quantitative, data ethics, grant writing, etc.). The first digital history methods course focuses on core principles in data science and computational history, with an emphasis on creating ethical historical data from primary sources, reproducible research practices, visualizations, and various analytical techniques. The second builds on these skills by introducing students to more advanced programming concepts needed to build interactive data-driven visualizations, as well as an introduction to advanced machine learning concepts.[16] The digital historiography course presents an overview of key theories of digital analysis, focusing on the various computational techniques used by historians. The digital research seminar concentrates on specific research questions and forms of scholarly communication using sources relevant to the student's dissertation research.

One aim of a digital history program based in a history department is teaching disciplinary-based ways of thinking about data not just how to use tools. The data sets, digital projects, and metadata that digital historians compile or create are now being recognized as a valuable part of their scholarly record. As Christine Borgman states, "When publications were viewed as the sole end product of scholarship, few incentives existed to curate data for use by other researchers," but, she continues, "As opportunities for data reuse increased, more scholars began to recognize the inherent value in their data. Data from multiple research projects can be combined or compared, and results can be replicated or validated. Data- and text-mining methods enable new research to be done with old data" (*Scholarship in the Digital Age*, 182). A department with a digital history doctoral program has the responsibility to recognize a place for data within the traditional definitions of historical scholarship.

The increase in the size and digital nature of historical collections makes possible and often necessitates new ways to search and analyze sources. As Robertson notes, the "closed and sometimes shrouded character of commercial products has encouraged historians and other humanities scholars to be simply consumers of digital content, to accept the search interfaces provided by vendors as the means by which to conduct research using digitized sources rather than looking to tools like topic modeling software" ("Differences between Digital," 297). As historians, we have the opportunity to use new technologies in our work and to reflect on our own participation in the two-way interactions between technological change and societies. Historians must be able to recognize the built-in biases of digitized collections and the algorithms used to create and access their content.[17] To do this they will need to develop a familiarity with databases that extends beyond simply knowing how to use them into understanding how they are made and how they transform data (Schmidt, "Do Digital Humanists Need?"). Likewise, data ethics and privacy will be even greater concerns as archivists and historians decide what to collect, whom to provide access to, and how to present this information in ways that do not jeopardize the privacy and safety of individuals.[18]

Elective courses provide students with opportunities to explore and master digital history methods and techniques necessary for their particular focus. For example, digital technologies have enabled spatial analysis to develop from just the simple plotting of events into the creation of spatial narratives and what historian David Bodenhamer has dubbed "deep maps" containing links to the data that they represent ("Narrating Space and Place," 21–23). Rather than using maps to simply illustrate data in support of an argument made in writing, deep maps and spatial narratives allow both scholars and their audiences to create new knowledge and discover new meanings through sophisticated spatial analysis. The boundaries between maps and visualizations of data have blurred, making deep maps an analytical tool central to understanding spatiotemporal patterns.

Historians are increasingly employing distant reading in conjunction with traditional close reading and are finding value in utilizing textual analysis tools to reveal patterns and connections within and across corpora.[19] Although network analysis is not a new approach, the advent of social media is pushing more historians to become aware of its value and requiring that they understand and can create and interpret visualizations that may contain many more nodes and edges than they could review by hand. As Lauren Tilton's work with statistician Taylor Arnold demonstrates, types of sources, such as the ubiquitous social media post and the tremendous amount of visual data available for analysis from photographs and television shows, have facilitated the opportunity for historians to collaborate with experts from disciplines beyond the humanities and social sciences. Such collaborations allow for the creative adaptation and application of traditionally discipline-bound methodologies to bring fresh insight to historical questions (Arnold and Tilton, "Distant Viewing Lab"; Wexler et al., "Photogrammar").

One way to foster innovative collaboration is for a digital history PhD program to accept students from a variety of backgrounds. The range of skills that students bring from master's degrees in different fields provides diverse perspectives and approaches for thinking about using digital methods to make historical arguments. A flexible curriculum would allow students whose graduate degree is not in history to take the foundation courses typically taught in a history MA program, and those with more of a background in history would immediately focus on the digital curriculum. Cohorts of students can work closely and learn from each other's diverse backgrounds in areas such as computer science, cultural studies, philosophy, library and information science, law, and English while focusing on history. Program learning outcomes for a doctoral program in digital history must represent both digital and traditional methods but also foreground ethical and historiographical training and practice.

In addition to the required digital courses, students would take or transfer in traditional historical methods and historiography courses, complete a major field of history, choose a concentration field, seek an internship, and participate in a digital history "salon" course that features guest presentations from leading digital history practitioners from the home and other institutions. Such a program should fully fund each student who needs funding and provide them with assistantships, internships, and opportunities to teach. Experience both inside and outside of academia will enrich the thinking of students. To prepare students to think more broadly about the uses of historical training beyond the professoriate, we recommend that a digital history program requires an internship in a professional setting. Although many programs offer internship opportunities at the undergraduate level, as of academic year 2011–2012 (which marks the most recent humanities indicators survey data from the American Academy of Arts and Sciences), no history departments in the United States did so on the PhD level.[20] Faculty involved in teaching digital history will use their professional networks to help students arrange these valuable experiences in libraries, archives, and museums as well as in industry and through participation in existing digital history projects at other institutions. These will be separate from opportunities for students to work on faculty projects at their own institution as part of their assistantship. We do not pretend that this is the answer to declining job prospects for history PhDs, but we intend to equip our students to work with us to find new opportunities.

A digital history PhD program based in a history department prompts a rethinking of department, university, and disciplinary norms instead of leaving each student to swim upstream through established expectations. Such a program will teach students to ethically and professionally conduct archival research and collect, analyze, and visualize materials using traditional as well as digital techniques. Students will demonstrate knowledge of the historiographical literature in digital history and two other fields of history and demonstrate proficiency in at least two digital history methods. Students will make an original contribution to their field of history via a final dissertation project based significantly upon the use of digital methods and presented in written or digital form.

Creating a digital history doctoral program in a history department brings the way we train historians in line with the changes in research and scholarly communication. As the creation of new sources, the format of traditional sources, and the preservation of historical sources continue to change, the training of historians must be modified to meet these new realities. While many of the key elements of historical research such as the close reading of archival manuscripts will remain the foundation of the discipline, technological developments and institutional and cultural changes require that historians develop additional research skills, methods of analysis, and forms of scholarly presentation. A doctoral program focused on digital history provides the opportunity to fully integrate digital methodologies into the study of history. Finally, a PhD in digital history makes it possible to focus on opportunities afforded by the digital turn in our discipline so we can see what history students and faculty can do with professional training in digital methods.

Notes

1. For more on argument-driven historical scholarship, see Robertson and Mullen, "Digital History and Argument."

2. For a discussion on the pace of fulfilling the promise of digital history see Ayers, "Does Digital Scholarship Have a Future?" and "Doing Scholarship on the Web"; Blevins, "Digital History's Perpetual Future Tense."

3. In particular, consider efforts sponsored by the American Historical Association, including "Gutenberg-e Program," available at https://www.historians.org/about-aha-and -membership/aha-history-and-archives/historical-archives/gutenberg-e-program.; Ethington, "Los Angeles and the Problem"; Thomas and Ayers, "Overview"; Censer and Hunt,

"Imaging the French Revolution." See also Omohundro Institute, "OI Reader," available at https://oireader.wm.edu/.

4. Although digital history has demonstrated the potential to play a central role both in the development of historical arguments for historians as well as in the ways the discipline communicates with the broader public, we recognize that putting something online does not mean that it is public history. Both public and digital history can advance historical arguments, but not all digital history is public history.

5. Other disciplinary assessments include Townsend, "How Is New Media Reshaping?"; Townsend, "Report Claims History Discipline Failing"; Townsend, "Historians and the Technologies."

6. For the AHA guidelines see "Guidelines for the Professional Evaluation," available at https://www.historians.org/teaching-and-learning/digital-history-resources /evaluation-of-digital-scholarship-in-history/guidelines-for-the-professional-evaluation-of -digital-scholarship-by-historians. For the MLA guidelines, see "Guidelines for Evaluating Work," available at https://www.mla.org/About-Us/Governance/Committees/Commit tee-Listings/Professional-Issues/Committee-on-Information-Technology/Guidelines-for -Evaluating-Work-in-Digital-Humanities-and-Digital-Media.

7. See Thaller, "Notes on Digital Groundhog Day" in chapter 6 in this volume.

8. See Crossley, Regan, and Catalano, "Graduate Assistantships in the Digital Humanities" in chapter 13 in this volume.

9. For example, George Mason University has also started a certificate program in digital public humanities. See Robertson, "Teaching Digital Humanities Online" in chapter 9 in this volume.

10. For a discussion on the unrealized potential of digital history see Blevins, "Digital History's Perpetual Future Tense;" Ayers, "Doing Scholarship on the Web."

11. Roy Rosenzweig founded the Center for History and New Media (CHNM) in the Department of History and Art History at GMU in the fall of 1994. The Virginia Center for Digital History, founded in 1998 by Edward L. Ayers and William G. Thomas III, is credited with coining the term "Digital History"; the CDRH was formally established at the University of Nebraska-Lincoln in 2005.

12. As Crossley, Regan, and Catalano argue in this volume, balancing grant deliverables and providing meaningful graduate training are often at odds.

13. See the *AHA Directory of History Departments and Organizations Institution Search,* available at https://secure.historians.org/members/services/cgi-bin/memberdll.dll /openpage?wrp=search_institution.htm; see also American Academy of Arts and Sciences, "Digital Engagement," which was created using data from White et al., *2012–13 Survey.* For a global list of institutions that offer advanced degrees in digital humanities, see Digital Humanities Notes, "Advanced Degrees in Digital Humanities" at https://github.com/dh -notes/dhnotes/blob/master/pages/dh-programs.md.

14. For how digitization is changing what we study, see Milligan, "Illusionary Order" and *History in the Age of Abundance?*; for an example of how something as simple as

text search is reshaping transnational research, see Putnam, "Transnational and the Text-Searchable"; for an archival perspective, see Owens, *Theory and Craft of Digital Preservation.*

15. See Bussell and Helton, "Why Our Digital Humanities Program Died and What You Can Learn about Saving Yours" in chapter 5 in this volume.

16. The framing of these two methods courses is inspired by the Clio I and Clio II courses that have been offered GMU and discussed in greater detail by Crossley, Regan, and Catalano in chapter 13 in this volume.

17. For more on bias and other challenges exacerbated by new search technology, see Noble, *Algorithms of Oppression*; Halavais, *Search Engine Society*; Padilla and Arroyo-Ramirez, "Bias, Perception, and Archival Praxis"; and Watson, "Bias and Inclusivity in Metadata."

18. For example, see Society of American Archivists, "SAA Core Values Statement and Code of Ethics," available at https://www2.archivists.org/statements/saa-core-values-statement-and-code-of-ethics.

19. For the use of digital methods to form historical arguments, see the recently created journal *Current Research in Digital History,* available at https://crdh.rrchnm.org/.

20. See "Occupationally Oriented Activities for Doctoral Students, 2011–12 Academic Year (Nonacademic Employment Only)," created using data from White, Chu, and Czujko. Accessible at https://www.humanitiesindicators.org/content/indicatordoc.aspx?i=526.

Bibliography

American Academy of Arts and Sciences. "Digital Engagement in Humanities Departments." Accessed March 23, 2022. https://www.amacad.org/humanities-indicators/higher-education-surveys/digital-engagement-humanities-departments.

Arnold, Taylor, and Lauren Tilton. "Distant Viewing Lab." Accessed August 6, 2020. https://www.distantviewing.org/.

Ayers, Edward L. "Does Digital Scholarship Have a Future?" *Educause Review* 48, no. 4 (July/August 2013): 24–34.

Ayers, Edward L. "Doing Scholarship on the Web: Ten Years of Triumphs—and a Disappointment." *Journal of Scholarly Publishing* 35, no. 3 (April 2004): 143–47.

Blevins, Cameron. "Digital History's Perpetual Future Tense." In *Debates in the Digital Humanities 2016,* edited by Matthew K. Gold and Lauren F. Klein, 308–24. Minneapolis: University of Minnesota Press, 2016.

Bodenhamer, David. "Narrating Space and Place." In *Deep Maps and Spatial Narratives,* edited by David Bodenhamer, John Corrigan, and Trevor Harris, 7–27. Bloomington: Indiana University Press, 2015.

Borgman, Christine. *Scholarship in the Digital Age: Information, Infrastructure, and the Internet.* Cambridge, Mass.: The MIT Press, 2007.

Censer, Jack, and Lynn Hunt. "Imaging the French Revolution: Depictions of the French Revolutionary Crowd." *The American Historical Review* 110, no. 1 (February 2005): 38–45.

Ethington, Philip J. "Los Angeles and the Problem of Urban Historical Knowledge." Roy Rosenzweig Center for History and New Media, George Mason University. Accessed March 23, 2022. http://chnm.gmu.edu/digitalhistory/links/cached/introduction/link0 .23.LAurbanhistoricalknowledge.html.

Halavais, Alexander. *Search Engine Society.* 2nd ed. Malden, Mass.: Polity, 2018.

Milligan, Ian. *History in the Age of Abundance? How the Web Is Transforming Historical Research.* Chicago: McGill-Queen's University Press, 2019.

Milligan, Ian. "Illusionary Order: Online Databases, Optical Character Recognition, and Canadian History, 1997—2010." *The Canadian Historical Review* 94, no. 4 (2013): 540–69.

Noble, Safiya. *Algorithms of Oppression: How Search Engines Reinforce Racism.* New York: New York University Press, 2018.

Owens, Trevor. *The Theory and Craft of Digital Preservation.* Baltimore: Johns Hopkins University Press, 2018.

Padilla, Thomas, and Elvia Arroyo-Ramirez. "Bias, Perception, and Archival Praxis." *Dh+lib* (blog), September 13, 2017. Accessed March 23, 2022. https://acrl.ala.org/dh/2017 /09/13/archivalpraxis/.

Paju, Petri, Mila Oiva, and Mats Fridlund. "Digital and Distant Histories: Emergent Approaches within the New Digital History." In *Digital Histories: Emergent Approaches within the New Digital History,* edited by Mats Fridlund, Mila Oiva, and Petri Paju. Helsinki University Press, 2020. https://hup.fi/site/chapters/e/10.33134/HUP-5-1/.

Putnam, Lara. "The Transnational and the Text-Searchable: Digitized Sources and the Shadows They Cast." *American Historical Review* 121, no. 2 (April 2016): 377–402.

Robertson, Stephen. "The Differences between Digital History and Digital Humanities." May 23, 2014. Accessed June 20, 2021. https://drstephenrobertson.com/blog-post/the -differences-between-digital-history-and-digital-humanities/.

Robertson, Stephen. "The Differences between Digital Humanities and Digital History." In *Debates in the Digital Humanities 2016,* edited by Matthew K. Gold and Lauren F. Klein, 289–307. Minneapolis: University of Minnesota Press, 2016.

Robertson, Stephen, and Lincoln Mullen. "Digital History and Argument White Paper." Arguing with Digital History Workshop, Roy Rosenzweig Center for History and New Media, George Mason University. November 13, 2017. https://rrchnm.org/argument -white-paper/.

Rosenzweig, Roy. "Scarcity or Abundance? Preserving the Past in a Digital Era." *American Historical Review* 108, no. 3 (June 2003): 735–62.

Rumsey, Abby Smith. "New-Model Scholarly Communication: Road Map for Change." White Paper. Scholarly Communication Institute Reports, University of Virginia Library, July 13, 2011. http://uvasci.org/institutes-2003-2011/SCI-9-Road-Map-for -Change.pdf.

Schmidt, Benjamin. "Do Digital Humanists Need to Understand Algorithms?" In *Debates in the Digital Humanities 2016,* 546–55. Minneapolis: University of Minnesota Press, 2016.

Schmidt, Benjamin. "Two Volumes: The Lessons of Time on the Cross." December 5, 2019. Accessed June 20, 2021. http://benschmidt.org/post/2019-12-05-totc/2019-aha/.

Thomas, William G., and Edward L. Ayers. "An Overview: The Differences Slavery Made: A Close Analysis of Two American Communities." *The American Historical Review* 108, no. 5 (December 1, 2003): 1299–1307.

Townsend, Robert B. "Historians and the Technologies of Research." *Perspectives on History*. October 1, 2017. https://www.historians.org/perspectives-article/historians-and -the-technologies-of-research-october-2017/.

Townsend, Robert B. "How Is New Media Reshaping the Work of Historians?" *Perspectives on History*. November 1, 2010. https://www.historians.org/perspectives-article /how-is-new-media-reshaping-the-work-of-historians-november-2010/.

Townsend, Robert B. "Report Claims History Discipline Failing in Modern Research Practices." *Perspectives on History*. February 1, 2013. https://www.historians.org /perspectives-article/report-claims-history-discipline-failing-in-modern-research -practices-february-2013/.

Watson, Brian M. "Bias and Inclusivity in Metadata." Society of American Archivists. Accessed January 9, 2021. https://mydigitalpublication.com/article/Bias+and+Inclus ivity+in+Metadata/3426311/601234/article.html.

Wexler, Laura, Lauren Tilton, and Taylor Arnold. "Photogrammar." Accessed August 6, 2020. http://photogrammar.yale.edu/.

White, Susan, Raymond Chu, and Roman Czujko. *The 2012–13 Survey of Humanities Departments at Four-Year Institutions.* College Park, Md.: Statistical Research Center, American Institute of Physics, 2014.

Remediating Digital Humanities Graduate Training

SERENITY SUTHERLAND

The introduction of digital methodologies in graduate education has led to a refashioning of the tools and approaches scholars use to create new knowledge. Graduate students are often at the forefront of this new knowledge and tool creation when they serve as project managers, interns, and research assistants on digital humanities projects or when they plumb the depths of their home disciplines and study digital methodologies in research seminars. While studying digital humanities methods and epistemologies, graduate students also engage in the act of digital media creation when they work on digital projects. Thus, graduate students embody two roles: that of learner and consumer of theories and models about the discipline and that of creator of new work, typically digital media in the form of tools, projects, and software. Digital media scholars have already enjoined the disciplines of media studies and digital humanities in academic conversation, most notably in Jentery Sayers's edited volume, *The Routledge Companion to Media Studies and Digital Humanities,* as well as others elsewhere (McPherson; Kraus; Mittell; Ferguson). There is little conversation, though, about what media studies can do for digital humanities graduate education. Although some scholars are addressing graduate education in the digital humanities, there is scant attention paid to how media studies plays a role (Huet and Taylor; Opel and Simeone; Reid; Selisker; Sutherland). Working within the space created for this conversation, my goal is to present the phenomenon of remediation as a metaphor for graduate education in digital humanities to urge a more central position for media studies as a necessary component within graduate education training. Media studies provides a way of assessing digital humanities products as media artifacts and offers a theoretical framework for doing so.

There are some tensions between media studies and digital humanities. Sayers proposes this tension may be because digital humanities takes as their topics of study material typically in textual form from before the 1800s, whereas media studies seldom looks before 1800 and studies multimodal texts. Additionally, although media studies takes media products as its central study, digital humanities integrates media into its processes and methods. Such tensions, although not trivial, are not insurmountable and reinforce that we are not separate from media, but rather, as Sayers notes, entangled in their production, consumption, and analysis. Likewise, I emphasize that media are entangled with graduate student research and training.

Digital humanities has become a somewhat permanent discipline; certain universities offer MA and PhD positions in digital humanities and may have a coterie of fully onboard educators who "get" digital humanities. Students who work from disciplines outside those with scholars friendly to digital humanities are likely to encounter thesis members, tenured faculty, endowed chairs, and people occupying otherwise impressive positions of academic power, who dismiss digital humanities. This is not a trivial experience for graduate students defending their research. It is to both of these imagined subsets of graduate students that I argue media studies as a discipline might offer instruction on how to position and defend one's research and how the field itself can aid in furthering digital humanities epistemologies.

The scholars Jay Bolter and Richard Grusin employ the term "remediation" to indicate a refashioning of traditional media to address how new media, like the internet, build on and improve upon older forms of media, like film. Bolter and Grusin argue in *Remediation: Understanding New Media*, a work stemming from a series of graduate courses they both taught at Georgia Tech, that the outcome of media studies is not to serially displace "old" media with "new" media. In fact, such distinctions between old and new media are not all that useful. Instead, they maintain, "What is new about new media comes from the particular ways in which they refashion older media and the ways in which older media refashion themselves to answer the challenges of new media" (15). Similarly, Lev Manovich argues that all new media relies on the conventions of old media, thus complicating the terms old and new. Using the interplay between new and old medias as our metaphor, then, new graduate pedagogical approaches do not make old ones obsolete. Rather, there exists the potential to transform older pedagogies, retaining some features while discarding others. Through this perspective, the notion of remediation serves as a bridge between subfields in the humanities and can transform and reenergize disciplines. Furthermore, using media studies as an analogy and metaphor may offer graduate students a position of strength to articulate to themselves and those resistant to their efforts why their digital humanities work matters.

In the last ten years, digital humanities scholars have shifted their thinking about interdisciplinary work in the digital humanities from the metaphor of the Big Tent to the more recent "zonas de contacto" (Pannapacker; Ortega). In response to the gathering of disciplines and approaches brought into the DH community, Elika Ortega argues for a "synthesis of multiple" models of knowledge production because "a single hegemonic epistemic model is insufficient" to fully capture the interdisciplinarity of digital humanities works (Ortega, "Zonas de Contacto," 180). Within the context of contact zones, there are two principal ways that media studies can help illuminate digital humanities graduate education. First, media studies and digital humanities are both embedded within and easily reach out to other disciplines, such as English and history, and create pathways for interdisciplinary connections. Second, media studies can help explain digital humanities artifacts and help digital humanities projects and products become objects of analysis and sites of new knowledge production about the nature of digital media and the production of knowledge.

Media studies is an interdisciplinary discipline. After the Second World War, media studies grew, taking many of its cues from more established fields like psychology and sociology with a sharp eye toward early information theory outlined by Claude Shannon and Warren Weaver. The critical study of media burgeoned in the 1970s and 1980s and took inspiration from literary studies, feminist criticism, film and television studies, science and technology studies, and critical cultural studies. Although these approaches could contradict one another at times, they have a long history of integration with media studies, furthering the discipline and at the same time facilitating pathways for media studies to be situated within academia (Ouellette and Gray, *Keywords for Media Studies,* 2–3). Allegorically, media studies can be seen as an older, world-wise academic sibling within the interdisciplinary family, one who has already been parented and forged an academically institutionalized path.

Part of the origin story of media studies, then, much like digital humanities, is an emphasis on interdisciplinarity and collaboration across disciplines. Mentioned so often it may now sound trite, digital humanities scholars time and again note the strength of interdisciplinary collaboration. Tara McPherson, in her description of intersections between media studies and digital humanities, inscribes this interdisciplinary collaborator as the "multimodal scholar" who "complements rather than replaces" other types of digital humanists, and indeed other humanists generally ("Introduction," 120). Working with different tools and products—visualizations, databases, video games, and films—the multimodal scholar seeks to analyze ways of knowing and create new ways of seeing the world; in other words, the multimodal scholar is in the work of creating media and assessing epistemologies in whatever modality she encounters them. But how does such a multimodal scholar pursue her training, or how is a multimodal scholar made? What formalized pedagogical trends in graduate education promote and encourage such interdisciplinary multimodality? More importantly, where do graduate programs stand with training multimodal scholars, or is this burden of educating themselves as multimodal scholars something graduate students pursue outside their formalized disciplinary training? Part of the process of remediating the future of graduate education will be answering these questions, but one immediate response is the role media theories can play in assessing media artifacts. For example, social network analysis, which is a theoretical concept stemming from communication studies, is increasingly used to analyze humanistic phenomena such as networks of British luminaries (Kindred Britain) and the lineages between jazz musicians (Linked Jazz).[1] Built within social network analysis is not only the theory of why nodes, edges, and connections are significant but also a pathway for recognizing network analysis as a reductive tool of western categorization intent on capturing a static moment in time (Drucker, "Graphical Approaches"). Thus, within social network analysis, instruction on creating a tool that integrates humanities data as well as a mode of analysis for critiquing the tool as an "object of inquiry" can be found.[2]

In his explanation of the intersections between digital humanities and media studies, Sayers emphasizes that one fruitful area of analysis is not just asking "what media *are*," but also "what media *do*" (*Routledge Companion*, 3). This approach employs media studies and digital humanities as a matter of politics, or in other words, as a way to unpack the power structures embedded within our technologies and media. As digital humanities products become increasingly multimodal and move beyond the remediation of print texts to also include sound, maps, visualizations, and archives, studying these artifacts as media can be instructive for locating politics of labor, race, gender, and class.

To further explore the above concepts (interdisciplinarity embedded in DH work, the entanglement of DH and media studies, and the usefulness of viewing DH projects as media artifacts) within the context of graduate education, I will present my experiences of working on a digital humanities project outside my home discipline of history—one that proved instrumental to my education in media studies and the "learning by doing" inherent in digital humanities projects. Re-Envisioning Japan: Japan as Destination in 20th-Century Visual and Material Culture is a digital archive of material objects documenting changing representations of Japan from the early to mid-twentieth century; it is headed by Joanne Bernardi in the University of Rochester's Department of Modern Languages and Cultures (Bernardi and Dimmock, "Creative Curating"). The archive contains postcards, sheet music, small gauge films (8–16mm), glass slides, photographs, print ephemera, and three-dimensional material objects such as a souvenir doll, Japanese fans, and as I will examine in greater detail below, a nutshell containing a tiny booklet of scenes from the 1933 Chicago World's Fair.

As part of an Andrew W. Mellon predoctoral fellowship in digital humanities, I worked on Re-Envisioning Japan as a member of the digital archive's redesign team and as a teaching assistant in Tourist Japan, a course that complements the archive. At the heart of the redesign was the question of how to best portray three-dimensional objects in a web-based space. Many of the objects begged for tactile interaction, such as the smooth feel of the pages of a book made of Japanese crepe paper, the heft of the souvenir Hanako doll, and the fragility of a small nutshell containing tiny pages. We were conscious, too, that the photos taken of these objects had their own media specificity distinct from the actual objects. Understanding that the digital surrogate could not replace the material object, how could we compose an experience for our digital archive user that communicated the nutshell's material characteristics? This caused us to think about two central issues: first, the affordances and limitations of web-based digital media, and second, the characteristics of the material object itself. For the latter, we engaged in a detailed Prownian analysis to explore the nutshell (Prown and Haltman, *American Arti-facts*). Sitting in a circle, we each looked closely at the object and verbally analyzed the following: description, deduction, speculation, research, and interpretive analysis. As we progressed, we created a narrative that summarized our experience of the nutshell as an object and media artifact, as well as a contextual analysis of the nutshell's time and place in history.

Because the nutshell contained a small paper booklet detailing the attractions at the 1933 World's Fair, our analysis and subsequent narrative from the start blended both language about the object and the printed paper media embedded within the object. Such close reading illuminated the object's history, materiality, and cultural significance. We then began to think about the digital characteristics of this object displayed on the web and imagine web-based media afforded a similar, albeit non-tactile, experience, especially if the encounter focused on storytelling via a photo-essay type gallery and close description of the object. Built into this plan was the understanding that the digital encounter was its own media artifact that had value not only as Japanese material culture and history but also as digital media. Central to distinguishing the material object and the digital surrogate was the rich Dublin Core metadata that outlined the digital media surrogate and its description of who contributed the labor to digitize this object, the technologies required to create the surrogate, and when the digital object was created, as well as key metadata about the analog object.

As a predoctoral student in history, I was unfamiliar with Prownian analysis and thinking of objects as media. As I watched others in the group who had greater familiarity with media studies, visual and cultural studies, and digital media, as well as course subject expertise in Japanese material culture, I began to see that this educational experience was for me as much about learning how to intellectually engage with material objects as it was about learning the language of other disciplines and how they applied theoretical frameworks. In this way, our attempts to remediate the nutshell—to transform an analog nutshell into a digital media artifact—became a true contact zone à la Ortega. For this type of graduate education to happen, two factors needed to exist: first, an interdisciplinary ethos and space for cross-disciplinary activities, and second, a focus that emphasized both the material object and the digital surrogate as not only products of our work but as media artifacts themselves. To the former, Sean Weidman's point about the vulnerability and precariousness of graduate students occupying in-between spaces of DH's intradisciplinarity is especially salient. As Weidman argues in chapter 16 in this volume, the efficacy of this in-between work varies from institution to institution and even more granularly from department to department. From my experience, the presence of the Digital Scholarship Lab at the University of Rochester centered our institution's DH work and provided a physical in-between space that was essential. Secondly, the formalization of DH graduate student fellowships via the Andrew W. Mellon predoctoral fellowships in the digital humanities provided the pathway for experiencing digital humanities and interdisciplinarity perspectives.[3]

In important ways, this example shows what digital humanities is (a process of collaboration, an archive) and what digital humanities does (inspire collaborators to consider their disciplinary biases) and how these are entangled with media studies. Although this example is personal to me, other examples of graduate students engaging with digital humanities artifacts as media do exist, for example, the Blake Archive's XML transcriptions of William Blake's illuminated manuscripts (Reed, "Managing an Established Digital Humanities Project"), a television archive (Van Gorp and Bron, "Building Bridges"), and a Native American video game focusing on indigenous storytelling to portray the history of native experiences of colonization.[4] Through creating media objects, students explored what media are as artifacts and what media do as sites of collaboration, knowledge production, and political power. There are debates about what constitutes "making" within the digital humanities, and I do not have space to address this here other than to say that embedding media studies within DH graduate education not only emphasizes the process of students building digital things (experiential learning), but also on the object itself and what it took to "build" that object within its time and place (i.e., papermaking, bookbinding, ink production, and gathering real nutshells).

Jamie "Skye" Bianco, in an argument for a "digital humanities which is not one," notes that digital humanities is "radically heterogeneous" and "multimodally layered" ("This Digital Humanities," 109). It is this richness of perspective that addresses "the contexts and conditions in which we find ourselves" that gives digital humanities and its upcoming practitioners (i.e., graduate students) political power in their creation and critique of media. The metaphor of remediation illustrates that a refashioning of pedagogical approaches does not automatically render old graduate pedagogies obsolete. Instead, remediation allows graduate students to cultivate a more productive, multimodally layered conversation with emerging, transformed pedagogies. It allows us to respond to the ultimate critique of the digital humanities and answer with the new knowledge we discover in our endeavors.

Notes

1. See http://kindred.stanford.edu and https://linkedjazz.org/network/ for examples of social media networks that serve as both a media artifact and ongoing scholarship.

2. Sayers uses the idea of "objects of inquiry" as one pathway to understanding the making of DH artifacts and as a pathway through media studies in two different volumes he has edited—first in 2018 in *The Routledge Companion to Media Studies and the Digital Humanities* and then in 2019 in *Making Things and Drawing Boundaries*.

3. See chapter 25 in this volume, "A Tale of Three Disciplines: Considering the (Digital) Future of the Mid-Doc Fellowship in Graduate Programs" by Daniel Gorman Jr., Erin Francisco, Madeline Ullrich, and Alexander J. Zawacki.

4. Examples of digital media that employ this use of graduate scholarship include The Blake Archive, http://www.blakearchive.org/ and Terra Nova, by Maize Longboat. https://maizelongboat.itch.io/terra-nova.

Bibliography

Bernardi, Joanne, and Nora Dimmock. "Creative Curating: The Digital Archive as Argument." In *Making Things and Drawing Boundaries: Experiments in the Digital Humanities,* edited by Jentery Sayers, 187–97. Minneapolis: University of Minnesota Press, 2017.

Bianco, Jamie Skye. "This Digital Humanities Which Is Not One." In *Debates in the Digital Humanities,* edited by Matthew K. Gold, 96–112. Minneapolis: University of Minnesota Press, 2012.

Bolter, Jay David, and Richard Grusin. *Remediation: Understanding New Media.* Cambridge, Mass.: The MIT Press, 1999.

Drucker, Johana. "Graphical Approaches to the Digital Humanities." In *A New Companion to Digital Humanities,* edited by Susan Schreibman, Ray Siemens, and John Unsworth, 238–50. Oxford: John Wiley, 2015.

Endres, Bill. "A Literacy of Building: Making in the Digital Humanities." In *Making Things and Drawing Boundaries: Experiments in the Digital Humanities,* edited by Jentery Sayers, 44–54. Minneapolis: University of Minnesota Press, 2017.

Ferguson, Kevin L. "Volumetric Cinema." In *Debates in the Digital Humanities 2019,* edited by Matthew K. Gold and Lauren Klein. Minneapolis: University of Minnesota Press, 2019. https://dhdebates.gc.cuny.edu/read/untitled-f2acf72c-a469-49d8-be35-67f9ac1e 3a60/section/a214af4f-2d31-4967-8686-738987c02ddf.

Gaertner, David, and Melissa Haberl. "Recoding Relations: Dispatches from the Symposium for Indigenous New Media." *Critical Inquiry* (blog), January 21, 2020. https:// critinq.wordpress.com/2020/01/21/recoding-relations-dispatches-from-the-sympo sium-for-indigenous-new-media/.

Huet, Hélène, and Laurie N. Taylor. "Teaching Together for the Digital Humanities Graduate Certificate." In *Quick Hits for Teaching with Digital Humanities,* edited by Christopher J. Young, Michael Morrone, Thomas C. Wilson, and Emma Annette Wilson, 88–93. Bloomington: Indiana University Press, 2020.

Kraus, Kari. "The Care of Enchanted Things." In *Debates in the Digital Humanities 2019,* edited by Matthew K. Gold and Lauren Klein. Minneapolis: University of Minnesota Press, 2019. https://dhdebates.gc.cuny.edu/read/untitled-f2acf72c-a469-49d8-be35 -67f9ac1e3a60/section/d74d1f76-372e-4427-8835-36c9baf7ebaa.

Manovich, Lev. *The Language of New Media.* Cambridge, Mass.: The MIT Press, 2001.

McPherson, Tara. "Introduction: Media Studies and the Digital Humanities." *Cinema Journal* 48, no. 2 (2009): 119–23.

Mittell, Jason. "Videographic Criticism as a Digital Humanities Method." In *Debates in the Digital Humanities 2019,* edited by Matthew K. Gold and Lauren Klein. Minneapolis:

University of Minnesota Press, 2019. https://dhdebates.gc.cuny.edu/read/untitled -f2acf72c-a469-49d8-be35-67f9ac1e3a60/section/b6dea70a-9940-497e-b7c5 -930126fbd180.

Opel, Dawn, and Michael Simeone. "The Invisible Work of the Digital Humanities Lab: Preparing Graduate Students for Emergent Intellectual and Professional Work." *Digital Humanities Quarterly* 13, no. 2 (2019). http://www.digitalhumanities.org/dhq/vol /13/2/000421/000421.html.

Ortega, Élika. "Zonas de Contacto: A Digital Humanities Ecology of Knowledges." In *Debates in the Digital Humanities 2019,* edited by Matthew K. Gold and Lauren Klein. Minneapolis: University of Minnesota Press, 2019. https://dhdebates.gc.cuny.edu/read /untitled-f2acf72c-a469-49d8-be35-67f9ac1e3a60/section/aeee46e3-dddc-4668 -a1b3-c8983ba4d70a.

Ouellette, Laurie, and Jonathan Gray. *Keywords for Media Studies.* New York: New York University Press, 2017.

Pannapacker, William. "'Big Tent Digital Humanities': A View from the Edge, Part I." *Chronicle of Higher Education,* July 31, 2011. https://www.chronicle.com/article/Big -Tent-Digital-Humanities/128434.

Prown, Jules David, and Kenneth Haltman. *American Artifacts: Essays in Material Culture.* East Lansing: Michigan State University Press, 2000.

Reed, Ashley. "Managing an Established Digital Humanities Project: Principles and Practices from the Twentieth Year of the William Blake Archive." *Digital Humanities Quarterly* 8, no. 1 (2014). http://www.digitalhumanities.org/dhq/vol/8/1/000174/000174. html.

Re-Envisioning Japan. https://rej.lib.rochester.edu/.

Reid, Alexander. "Graduate Education and Ethics of the Digital Humanities." In *Debates in the Digital Humanities,* edited by Matthew K. Gold, 350–67. Minneapolis: University of Minnesota Press, 2012.

Sayers, Jentery, ed. *The Routledge Companion to Media Studies and Digital Humanities.* New York: Routledge, Taylor & Francis, 2018.

Selisker, Scott. "Digital Humanities Knowledge: Reflections on the Introductory Graduate Syllabus." In *Debates in the Digital Humanities 2016,* edited by Matthew K. Gold and Lauren F. Klein. Minneapolis: University of Minnesota Press, 2016. https://dhdebates .gc.cuny.edu/read/untitled/section/2328bdb8-b7ea-4931-8258-12e220b3d767.

Sutherland, Serenity. "Graduate Training in the Digital Archive." In *Quick Hits for Teaching with Digital Humanities,* edited by Christopher J. Youn, Michael Morrone, Thomas C. Wilson, and Emma Annette Wilson, 94–99. Bloomington: Indiana University Press, 2020.

Van Gorp, Jasmijn, and Marc Bron. "Building Bridges: Collaboration between Computer Sciences and Media Studies in a Television Archive Project." *Digital Humanities Quarterly* 13, no. 3 (2019). http://www.digitalhumanities.org/dhq/vol/13/3/000375/000375 .html.

Afterword

KENNETH M. PRICE

In February 1950, Waldemar Kaempffert, the science editor of the *New York Times*, published an article titled "Miracles You'll See in the Next Fifty Years," and—as could be guessed—he was often spectacularly wrong.[1] He predicted that in the year 2000, houses would be made of metal, plastic sheets, and aerated clay resembling a petrified sponge. He thought a house would cost only about five thousand dollars. And he asserted that "because everything in her home is waterproof, [the future housewife of 2000] can do her daily cleaning with a hose." Kaempffert imagined massive change in building materials but not in gender roles. He is instructive when he is wrong because his imagined future underscores the need to foresee technological change as one strand in a whole fabric of change.

Future changes in digital scholarship and pedagogy will be shaped by larger forces, all of them difficult to predict, in the academy and beyond. Unlike the upbeat Kaempffert, the writers contributing to this volume are sober and reflective, displaying little, if any, of the unbounded enthusiasm that marked some earlier phases of digital humanities, or "humanities computing," as it was commonly called in the 1990s. At that time, though early adopters faced skepticism and resistance, the vast possibilities of computationally assisted work nonetheless were also thrilling, even intoxicating. By contrast, the restrained tone that marks these essays is suited to shrinking enrollments in the humanities, dwindling support for public education, and a declining professoriate job market that has gone from meager to almost nonexistent. These essays are, nevertheless, written with social change as a major preoccupation—including the pandemic, the increasingly urgent calls for racial justice, and the underfunding of the academy. The editors of *Digital Futures of Graduate Study in the Humanities*, Gabriel Hankins, Anouk Lang, and Simon Appleford, offer in this volume a "series of meditations in an emergency." By their nature, emergencies tend to pass, but we should not, therefore, conclude that the essays presented here will quickly date just because of changing circumstances. The current crisis has brought lasting issues in higher education into bold relief. And, as Katina Rogers observes, we are also in a rare moment in which we have seen abrupt and radical change occur in how education is understood and delivered, indicating that other big changes larger than ordinarily contemplated are actually possible.

I am pleased to have been asked to provide this afterword. It is not feasible to comment on each argument—many of them excellent—so instead, I address what I see as some of the key issues brought to mind by this volume. My own vantage point is worth noting—I am a fully promoted white male teaching at a midwestern state university in the United States (University of Nebraska-Lincoln) that has invested in digital humanities. My experiences no doubt enable some perceptions and blind me to others. My involvement in digital scholarship dates to the mid-1990s when I wished to address research questions that defied adequate treatment in print: specifically, through The Walt Whitman Archive, initiated in 1995, I wanted to collaborate with others to treat a poet whose writings and restless revisions spanned six distinct editions and also included manuscript drafts, notebooks, corrected proofs, and much else. Along the way, I have gained other perspectives on DH through codirecting the Center for Digital Research in the Humanities at Nebraska. I have also had the opportunity to codirect Civil War Washington, an interdisciplinary study of the massive transformation of the nation's capital during four years of war. This project, including its transcription of the emancipation petitions of approximately three thousand enslaved people in the nation's capital, underscored my growing interest in how DH could address issues involving race and social justice. My other recent efforts—I have recently begun coediting the African American writer Charles Chesnutt, and I served as a co-convener on an American Council of Learned Societies-funded digital ethnic studies summer institute involving wide-ranging consultations and partnerships with minority-serving institutions—were motivated in part by revulsion at the endorsement of white supremacist ideas at the highest levels of government.[2]

Not surprisingly, I am particularly drawn to the numerous essays compiled here addressing racial justice, diversity, and inclusion. In their introduction, the editors follow Christopher Newfield in highlighting a connection between U.S. higher education and whiteness: "Public investment in higher education was tightly linked to the expanding white middle classes that were its primary beneficiaries, a link that has slowly come undone." The disinvestment in education raises significant and worrisome issues at many levels. Although not the only cause of the crisis of the job market, this disinvestment worsens it. Going forward, as we contemplate how our choices and policies impact the future of graduate education, we need to keep both the job market and our relation to a diverse public very much in mind. Digital humanities has extraordinary potential to expand public access to education, and we have much to offer in efforts to restore the frayed relation between the academy and the public. Regrettably, we have lived through what Eric Hayot calls a "50-year culture war against the academy in general and the humanities in particular." A destructive narrative has tried to dismantle the welfare state while conveying false information, including that "majoring in the humanities leads to lower salaries and higher unemployment" ("Humanities Have a Marketing Problem"). This is not in fact the case, but it has taken firm hold as entrenched understanding, and the idea surfaces regularly in popular culture, to our detriment (Schmidt, "Humanities Are in Crisis").[3]

In recent years, much commentary has lamented the "whiteness" of DH (Bailey, "All the Digital Humanists Are White"; McPherson, "Why Are the Digital Humanities So White?"). Once accurate, that characterization of digital humanities grows increasingly less so thanks to the energizing work of many scholars and efforts by organizations such as Alliance of Digital Humanities Organizations and ACH to promote diversity and inclusion. As Brandon Walsh argues in this volume, digital humanities has been strengthened also by the "work of activists involved in the creation of #TransformDH, Postcolonial Digital Humanities, and DHWOGEM," an email list for women and gender minorities in digital humanities. Many other projects could be mentioned, including Black Covid, the Transgender Archive, Torn Apart/Separados, and Mukurtu CMS, an open-source platform developed with Indigenous communities to share, exchange, and manage digital cultural heritage. Also notable has been a turn toward more progressive policies seen in both foundations, including Mellon, Spencer, ACLS, and Ford, and in some of the newly articulated priorities of government funding agencies, including the National Endowment for the Humanities and the National Historical Publications and Records Commission. I agree with Alison Booth and Miriam Posner who remark that in the future, DH pedagogy "must concern itself deeply with race, gender, disability, economic and linguistic access, and other intersecting axes of power embedded in our materials and methods, as demanded by this troubled moment in the world" ("Materials at Hand," 10).

How can we put such an approach into effect in practical ways? Here are some possibilities to consider. As we teach in our graduate programs and shape their policies, we should be attentive to how they may inadvertently produce or reproduce biases. For example, do our admissions processes value previous experience when in fact DH curricula and other opportunities are limited in most undergraduate programs and particularly at minority-serving institutions? Do past hiring practices that led to a lack of racial diversity among DH faculty in most institutions produce biases and weaknesses in our teaching and thus risk reinscribing a limited perspective within DH? Does our reliance on software produced by a segment of the population yield bias in our results (Noble, *Algorithms of Oppression*)? Are we poorly serving women, people of color, and those who are economically disadvantaged? How can we make DH more welcoming and appealing to those who in the past have been on the outside? Can we do more to cut across educational hierarchies, in ways discussed by Olivia Quintanilla and Jeanelle Horcasitas, so that we promote new alliances that address the needs of people of color?

Even a rich and extensive collection like this one cannot discuss everything. I find myself wishing for a substantive discussion of minimal computing given the promise of this approach for both sustainability and equity issues.[4] Minimal computing can lower the barriers to DH and can be deployed in a wide range of settings. The approach thus has appeal on various grounds, including ease of maintenance, control of cost, and the advancement of equity. For cash-strapped graduate students everywhere and for faculty members with limited financial and technical support, we need reasonable and attainable approaches. Minimal computing makes sense both for getting started and for sustainability over the long run. The general principle animating minimal computing is sound: we should employ just enough technology to address scholarly problems without acquiring unsustainable technological, financial, and administrative burdens.

Manfred Thaller suggests another facet of DH that is less frequently considered; in his contribution to this volume, he reminds us that computer and humanities courses have been offered for fifty years, yet paradoxically, they still have an aura of being new. He unearths a disturbing trend when he asks: "Why have so many programs failed, and why do the discussions seem to form an endless loop?" Thaller would like to see a "clearer sharpness of profile of the degrees offered." I understand this wish, but it may well be that DH is strengthened by its protean nature and its ability to lodge itself within and across disciplinary niches. The extraordinary diversity and proliferation of forms of digital humanities strengthens the overall ecosystem. There are, of course, forces that make it difficult for DH to establish itself, as Thaller notes, but other characteristics of DH contribute to its ongoing appeal. As Booth and Posner remark, DH "prizes *interdisciplinary collaboration and technical experimentation*" (emphasis in the original), and DH is most worthwhile if it also "promotes public engagement and humanistic knowledge and understanding" ("Materials at Hand," 10). In her essay in this volume, Booth recognizes that we take certain risks if we advocate for digital graduate study because of its usefulness. I would argue, though, that high-minded and practical arguments alike are valid: what should be emphasized at any time must suit the moment and immediate context.

As noted, DH is situated in remarkably varied institutional settings, but regardless of that variety/diversity, those who teach need to be concerned with the prospects for graduate students. Leonard Cassuto holds that the anti-utilitarian case for humanities should give way so we make progress "in search of a usable future."[5] Too many of us, as faculty members, remain inattentive to the large academic-adjacent market, and so we often fail to guide our students toward these opportunities. We need to remedy that and adjust our mentoring to instill flexibility in students and promote career diversity. In good conscience, we can only continue to train students for vanishing tenure-track jobs if we also prepare them for a broader array of rewarding and productive jobs. Doing so may force tenured faculty to quell our own anxieties about deprofessionalization.

Several essays here argue persuasively that we should normalize preparation for multiple career pathways. Rogers notes that such an approach should be reinforced in various ways: credit for interdisciplinary projects; credit for group-based, public-oriented work; a recommitment to teaching; and listing of all jobs obtained by their graduates as opposed to the usual tenure-track placement list ("Cultivating a Joyful Workplace," 227–31). Mentorship should be extended beyond a student's home department and ideally even beyond the university. A low-stakes, one-credit seminar could be developed featuring speakers who could present either in person or remotely to highlight the possibilities for meaningful and rewarding lives beyond the academy.

In response to the disinvestment in public education, I would urge us to consider doing more to involve ordinary citizens in our work so that they share to some degree in the creation of knowledge and become more invested in colleges and universities. Engaging the public with our research, and enabling them to partner in it, can strengthen ties. Ordinary citizens value freely available online resources and thus often jump at the opportunity to help create them across divergent subjects, as seen in such successes as the University of Iowa's effort to engage the public in transcribing Civil War notebooks, the U.S. National Archives project to involve the public in transcribing census records, and the New York Public Library's work with the public on their collection of historic menus. What can we do to shape our institutions so that they bolster faculty engagement with the public while also being attentive to underserved communities? Crowdsourcing projects offer a way for public-facing humanities projects to engage in cocreation with the interested public. Contributions by nonprofessionals hold great promise where both strong organization and well-developed systems for vetting content are present. We would also be wise, of course, to reduce our own posturing and needless jargon in an effort to limit hierarchies and increase access to knowledge. Crowdsourcing is especially good for massive, labor-intensive undertakings, and work in this area does not have to be undertheorized. Learning how to communicate beyond academic-speak to reach interested lay people is enormously valuable, as is grappling with the complexities of crowdsourcing so that it can be pursued ethically.[6]

One approach I would advocate for is project-based digital humanities pedagogy, mentioned at least in passing in several essays. Specifically, I think there are great advantages in having a class, or a series of classes over a span of years, contribute to a genuine project. Having students learn in such a hands-on way encourages them to think beyond individual achievement (and competition) toward collective action and accomplishment. An ideal project—something bold and self-evidently important—can inspire students if it is something both significant and too big for any one person to attempt but remains an achievable goal if many people work in a coordinated way over several years. I think such a marriage of research and teaching is most likely to work when students can delve into matters of local cultural history that also resonate with meaning for that area and beyond. For example, Georgetown University students could delve into the case of Patrick Francis Healy, a person born enslaved who "passed" his way to the presidency of Georgetown University (Greene,

"Born Enslaved"). What can church records, the university archives, Healy's personal papers, and city ordinances tell us about this individual, and how does he fit into broader stories about race and passing in America? Or at the University of Minnesota, Morris, what can be learned about education in a place that was home to the Dakota people and later the Ojibwe people? Could a decolonial archive be built with and in consultation with the descendant communities, yielding new insight into the history and legacy of American Indian boarding schools as they were operated, in this case, by the Sisters of Mercy and the U.S. government (1887–1909)?[7] Or students at Fisk University in Nashville, home of the Fisk Jubilee Singers who saved that distinguished HBCU from financial ruin, could study how "music city" nonetheless became associated overwhelmingly with white country music despite the remarkable achievement of the Jubilee Singers. At California State University, Fresno, students could transcribe oral histories from Manzanar, the famous concentration camp where Japanese Americans were incarcerated during World War II. Or at California State University, Chico, a project focused on wildfires could be developed, tracking their location, changing frequency over time, known or suspected cause; gathering oral history testimonials of loss and heroism; documenting the use (and abuse?) of imprisoned laborers; and analyzing political commentary from the good to the incomprehensibly ill-informed. Such a site would require a multidisciplinary team drawing on experts in mapping and GIS, forest management, web design, oral history, archival theory, and other domains. In fact, all types of climate disasters raise opportunities to document similar changes over time and effects on the local community. This can yield socially useful information and engage the public in broad matters of common concern. A creative response along these lines has emerged at Xavier University of Louisiana studying recovery itself by recording ordinary people and their resilience in the face of Hurricane Katrina's destruction. My Nola, My Story is a project developed by Shearon Roberts and her students "to record and share the stories of people of color in New Orleans. These stories reflect snapshots of lived experiences of communities of color who have called New Orleans home. It serves as a testament that they were here, are here, and shaped the fabric of this historic, cultural space" ("My Nola, My Story"). Some projects like those I have mostly imagined in this paragraph are underway.[8] The model etched out here is not meant to replicate a workshop or apprentice model with the teacher/master owning the labor. Rather, this is meant to be a collective undertaking with a teacher's guidance and with crediting that reflects the roles and contributions of those involved.

Many of the projects I have just suggested are archival and rely heavily on data gathering. An unsympathetic colleague could argue that they lack the analytical edge that is prized in humanities projects, but that view is shortsighted if the projects display a creative and compelling reformulation of what should be remembered, recorded, archived, and highlighted. Because of past neglect, violence, and destruction, there are significant gaps in the cultural record, and it requires acumen to reconstruct a past littered with distortions and absences. Such efforts are consistent with what Cecily Raynor calls "project-based deep learning in digital humanities," with humanities content, skills, methods, and theory all learned in context while contributing to a project, rather than acquired in the abstract. This type of teaching-as-research offers students the opportunity to engage in large-scale project management and confront and grapple with digital preservation issues, copyright negotiations, crediting questions, collaborative achievements and frictions, and, depending on the topic, politically fraught decision making. As Walsh asks, "How do we teach right now? Why do we teach now? And, for this audience, what might DH pedagogy, in particular, have to do with and for this moment?" He argues that a sense of urgency always should have been key to our practice.

Another pressing issue is that of data justice. What information is collected, why, and what use is it put to? Gaps in what we know provide pedagogical and research opportunities to be seized. There is a great deal of attention paid now to decolonizing and anti-racist editorial and archival practices, and we can energize students by providing them with opportunities to contribute to these efforts. As we do so, we need to cultivate in students a self-conscious awareness, a critical stance, toward the medium in which research takes place, itself a worthy subject of inquiry.

In their different ways, the essays collected here speak to these and other pressing concerns that both animate the present and foreshadow potential futures of graduate studies in digital humanities. Despite the challenges we face, it seems wise for us to be as bold as possible, because digital humanities pedagogy has much to offer higher education and the broader public. In the coming years, we will see established disciplines in the humanities even more thoroughly remade as we work with ever-growing troves of digital texts and artifacts. And we will see new programs emerge, as is already happening, in data and society and in data science. Digital humanists can bring a critical consciousness to these developments as we remind ourselves and others of the omissions and distortions that make the entirety of the digitized text, as Lara Putnam notes, "anything but representative of the temporal and geographic contours of human life in the past" ("Transnational and the Text-Searchable," 389). As Putnam suggests, we need to do all we can to recover lost histories, many of them painful and repressed, as we strive for a more fully informed and ethically directed society.

Notes

1. In fairness to Kaempffert, it should also be said that he could be strikingly accurate in his predictions, too. For example, he foresaw the interstate highway system, medical imaging devices akin to CAT scans, and weather-forecasting supercomputers.

2. Specifically, following a listening tour to eight minority-serving institutions, we developed a plan for a digital ethnic studies summer institute to support research and teaching. We hoped to help alleviate unequal access to new means of expression and

336] KENNETH M. PRICE

analysis. Digital humanities—including the production of online archives, animations, dynamic maps, data mining applications, visualizations, video games, and more—has revolutionized the way scholars conceive of history, literary study, and culture, yet access to the field has remained stubbornly limited to the largest research universities and the wealthiest institutions. There remains a disproportionate whiteness of the field in terms of practitioners and the dominance of predominantly white institutions in producing digital scholarship. Too often, stories are being left untold and rich heritages ignored in the digital environment.

3. Schmidt points out that "students aren't fleeing degrees with poor job prospects. They're fleeing humanities and related fields specifically because they think they have poor job prospects"; see "Humanities are in Crisis."

4. For more information see the home page, a github site, for Minimal Computing. The chapter by Afanador-Llach and Martínez in this volume implicitly touches on the importance of minimal computing when noting the disparities in digital infrastructure between those doing DH in Latin America and those in the Global North.

5. This perspective of Cassuto's is quoted in the introduction to this volume.

6. One of my favorite examples of an effective crowdsourcing project is the government-funded Australian Newspapers Digitization Program, part of Trove, a project with more than thirty thousand volunteers who have corrected lines of text. No special knowledge is required, only the ability to decipher often poorly reproduced page images derived from microfilm copy of old newspapers. Often produced originally by poor quality printing presses that had been taken out of service in Britain, the newspapers were sometimes further marred by creases, gaps, and other types of damage. The manager of the newspaper digitization project, Rose Holley, wished to work "with" users rather than "doing things 'to' or 'for' them." In explaining their success, she notes the straightforwardness of the task, its addictiveness, and the wish of volunteers to help a worthy Australian cause. See Holley, "Crowdsourcing and Social Engagement."

7. The University of Minnesota, Morris honors an agreement to provide a federal- and state-mandated tuition-free education to eligible American Indian students.

8. Katherine Harris of California State University, San Jose recently encouraged her students to rethink British Romanticism in ways that reflected their own identities and subject positions. The result was a collaborative digital humanities project titled The Bengal Annual: A Digital Exploration of Non-Canonical British Romantic Literature; see Dirilo et al., *Bengal Annual.*

Bibliography

Bailey, Moya. "All the Digital Humanists Are White, All the Nerds Are Men, But Some of Us Are Brave." *Journal of Digital Humanities* 1, no. 1 (Winter 2011). http://journalof digitalhumanities.org/1%E2%80%931/all-the-digital-humanists-are-white-all-the -nerds-are-men-but-some-of-us-are-brave-by-moya-z-bailey/.

Booth, Alison, and Miriam Posner. "The Materials at Hand." *PMLA* 135, no. 1 (January 2020): 9–22.

Dirilo, Dan Jerome, Marisa Plumb, Katherine D. Harris, Keith Giles, Taylor-Dawn Francis, and Samantha Douglas. *The Bengal Annual: A Digital Exploration of Non-Canonical British Romantic Literature.* The Bengal Annual: A Literary Keepsake for 1830. Last updated October 21, 2020. http://scalar.usc.edu/works/the-bengal-annual/index.

Greene, Bryan. "Born Enslaved, Patrick Francis Healy 'Passed' His Way to Lead Georgetown University." *Smithsonian Magazine,* September 2020. https://www.smithsonian mag.com/history/born-enslaved-patrick-francis-healy-passed-his-way-lead-george town-university-180975738/.

Hayot, Eric. "The Humanities Have a Marketing Problem." *Chronicle of Higher Education,* March 22, 2021. https://www.chronicle.com/article/the-humanities-have-a-marketing -problem.

Holley, Rose. "Crowdsourcing and Social Engagement in Libraries: The State of Play." *ALIA Sydney* (blog), June 29, 2011. http://aliasydney.blogspot.com/2011/06/crowdsourcing -and-social-engagement-in.html.

Kaempffert, Waldemar. "Miracles You'll See In The Next Fifty Years." *Popular Mechanics* 93, no. 2 (February 1950): 112–18; 264–72.

McPherson, Tara. "Why Are the Digital Humanities So White? Or Thinking the Histories of Race and Computation." In *Debates in the Digital Humanities,* edited by Matthew K. Gold, 139–60. Minneapolis: University of Minnesota Press, 2012.

Noble, Safiya. *Algorithms of Oppression: How Search Engines Reinforce Racism.* New York: New York University Press, 2018.

Putnam, Lara. "The Transnational and the Text-Searchable: Digitized Sources and the Shadows They Cast." *The American Historical Review* 121, no. 2 (April 2016): 377–402.

Roberts, Shearon. "My Nola, My Story." Digital Library of the Caribbean. Accessed April 2024. https://nehcaribbean.domains.uflib.ufl.edu/tag/shearon-roberts/.

Rogers, Katina L. "Cultivating a Joyful Workplace through Trust, Support, and a Shared Mission." In *Graduate Education for a Thriving Humanities Ecosystem,* edited by Stacy Hartman and Yevgenya Strakovsky. New York: The Modern Language Association, 2023.

Schmidt, Benjamin. "The Humanities are in Crisis." *The Atlantic,* August 23, 2018. https://www.theatlantic.com/ideas/archive/2018/08/the-humanities-face-a-crisisof -confidence/567565/.

A Commemoration of Rebecca Munson

NATALIA ERMOLAEV AND MEREDITH MARTIN

On August 13, 2021, the digital humanities community lost Rebecca Munson, a beloved colleague, scholar, mentor, and friend. Rebecca lived her entire life surrounded by books, and her passion for literature—and storytelling of all kinds—sustained her intellectual curiosity and inspired her professional path. Rebecca attended Columbia University, where she majored in English literature, and she studied Shakespeare and early modern drama for her master's (Oxford) and PhD (University of California, Berkeley). Rebecca held several postdocs before moving to Princeton in 2016, where she started out as the digital humanities project manager at the Center for Digital Humanities (CDH). In early 2021, she was promoted to CDH assistant director of interdisciplinary education.

Working with graduate students was Rebecca's favorite part of her job. She designed and led the CDH's grants, fellowships, and training programs that gave graduate students a chance to explore new scholarly avenues. She taught classes, gave talks, and published essays on topics ranging from marginalia in early printed books, to data models, to feminist theory, to the ethics of project management. She organized lunches, dinners, and parties for students and thrived on connecting people and creating community. She was a proud and committed mentor who cherished opportunities to guide students through the difficult terrain of graduate school.

In early 2019, when she was 34 years old, Rebecca was diagnosed with a rare and aggressive form of metastatic breast cancer. The honesty, vulnerability, and determination she showed while juggling work, research, advocacy, and cancer treatments—all during a global pandemic—made an indelible mark on all who knew her. Rebecca's generosity, kindness, integrity, and empathy live on in the writing she left behind, from her many tweets, to the personal reflections she published on her blog, and to her scholarly essays, such as the one included in this volume.

MARIA JOSÉ AFANADOR-LLACH is assistant professor of digital humanities in the School of Arts and Humanities at Universidad de los Andes, Bogotá, Colombia. She is also a member of the editorial team of *The Programming Historian* en español.

MARIA K. ALBERTO is a PhD candidate in the Department of English at the University of Utah, where she is working on her dissertation on canons in popular culture.

SIMON APPLEFORD is associate professor of history at Creighton University and associate director of the Creighton Digital Humanities Initiative. He is author of *Drawing Liberalism: Herblock's Political Cartoons in Postwar America*; coauthor of DevDH.org, an online resource for digital humanities project development; and project director of The Natural Face of North America.

AGNIESZKA BACKMAN earned her PhD in Scandinavian languages from Uppsala University with a dissertation titled "The Materiality of the Manuscript: Studies in Codex Holmiensis D 3, the Old Swedish Multitext Manuscript Fru Elins bok." She has worked on the Norse Perception of the World project, helping develop a digital platform for onomastics research with interactive maps, Norse World.

TRAVIS M. BARTLEY is a PhD candidate in English at the CUNY Graduate Center, where he researches critical digital infrastructure and language technology.

PEGGY BOCKWINKEL is a doctoral researcher at the University of Stuttgart Department of Digital Humanities. In her dissertation, she investigates how different quantities of deictic expressions affect literary texts.

ALISON BOOTH is Brown-Forman Professor of English and faculty director of the Library DH Center, University of Virginia, where she codirected the Graduate Digital Humanities Certificate from 2017 until 2023. Her database, Collective Biographies of Women, is based on her book *How to Make It As a Woman: Collective Biographical History from Victoria to the Present*. Her other books include *Homes and Haunts: Touring Writers' Shrines and Countries*.

DONNA ALFANO BUSSELL is professor and chair of the Department of English at the University of Illinois Springfield. As a scholar of medieval literature and liturgy, she has published and presented work on Barking Abbey, including a GIS map of the abbey. She is currently researching the liturgies of Mary Magdalene in medieval England.

JOSHUA CASMIR CATALANO is assistant professor of history at Clemson University and serves as coordinator of the public history program.

LAURA CROSSLEY is a history PhD candidate at George Mason University in Fairfax, Virginia, specializing in digital history and Indigenous histories.

QUINN DOMBROWSKI supports non-English digital humanities as the academic technology specialist in the Library and the Division of Literatures, Cultures, and Languages at Stanford University and serves as co–vice president of the Association for Computers and the Humanities.

STUART DUNN is professor of spatial humanities at King's College London, where he is also head of the Humanities Cluster. He is author of *A History of Place in the Digital Age* and coeditor of *The Routledge International Handbook of Research Methods in Digital Humanities*.

JENNIFER EDMOND is professor in digital humanities at Trinity College Dublin, codirector of the Trinity Centre for Digital Humanities, director of the MPhil in Digital Humanities and Culture, and a funded investigator of the SFI ADAPT Centre.

NATALIA ERMOLAEV is executive director of the Center for Digital Humanities at Princeton University. She is co–principal investigator on New Languages for NLP: Building Linguistic Diversity to the Digital Humanities, an initiative funded by the National Endowment for the Humanities and a collaboration with DARIAH-EU.

LAURA ESTILL is Canada Research Chair in Digital Humanities and professor of English at St. Francis Xavier University. She is author of *Dramatic Extracts in Seventeenth-Century English Manuscripts* and coeditor of *Early Modern Studies after the Digital Turn, Early British Drama in Manuscript*, and *Digital Humanities Workshops: Lessons Learned*.

MALTE GÄCKLE-HECKELEN earned a PhD from the Department of Digital Humanities of the University of Stuttgart and is a visual data manager at BurdaForward.

VICKY GARNETT has a PhD in sociolinguistics from Trinity College Dublin, Ireland, where she is also based as the Training and Education Officer for DARIAH-EU.

DANIEL GORMAN JR. is a history PhD graduate of the University of Rochester, where he specialized in U.S. religion and culture. He has worked on digital projects that include The Hill Cumorah Legacy Project, Digitizing Rochester's Religions, the William Blake Archive, Remembering WWI, and the Seward Family Digital Archive.

SABRINA T. GRIMBERG is a lecturer in the Spanish Language Program and coordinator of the Accelerated Spanish Language Program at Stanford University. Sabrina holds degrees in linguistics from Stanford University and linguistics, comparative literature, and classics from the University of Buenos Aires.

GABRIEL HANKINS is associate professor of English at Clemson University. He is series coeditor of Cambridge University's *Elements in Digital Literary Studies.*

TENA L. HELTON is professor of English and interim associate vice chancellor for undergraduate education at the University of Illinois Springfield. As a scholar of early American literature and culture, she has published articles on African American, Native American, and Asian American literature, history, and film, as well as online teaching of American literature.

JEANELLE HORCASITAS is a Senior Regulatory Adherence Consultant at Delta Dental California. She received her PhD in literature/cultural studies from UC San Diego and her undergraduate degree in English from UC Los Angeles.

MELISSA A. HOSEK is a lecturer in Stanford University's program for civic, liberal, and global education.

HOYEOL KIM received his PhD in English with a focus on computational literary studies from Texas A&M University. His articles "Sentiment Analysis: Limits and Progress of the Syuzhet Package and Its Lexicons" and "*Victorian400*: Colorizing Victorian Illustrations" were published by *Digital Humanities Quarterly* and the *International Journal of Humanities and Arts Computing*, respectively.

BRADY KRIEN is completing his PhD in English and is a graduate careers and fellowships adviser at the Graduate College, University of Iowa. His research combines environmental literature, digital humanities, and print and information culture.

ANOUK LANG is a senior lecturer in the Department of English and Scottish Literature at the University of Edinburgh. She is the editor of *From Codex to Hypertext: Reading at the Turn of the Twenty-First Century* and coeditor of *Patrick White Beyond the Grave: New Critical Perspectives.*

BENJAMIN CHARLES GERMAIN LEE is assistant professor in the Information School at the University of Washington.

PAMELA E. MACK is emeritus professor at Clemson University, retired from the Department of History and Geography. She is author of *Viewing the Earth: The Social Construction of the Landsat Satellite System.*

MEREDITH MARTIN is professor of English at Princeton University, where she directs the Center for Digital Humanities. She is principal investigator on the Princeton Prosody Archive and author of *The Rise and Fall of Meter: Poetry and English National Culture, 1860–1930.*

GERMÁN CAMILO MARTÍNEZ PEÑALOZA is coordinator of the Banco de Archivos Digitales de Artes en Colombia and professor of digital humanities in the School of Arts and Humanities, Universidad de los Andes, Bogotá, Colombia.

E. L. MESZAROS is a PhD candidate in the history of the exact sciences in antiquity at Brown University.

SARA MOHR is an Assyriologist and a digital humanist and digital scholarship librarian at Hamilton College.

SETHUNYA MOKOKO is completing his PhD in rhetoric, communication, and information design and is assistant director of the Writing Lab and Dean's Advisory Council member at Clemson University.

REBECCA MUNSON was assistant director of interdisciplinary education at the Center for Digital Humanities at Princeton University. A commemoration of her life and contribution to digital humanities concludes this volume.

ERIN FRANCISCO OPALICH is a PhD candidate in English at the University of Rochester and assistant director of DEI Projects and Initiatives at SUNY Oneonta. Her dissertation focuses on the intersections of environmental and social justice in twentieth-century American fiction. Her ongoing digital humanities project is Food Apartheid ROC, an interactive digital mapping initiative that seeks to narrate and visually render the landscape of food access inequities across the city of Rochester, New York.

KENNETH M. PRICE is Hillegass University Professor at the University of Nebraska–Lincoln and codirector of The Walt Whitman Archive, The Charles W. Chesnutt Archive, and the Center for Digital Research in the Humanities. His latest study is *Whitman in Washington: Becoming the National Poet in the Federal City.*

OLIVIA QUINTANILLA is a Chamoru scholar, professor in the Department of Ethnic Studies at MiraCosta College in Oceanside, California, and a Digital Humanities Research Institute Fellow.

CECILY RAYNOR is associate professor of Hispanic studies and digital humanities at McGill University. She is author of *Latin American Literature at the Millennium: Local Lives, Global Spaces* and coeditor of *Digital Encounters: Envisioning Connectivity in Latin American Cultural Production.*

AMANDA E. REGAN is assistant professor in the Department of History and Geography at Clemson University. She is co–project director and digital historian on Mapping the Gay Guides, an NEH-funded digital history project that seeks to map entries from historical LGBTQ guidebooks.

HEATHER RICHARDS-RISSETTO is associate professor of anthropology in the School of Global Integrative Studies and faculty fellow of the Center for Digital Research in the Humanities at the University of Nebraska–Lincoln. She has published on multisensory archaeology, 3D WebGIS, Virtual Reality, 3D data preservation and access, machine learning, and collaborative web-based archaeology.

JACOB D. RICHTER is a teaching assistant professor of writing at George Washington University. His research on composition pedagogy, writing in networked environments, digital rhetoric, and social media's utility for education has been published in *College Composition and Communication, Computers & Composition, Composition Forum, Convergence,* and *Prompt.*

STEPHEN ROBERTSON is professor in the Department of History and Art History at George Mason University, coeditor of the open-access online journal *Current Research in Digital History,* and author of the digital monograph *Harlem in Disorder: A Spatial History of How Racial Violence Changed in 1935.*

KATINA L. ROGERS is author of *Putting the Humanities PhD to Work: Thriving in and beyond the Classroom* and *Presence of Absence: Meditations on the Unsayable in Writing.* In 2021, she founded Inkcap Consulting to work with colleges and universities to design and implement creative, sustainable, and equitable structures for humanities education.

CLAUS-MICHAEL SCHLESINGER is a digital scholarship expert for the humanities at the University Library at Humboldt University Berlin.

DOUGLAS SEEFELDT is director of the digital history PhD program and associate professor of history at Clemson University, codirector of the William F. Cody Archive, and editor of the Cody Studies Digital Research Platform.

KAYLA SHIPP is digital humanities program manager for the Yale Digital Humanities Lab, where she designs and manages digital cultural heritage projects in collaboration with researchers, collections, and community partners.

SERENITY SUTHERLAND is associate professor of communication studies at SUNY Oswego. She is a member of the NHPRC and Mellon-funded Primary Source Cooperative, a publishing platform for digital editions, and editor of the Ellen Swallow Richards Papers. She copublished the digital humanities project Visualizing Women in Science at the American Philosophical Society.

TOMA TASOVAC is director of the Belgrade Center for Digital Humanities and president of the board of directors of DARIAH-EU. His areas of scholarly expertise include historical and electronic lexicography, data modeling, and digital editions.

HANNAH TAYLOR is faculty in the Thompson Writing Program at Duke University. Her research focuses on digital activism and reproductive justice and has been featured or is forthcoming in *College English, Peitho,* and *Women's Studies in Communication.*

MANFRED THALLER is professor emeritus of Historisch-Kulturwissenschaftliche Informationsverarbeitung (Humanities Computer Science) at the Universität zu Köln, Germany.

MADELINE ULLRICH is a PhD candidate in the Graduate Program in Visual and Cultural Studies at the University of Rochester. Her research explores television, contemporary female subjects, and audiences in relation to feminism, postfeminism, neoliberalism, and "quality" TV.

TED UNDERWOOD is professor of information sciences and English at the University of Illinois Urbana–Champaign. His most recent book is *Distant Horizons: Digital Evidence and Literary Change.*

GABRIEL VIEHHAUSER is professor of digital humanities at the University of Stuttgart. His main research interests encompass digital editions and digital text analysis.

BRANDON WALSH is head of student programs in the Scholars' Lab, University of Virginia Library. He serves on the editorial board of *The Journal of Interactive Technology and Pedagogy* and is a regular instructor at Humanities Intensive Learning and Teaching.

SEAN WEIDMAN is visiting assistant professor of English at the University of Wisconsin–Eau Claire. He has published in *Digital Humanities Quarterly, Digital Scholarship in the Humanities, Modernism/modernity,* and *English Literary History.*

ALEX WERMER-COLAN is academic and research director at Temple University Libraries' Loretta C. Duckworth Scholars Studio. He is managing editor for *The Programming Historian* in English, and his writing has been published in *Twentieth-Century Literature, The Yearbook of Comparative Literature, PAJ: A Journal of Performance and Art, dh+lib,* and *The Journal of Interactive Technology and Pedagogy.*

ADRIAN S. WISNICKI is associate professor of English and faculty fellow of the Center for Digital Research in the Humanities at the University of Nebraska–Lincoln. He is a founding developer of Undisciplining the Victorian Classroom, lead developer of One More Voice, and director of Livingstone Online. He is the author of *Fieldwork of Empire, 1840–1900: Intercultural Dynamics in the Production of British Expeditionary Literature.*

ALEXANDER J. ZAWACKI is a lecturer in digital humanities and an imaging scientist at the University of Göttingen. His work employs multispectral imaging and statistical processing software to digitally recover damaged manuscripts and cultural heritage objects. His research focuses on ghosts, the supernatural, and hermeneutics in the Middle Ages.